The Mask of the Parasite

The Mask of the Parasite

A Pathology of Roman Patronage

Cynthia Damon

Ann Arbor

THE UNIVERSITY OF MICHIGAN PRESS

DG83.3
.D36
1997

2000   1999   1998   1997   4   3   2   1

A CIP catalog record for this book is available from the British Library.

Library of Congress Cataloging-in-Publication Data

Damon, Cynthia, 1957–
    The mask of the parasite : a pathology of Roman patronage /
Cynthia Damon.
       p.   cm.
    Based on the author's thesis (doctoral—Stanford University,
1990).
    Includes bibliographical references and index.
    ISBN 0-472-10760-7 (cloth)
    1. Patron and client—Rome.   2. Rome—Social conditions.   3. Latin
literature—History and criticism.   4. Authors and patrons—Rome.
5. Oratory—Rome.   I. Title.
DG83.3.D36   1997
870.9'001—dc21   97-33297
                                                               CIP

For my mother and father

Acknowledgments

This book has been a long time in the making. It reached its first developmental milestone in 1990 as a dissertation at Stanford University. Since then it has matured, I hope, into a book.

Over the years I have been fortunate in my fellow students, my teachers, and my colleagues past and present. Without their questions and suggestions this book, and indeed all my work, would be the poorer. Boston College's M.A. program enabled me to enter the field of classics, the Classics Department at Stanford provided a wonderful environment for graduate study, and the Department of the Classics at Harvard offered matchless opportunities for a beginning assistant professor. At Amherst College I enjoy the benefits of collegiality both within and beyond the bounds of my own department. Particular thanks go to the members of my dissertation committee, Ted Courtney, Susan Treggiari, and Elaine Fantham. The standards they set, both scholarly and professional, are an important part of the value I see in our field. I am grateful, too, to those who have read or discussed with me successive revisions: John Bodel, Adrian Gratwick, Bob Kaster, David Konstan, James Rives, Richard Tarrant, Elizabeth Tylawsky. Welcome new perspectives accrued from participation in conferences on "Greece in Rome" (Harvard University, 1994) and "Roman Non-Elites" (New York University, 1995), so my thanks go to their organizers, Christopher Jones, Richard Thomas, Michèle Lowrie, Michael Peachin. The scholars who read the manuscript for the Press made the final draft much better than the initial one; errors and inadequacies remain my own. My editor, Ellen Bauerle, James Laforest, and the staff of the University of Michigan Press have made the process of transforming manuscript to book as painless as possible, and for that I thank them all. Funding for the preparation of the indices—ably managed by David Bloch, Amherst '97—came from the Amherst College Faculty Research fund. For the time in which to profit from all this I have to thank the Whiting Foundation, for a dissertation fellowship, and Harvard University, for a term of leave at a crucial stage in the rewriting process. But for the strength I thank my family, Dick, JD, Emily.

Contents

Introduction: Why Parasites?

> Hold thee, Mosca,
> Take of my hand; thou strikest truth in all
> And they are envious term thee parasite.
> —Ben Jonson *Volpone* 1.1.67–69

During this century historians have credited Roman patronage with increasingly comprehensive functions in providing conduits for the downward distribution of power and resources and in reinforcing the ties that kept the lower orders looking to their social superiors rather than to their peers for such goods as society could provide. In drawing this picture historians are faithful to the rhetoric, if not the reality, of the period: there is no dearth of passages in which the vocabulary of patronage is applied to the relationship between a powerful Roman and entities as populous and disparate as towns, cities, tribes, provinces, and even whole social orders. The patron-client dyad was a kind of moral archetype that was used both to legitimize such relationships and to endow them with affective appeal. Recent work has shed light on the gap between the patronal terminology and the underlying realities; the present study focuses instead on the archetype, on the relationship between an individual patron and his dependent.[1]

Dionysius of Halicarnassus' description of the original form of this relationship is much quoted.

> He [sc. Romulus] placed the plebeians as a trust in the hands of the patricians, by allowing every plebeian to choose for his patron any patrician whom he himself wished. . . . Romulus not only recommended the relationship by a handsome designation, calling this protection of the poor and lowly a "patronage," but he also assigned friendly offices to both parties, thus making the

---

1. A balanced assessment of the role of patronage in Roman life is given in Brunt 1988, 382–442. Wallace-Hadrill 1989, 63–87, has a useful discussion of the distinction between the rhetoric and the reality of patronage. I owe the phrase *moral archetype* to a sociologist of patronage, Luis Roniger (1988, 89).

connection between them a bond of kindness befitting fellow citizens. . . . It was a matter of great praise to men of illustrious families to have as many clients as possible and not only to preserve
the succession of hereditary patronages but also by their own
merit to acquire others. And it is incredible how great the contest
of goodwill was between the patrons and clients, as each side
strove not to be outdone by the other in kindness. (*Roman Antiquities* 2.9.2–3, 10.4, trans. E. Cary)

That Dionysius is creating (or reproducing) an ideal past for a contemporary phenomenon is often noted, but the positive light in which he
bathes this piece of the "past" is still perceptible in modern descriptions
of the Roman patron/client relationship. Scholars rightly try to understand Roman society on its own terms, but the effort of turning an unbi-
ased eye toward a system that is essentially foreign has resulted both in
an overemphasis on the fact that the Romans made the system work
and in a corresponding inattention to the problems they themselves
perceived in it. The figure of the parasite, the subject of this book, helps
redress the balance.

The pairing of the terms *parasite* and *patronage* in the title of this book
is at first sight unlikely. Parasites evoke the literary world of comedy, a
cultural tradition indebted to the Greeks, a physical setting of masks
and illusion, a festival atmosphere. Patronage, however, seems both
real and Roman—so Roman as to be ascribed to Romulus' arrangements for his new city, so real as to have attracted historians' scrutiny
in ever-increasing measure over the course of recent decades. The common ground between the two lies in the third substantive of the title,
pathology. For I argue that the stock character of the parasite that the
Romans knew from Greek plays became in Latin authors a symbol for
unhealthy aspects of patronage relationships in their own real world.
The figure of the parasite opens up for us a pathology of Roman patronage.

Put another way, the question I address is, How real is the parasite?
This question used to be dismissed out of hand. The parasites that we
find in Roman comedy and in Latin literature more generally, it was
said, are Greek through and through, carryovers from Greek literature
that reflect nothing real in Roman life. An "import product," Fraenkel
calls them; "foreign to the audiences of Plautus," says Gilbert Highet;
"there is no evidence that these creatures had as yet made their way to

Rome," says Tenney Frank. Various explanations are given for the importation of this foreigner into Roman comedy, ranging from the simple "because he was there in the original" to more thoughtful accounts that make reference to the parasite's habit of delivering monologues (which was useful in covering up breaks between acts in the original) or to his abusability (which offered farcical filler for plays that were otherwise too dull). All of these reasons are valid, at least for comedy, but they are not necessarily sufficient even for that genre, and they certainly do not account for the spread of the type into new genres, particularly into the very Roman genre of satire, where we find him from Ennius onward.[2]

A counterbalance to this dismissive approach is found in a book by Michel Serres entitled *Le Parasite*. Serres is a professor of the history of science and a philosopher, not a classicist, but he sets the classical figure of the parasite at the center of his analyses of human behavior. "L'homme est le parasite universel"—that is the essence of his message.[3] In his view, all human systems, from forms as small as personal relationships to agglomerations as vast and complex as economies, societies, or governments, are based on a parasitic exchange of something for nothing. Nice distinctions between the Greek and the Roman, ancient and modern, animal and human, even physical and biological, do not figure in his model. His view of the parasite is overinclusive, but it is not without utility.

Serres' principal contribution to the topic is to insist that the parasite be examined as an element in a system. The parasite—whether the figure from Greek comedy, the biological phenomenon, or the static in communications signals that is, so conveniently for Serres, called *parasite* in French—cannot exist without a host. Serres shows that he must

---

2. Fraenkel, though he speaks of the parasite as "merce d'importazione," is not without his doubts: "non è però escluso che già allora distinti signori romani invitassero occasionalmente buffoni o giocolieri" (1960, 183 and n. 2), but Highet (1949, 600 n. 30) and Frank (1957, 79) are dogmatic. Somewhat more nuanced is the view of Danek (1988, 226 n. 8): "Der Römer empfand den Parasiten der Palliata wohl als Mischung aus dem grotesk überzeichneten Fresser Bucco der Atellane und dem nur in der sprichwörtlichen griechischen Dekadenz vorstellbaren Parasitentypus der attischen Komödie; die Gestalt war der römischen Alltagserfahrung völlig fremd." D'Agostino (1937, 109), however, takes it as a matter of course that parasites of some sort existed in Roman society.

3. Serres 1980, 38.

be studied in situ, in his relationship with the organism that supports him.

If we strip the system that is composed of the comic parasite and his host to its barest essentials, we find a system in which words and services are exchanged for food. There are varieties of words (the parasite tells jokes, teases his fellow diners, flatters his host, and so on) and varieties of services (he can do the shopping, take messages to girls, brush dandruff off his patron's cloak, or simply offer himself as a butt of abuse), but what the various words and services have in common is their cheapness: they cost the parasite nothing. And what does he get in return for these insignificant offerings? The most indispensable of goods, namely, food.

For Serres this something-for-nothing creature is the emblem of all evil, the source of all that is wrong with our world; if we could shut out the parasite, we would be living the existence of the gods, serene, amply supplied with ambrosia, immortal. He uses a story to show why he feels this is so.[4]

The story takes place outside the kitchen window of a crowded restaurant. It is cold and dark out, but a smell of rich cooking fills the street. Along comes a vagrant, famished and cold. He lingers to enjoy the smells. A cook sees him and comes outside. He demands that the vagrant pay for what he has enjoyed. They are about to come to blows when a third person happens along. They ask him to arbitrate. He hears the two sides, ponders a bit, then asks the vagrant for a coin. The man produces one, reluctantly. The third man drops the coin on the street so that it makes a clinking sound. He kicks it about a bit, making more noise, then picks it up and returns it to the vagrant. To the cook he says, "There, now you've been paid." He had given him a sound in return for a smell.

The moral of the story, and the premise of this kind of economy, is that goods exchanged must be of the same order, one insubstantial for another, or real food for real coin. The parasite and his host exchange goods of different orders, a trivial offering gets a substantial reward. Hence comes all evil (according to Serres, anyway). A system in which nothing (or nearly nothing) can be exchanged for something has got a faulty scale.

This little story gives a vivid picture of a model economy, a model

---

4. Ibid., 49–50.

that condemns the parasite as an aberration, a glitch in the system, static in the signal. By viewing the parasite in the context of a system, we can see that the essence of the parasitic lies not so much in the character of the sponger as in the process of exchange. Anyone could do as Serres' vagrant did. What makes an exchange parasitic, in this view, is the relative value of the goods. But Serres' story raises as many questions as it settles. One can question the premise about the nature of the goods exchanged, for example: it would be a very limited economy in which goods had to be exchanged for others of precisely the same order. Then again, one may ask how the arbiter determines the rate of exchange. And, more fundamentally, one must ask why we humans fail to shut out the parasite, why we tolerate him in the first place if he prevents us from living like the gods. Serres' response to this last question is particularly unsatisfactory: the hosts he describes are always constrained in some way, "drogué d'une sorte de fascination," he says, or, in another story, "blinded by lightning," or, like Prometheus, chained to a cliff for the eagle to feed on.[5]

Serres' book explores the implications of his premise that all human systems incorporate a parasite. For him, the parasite is very real indeed, but his analysis leaves some important questions unanswered. What one needs to ask, it seems, is not how real the parasite is but how the parasite is real. The most efficient approach to this question lies through another story, one told by Xenophon in the *Memorabilia* (2.9).

In Athens one day long ago, a wealthy man was venting his annoyance at the groundless lawsuits with which he was threatened. A wise friend asked him if he kept dogs to protect his sheep from wolves. "Of course I do," replied the man, "and they earn their keep, too." Now there was in Athens at that time a man who was quite a competent speaker but poor. The wealthy man, taking his wise friend's hint, began a series of small kindnesses toward the poor man: whenever the wealthy man was getting in his crops, he would send the poor man a portion; when the wealthy man sacrificed, he invited the poor man to dinner; and so on. In time, the poor man realized that the wealthy man's goodwill was worth cultivating; the wealthy man's house had become for the poor man a kind of refuge. So he took it on himself to initiate legal proceedings against one of the annoying accusers, with the result that the accuser withdrew his case. One case led to another,

---

5. Ibid., 14, 54, 20.

and in time the wealthy man's wealthy friends wanted protection too; the poor man was happy to oblige. Not everyone looked so kindly on his activities, of course: his enemies reproached him with earning his keep by "playing the parasite" to the wealthy man.

These are the bare bones of a story told by Xenophon about Crito (the wealthy man), Socrates (the wise friend), and Archedemus (the poor man). It reveals with admirable succinctness the connection between the parasite and the real world: *parasite* is an unflattering label that is applied, in this case, to a dependent who makes himself useful.[6] Let us look more closely at how this relationship works.

Crito is well-off and willing to pay for his comforts, Archedemus is well educated and capable, but he lacks capital and is insufficiently ruthless to make his own way in the world. He is the sort of man, says Socrates, who prefers doing favors for the great to making enemies of them. The animal parable draws the lines clearly: "Tell me, Crito, you keep dogs (κύνας δὲ τρέφεις), don't you?" The verb τρέφειν, "support" (i.e., feed and tend), gives concrete expression to several important points: that Archedemus depends on Crito for his livelihood, that the livelihood consists largely of foodstuffs, and that Crito expects a return on his investment like the return he would get from raising any other sort of domestic beast: "I turn a better profit if I support them than I would if I didn't do so" (μᾶλλον γάρ μοι λυσιτελεῖ τρέφειν ἢ μή).

Xenophon's attitude toward the relationship between Archedemus and Crito is more favorable than otherwise: the story, taken from the *Memorabilia*, is meant to be evidence of Socrates' wisdom. But it emerges that Archedemus had his critics: those who disliked him reproached him with getting ahead with Crito's help and then playing the parasite to him (ὡς ὑπὸ Κρίτωνος ὠφελούμενος κολακεύοι αὐτόν). The core of the reproach, which I have translated "plays the parasite to him," requires a little glossing. A more ordinary translation would be "flatters him," but there is not a trace of flattery in Xenophon's account. What Xenophon is in fact referring to with κολακεύοι αὐτόν is the behavior of the κόλαξ, a type that comic poets had been putting on the stage ever since the early fifth century. The κόλαξ was a hanger-on characterized by his willingness to perform any and all services in hopes of a return, and Archedemus looked like this type to his critics.

---

6. The resemblance of Xenophon's Archedemus to the comic parasite is noted in an earlier study of the type: Lofberg 1920, 71. On the real Archedemus, see Osborne 1990, 83–102.

In other words, Xenophon has Archedemus' critics use a comic type to describe and insult their contemporary.[7]

Xenophon's story illustrates a fundamental point, that *parasite* is an insult that may be applied to a man in dependent circumstances but is not a precise or complete description of him. The corollary is that the parasite has no counterpart in real life. Whenever the figure of the parasite is evoked to represent a real person, we must realize that an effort of interpretation is underway. This means that the statement "he is a parasite" is fundamentally different from the statement "he is a slave," for example. The latter might mean "he has a servile disposition" (which could be applied to anyone), but it might also be a simple reference to a real slave's legal status ("he is a slave, and therefore he cannot marry, can't own property, can't serve in the army, and so on"). There is no equivalent to this latter meaning for the statement "he is a parasite" (except, of course, in references to the characters in the plays themselves, to Plautus' Gelasimus or Saturio, say, or to Terence's Gnatho—a trivial exception). It is rather like calling someone a clown. You might be speaking literally and referring to someone who works in a circus, but you are much more likely to be referring to someone who behaves in a foolish or attention-getting way. In this case *clown* is a label for a behavior, not for a person. Xenophon's little story shows that the same is true of *parasite.* But there is one difference: one can use *clown* either approvingly or disapprovingly, but *parasite* is exclusively negative; only Archedemus' critics viewed him as a parasite.

The parasite is in fact a conveniently compact personified form of something quite abstract, of a complicated nexus of social irritants including flattery, favoritism, and dependency. These irritants existed in both Greek and Roman society, and the parasite provided a focus for reaction to and discussion of them. Paul Millett has given a preliminary

---

7. A century and more after Xenophon, the term κόλαξ was popular as an insulting reference to the associates of monarchs. In one section of his lengthy chapter on parasites, Athenaeus mentions nineteen historians who had discussed monarchs, both foreign (Persian, Celtic, Arab) and Greek (Dionysius I, Dionysius II, Hieron, Philip II, Alexander, and a number of his successors), along with their parasites and flatterers (6.246c–253d). Xenophon's story suits my purposes better than any of those preserved by Athenaeus, because the Roman relationships that I examine in parts 2 and 3 involve not the man at the top of society and his circle but ordinary patrons and clients at various middling positions within the Roman social order.

sketch of the figure of the parasite in democratic Athens;[8] my focus is on the Roman world. The parasite of Latin literature, I argue, is a negative reflection of the *cliens:* there were real people in Rome who seemed to hostile eyes to participate in a relationship with a superior on terms comparable to the something-for-nothing economy of the comic parasite and his host, his *rex.* The behaviors ascribed to this parasite are, it seems to me, vivid indicators of where and how the patronage system grated on those who lived in (and by) it.

The connection between parasite and *cliens* is also seen by Peter White in his recent book on literary patronage.[9] But when he says that *parasite* and terms of that sort are "partial, negative, or distorted images," he implies that such characterizations—which he estimates appear in "well under 20 percent of the references to the kinds of attachments which are formed in Roman social life"—are inaccurate. I would rather say that the relationship looked different from different points of view and that every point of view needs to be considered if we are to assess the Romans' experience of patronage.

Providing as complete a picture of the Roman relationship as is possible given the state of our sources is a project whose importance extends beyond the borders of classics as a field, for the Roman dyad is often taken as a historical archetype for more modern instantiations of patronage. The standard positive view of the Roman relationship now makes it seem an anomaly to Luis Roniger, a sociologist who has been publishing on patronage for many years, who writes: "Basically, clientelism creates an inherently contradictory situation. Asymmetrical power and/or inequality is combined with solidarity, and potential and/or actual coercion coexists with an ideological emphasis on the voluntary nature of the attachment. . . . These arrangements are maintained through perpetual contest, resource manipulation, and instability. Whereas in antiquity patronage formed part of the *mos maiorum* and could hardly be thought of as conflicting with legal institutions, in modern societies it is in fact built around such conflict."[10] By studying the Roman use of the parasite, I hope to show that the Romans were in fact aware of a wide range of conflicts inherent in the institution.

This project is an exercise at the intersection of literature and society in ancient Rome, but neither the parasite nor patronage is confined to

8. Millet 1989, 15–47.
9. White 1993, 29–30.
10. Roniger and Günes-Ayata 1994, 4.

the Roman world (as I try to suggest with the epigraphs to each chapter). I hope that my discussion will stimulate scholars in other fields as I have been stimulated by discussions of societies as far from Rome as Elizabethan England and modern-day Malta. Like Ben Jonson's character Volpone, a wealthy man who uses a parasite named Mosca ("The Fly") to help him spot the insincere among the well-wishers that crowd around him, I find Mosca and his forebears an aid to understanding.

Discomforts arising from the functioning of patronage in Roman society are attested in many forms: in Cato's objection to the habit provincial governors had of using state resources to service their personal networks, for example; in the repeated attempts to curb payment for legal services; in Marius' annoyance at being publicly claimed as a *cliens;* in Cicero's detailed criteria for distinguishing between flatterer and friend; and so on. But such attestations are essentially strays, whereas parasites appear in the earliest complete work of Latin literature from the period after Roman comedy (Cato's *de Agricultura*) and show up quite regularly thereafter in the literary genres that take contemporaries as their matter and invective as their manner—that is, in satire and oratory.

The parasites that we will encounter in parts 2 (satire) and 3 (oratory) of this study are varied and plentiful because the type, a far-from-ideal reflection of a social role traditionally associated with such social virtues as fidelity, humility, and gratitude (see, e.g., Cic. *Off.* 1.45–46), served Roman authors well when they wanted to evoke the frustration, envy, and outrage that could arise from frictions due to the functioning of patronage. If the parasite is always a mask and if the fit between the mask and its wearer lies in the eyes of the beholder, that the mask seemed to fit people in so many different situations—in parts 2 and 3 we will find it on property managers, tax farmers, female companions, philosophers, poets, and many others—indicates how well it satisfied those who wanted to complain about or criticize the system.

To be sure, the world that satire reflects is stylized and even literary, and Cicero (the only orator from whom we have complete speeches extant) is not a social critic but a pleader who reshapes reality for the purposes of his case. Yet neither satire nor oratory achieves its purpose unless it reveals something that people will take to be valid about reality. The worlds created are not impossible fictions but interpretations of the familiar; the process is overt in satire, carefully concealed in

Cicero's speeches. To show how this process works for the parasite/ patron pairs studied in parts 2 and 3, I adduce wherever possible relationships that are in essentials the same as the one labeled parasitic but that are interpreted differently. The two genres are treated in what might seem to be the reverse of chronological order (the bulk of satire postdates Cicero, though its earliest authors preceded him) because satire's generic ties to comedy are much clearer than are those of oratory.

Other genres do not yield many parasites. One can certainly find unappealing dependents in the sober texts of the historians. Consider Tacitus' P. Egnatius Celer, for example: "Soranus's *cliens*, [Celer] was suborned into ruining his friend"; "[Celer was] a treacherous and tricky man who kept his greed and lust well hidden" (*Ann.* 16.32). But such dependents are not attacked via the comic type by their authors, who generally preserve a seemly distance from their subject matter. Even villains like Celer are treated in the high style by Tacitus. The parasite qua type is even more foreign to the sublimity of epic, particularly Latin epic.[11] Lyric poetry, with its focus on the *ego* and his relationship with a particular *tu*, is not a suitable stage for type characters of any sort. Horace, though fertile of parasites in the *Satires*, makes no call on the type in the *Odes*.[12] Letters, too, are so imbued with the particulars of historical context that they do not readily adopt the strategy of analysis by types.[13]

Elegy is another matter altogether. The elegiac lover's debt to the parasites of comedy has in fact already formed the subject of two substantial discussions. Netta Zagagi focuses on the topoi of flattery, while Mario Labate treats the lover's technique more generally as a lesson learned from the ingratiating parasite.[14] But the presence of parasite material (suitably adapted) in elegy, while excellent testimony to the lasting appeal of the type for Roman authors very far removed from the

---

11. The parasite does have some affinity to the beggar Irus of the *Odyssey*, however. The connection is developed in Monteverdi's *Il ritorno d'Ulisse in patria*, where Iro opens act 3 with a long lament replete with comic topoi on the theme of hunger (see Rosand 1989, a reference I owe to R.J. Tarrant).

12. For a revealing near miss see the discussion of *Odes* 2.20.6.

13. This is more true of the letters of Cicero and Pliny than of those of Seneca. The parasites of the *Epistulae Morales* are interesting for terminology; they make a brief appearance later in this introduction.

14. Zagagi 1980; Labate 1984.

stage, is not directly relevant to my theme, for it is possible to understand that borrowing as a purely literary one.[15] The lover of elegy, particularly of Ovidian elegy, where the parasite element is the strongest, is as much a type as the parasite; that is, the parasite is not being used in a purposefully negative interpretation of reality (as, I argue, is the case in satire and oratory) but is itself adapted to fit another literary framework. "Purely literary" is no doubt an overstatement, and it would almost certainly be worthwhile to investigate the intersection of the patron/client relationship with the various relationships involved in elegiac love. In the present work, however, I focus on parasites in genres that engage contemporary reality more directly.

Parts 2 and 3 of this study, then, examine the uses to which Latin authors put the figure of the parasite that had been transplanted from Greece to Rome by the authors of Roman comedy. The necessary groundwork is laid in part 1, which assembles a composite picture of the comic parasite, using evidence from the fragments of Greek comedy, from Greek writers of the imperial period whose works reflect the comic tradition, and from the ten complete plays of Roman comedy in which a parasite appears. But before we can begin, some matters of terminology, both Greek and Latin, need to be addressed.

Κόλαξ—the term used by Archedemus' enemies—was the regular name for witty, obsequious, and hungry hangers-on in Greek comedy until the middle of the fourth century.[16] Otto Ribbeck suggested that the original meaning of κόλαξ was "companion."[17] If this is true, it was a consequence of the status differences inherent in ancient society that "companion" came to mean "flatterer." For when κόλακες take the comic stage, they are characterized not only by their willingness to provide companionship but also by a desire to feed themselves at someone else's expense and by their use of flattery. The more negative traits of

15. The case of the parasites of declamation is analogous; for references see appendix 1.

16. The most recent survey of the Greek comic material is Nuchelmans 1977, but neither this article nor the much earlier piece by Giese (1908) adds anything substantial to the picture provided by Ribbeck in his ground-laying *Kolax, eine ethologische Studie* (1883), a work that constituted a great advance over Beaufils 1861. The *RE* article by E. Wüst and A. Hug (1949) is, however, useful, and H.-G. Nesselrath's 1985 book on Lucian's *On the parasite* contains a lengthy review of Lucian's comic sources. Nesselrath returned to the parasite in a subsequent book (1990, 309–17).

17. Ribbeck 1883, 3–5.

the type—the obsequious disposition and the hunger—in fact take precedence over companionship in the three ancient etymologies of κόλαξ that Athenaeus preserves: it is suggested that the word derives from τὸ κόλον, "nourishment"; from προσκολλᾶσθαι ταῖς ὁμιλίαις, "to be affixed to gatherings"; or from εὐκολία, "good temper" (i.e., tolerance of maltreatment).[18]

The type seems to have increased in popularity as comedy became less political and more social in orientation in the early fourth century. Sometime near the middle of that century, the type acquired a second name. The term *parasite* (παράσιτος, from παρά, "beside," and σῖτος, "food") was, it appears, first jokingly applied to the κόλαξ as a nickname; παράσιτος was properly the title of temple officials who participated in feasts offered to the resident divinity.[19] As a nickname for the κόλαξ, it was a tongue-in-cheek honorific. The joke—first found in Middle Comedy—recommended itself, and the type appears under both names thereafter.

Various attempts have been made to analyze the genus of hanger-on into separate species. Heinz-Gunther Nesselrath, in his admirably thorough commentary on Lucian's satirical dialogue *On the parasite*, for example, traces the presentation of the characters and the use of the terms κόλαξ and παράσιτος in Epicharmus, in Attic comedy (Old, Middle, and New), and in philosophical writers down to the Age of Lucian. He shows that in Old Comedy, that is, before the term παράσιτος had been appropriated from the sphere of cult officials and public honorands for the hungry sponger, the term κόλαξ referred to two distinct types: the private type who preyed on wealthy individuals and who had in view relatively petty material ends (such as satisfying his hunger), and the political type, a caricature of the Athenian demagogue.[20] In the early period of Middle Comedy, the terms κόλαξ, κολακεία (meaning "the behavior of the κόλαξ"), and κολακεύειν

---

18. Ath. 6.258b, 262a. Frisk (1960, s.v.) declines to explain the derivation of κόλαξ, but the ancients did not admit ignorance.

19. Arnott (1968) credits Alexis with the joke, Nesselrath (1985, 102 n. 314) argues Araros' claim. Wüst 1949, col. 1378, has a list of the deities who supported παράσιτοι in Athens. The term was also used for public honorands of uncertain function: cf. Solon's use of παρασιτεῖν (Plut. *Solon* 24.5) and Aristotle fr. 551 Rose (Teubner ed.) for παράσιτος as a state official at Methone. Other examples may be found at Ath. 6.234d–235e.

20. Aristophanes *Knights* 48, 869–911, *Acharnians* 134 ff., *Wasps* 418, etc. Cf. also Plato *Alc.* 120b, Aristotle *Pol.* 1292a15–28, 1313b39–41.

(meaning "to be a κόλαξ") were applied to hungry parasites and to flattering ones alike, as we have seen, but eventually (by the time of Anaxandrides, according to Nesselrath) the types and the terms had been differentiated, with the fellow with the food interest going by the name of παράσιτος, while the obsequious fellow became the κόλαξ par excellence. Nesselrath claims that the distinction was maintained and sharpened in New Comedy, the κόλαξ becoming a "rabenschwarze Figur," the παράσιτος a relatively harmless, if morally unrecommendable, type.[21]

A century before Nesselrath, Otto Ribbeck used a different (and for our purposes more useful) approach to distinguish the two types. He believed that by the time of Menander the παράσιτος was particularly associated with civilian patrons, the κόλαξ with the boastful soldier.[22] Ribbeck's distinctions are more functional than terminological, however: the soldier is flattered and requites his flatterer with a variety of rewards, while the private host is coaxed by a variety of tactics into providing specifically edible perquisites. The constant in one case is the tactic, in the other the reward. These functional distinctions are useful; that is, it is useful to recognize that there are two basic techniques that a dependent might use to attract benefits from a patron, namely, flattery and service. In the real world, of course, there were not distinct sets of dependents, one comprising men who were serviceable without indulging in flattery, another those who relied on flattery rather than service. Rather, the comic poets created distinct embodiments of techniques used in tandem by any ordinary dependent to gain and keep his place.

When these hangers-on were transplanted from Greek comedy to Roman, the terminological distinctions that interested Nesselrath got lost.[23] Parasites (parasiti, not kolakes) flatter the soldiers to whom they were attached: "In comedies we wouldn't find the parasites' flattery

---

21. Nesselrath 1985, 108, but see the critique in Brown 1992, 98–106.

22. Ribbeck 1883, 21. Wüst (1949, col. 1393) adduced the difference in the masks of παράσιτος and κόλαξ described by Pollux (κόλαξ δὲ καὶ παράσιτος μέλανες, οὐ μὴν ἔξω παλαίστρας, ἐπίγρυποι, εὐπαθεῖς· τῶι δὲ παρασίτωι μᾶλλον κατέαγε τὰ ὦτα, καὶ φαιδρότερός ἐστιν, ὥσπερ ὁ κόλαξ ἀνατέταται κακοηθεστέρως τὰς ὀφρῦς, 4.148) in support of Ribbeck's observation. For the little-understood third category of parasite mask, ὁ Σικελικός, see Woytek's note to Persa 395 (Woytek 1982).

23. The best short discussion of the parasite in Roman comedy is Lowe 1989a, 161–69. See also D'Agostino 1937, Brinkhoff 1948, Gil 1981–83, and Castillo 1987.

funny if the soldiers weren't such braggarts," says Cicero.[24] We can see
an instance of what he is referring to in Plautus' play *The Boastful Soldier*, where a *parasitus* named Artotrogus ("Crust-muncher") flatters
the soldier Pyrgopolinices quite energetically.[25] As his name would
lead one to expect, Artotrogus has a strong interest in food, and the
topic comes up repeatedly during his one scene on stage. In the relationship between this parasite and his soldier, it is clear that Ribbeck's
functional distinctions are no longer operative: Artotrogus flatters his
soldier shamelessly to gratify his palate and fill his belly. Something
similar may be seen in Terence's play *The Eunuch*, with the character
labeled "a parasitic flatterer," a *parasitus kolax* (*Eun.* 30). This fellow,
Gnatho ("The Jaw") by name, has, like Artotrogus, both a hearty
appetite and expertise in flattery.[26] But the word *kolax* was never taken
up into Latin: apart from Terence's line and the ancient commentaries
on it, *kolax* does not occur except in glossaries or as a play title.[27] In
Roman comedy the word *parasitus* is the regular name for all varieties
of the type. The all-purpose nature of the word is reflected in the etymologies that were derived for it.

> *Parasite* means "someone who takes his food with me or at my
> house," because παρά means "beside" and σῖτος "food." Or else
> the parasite gets this name from obeying (*parendo*) and staying
> beside someone (*assistendo*), since they stay beside their social
> superiors and cater to their pleasure with flattery.[28]

In Latin, then, there is no easily identifiable boundary between the parasite and the flatterer. Both will be considered in what follows and will

---

24. nec parasitorum in comoediis assentatio faceta nobis videretur nisi
essent milites gloriosi (Cic. *Amic.* 98).

25. Pyrgopolinices calls him a parasite: nam ego hodie ad Seleucum regem
misi parasitum meum (Plaut. *M.g.* 948).

26. Cf. Donatus on Ter. *Eun.* 391: sermo continet . . . assentationem parasiti-
cam et stultitiam . . . militis.

27. It is glossed as *parasitus, adulator, assentator, blandus,* or *fallax, furax aut cir-
cumventor,* see *TLL* s.v.). It does occur as a personal name, however: *CIL* 6.5682
P. Alfenus P.l. Colax, 6.22495 M. Minatius (mul.) l. Colax.

28. parasitus sonat mecum cibatus vel apud me, quia παρά apud, σῖτος
cibus dictus est; vel parasiti dicuntur a parendo et assistendo eo, quod assi-
dentes ipsi maioribus personis illorum voluptati per adulationem obsequuntur
(Schol. Ter. p. 98.18 Schlee). Cf. [Acron] *ad* Hor. *Epist.* 2.1.173: parasiti vocantur,
qui quaestu gulae dominis favent, id est adulantur.

generally be termed "parasites." But we need to look just a little further into the question of how Latin authors referred to this unsavory fellow.

In comedy the term *parasitus* is the *vox propria:* it is used by patrons of their parasites and by parasites of themselves.[29] The word is nearly neutral in tone in this genre. In Plautus' *Curculio,* for example, when the *adulescens* says, "I sent my parasite off to Caria to try to get a loan for me," he does not mean to belittle his emissary. He is simply stating a fact in the most efficient format available to him. But the term could also be used as a reference to someone who was not ostensibly a parasite, in which case it was indeed insulting. We can see such an insult in Plautus' *Mostellaria.* "Stand still won't you, you foul parasite!" says Pinacium to a hungry slave named Phaniscus. When Phaniscus asks, "Why parasite?" Pinacium justifies his expression by saying, "I'll tell you why: because with food as bait you could be made to go anywhere."[30] Pinacium's strategy here is an early example of a tactic that we will see a great deal of in parts 2 and 3.

But we will not find these later instances of Pinacium's strategy by looking for the term *parasitus,* for *parasitus,* though occurring more often than *kolax,* never became fully naturalized as a Latin word. (Appendix 1 contains a list of its occurrences outside of comedy and references to comedy in the period from Plautus to Apuleius.)[31] The only new genre in which *parasitus* made itself at home was declamation, where the parasite joins other stock types, such as the angry father, the virgin, the pimp, the pirate, the poor man, and the rich man.

---

29. *Parasitus* is used of parasites by patrons at *Curc.* 67, 206, 629, *Men.* 901, *M.g.* 948, *Stich.* 458, 574; by others at *Curc.* 225, 252, 275, 277, 599, *Men.* 281, 285, 321, 389, 421, *Stich.* 150, 196, 331, Ter. *Eun.* 228, 348, *Phorm.* 122. Other forms of reference (besides the parasite's name) are *homo* (*Stich.* 575, 578, Ter. *Phorm.* 305), *homo confidens* (Ter. *Phorm.* 122), *ridiculus homo* (*Stich.* 171), *congerro meus* (*Persa* 89). *Parasitus* is never used in direct address (though nearly so at *Stich.* 628); the parasite's name is used instead (*Men.* 196, *Persa* 101, 725, Ter. *Ph.* 437 etc.) or a phrase like *o mea opportunitas* (*Curc.* 305; cf. *Men.* 137). The etiquette of address is nicely illustrated by Afranius 366–68 Ribbeck: equidem te numquam mihi / parasitum verum amicum aequalem atque hospitem / cotidianum et lautum convivam domi.

30. PINACIUM: manesne ilico, inpure parasite? PHANISCUS: qui parasitus sum? PI: ego enim dicam: cibo perduci poteris quovis (Plaut. *Most.* 887a–88).

31. By "references to comedy" I mean such passages as Horace's comment on Plautus and his parasites at *Epist.* 2.1.173: quantus sit Dossennus edacibus in parasitis.

Seneca the Elder preserves a declamation passage that shows with particular clarity the sometime parity of clients and parasites: "That
wealthy man was, by his own admission, both powerful and influential. . . . He comes with his crowd of clients and parasites and pours out
his kingly wealth against my poverty."[32] But outside of declamation the
term is most common in the phrase "parasites of Apollo" (*parasiti
Apollinis*), the official name of a guild of mime-actors under the protection of Apollo, who could therefore be called, in a reversion to the origin of the term, "companions at Apollo's feast."[33] In the period after the
chronological limits of this study—roughly Plautus to Juvenal—the
term took a new lease on life, as, on the one hand, the term for a type of
jester in the imperial household (a usage that one can find in the imperial biographies of the *Historia Augusta*, for instance) and, on the other,
an all-purpose term of abuse that Christian authors used in their
attacks on contemporary morals (and especially on one another).[34] In
the period with which I am concerned, however, the word had a rather
tenuous existence. But reluctance to use the term *parasitus* did not keep
Roman authors from evoking the type.

One could use the name of a comic parasite as an insulting form of
reference, for example. In the second *Philippic*, Cicero does just this:
"Antony's not going to join us in the Senate today," he says. "Why?
Well, he's giving a garden party for someone's birthday. Whose? I
won't name any names. Let's call him Phormio, or Gnatho, or even Ballio."[35] Phormio and Gnatho are Terence's two parasites; Ballio, a Plautine pimp, is the odd man out.

One could also characterize someone as a parasite by labeling his

32. potens iste et gratiosus, quod ne ipse quidem negat, dives fuit . . . venit
iste cum turba clientium ac parasitorum et adversus paupertatem totam regiam
suam effundit (Sen. *Contr.* 10.1.7).

33. On the guild see Müller 1904. The full phrase is usually used, but there
are occasional inscriptional mentions of *parasiti* without modifier that are most
likely members of the guild as well (see Jory 1970). A similar retroversion to the
origin may be seen in the inscription of the "parasite" of M. Antonius, one
Aphrodisius: Ἀντώνιον μέγαν | κἀμίμητον Ἀφροδίσιος | παράσιτος τὴν
ἑαυτοῦ θεόν | καὶ εὐεργέτην (Dittenberger, 1903–5, 195).

34. See *TLL* s.v.

35. Hodie non descendit Antonius. Cur? Dat natalicium in hortis. Cui? Neminem nominabo: putate tum Phormioni alicui, tum Gnathoni, tum etiam Bal-
lioni (Cic. *Phil.* 2.15). Cf. the metaphorical leftovers—parasite provender—mentioned earlier in the speech: . . . praesertim cum tu reliquias rei publicae
dissipavisses (2.6).

patron *rex*, "king," the flattering term used by comic parasites of their patrons, as, for example, in a passage of Plautus' *Asinaria* where a parasite explains why he is so helpful about procuring a girl for his patron: "If I can't do it, I'll have lost me a *rex* [*regem perdidi*], for the man's a blaze of passion."[36] Horace makes use of the term *rex* when he defends himself against a charge of ingratitude to Maecenas, reminding Maecenas that he (Horace) had been in the habit of making verbal acknowledgment of his debt by speaking of Maecenas as his "patron and parent" (*rexque paterque*, *Epist.* 1.7.37). And the declamation speaker quoted by Seneca the Elder evokes the comic *rex* when he refers to his opponent's "kingly wealth" (*regiam suam*, *Contr.* 10.1.7, previously cited).

Comic names and references to "kings" were two possibilities for the use of the term *parasitus*, then. The Romans also devised some Latin terms for hangers-on. *Adsecula* (meaning "follower," with a patronizing diminutive suffix) has perhaps the best claim to represent the type in general usage; it is one of Cicero's favorite labels for the subordinates of his enemies.[37] Other terms are *adsentator* and *adulator* (both meaning "flatterer").[38] *Adsectator* (like *adsecula*, meaning "follower," though with a suffix indicating assiduity but not contempt) is a more flexible term: one could call a man an *adsectator* of another without insulting him, but it was quite another thing to call him an *adsectator* of good dinners (Sen. *Ep.* 122.12).[39] *Scurra* is another term that will appear in the passages we examine.

Most often, however, the type is evoked by means of its characteristics. In the speech on behalf of L. Valerius Flaccus, for example, Cicero stigmatizes the witnesses who appeared against his client by saying,

---

36. *Asin.* 919. Other parasites speak of their *reges* at *Capt.* 92, *Stich.* 455; cf. *Men.* 901–2 and Ter. *Eun.* 338).

37. *Ver.* 1.65, 2.3.30, 2.3.34, *Sest.* 135, *Att.* 6.3.6, *Div.* 2.79; cf. Nepos *Att.* 6.4. The imitator of Cicero who produced the *Invectiva in Sallustium* shows that he has studied his model carefully when he calls Sallust *omnium mensarum adsecula* (21).

38. For *adsentator* see, e.g., Vell. 2.83 and Cic. *Amic.* passim. A word of similar meaning and design, *subsentator* (*subdoli subsentatores, regi qui sunt proximi,* Plaut. fr. 53), was an ephemeral coinage. For *adulator* see Petron. *Sat.* 3: . . . sicut adulatores cum cenas divitum captant, where note the convivial context.

39. Cic. *Ver.* 2.28, *Mur.* 34, Pliny *Ep.* 8.23.5; cf. also Enn. *Inc.* 8V: adsectari se omnes cupiunt. *Adsectator* was also the appropriate term for an adherent to a philosophical or rhetorical school: Pliny *HN* 20.160, 24.167, Gell. 5.10.7, etc.

"Mithridates influences that crowd not by virtue of his *auctoritas* but by keeping their food troughs full."[40] The allusion to the comic type that he was making here was not lost on the scholiast, who says that Cicero undermines the credibility of the hostile witnesses by suggesting that they, like parasites, can be corrupted via their bellies (i.e., that their testimony can be bought for the price of feeding them).[41] Horace makes use of the same technique in *Satire* 2.7, where he has one Mulvius confess that he is "a lightweight who is governed by his belly," a man whose head tilts way back when his nose is tracking the smell of cooking.[42] Subservience to one's belly and hunting skills are, as we shall see in part 1, marks of the parasite. So is the quest of invitations to dinner that Catullus refers to in his attack on Porcius and Socration: Catullus' friends Veranius and Fabullus, who are reduced to cadging invitations at the crossroads (*quaerunt in trivio vocationes*, 47.7), have changed roles with two men whose names—"the Hog" and "the Greekling"—do duty for the comic mask.[43] Similarly parasite-like is the obsequiousness that Petronius has in mind when he describes a character in his *Satyricon*—the schoolteacher Agamemnon—as someone "who knows what kinds of behavior will get him invited back for another dinner."[44]

40. qui [sc. Mithridates] multitudinem illam non auctoritate sua, sed sagina tenebat (*Flac.* 17).

41. De Mithridate Pergameno loquitur, a quo vehementer adseverat testes esse corruptos. et quo magis eorum levitas et paene obsequium servile detegeretur: "quam multitudinem" inquit "non auctoritate sua, sed sagina tenebat," ne quid fidei hominibus adsit, qui parasitorum in modo vel solo possint ventre corrumpi, ad gylae blandimenta venales (Schol. Bob. 99.16 Stangl).

42. Hor. *Sat.* 2.7.37–39.

43. The image is well explicated in Wiseman 1982, 40–41. On the function of the invective in this poem (and in 28, 29, and 57) see also Skinner 1979. I cannot agree, however, when she says that in poem 29 "Mamurra can function as an archetype of a successful parasite" (145). As he is presented in that poem, he is far too independent an operator (in both dining room and bedroom) to qualify as a parasite.

44. sciebat quibus meritis revocaretur ad cenam (Petron. *Sat.* 52). Agamemnon begins a narrative when bidden to do so (48), compliments his host on a (feeble) witticism (48), and prepares the way for his host's disquisition on Corinthian ware: . . . poculumque in lance accepit [sc. cocus] Corinthia. Quam cum Agamemnon propius consideraret, ait Trimalchio . . . (50). Agamemnon's familiarity with the comic model for his role is announced early in what we have of the *Satyricon*, in his comment on the tactics of declamation masters: sicut adulatores cum cenas divitum captant, nihil prius meditantur quam id quod putant gratissimum auditoribus fore (3).

Seneca refers to verbal skills of a different sort to make it clear that the man he called "a follower of good dinners" (*cenarum bonarum adsectator, Ep.* 122.12) is to be viewed as a latter-day parasite: he says that the man earned his dinners "by the naughty wit of his tongue."[45] And the parasite's habit of profiting his stomach at the expense of fools is neatly captured in the expression Seneca uses of another contemporary, Satellius Quadratus, who "nibbled at wealthy fools" (*stultorum divitum adrosor, Ep.* 27.7). Authors who evoke the type by means of its characteristics are drawing on the comic tradition, and in part 1 I turn to this tradition, the source of all our parasites.

---

45. Varus eques Romanus M. Vinicii comes, cenarum bonarum adsectator, quas improbitate linguae merebatur (Sen. *Ep.* 122.12).

Part 1: Comedy

1

The Compleat Parasite

TIMON: Uncover, dogs, and lap!
SOME GUESTS: What does his lordship mean?
OTHERS: I know not.
TIMON: May you a better feast never behold,
You knot of mouth-friends! Smoke and lukewarm water
Is your perfection. This is Timon's last
Who, stuck and spangled <with your> flatteries,
Washes it off, and sprinkles in your faces
Your stinking villainy. Live loathed and long
Most smiling, smooth, detested parasites.
Courteous destroyers, affable wolves, meek bears,
You fools of fortune, trencher-friends, time's flies,
Cap-and-knee slaves, vapors and minute-jacks.
Of man and beast the infinite malady
Crust you quite o'er.
　　　　　—William Shakespeare *Timon of Athens* 3.6.85–99

"Mouth-friends" the misanthrope Timon of Shakespeare's *Timon of Athens* calls the parasites who have tainted his feelings for the human race (3.6.89). As a brief definition, it is a good one, touching on several essential features of the type: the verbal skills, the lusty plying of hungry jaws, and the pretense of friendship. "Uncover, dogs, and lap!" he says to them (3.6.85). What they are meant to lap up is the banquet of "smoke and lukewarm water" that he offers as fit recompense for their services to him (3.6.89). Timon had thought that the lavish generosity he had shown in the past would win him help when he was in need himself ("I am wealthy in my friends," 2.2.190; cf. 4.3.260–63), but what he received instead was excuses, promises, and regrets—help as insubstantial as smoke and lukewarm water. In writing this speech for Timon, Shakespeare culled parasite traits from the literary tradition and from contemporary experience; when Roman authors such as Cicero, Horace, Martial, and Juvenal used the figure of the parasite in their depictions of dependent individuals, they too were working from a combination of literary inheritance and contemporary observation. The most important part of the literary background behind the parasites we will meet in parts 2 and 3 of this study was the Greek and Roman amalgam that is Roman comedy.

Roman comedy, then, is the place to begin. But we will also need to look back beyond what survives for us of Roman comedy (some twenty-seven plays and a collection of fragments, most of it dating from the very end of the third and the first half of the second century B.C.) to the Greek tradition on which it was based. The parasites of Greek comedy are for the most part directly accessible only via fragments; indirect access is occasionally possible through Greek writers of the imperial period (Plutarch, Lucian, Alciphron) who reflect the comic tradition in their own very different works.

Putting together a composite picture of the comic parasite is the task of part 1 of this study. Given the nature of the material—hundreds of fragments, primarily Greek, in which parasites speak, are spoken to, or are spoken about; and ten essentially complete plays, all Roman, in which a parasite appears on stage—the process has two phases. I begin in the present chapter with a review of the most common parasite characteristics, drawing most of my illustrations from the fragments. It is important to have the identifying features of the type clearly in mind, because, as we have seen, many postcomedy references to parasites evoke the type by its distinguishing characteristics or behaviors rather than by the label *parasitus* or by a parasite name. In the interests of efficiency, each parasite trait is illustrated by a small selection of passages; further references are supplied in the footnotes. In the second and third chapters I turn to the parasites in the plays of Plautus and Terence, for characters, even type-characters like the parasite, are not just assorted bundles of standard traits; they also participate in a play's action. And in making the parasite act, that is, in working out the behavioral consequences of his traits, the comic poets proved themselves highly innovative. New techniques, new areas of involvement, new complications—all of these are devised for the parasite as he processes through Greek and Roman comedy. Innovations are necessarily hard to trace in a body of fragments—many of the parasites of the fragments are only identifiable as parasites because they have traits common to their type—so to see how comic parasites behave we will look at each of the ten parasites from the more-or-less completely extant plays in context.[1] The chapters

---

1. For a chronological survey of the relevant fragments from Araros (the earliest of the authors known to have used the term παράσιτος) through one of the latest exponents of New Comedy, the mid-second-century B.C. author Nicolaus,

on Roman comedy (chaps. 2 and 3) function as a hinge between the Greek type (chap. 1) and the Roman (chaps. 4 through 7). Some of the behaviors that Plautus and Terence ascribe to their parasites were inherited from comic predecessors, but others seem designed to exploit the Roman setting in which the plays were performed: both Plautus and Terence can be seen searching for a functional equivalent in Roman society for the parasite of Greek literature. Neither makes the connection between Roman *cliens* and comic parasite that would prove so fertile in other genres, but their interest in and development of the type was crucial to its survival in Latin literature and beyond.

To reveal the first of the parasite's features, his dependency on his patron for food, the comic poets made him hungry, indeed insatiable.[2] The *parasitus edax* is listed by Terence among the stock types of comedy, beside hurrying slaves, angry old men, greedy brothel keepers, virtuous matrons, not-so-virtuous courtesans, boastful soldiers, and shameless sycophants (*Eun.* 36–38, *Heaut.* 31–39; cf. Hor. *Epist.* 2.1.170–74). Hunger is obvious in a parasite who complains of his tyrannical belly— "the source of all evils," according to one of Alexis' parasites—or who likens himself to a fish proverbial for having an empty stomach on capture, the "fasting mullet" (νῆστις κεστρεύς).[3] Plautus' parasite Gelasimus claims to be the son of Hunger: "My mother [sc. *Fames*] carried me in her belly for ten months, but I've been carrying her in my

---

see Nesselrath 1990, 309–17. Unless otherwise indicated, fragments of Greek comedy are cited according to the edition of Kassel and Austin (1983–). Volumes 2, 3.2, 4, 5, and 7 were available to me. In subsequent notes in this chapter fragments are arranged in the following order: Epicharmus; Old Comedy; Middle and New Comedy (alphabetical by author); Plautus (alphabetical by play); Terence (alphabetical by play).

2. Insatiable hunger and/or large appetites: Epicharmus 35.7 Kaibel; Eupolis 166; Alexis 183, 233, 263, Antiphanes 82, Aristophon 10, Axionicus 6, Diphilus 61, Epigenes 2, Eubulus 117.1–4, Sophilus 7–8, Timocles 13, 31; Plaut. *Capt.* 177, *Curc.* 309–25, *Men.* 222–23, *M.g.* 24, 33–34, 49, *Persa* 59–60, *Stich.* 575. The hungry parasite also appeared in *Atellana:* Pomponius 151–52 Ribbeck.

3. For the γαστήρ as the source of all evils see Alexis 215; cf. also Diphilus 60, Nicolaus 1.7, 43. In Roman comedy: Plaut. *Bacaria* fr. 1 (cf. Macrob. *Sat.* 3.16.1 for the parasite in this play). Plutarch reports a belly-joke made by a parasite named Melanthius, who, when asked how his patron was killed, replied "the weapon went through his chest into my belly" (*Mor.* 50d). For the νῆστις κεστρεύς see Alexis 258, Amipsias 1, Anaxandrides 35, Diphilus 53.

belly for more than ten years now."[4] The parasite in Plautus' *Captivi* is so hungry that he elevates satiety to the level of the gods, uttering an oath by "Divine Fullness" (*Sancta Saturitas*, 877), a state more often desired than achieved by comic parasites, who take the voracious Heracles as their patron deity.[5]

The hunger theme generated a large crop of offshoots. For example, the parasite's organs of consumption hypostatize. According to Plutarch (who had much to say about parasites in his treatise "How to Distinguish a Flatterer from a Friend," *Mor.* 48e–74e), the belly was more than just the focal point of the parasite's existence: "The belly is all there is to his body. It's an eye that looks high and low, a beast that creeps along on its teeth."[6] The throat, not the belly, comes to the fore in Plautus' parasite Curculio ("Weevil"), if Varro's etymology for his name was traditional: "In *curculio* there has been a substitution of letters. The weevil's name ought to be *gurgulio*, since it is practically all throat [*guttur*]."[7] Related is the parasite name *Gnatho* ("The Jaw") used by Terence in the *Eunuchus*.[8]

Another offshoot of the hunger theme is the parasite's painful eagerness for the arrival of the dinner hour.[9] The parasite in the surviving fragment of Plautus' *Boeotia*, for example, calls down imprecations on the inventor of the sundial that now regulates his access to the dining room: "nowadays one can't eat until the sun says it's time to."[10] The

---

4. nam illa me in aluo menses gestauit decem, / at ego illam in aluo gesto plus annos decem (Plaut. *Stich.* 159–60, with thematic variations throughout 155–71).

5. Diodorus 2.31; Naev. *Colax* 27–29 Ribbeck, Plaut. *Curc.* 358, *Stich.* 233, 386, 395. On the connection between Heracles and parasites see Fraenkel 1960, 272 n. 1, where he argues that it is a Plautine innovation. Arnott (1972, 78 n. 45) provides evidence that "Greek parasites too had a special relationship with Heracles."

6. γαστὴρ ὅλον τὸ σῶμα, πανταχῆ βλέπων / ὀφθαλμός, ἕρπον τοῖς ὀδοῦσι θηρίον (applied to a crab at *Carm. pop.* 15 Diehl, to a parasite at Plut. *Mor.* 54b). See further the discussion of Ter. *Phorm.* 988.

7. curculio per antistoichon dictum, quasi gurgulio, quoniam paene nihil est nisi guttur (*ap.* Serv. *ad G.* 1.186). See Gratwick 1981, 339–42.

8. For his Menandrian original see Gomme and Sandbach 1973, 420–21, and, most recently, Brown 1992, 98–102.

9. Passages referring an early arrival for dinner: Alexis 259, Amphis 39, Aristophon 5, Eubulus 117, Menander 304 Körte-Thierfelder [K-Th]; perhaps Aristophanes fr. 695. Cf. also Plaut. *Capt.* 183, *Men.* 154–55, *Persa* 112, 139.

10. non estur nisi Soli lubet. On this fragment, which is quoted and commented on by Gellius at *NA* 3.3.5, see Gratwick 1979.

parasite's hungry plight was the more woeful if he was a connoisseur of good eating, as many parasites were.[11] The parasite in Lucian's dialogue *On the Parasite* "understood what was good and bad in food and had busied himself with cookery."[12] Terence's "Jaw" knew his way around the marketplace, too (*Eun.* 255–59). But it is a rare parasite who can indulge his tastes without a patron footing the bill.

> A well-stocked market is a delightful sight, if you are in funds. If not, there's nothing more distressing. Once Corydos was shopping for food to eat at home—I guess he wasn't invited out that day. It was a laugh to see him, a man with all of four bits in his pockets, eyeing eels (two sorts), fresh tuna, and crayfish with his mouth all a-water. He asked the price of one thing after another. When he found out how much, why, back he went to the sprats.[13]

Without a patron this parasite of Timocles' was reduced to economy fare.[14] Equally pitiable is the parasite-connoisseur who had to be content with leftovers, for ancient leftovers seem to have been a mince of what diners left on their plates or threw back into the pot, together with food that was old and tired before it ever left the kitchen.[15] It is no wonder that the parasite's appetite is at times termed bestial: the parasite of Sophilus 7–8 uses the verb χορτασθήσομαι (meaning "I'll get fattened up")—a term properly used of the feeding of animals—to describe his

---

11. Connoisseur: Plaut. *Capt.* 846–51, 894–918, *Persa* 92–98. Good taste is implicit in the εὔοψος ἀγορά associated with parasites in Crito 3, Timocles 11, and Plaut. *M.g.* 667. See Nesselrath 1985, 32–36.

12. τὸ ἐπίστασθαι τὰς ἀρετὰς καὶ κακίας τῶν σιτίων καὶ τῶν ὄψων πολυπραγμοσύνην (Lucian *Par.* 5).

13. ἀγορὰν ἰδεῖν εὔοψον εὐποροῦντι μὲν
ἥδιστον, ἂν δ᾽ ἀπορῆι τις, ἀθλιώτατον.
ὁ γοῦν Κόρυδος ἄκλητος, ὡς ἐμοὶ δοκεῖ,
γενόμενος ὠψώνει παρ᾽ αὐτὸν οἴκαδε.
ἦν δὲ τὸ πάθος γελοῖον, οἴμοι, τέτταρας
χαλκοῦς ἔχων ἄνθρωπος, ἐγχέλεις ὁρῶν,
θύννεια, νάρκας, καράβους ἡμωδία.
καὶ ταῦτα πάντηι μὲν περιελθὼν ἤρετο
ὁπόσου, πυθόμενος δ᾽ ἀπέτρεχ᾽ εἰς τὰς μεμβράδας.

(Timocles 11)

14. Economy fare: Alexis 200, Amipsias 18.

15. Leftovers (documented better in Roman comedy than in Greek): Axionicus 6.14–15, Plaut. *Curc.* 321, 388, *Men.* 209–13, *Persa* 77–79, 138, *Stich.* 231, 496,

own consumption. A similar point underlies the "feeding trough" mentioned in connection with Plautus' Curculio (*praesepes*, *Curc.* 228).[16]

Many of the traits listed so far fit the glutton as well as the parasite, so further characteristics make the distinction. To reveal his dependency, for example, the parasite is made poor.[17] The parasite's hungry eagerness for the arrival of the dinner hour also shows that he has few resources at home. As does the fact that he does not contribute to the provisions if a party is in the offing (the term for not contributing is ἀσύμβολος).[18] And unlike the glutton, the parasite has to struggle to gain his place at the table. The parasite of Greek comedy would scout out an establishment at which a special meal was being made ready—by keeping an eye on who was hiring cooks in the agora (Alexis 259) or by scanning the sky for telltale chimney smoke (Diodorus 2.14ff.)—and present himself at the hospitably

---

594; Titinius fr. 83 Ribbeck. On their quality see Horace *Sat.* 1.3.80–83, where Horace mentions half-eaten fish that would have been saved for later if a slave had not eaten them on the sly, and Martial 7.20.11–16, where leftovers-to-be include an *excavatae pellis indecens volvae*, a *lippa fucus*, a *debilis boletus, rosi spondyli*, and a *devorato capite truncus turtur*. For partially eaten food see also Suet. *Galba* 22 and Juv. 14.127–34. The expected beneficiaries were slaves (Hor. *Sat.* 2.6.66, Petron. *Sat.* 64.13, 67.2, Sen. *Ep.* 77.8; see D'Arms 1991).

16. Beastlike: Anaxilas 32 (maggot), Antiphanes 193.7 (fly), Aristophon 10 (frog, caterpillar, various birds, cicada), Epigenes 2 (goose), Menander 698 K-Th (with Aelian's introduction to the fragment: καὶ ὁ μὲν τοῦ Μενάνδρου Θήρων μέγα φρονεῖ ὅτι ῥινῶν ἀνθρώπους φάτνην αὐτοὺς ἐκείνους εἶχε, *de Nat. Anim.* 9.7); Plaut. *Capt.* 77 (= *Persa* 58), 80, 85–86, 184, 844, Ter. *Phorm.* 330. At Plaut. *Men.* 163–70 the parasite has to "smell out" what his patron has been doing (cf. *praeolat* at *M.g.* 41). Much later Apuleius turns the metaphor around and applies the term *parasitus* to a man who has been turned into an ass (*Met.* 10.16; at 10.13–14 this ass regales himself on leftovers).

17. Poverty (perhaps so obvious that it was rarely stated): Epicharmus 35 Kaibel; Alexis 121.13, 164, 205, Diphilus 62, Timocles 11. Amipsias 9 illustrates the point by contrast when Socrates is praised because although poor he will not deign to flatter. In Roman comedy: Plaut. *Capt.* 172–75, *Curc.* 144, *Men.* 105, 665, *Persa* 120, *Stich.* 177; also Pomponius 80–81 Ribbeck.

18. Guests described as ἀσύμβολος or said to be fed at someone else's expense (τἀλλότρια δειπνεῖν), the implication being that they do not deserve to be: Phrynichus 60, Theopompus 35; Alexis 213, 259, Amphis 39, Anaxandrides 10, Antiphanes 208, 227, 252, Diodorus 2.13, Diphilus 74, Dromon 1, Eubulus 72, Timocles 8, 10.4–5, 31, Nicolaus 1.15–16, 1.42. Cf. Crobylus 1. *Alienus cibus* is referred to at Plaut. *Capt.* 77 (= *Persa* 58), 136–37; Ter. *Eun.* 265. Cf. Caecilius 16 Ribbeck: nihilne, nil tibi esse quod edim? At Plutarch *Mor.* 547d, the parasite's tolerance of his host's ill behavior is the contribution he makes to the party (συμβολὰς . . . μεγίστας; illustrated by Men. 746 K-Th).

open front door. He might suffer reproach for being ἄκλητος (uninvited), but he hoped the host would feel it incumbent on his own social position to receive him.[19] When the wit Philippus arrives uninvited at the party described in Xenophon's *Symposium*, for example, the wealthy young host Callias admits him, saying, "only a lout would begrudge you a place."[20] Greek parasites, then, preyed on whoever was offering a good meal on any given day.[21] Roman parasites, as we shall see, tended to have one particular patron and to take regular potluck at his house.

Once in, the parasite also had to exert himself to retain his place. Parasites are thus bold in drawing attention to themselves and willing to perform degrading services. They are amusing at dinner and shamelessly tolerant of insult and injury. A parasite in Antiphanes' *Lemnian Women* stresses the entertainment that he and his peers provide: "The parasite lives amid laughter and luxury. What we work hardest at is making jokes. Laughing out loud, poking fun, drinking lots—sounds nice, doesn't it?"[22] In other gatherings the entertainment required was of a more physical nature: "A veritable storm of punches and dishes

---

19. The parasite at Alciphron 3.13.3 insists (not surprisingly) that he and his colleagues should be not merely tolerated but required at festal gatherings: δεῖ γὰρ θυμηδίας καὶ παρασίτων τοῖς γάμοις καὶ ἄνευ ἡμῶν ἀνέορτα πάντα καὶ συῶν οὐκ ἀνθρώπων πανήγυρις. Plutarch's view, however, is that the essential components of a good party are food, wine, and the appropriate furniture; other amusements, such as wits like Philippus, are pleasant but not missed if absent (*Mor.* 629c).

20. αἰσχρὸν στέγης γε φθονῆσαι· εἰσίτω οὖν (Xen. *Symp.* 1.12). See Dover 1974, 177–80, and, under the heading of ἐλευθεριότης, Bolkestein 1939. See also Plut. *Mor.* 666e: λέγει δὲ τοὺς ἀγομένους γυναῖκας πολλοὺς παρακαλεῖν ἐπὶ τὴν ἑστίασιν, ἵνα πολλοὶ συνειδῶσι καὶ μαρτυρῶσιν ἐλευθέροις οὖσι καὶ παρ' ἐλευθέρων γαμοῦσι. The host at Theophrastus *Char.* 20.10, who shows off his parasite as well as his material luxuries, demonstrates his ἀηδία by doing so openly, but the incident shows that a more discreet man might have gained some honor from this evidence of hospitality.

21. Aristophanes 284, Cratinus 46; Alexis 213, 241 (one was invited, eighteen others show up too), 259, 263, Antiphanes 193, 227, Apollodorus 29, 31.

22. ἡμῖν δὲ μετὰ γέλωτος ὁ βίος καὶ τρυφῆς·
οὐ γὰρ τὸ μέγιστον ἔργον ἐστὶ παιδιά,
ἁδρὸν γελάσαι, σκῶψαί τιν', ἐμπιεῖν πολύν,
οὐχ ἡδύ;

(Antiphanes 142)

Parasite as γελωτοποιός: Epicharmus 35 Kaibel; Eupolis 172.12–16; Anaxandrides 10, Antiphanes 142, Diphilus 63. Also Philippus at Xenophon *Symp.*

and bones came my way; sometimes I was wounded in eight spots or more."[23] In Terence's *Eunuchus* a poor acquaintance explains his incapacity for Gnatho's parasitic profession by saying, "But my wretched state is such that I can't play the fool or take a beating."[24] In Plautus' *Persa* the parasite Saturio boasts of a long line of forebears whose success was predicated on one thing, their hard heads: *duri Capitones* (or, better, *Duricapitones*) they were called (*Persa* 60). On occasion the abuse is verbal.[25] Lively young men liked to assign parasites homely nicknames: "Dory," for example, and "Lightning," "Soup," "Thunder," "Call Girl," "Sponge," and "Numbskull."[26] The victims insist that the names do not bother them—indeed, some parasites even take such nicknames on themselves—for public opinion means nothing to a parasite as long as he has his patron's approval.[27]

Patronal approval is won not only by providing entertainment (whether by one's own efforts or by suffering the abuse dished out by others) but also by a variety of personal services. Flattery is foremost in this category, of course, but other services are attested as well. Some of the services attested are both degrading and utterly unnecessary: Aristophanes has one parasite picking off dandruff and plucking gray hairs from his host's beard (fr. 416) and another removing fuzz from his patron's cloak (fr. 689).[28] But in other cases the services are more useful.

1.11–2.23, 3.11, 4.5, 6.8–7.1. We will see the wit of Roman parasites in action in chaps. 2 and 3.

   23. πληγὰς ὑπέμενον κονδύλων καὶ τρυβλίων
       ὀστῶν τε τὸ μέγεθος τοσαύτας ὥστε με
       ἐνίοτε τοὐλάχιστον ὀκτὼ τραύματα
       ἔχειν.

(Axionicus 6.3–6)

Other references to physical abuse suffered by parasites: Epicharmus 35 Kaibel, Aristophon 5, Nicolaus 1.29, Timocles 31; Plaut. *Bacch.* 595–96, *Capt.* 88–89, *Curc.* 398, *Stich.* 624–25; Ter. *Phorm.* 988–89.

   24. at ego infelix neque ridiculus esse neque plagas pati / possum (*Eun.* 244–45).

   25. Alexis 183, Antiphanes 193, Axionicus 6.9–11, Nicolaus 1.31–32.

   26. Anaxandrides 35, Antiphanes 193, Aristophon 5, Anaxippus 3; Plaut. *Capt.* 69–70, *Men.* 77–78, *Persa* 60, respectively. On Παράσιτος itself as a nickname in Alexis 183, see my introduction.

   27. Plaut. *Curc.* 413–16, *Persa* 108, *Stich.* 242.

   28. Cf. *Knights* 869–911, where flatterers perform a variety of intimate services for Demos.

Suppose someone's drunk at a party and needs to be carried out:
you'll see me an Argive wrestler. If there's an attack to be made on
somebody's house, I'm a ram. I'm a Capaneus for climbing lad-
ders; I feel blows no more than an anvil does; I'm a Telamon at
wielding my fists, and smoke for finding beauty.[29]

The same idea is presented more succinctly in Antiphanes' *Twins*,
where the parasite is called "a good soldier" (στρατιώτης ἀγαθός,
80.11). Alexis has a parasite escorting a hurrying patron about the city
(205); one of Timocles' parasites makes it a rule to be "involved in
whatever comes up" (συμπαρὼν ὅ τι ἂν δέηι, 8). Patrons commonly
had parasites do the shopping—a sensible way to exploit the parasite's
connoisseurship.[30] When the parasite made arrangements with a pimp
about a girl for his patron, it preserved appearances for the patron.[31]
That parasites were regularly involved in their patron's amatory
affairs is indicated by the fact that in Plautus' *Amphitruo* the phrase
that Mercury uses to refer to his messenger service between Juppiter
and Alcumena is "I'll be my father's parasite" (*subparasitabor patri*, 515;
cf. 521, *prima parasitatio*).[32] The parasites of Aristophanes who bear
false witness for their patron at a trial provide a useful service (fr. 452),
and Antiphanes has parasites who in addition to giving evidence are
willing to strangle and stab (193). Menander's parasites in particular
tend to take practical (though still demeaning) action on their patrons'
behalf. In the *Dyscolus* Sostratos assumes that his parasite Chaireas—
whom he judges "a particularly useful friend" (καὶ φίλον καὶ πρακ-
τικὸν κρίνας μάλιστα, 56–57)—can and will help him with a love
affair, and in the *Sicyonius* the parasite Theron is deputed to persuade
a down-and-out citizen to swear that Stratophanes' girl is his daugh-

---

29. δεῖ τιν' ἄρασθαι μέσον
    τῶν παροινούντων, παλαιστὴν νόμισον Ἀργεῖόν μ' ὁρᾶν.
    προσβαλεῖν πρὸς οἰκίαν δεῖ, κριός· ἀναβῆναί τι πρὸς
    κλιμάκιον . . . Καπανεύς· ὑπομένειν πληγὰς ἄκμων·
    κονδύλους πλάττειν δὲ Τελαμών· τοὺς καλοὺς πειρᾶν καπνός.
                                   (Aristophon 5)

30. Shopping: Plaut. *Capt.* 474, *M.g.* 667; cf. *Capt.* 894–95.

31. Such was the assignment of Gnatho in Terence's *Eunuchus* and of the
unnamed parasite at *Bacch.* 573–605; Artotrogus is a go-between at *M.g.* 59–71.
Cf. also Titinius 45–46 Ribbeck.

32. Cf. Timocles 8.6: ἐρᾷς, συνεραστὴς ἀποφάσιστος γίγνεται.

ter.[33] If the help that Menander's parasites offer is not overly effective—Chaireas puts off helping Sostratos get his girl until "tomorrow" (131–32), by which time that young man is already happily betrothed to her; and Stratophanes' girl actually is the citizen's daughter—that is another matter. The services that Roman parasites provided their patrons will emerge from the discussions of the individual plays in chapters 2 and 3.

Servility is a reproach frequently incurred by parasites: the verb *praeservire*, "play the slave," is applied to Mercury's *parasitatio*, for example (Plaut. *Amph.* 126).[34] References to a parasite's pursuits as a "job" (ἔργον; Alexis 200, Amipsias 1, Diphilus 76) and to self-sale (Plaut. *Persa* 145–46, *Stich.* 172, 195) draw on the same topos. Another indication of the parasite's slavelike position was that he could never allow himself to display anger. In Plautus' *Stichus* the parasite cannot even object to the teasing that he receives from his patron's slaves without being brought up short: "PARASITE: [*aside*] For a long time now I've put up with undeserved insults from him. [*to the slave*] If you annoy me any further. . . . SLAVE: You'll be terribly hungry."[35] Occasionally his servility is revealed through the play's action. There is a purposeful parallelism between parasites and slaves in the *Dyscolus*, for example, where Sostratos expects his parasite Chaireas to help with his love affair but uses his slave Pyrrhias for the same purpose (*Dysc.* 70–74). At *Sicyonius* 141–49 Stratophanes issues orders to slave and parasite in the same tone. And in the *Stichus*, based on Menander's first *Adelphoe*, not only

---

33. For the *Dyscolus* cf. Chaireas' long advertisement of his versatility as an amatory aide-de-camp (lines 57–68). The status of Chaireas is much disputed. Gomme and Sandbach (1973, 130–32) and Handley (1965, *ad* 57ff.) consider Chaireas a parasite, albeit an unusual one, but Aloni (1972) and Arnott (cast list to Loeb translation) dissent.

34. Plaut. *Curc.* 623, *Men.* 87–92 (cf. 97: *ultro eo ut me vinciret*); Ter. *Phorm.* 336. Cf. Axionicus 6: ἥττων εἰμὶ γὰρ τῆς ἡδονῆς. The grammarian Nonius explains Caecilius' use of the adverb *verniliter* (meaning literally "in the manner of a homebred slave") as follows: verniliter pro adulatorie, a vernis quibus haec vivendi ars est (131 Ribbeck).

35. GELASIMUS: iam dudum ego istum patior dicere iniuste mihi. / praeterhac si me inritassis— PINACIUM: edepol essuries male (*Stich.* 344–45). A character in Diphilus' play Συνωρίς ("Yokemates") has trouble believing his ears when he hears of an angry parasite: A: ὀργίζεται· παράσιτος ὢν ὀργίζεται; B: οὐκ ἀλλ᾿ ἀλείψας τὴν τράπεζαν τῇ χολῇ ὥσπερ τὰ παιδί᾿ αὐτὸν ἀπογαλακτιεῖ (Diphilus 75).

does the *matrona* Panegyris want to send the parasite Gelasimus on an errand that she has already commissioned a slave to do (150–54), but she tells him (when he asks if she would like him to supervise her housecleaning) that she has enough slaves at home (*sat servorum habeo domi*, 397). In another play based on a Menandrean original, the *Bacchides*, a parasite and a slave are sent to fetch a girl for their respective patrons. The parasite fails, but the slave succeeds in the tricks necessary to get the girl for *his* master not once but twice (*Bacch.* 579–83).[36]

These parallels between parasite (ostensibly a free man) and slave (legally bound) are evident to the audience, but not to the parasites themselves, who make a habit of boasting of their profession, often in an extended monologue, such as this one from Antiphanes' *Twins*.

If you look closely, you'll see that the parasite shares his host's lot and his life. No parasite wishes to see his friends in trouble. On the contrary, they pray that their friends enjoy perpetual good fortune. If someone lives particularly well, the parasite doesn't get envious. He's happy to stay alongside and get a share of it all. He's a worthy friend, unshakably loyal, not contentious, not harsh; he doesn't wish you ill. If you get mad he puts up with it; if you make a joke he laughs. He's good at love affairs and laughter; his manner is lively; he'll soldier on just wonderfully well if you give him a nice dinner for rations.[37]

---

36. Cf. Menander *Dis Exapaton* fr. 3 Sandbach, and Barsby 1986, ad loc., for the presence of this incident in the original.

37. ὁ γὰρ παράσιτός ἐστιν, ἂν ὀρθῶς σκοπῆις,
κοινωνὸς ἀμφοῖν, τῆς τύχης καὶ τοῦ βίου.
οὐδεὶς παράσιτος εὔχετ᾽ ἀτυχεῖν τοὺς φίλους,
τοὐναντίον δὲ πάντας εὐτυχεῖν ἀεί.
ἔστιν πολυτελὴς τῶι βίωι τις· οὐ φθονεῖ,
μετέχειν δὲ τούτων εὔχετ᾽ αὐτῶι συμπαρών.
κἄστιν φίλος γενναῖος ἀσφαλής θ᾽ ἅμα,
οὐ μάχιμος, οὐ πάροξυς, οὐχὶ βάσκανος,
ὀργὴν ἐνεγκεῖν ἀγαθός· ἂν σκώπτηις, γελᾶι·
ἐρωτικός, γελοῖος, ἱλαρὸς τῶι τρόπωι·
πάλιν στρατιώτης ἀγαθὸς εἰς ὑπερβολήν,
ἂν ἦι τὸ σιτάρχημα δεῖπνον εὐτρεπές.

(Antiphanes 80)

Professionalism: Eupolis 172, 173, Alexis 121, Anaxandrides 10, Antidotus 2, Antiphanes 80, 142, 193, Aristophon 5, Axionicus 6, Diodorus 2, Hegesippus 2. Plautus' parasites are more plaintive but no less forthright: *Capt.* 69–109, *Men.*

Parasites were expensive companions, not so much because of their large appetites, but because they encouraged their host to live extravagantly. Parasite maintenance was a standard item in lists of spendthrift largesse. Perhaps the most memorable illustration of the material damage done by parasites occurred quite early in the comic tradition, in *Flatterers* (Κόλακες), a play by Eupolis that was produced in 421 and won first prize. The title characters fastened on the young heir Callias shortly after he came into his inheritance, instigating the rapid dispersal of a large estate. Even from the extant fragments, we can appreciate Callias' losses: gold and silver utensils (fr. 162); fields, sheep, and cattle (fr. 163); a race horse (fr. 164); one hundred drachmas and wine (fr. 165); food (fr. 166); "a clean sweep" (fr. 167); ten talents (fr. 168); and napkins (fr. 169)—all of which are prepared for by fragment 161, which is part of the account of his new possessions that was given to the heir. This cautionary tale had a firm basis in reality, for according to J.K. Davies the value of the real Callias' holdings seems to have shown a precipitous decline, falling from at least two hundred talents (his grandfather's worth) in the late 420s to a mere two talents in 387.[38] The κόλακες of this play flatter their host (frr. 172.9–10, 181), but their principal effect seems to have been to encourage him to spend money on life's pleasures (drinking, fr. 158; eating, fr. 166; amusement, fr. 172.12–16; sex, frr. 174, 178). It is noteworthy that the moralists stress Callias' material losses, not his moral degradation, which would have been even more congenial to their theme.[39]

78–105, *M.g.* 31–35, *Stich.* 174–92. Terence's Gnatho and Phormio are as proud as any of the Greeks: *Eun.* 232–64, *Phorm.* 330–45. For a parasite who feels his fetters, see the discussion of Peniculus in Plautus' *Menaechmi*.

38. Davies 1971, 261–62. Nesselrath (1985, 96) argues that the κόλακες in this play were not stock types but real individuals observed (and attacked) by the dramatist. Young and recent heirs were frequently the prey of parasites (Plato *Soph.* 222e, Alciphron 1.9.3). Callias was the most prominent victim (according to Athenaeus his prodigality was cautionary material used by παίδων παιδαγωγοί, 169a; see n. 39), but another was Ischomachus (Araros 16, Ath. 12.537f). See Davies 1971, 265–68. Other references to the expense of parasites: Menander 304, 309, 698 K-Th; Plaut. *Curc.* 600, *Most.* 20–24, *Stich.* 374–88, 575, 628, *Truc.* 676–81. The topos made its way into declamatory texts as well: Sen. *Contr.* 2.6.9, [Quint.] *Decl. min.* 296.

39. References to the "moral" of Callias' story: Lys. 19.48, Ar. *Rhet.* 1405a19f., Heracleides of Pontus fr. 58 Wehrli, Max. Tyr. 14.7, Philostratus *VS* 2.25.3, Libanius fr. 50β2.

But the expense of parasite maintenance was not the real danger in associating with them: far greater risk lay in one's exposure to unrestrained flattery and in believing that a parasite was a friend.[40] We saw that the parasite in the *Twins* claimed to be his host's true friend, but the context of such passages (when we have a context) generally shows just how barren and self-serving the parasite's "friendship" really is.[41] The Roman comedies offer many instances.

In the epigraph to this chapter, I quoted Timon's description of his "smiling, smooth, detested parasites." In that passage Shakespeare captures in language more exciting than mine many of the distinctive features of the comic parasite: the strange pairing of a desperate, almost bestial hunger with a self-suppressing eagerness to please ("affable wolves, meek bears"), the servile behavior ("cap-and-knee slaves"), and the gloss of friendship that parasites apply to their single-minded pursuit of self-interest ("trencher-friends"). Timon curses the "stinking villainy" of those who deserted him when there was nothing left to prey on ("fools of fortune" and, even better, "time's flies"), and indeed the picture he gives is exceedingly negative. But *Timon of Athens* is a tragedy, and a pessimistic one at that, so the parasitical insincerity and "usuring kindness" (4.3.512) that provoke Timon's curse on humankind are not balanced by any more pleasant traits. In the ancient world, however, parasites were types of comedy, with at least a superficial brightness about them. When an eager-to-please Periplecomenus in Plautus' *Miles gloriosus* reels off a list of the associates a young man might find desirable, a "first-rate parasite with a flair for provisioning" is among them (*vel primarium parasitum atque opsonatorem optumum,*

---

40. False friendship emerges already in the earliest of the parasite-related fragments of Greek literature: ἦλθες οἷα δὴ φίλος, ἀλλά σεο γαστὴρ νόον τε καὶ φρένας παρήγαγεν εἰς ἀναιδείην (Archilochus 124b West [W]). The connection between extravagance, (false) friends, and moral decline is nicely illustrated by Menander 614–16 K-Th: a wealthy man who is willing to give is assured of "friends" (614), but wealth unwisely spent makes him ἀνόητος (615); indeed, it changes his character altogether (616).

41. Eupolis 172; Alexis 205, Anaxandrides 43, Anaxilas 32, Antiphanes 80, 193, Araros 16, Diphilus 23, Eubulus 117, Nicolaus 1.44–45, Timocles 8; Plaut. *Capt.* 140–41, 151–52, *Men.* 903 (with Gratwick 1993, ad loc.); Ter. *Phorm.* 562 (cf. 595–98). Cf. also Gomme and Sandbach 1973, *ad Dys.* 148: "But one of the points in this scene is that for all his boasts he [sc. Chaireas] proves to be quite useless."

M.g. 667).[42] Clearly an *adulescens* might feel that a parasite added to the fun of a party. To see how the type capitalized on this point of view and managed to survive at the expense of others, we must turn to the parasites that are found in action in the plays of Plautus and Terence.

---

42. Cf. Ephippus 6, where the verb κολακεύειν is used of behavior that is meant to be enjoyed.

2

Plautus' Parasites

But the yong lustie gallants he did chose
To follow, meete to whom he might disclose
His witless pleasaunce, and ill-pleasing vaine,
A thousand ways he them could entertaine,
With all the thriftless games, that may be found,
With mumming and with masking all around,
With dice, with cards, with balliards farre unfit,
With shuttlecocks, misseeming manlie wit,
With courtizans, and costly riotize,
Whereof still somewhat to his share did rize:
Ne, them to pleasure, would he sometimes scorne
A Pandares coate (so basely was he borne);
Thereto he could fine loving verses frame,
and play the poet oft.
　　—Edmund Spenser *Mother Hubbard's Tale* 797–810

Parasites appear in eight of Plautus' twenty-one extant plays. In some plays, the parasite's part is small and he functions as a single cog in the wheel of the plot (*Asinaria*, *Bacchides*) or as a mirror that reflects the character of his interlocutor (*Miles gloriosus*). But in *Curculio* he is the title character, and the parasites of *Persa*, *Menaechmi*, and *Captivi* are much on stage and each has at least one solo song of his own. Plautus' innovations with the type were recognized (if not admired) by Horace (*quantus sit Dossennus edacibus in parasitis*, Epist. 2.1.174). We will look at these plays in the order listed (except for *Bacchides*, whose parasite will have to wait in the wings until the end of the chapter).

The legal maneuvers of Xenophon's Archedemus are transplanted into the world of comedy in Plautus' *Asinaria*, where we meet an unnamed parasite drawing up a contract between a young man (Diabolus) and a procuress, a *lena* (746–809).[1] Diabolus is planning to pay 20 minas for

---

1. The unnamed character is never referred to as a *parasitus*. The services he provides are paralleled in other comic texts, but his most obvious parasite traits—dinner as his reward (914) and his *rex* (919)—do not emerge until late in his time onstage. The audience would not have known how to place him unless

the right to exclusive access to the *lena*'s daughter, Philaenium, for the period of a year, and he wants to dictate some rules to ensure that his access is exclusive. He has chosen an expert to help him in the matter: "Let's see what sort of a contract you came up with for the *lena,* the girl, and me. Read out the terms. You're an artist, the best there is for this sort of job."[2] But the first set of terms is not stringent enough to allay the worries of a jealous lover, so the parasite supplements them with a long series of prohibitions (756–73). After eighteen lines of these, Diabolus professes himself pleased (*sati' placet,* 773), but the parasite is not to be stopped. He continues in the same vein for thirty-three more lines, with Diabolus interjecting an occasional note of approval (773, 785, 802; cf. 809). The parasite produces a catalog of the amatory tactics that Philaenium is *not* to use (except with Diabolus, 787–88). Nearly two centuries later, the lovelorn speakers of elegy echo the parasite here.[3] They, of course, speak on their own behalf, whereas he is giving voice to the worries felt by his patron. All of the effort expended on these terms proves in vain, however, because Diabolus' rival Argyrippus (who is the sympathetic *adulescens* in the play) gets the cash to the *lena* first, thanks to the help of his remarkably complaisant father, Demaenetus. When Diabolus resolves to revenge himself on Demaenetus by summoning his wife, the parasite offers his services once again.

> PARASITE: Here is what I think ought to be done. It would look better if I'm the one who does the informing, rather than you. We don't want her to think that it is your love rather than her predicament that makes this so upsetting to you.
> DIABOLUS: Right you are. You go stir her up then, make her ready for a fight, tell her that he spends the day drinking with his own son with a single girl for the two of them, and that he is robbing her, to boot.

---

the actors were masked. No remains of masks from Rome of Plautus' day have yet come to light, but for Greek parasite masks see Webster 1995, 22–25, and Bieber 1961, 100.

2. Agedum istum ostende quem conscripsti syngraphum
    inter me et amicam et lenam. leges pellege.
    nam tu poeta es prosus ad eam rem unicus.

(Asin. 746–48)

The text of Plautus is from Lindsay 1904–5 unless otherwise indicated.

3. Zagagi 1980.

PA: Okay, okay. You don't need to tell me how. I'll take care of it.
DI: And I'll go home and wait for you there.[4]

This time the parasite is successful. When the outraged wife hounds her husband back home, the parasite can congratulate himself not only on having exacted the vengeance desired but also on having come up with a plan promising to satisfy his patron's amatory passions.

> That's the end of Demaenetus. Time for me to take myself off, too. It's going to be a lovely battle. I'll go see Diabolus, tell him that the job is done as he wanted it, suggest that we relax and have dinner while they fight it out here. Then tomorrow I'll persuade lover-boy to give 20 minas to the *lena* so that he can have at least part share in the girl. I hope Argyrippus can be persuaded to let him have her every other night. If I can't get him to agree, I've lost me a patron, for the man is a blaze of passion.[5]

Until the dust settles at the *lena*'s, however, he is well content to return to his accustomed place at Diabolus' dinner table.

The parasite in this play makes himself useful as his patron's mouth-piece and emissary and is rewarded with a place at his patron's table.

---

4. PA: ego sic faciundum censeo: me honestiust
   quam te palam hanc rem facere, ne illa existumet
   amoris caussa percitum id fecisse te
   magi' quam sua caussa. DI: at pol qui dixti rectius.
   tu ergo fac ut illi turbas, litis concias,
   cum suo sibi gnato unam ad amicam de die
   potare, illam expilare. PA: iam <iam>. ne mone.
   ego istuc curabo. DI: at ego te opperiar domi.

   (*Asin.* 820–27)

5. mortuos est Demaenetus.
   tempus est subducere hinc me; pulchre hoc gliscit proelium.
   ibo ad Diabolum, mandata dicam facta ut uoluerit,
   atque interea ut decumbamus suadebo, hi dum litigant.
   poste demum huc cras adducam ad lenam, ut uiginti minas
   ei det, in partem hac amanti ut liceat ei potirier.
   Argyrippus exorari spero poterit ut sinat
   sese alternas cum illo noctes hac frui. nam ni impetro,
   regem perdidi: ex amore tantum est homini incendium.

   (*Asin.* 911–19)

See further Lowe 1992, 170–74.

The two of them seem perfectly satisfied with their relationship. In the world of the play, of course, the sympathetic figures are those who give themselves up to love and leisure, not the grim standard-bearers of duty. But those who examine the matter through everyday lenses rather than festival glasses may think that the parasite is no less a corrupter of youth than is the complaisant Demaenetus.[6]

The art of Diabolus' parasite lay in turning his patron's weaknesses into a source of profit for himself. Legal expertise was the tool he brought to the task, supplemented by a keen sense of psychology. The parasite who preys on the vanity of the *miles gloriosus* Pyrgopolinices has a more mundane sort of equipment: he exercises a talent for flattery.[7]

Artotrogus ("Crust-muncher") serves his soldier as a repository of information about past battles, or, rather, about the stories that the two of them have built up around past battles.

> PYRGOPOLINICES: But where is that Crust-muncher of mine?
> ARTOTROGUS: He stands beside a man brave and blessed by good fortune, regal of bearing, a warrior. Mars himself would scarcely presume to call himself that or to equate his qualities with yours.
> PY: Didn't I rescue him in the Weevilian Fields, when I was fighting against the commander Bumbomachides Clutomestoridysarchides, grandson of Neptune himself?
> AR: I remember. Wasn't he the one with the weapons of gold, whose legions you scattered with a puff, as the wind scatters leaves or a brush <spreads> plaster?[8]

---

6. See lines 867, 875, and 932 for Demaenetus' bad influence on his son and 865–66 and 871 for the sort of behavior that would have entitled him to the epithet *frugi*.

7. For a detailed discussion of and bibliography on the first scene of the *Miles gloriosus* see Schaaf 1977, 130.

8. PY: sed ubi Artotrogus hic est? AR: stat propter uirum
fortem atque fortunatum et forma regia,
tum bellatorem—Mars haud ausit dicere
neque aequiperare suas uirtutes ad tuas.
PY: quemne ego seruaui in campis Curculionieis,
ubi Bumbomachides Clutomestoridysarchides
erat imperator summus, Neptuni nepos?
AR: memini. nempe illum dicis cum armis aureis,
quoius tu legiones difflauisti spiritu,

Artotrogus' "memory" is of course really a knack for retelling the old tales ever better than before.[9] Physical prowess, both military and amatory—the soldier's two sources of pride—provides the parasite with the themes for his fantasies. The "Battle of the Weevilian Fields" never happened, and the soldier's image of himself as a ladies' man is equally the product of his parasite's tongue.

> AR: All the women love you, and rightly so, given how good-looking you are. The ones who grabbed me by the cloak yesterday, for instance.
>
> PY: What did they say?
>
> AR: They had no end of questions. "Is this Achilles?" one of them asked. I said, "No, his brother." Then another one said, "That's why he's so good-looking, then, so grand. Just look at that head of hair! How lucky the women are who bed down with him!"
>
> PY: Did they really say that?
>
> AR: Why not? Didn't they both beg me to parade you in their direction today?
>
> PY: It's an awful nuisance being so good-looking.
>
> AR: Indeed it is. These women cause me all kinds of trouble: they make requests, hang around, beg to be allowed to see you, bid me invite you to them. They leave me no time for the job I'm doing for you.[10]

---

quasi uentus folia aut peniculum tectorium.

(M.g. 9–17)

Cf. 42–49, 52–54 for more flattery. On the insect imagery of this passage see Petrone 1989.

9. Note the presence in the story of a term from the parasite's own center of interest, *campis Curculioneis,* "Weevilian Fields." This procedure is taken further by "The Weevil" himself, Curculio, at *Curc.* 444. Martina 1980 suggests that Artotrogus' role is modeled on "una situazione storicamente e socialmente ben determinabile," that of the *poeta cliens.* Pace Martina, Artotrogus' language is no more poetic than that of other parasites (all of whom tend to speak with a certain flair), and the "records" that he keeps are explicitly unwritten (line 42); the *tabellae* mentioned at line 38 contain information pertaining to the newly hired mercenaries (cf. 72–74), not rough drafts of epics on the "brother" of Achilles (*M.g.* 62).

10. AR: amant ted omnes mulieres neque iniuria,
    qui sis tam pulcher ; uel illae quae here pallio
    me reprehenderunt. PY: quid eae dixerunt tibi?

Artotrogus' intimate knowledge of his victim allows him to anticipate needs that the *miles* cannot quite articulate, a skill that shows up in even the most trivial contexts.

PY: What was I saying?

AR: Well, I know what you were wanting to say. It was done, really; I remember that it was.

PY: But what was it?

AR: It was . . . whatever it was.

PY: Do you have . . .

AR: . . . You were wanting to ask for the tablets. I've got them, got a stylus, too.

PY: You are awfully good at figuring out what I have in mind.

AR: It is only right that I be studiously familiar with your ways and take care to be able to sniff out in advance what you want.[11]

AR: rogitabant: 'hicine Achilles est?' inquit mihi.
'immo eius frater' inquam 'est.' ibi illarum altera
'ergo mecastor pulcher est' inquit mihi
'et liberalis. uide caesaries quam decet.
ne illae sunt fortunatae quae cum isto cubant!'
PY: itane aibant tandem? AR: quaen me ambae opsecrauerint
ut te hodie quasi pompam illa praeterducerem?
PY: nimiast miseria nimi' pulchrum esse hominem. AR: immo itast.
molestae sunt: orant, ambiunt, exopsecrant
uidere ut liceat; ad sese arcessi iubent,
ut tuo non liceat dare operam negotio.

(*M.g.* 58–71; cf. 91–94)

11.   PY: quid illuc quod dico? AR: ehem, scio iam quid uis dicere.
factum herclest, memini fieri. PY: quid id est? AR: quidquid est.
PY: habes— AR: tabellas uis rogare. habeo, et stilum.
PY: facete aduortis tuom animum ad animum meum.
AR: nouisse mores tuos me meditate decet
curamque adhibere ut praeolat mihi quod tu uelis.

(*M.g.* 36–41)

Zwierlein (1991, 128–32) includes lines 37–41 in the long list of passages he would like to excise from this play. He has six principal objections to these lines. The first two, that *illuc* in line 36 ought to introduce a new theme more quickly than it does and that the *tabellae* mentioned in line 38 are not needed until line 73, disappear if one realizes that Pyrgopolinices comes on stage with the intention of going to the forum to gather up his recruits and go off to the campaign (71–78). He needs Artotrogus and the *tabellae* for this, and *illuc* refers

He keeps track of the record books, he remembers the stylus, and he even does the *miles'* addition for him (suitably inflated): 150 + 100 + 30 + 60 = 7000 (42–47). Artotrogus vanishes from the play early when he takes over a task the *miles* tells us he would ordinarily have done himself, delivering mercenaries to Seleucus. By so doing Artotrogus gives his patron the *otium* he needs to enjoy a recently acquired concubine (948–50). It is plain, in fact, that Artotrogus was in the habit of making himself agreeable in whatever way the occasion required.[12] His reward, however, always takes the form of provisions: "PY: As long as you behave the way you are doing now, you'll always have food, I'll always make a place for you at my table."[13]

Artotrogus' success is due to the soldier's vanity. If he could find someone even more puffed-up than Pyrgopolinices, he tells us, he would be inclined to sign himself up as that man's slave (21–23). Loss of independence is the price he is willing to pay for the wherewithal to satisfy the demands of his imperious insides: "My belly is the cause of all these miseries. I've got to drink this in with my ears lest my teeth have only each other to grind. I've got to go along with whatever lies the fellow comes up with."[14] Artotrogus is not a prepossessing figure— the parasite is only less despicable than the *miles* (as the audience sees it, anyway) because he makes his part of the exchange consciously,

---

back (appropriately enough) to the old purpose of going to the forum, not to a new theme. Zwierlein also suggests that *rogasne* would be a more Plautine locution than *uis rogare* (38), but the phrase need not be a question. The use of the possessive adjectives with *animum aduertere* (39) is justified by the *tuom/meum* contrast. *Praeolere* (instead of the more common *subolere*) is likewise tailored to its context. The final objection—to line 40—is based on its similarity to another suspect line (*Bacch.* 545), a dangerously circular argument.

12. Cf. the parasite's boast at *Men.* 140: commoditatis omnis articulos scio.

13. PY: dum tale facies quale adhuc, adsiduo edes, / communicabo semper te mensa mea (*M.g.* 50–51). For Artotrogus' interest in food see lines 24, 33–34, 49.

14. uenter creat omnis hasce aerumnas: auribus
     peraurienda sunt, ne dentes dentiant,
     et adsentandumst quidquid hic mentibitur.

                                                        (*M.g.* 33–35)
In line 34 I read *peraurienda* rather than *peraudienda*, as it is characteristic of parasite wit to use the vocabulary of eating for other objects and activities. Cf. *Bacch.* 595–98, *Capt.* 134–35, *Curc.* 600, *Trin.* 908 (where the sycophant is pretending to be Charmides' parasite); Ter. *Phorm.* 319; perhaps also Men. 746 K-Th (λεπτὸς γίνομ' εὐωχούμενος τὰ σκώμματα), though see Brown 1992, 93.

whereas the soldier is both blind and vain. As Cicero says, "in comedies we wouldn't find the parasites' flattery funny if the soldiers weren't such braggarts."[15]

Open-eyed abandonment of the responsibilities and prerogatives of an independent man—voluntary servitude, in short—is a parasite trait that we see again in the *Curculio*. The parasite of that play, Curculio ("Weevil"), does the job of a *servus callidus* in planning the central intrigue, and he is so helpful and so tricky that a character in the play infers (wrongly) that he is a slave in reality (623–24).[16] But Curculio is not a slave. Nor is he a supernumerary figure brought on to provide information and amusement for the audience (as Artotrogus and Diabolus' parasite were); his help is eagerly sought by both *adulescens* and *miles*.

The *adulescens* Phaedromus, who needs money to purchase his beloved from a brothel keeper, a *leno*, laid claim to Curculio's services even before the play began: "I have sent my parasite off to Caria to see if he can't get me a loan from a buddy of mine there."[17] The parasite (who clearly did not have the resources to provide the loan himself)[18] goes off to Caria so that Phaedromus can stay in Epidaurus near his beloved Planesium. A dinner party was to be Curculio's reward: Phaedromus had set a cook to planning the meal—a meal of leftovers, of course (251–54, 321; cf. 388)—even before the parasite's return, and when the newly arrived Curculio encounters his patron, he produces a lively demonstration of parasitical hunger to get a promise of that dinner before he divulges the bad news that there was no money to be had in Caria (309–27).[19] Instead of cash, however, he has a story and a plan.

---

15. nec parasitorum in comoediis assentatio faceta nobis videretur nisi essent milites gloriosi (Cic. *Amic.* 98).

16. The role reversal is symmetrical, since the slave Palinurus handles the selection of provisions for the meal (cf. *Capt.* 894, 901–18, for a parasite so engaged). Curculio is called "slave" at 623 and enacts a typical running-slave scene at 280–300 (Csapo 1989). In part the substitution of parasite for slave is due to the requirements of the plot, which needs an agent who can serve both *adulescens* and *miles*, but the similarity between the two roles is a theme touched on elsewhere in Plautus. In *Curculio* the same actor may even have played both parts (Conrad 1918).

17. nunc hinc parasitum in Cariam misi meum / petitum argentum a meo sodali mutuom (*Curc.* 67–68).

18. He had in fact "consumed" the property he once had: nulla [sc. res] est mihi, nam quam habui absumpsi celeriter (*Curc.* 600).

19. Zwierlein (1990, 245–50) would excise lines 310–18 as a post-Plautine addition. The lines contain an expansion of the "weak with hunger" theme of

Disappointed by the Carian *sodalis*, Curculio had taken himself off to the forum, where he saw a *miles* (suitable prey) and approached him (337–38). The *miles*, for his part, was looking for a man to do a job in Epidaurus: he wanted someone to collect some money he had deposited with a banker there (346–48). In the course of their negotiations, Curculio possessed himself of the soldier's seal ring, thinking that on returning to Epidaurus he would pretend to be an Artotrogus, an agent, that is, for the business transactions of the *miles* (another *gloriosus* one) Therapontigonus Platagidorus. This would enable him to use the soldier's deposit to purchase Planesium for Phaedromus.

Phaedromus is duly grateful. He welcomes Curculio back to Epidaurus eagerly—"Just the man I've been waiting for!" (*o mea opportunitas, Curculio exoptate*, 305–6)—and later he promises to safeguard his parasite "as I would myself and my divine protector" (*tamquam me et genium meum*, 628).[20] Better yet (from the parasite's point of view), Phaedromus feeds his parasite on credit, as it were.

> CURCULIO: Let's have a bite to eat first, ham, tripe, sweetbreads. These things (and bread and roast beef, a tall cup, a wide table) support the insides, so that one can plan properly. You deal with the tablets, this fellow will serve, I'll eat.[21]

---

line 309. They could be removed without detriment to the plot or the characterization of the parasite, but they do contribute to the characterization of the slave Palinurus, who has quite a sardonic eye for the free folk from whom his master seeks help in his amatory predicament (cf., apropos of the *lena*, lines 96–138; of Curculio, 223–28).

20. In Lindsay's text this phrase refers to the girl Planesium, not Curculio. But Lindsay suggests in the apparatus that the words *Phaedrome, opsecro, serua me* might be spoken by Curculio (who is being pummeled by the *miles* at this point) rather than by the girl, in which case Phaedromus promises to protect his parasite rather than his beloved. This reading makes better sense of the scene, since Planesium is in no immediate danger (Therapontigonus now wants fourfold damages, not the girl herself; see 619). Curculio had referred to Phaedromus as his *genius* earlier in the play (301; cf. *Pers.* 263, *Men.* 138).

21. CU: atque aliquid prius opstrudamus, pernam, sumen, glandium.
     haec sunt uentris stabilimenta, pane et assa bubula,
     poculum grande, aula magna, ut sati' consilia suppetant.
     tu tabellas consignato, hic ministrabit, ego edam.

                                   (*Curc.* 367–70)

Curculio makes the most of this opportunity, and at line 384 he emerges well stuffed and ready to work. But he is already thinking about the next meal: "Goodness! I certainly filled myself properly in there. I did leave one small nook empty in my belly, however, so as to be able to put away the leftovers of the leftovers."[22]

Needing assistance and generous with both recompense and recognition on receiving it, Phaedromus would be an ideal *rex* were it not for the precarious state of his finances. At the beginning of the play it even looked as though his self-indulgent lifestyle might have to be at least temporarily suspended (63–69, 329, 335). It is therefore not surprising that his parasite should approach a potential new patron (the *miles*) when the bid for a loan has failed. Parasites, after all, were known for their tendency to desert a patron who was out of funds. Once he figured out what could be done with the soldier's seal ring, of course, Curculio no longer needed Therapontigonus. But the relationship between them was not utterly abortive, for the plot that Curculio hatched to enable him to use Therapontigonus' money for Phaedromus' benefit required that he *pretend* to be Therapontigonus' parasite. He had to persuade the Epidaurian banker that he was the agent the soldier had arranged to send. He was equipped with tablets sealed by the all-important ring, of course, but he also did a little playacting to make his pretense plausible: the parasite plays the role of a parasite. He shows, for example, that he can produce the exaggerations that a *miles* likes to hear.

LYCO: Where is [Therapontigonus]? Why didn't he come himself?
CURCULIO: I'll tell you. It's because we arrived in Caria from India three days ago and he wants to get a statue made of solid gold (gold from the coins of Philip, no less), seven feet high, a monument to his deeds.
LY: Why that?
CU: I'll tell you. It's because he subjugated Persians, Paphlagonians, Chinese, Arabs, Carians, Cretans, Syrians, Rhodes, Lycia, the Lands of Gobble and Gulp, Centauromachia, Classia Uno-

---

22. edepol ne ego hic med intus expleui probe,
      et quidem reliqui in uentre cellae uni locum,
      ubi reliquiarum reliquias reconderem.

(*Curc.* 386–88)

mammia, the whole Libyan shore, all of Conterebromnia, half
of all nations everywhere, all within twenty days, alone.
LY: Bah!
CU: Why do you find it so amazing?
LY: Because even if they were all penned up like the sacred chick-
ens, one couldn't even walk around them in the space of a year.
Only someone coming from him would talk such nonsense.
CU: I'll tell you more if you like.[23]

The parasite's imitation of parasitical ways is a success—this story
alone sufficed to persuade Lyco that "Leaky," as the parasite names
himself—"Leaky because when I drink myself to sleep I take a leak in
the blankets" (416)[24]—was Therapontigonus' Artotrogus.

One further point about this clever and adaptable parasite requires
attention. To enhance the verisimilitude of his claim to represent the
miles, Curculio introduces himself to the banker as Therapontigonus'
freedman (413, 543, 582; cf. *salutem multam dicito patrono,* 524). This is
peculiar, as *libertini* are rare in Roman comedy.[25] In the *Captivi* the *senex*
Hegio has a freedman named Cordalus as a business connection (735),
in the *Eunuchus* the *adulescens* Chaerea has arranged a dinner party for

---

23. LY: ubi ipsus? qur non uenit? CU: ego dicam tibi:
     quia nudiusquartus uenimus in Cariam
     ex India; ibi nunc statuam uolt dare auream
     solidam faciundam ex auro Philippo, quae siet
     septempedalis, factis monumentum suis.
     LY: quam ob rem istuc? CU: dicam. quia enim Persas, Paphlagonas,
     Sinopas, Arabes, Caras, Cretanos, Syros,
     Rhodiam atque Lyciam, Perediam et Perbibesiam,
     Centauromachiam et Classiam Unomammiam,
     Libyamque oram <omnem>, omnem Conterebromniam,
     dimidiam partem nationum usque omnium
     subegit solus intra uiginti dies.
     LY: uah! CU: quid mirare? LY: quia enim in cauea si forent
     conclusi, itidem ut pulli gallinacei,
     ita non potuere uno anno circumirier.
     credo hercle te esse ab illo, nam ita nugas blatis.
     CU: immo etiam porro, si uis, dicam.
                                                    (*Curc.* 437–53)
     24. See chap. 1 n. 26 on nicknames. The derivation of the name *Summanus* is
disputed; I use Curculio's own definition. But see García Hernández 1992.
     25. Rawson 1993.

his friends at the house of a freedman named Discus (608). In both cases
a former master needs a service from his ex-slave. The label *freedman*
may have provided Roman poets with an easy explanation for the
patron's confidence that he would be served.[26] The Roman origin of
one freedman in Roman comedy is certain, at any rate. Donatus reports
that the expository dialogue between *senex* and *libertus* in Terence's
Andria (28–171) was adapted from a scene in which the conversants
were a *senex* and his wife. The freedman Sosia disappears from the play
after this scene, but the reason for his creation is apparent: the *senex*
needs someone on whose *fides* and *taciturnitas* he can rely (34). As
Donatus says, the *fides* guarantees that Sosia will accomplish the task
assigned him, while the *taciturnitas* keeps him quiet about the plot his
former master has devised (*ad* 34). The (fictional) freedman status of
"Leaky" has a precise purpose, too: it is a way of making the association between agent and employer look like a close one; that is, Curculio
creates a persona and a status for "Leaky" that makes him a plausible
emissary for the *miles*. Of interest here is not so much the equation of
parasitus and *libertus* (since, as we shall see, this particular equation is
not often made) but the fact that Plautus was trying to identify something in his audience's experience that corresponded in some degree to
the comic type that he had drawn so well in the *Miles gloriosus*.

Whereas Plautus calls on the Roman reality of ex-master/freedman
relationships to explain the parasite/*miles* connection, his contemporary Cato reverses the procedure in a striking passage in the *de Agricultura*, where he warns the absentee landowner to take care lest his farm
overseer support a parasite: *parasitum ne quem habeat* (*Agr.* 5.4). Cato's
use of the comic label is remarkable. It seems to be shorthand for a type
of behavior he had earlier warned against more fully: "The overseer
must not parade about, he must always keep sober, mustn't go out to
dinner parties" (*vilicus ne sit ambulator, sobrius siet semper, ad cenam
nequo eat*, 5.2). And the same goes for the housekeeper.

---

26. The situation in the *Poenulus* may be analogous if, as has been suggested,
the *advocati* (who are certainly ex-slaves, *Poen.* 519) are in fact the freedmen of
the *adulescens* (Rosivach 1983). Contra this reading see Lowe 1990 and Rawson
1993. In most instances comic references to the manumission of slaves are
prospective—it is held out as a potential reward for the successful completion
of an important task (*Amph.* 462, *Capt.* 408, 575, 713, *Epid.* 725–27, *M.g.* 961, *Pers.*
487, *Pseud.* 358).

She is not to be extravagant. She is to keep company as little as possible with women from the neighboring farms or elsewhere, and she is not to invite them to the farm. She is not to go out to dinner parties or to parade about.[27]

In short, Cato does not want the slaves in charge of the farm either to resemble or to patronize parasites.[28] Our sense of the interpenetration of comedy and reality here is reinforced when we turn to Plautus' *Persa*, in the opening scene of which we find a slave doing just what Cato warned against, inviting a friend to "a regal entertainment" at the expense of his absent master.

> TOXILUS: I'm a king in my own castle.
> SAGARISTIO: How's that?
> TO: My master is overseas.
> SA: Overseas, you say?
> TO: If you can allow yourself to be well-off, come on over. We'll spend some time together; you will be accommodated at the table of a king.[29]

The slave Toxilus is not simply holding out the prospect of regal (i.e., lavish) dinners here; he is offering to take Sagaristio on as his parasite. The adjective *basilicus*, "kingly," is a calque of the special sense of the Latin word *rex* that we have seen before, namely, "parasite's patron."[30]

---

27. ne nimium luxuriosa siet. Vicinas aliasque mulieres quam minimum utatur neve domum neve ad sese recipiat. Ad cenam nequo eat neve ambulatrix siet (Cato *Agr.* 143.1).

28. Columella tackles the problem as well: eidemque actori [sc. vilico] praecipiendum est, ne convictum cum domestico multoque minus cum extero habeat (*Rust.* 1.8.5).

29. TO: basilice agito eleutheria.
    SAG: quid iam? TO: quia erus peregri est. SAG: ain tu,
    peregri est? TO: si tut' tibi bene esse
    pote pati, ueni: uiues mecum,
    basilico accipiere uictu.

(*Persa* 29–31)

30. On the term *rex* see my introduction. Pace Harsh (1936) βασιλεύς and βασιλικός ("king" and "regal," respectively) do not have this sense in Greek, though they are used, as are *rex* and *regius*, to mean "a wealthy man" and "sumptuous." On the Roman origins of this usage, see Fraenkel 1960, 425, and, with further refinements, Shipp 1977, 7–9. Another bilingual pun involving

Sagaristio (himself a slave) never did become Toxilus' parasite, for he was not someone whose services needed to be bought but rather a true friend, helpful and loyal for all the right reasons.[31] But there was only so much he could do to help Toxilus. For a permanent solution to his predicament, Toxilus called on the services of a real parasite, Saturio.

TO: Why, there's the parasite whose help I need. I'll pretend not to see the man. That way I can get him interested. [*to servants inside the house*] Do what I asked, and do it quick. I don't want there to be any waiting when I return. Mix the honey wine, and get the fruit plate ready; warm it up well and dash on the spice. He'll soon be here, I think, my fellow funster.

SATURIO: He means me. Hallelujah!

TO: I imagine he'll be here soon, after a stop at the baths.

SAT: Right on the mark!

TO: Make sure the noodles and meat are stewing—I want them fully cooked.

SAT: He's got it right. Underdone, they're awful. You want them soft when you swallow them down. You want the noodles to have a thick broth to them, too. That see-through thin stuff isn't worth a thing. A noodle dish ought to be like [the text is corrupt]. I want something for the belly, not the bladder.

TO: I hear someone talking nearby.

SAT: Jupiter mine, your earthbound fellow diner salutes you.

---

parasites appears at line 99, where Saturio refers to himself as the terrestrial *coepulonus* (dinner companion) of "Jupiter" (Toxilus). This is a reference to a newly instituted board of priests of the Capitoline triad, the *coepuloni* (see Woytek 1982, ad loc.), but it gains additional point from the fact that παράσιτος, too, was originally a cult title. The Greek term was applied as a nickname, to the sponger of comedy (see my introduction); Plautus was trying to reproduce the joke in Latin. It never caught on.

31. *Persa* 21, 255, 263, 265, 595, 614. At line 41, however, Toxilus tells Sagaristio that he will "buy" his (Toxilus') friendship if he comes up with the money that Toxilus needs to free his *amica*. Woytek 1982 objects to the crudity of the language and argues that *emere* is a late interpolation for *facere*, but I think it is a sardonic comment on friendship rather than a parallel for *Asin.* 72 and 673 or *Trin.* 1056. The financial metaphor is renewed in line 46 with *ueneam*. The frank tone of *emere* is well suited to a character who is at least as much tricky slave as infatuated *adulescens*.

TO: Saturio my friend, how lucky for me that you've come just now![32]

The fortunate parasites of the *Asinaria, Miles gloriosus,* and *Curculio* had either wealthy (or at least wellborn) young men or military types as patrons. Saturio is parasite to a slave and is treated rather more roughly. Toxilus' plan for cheating the *leno* in fact tests (but does not find) the limits of parasitical willingness to suffer injury to be fed.[33]

Saturio alone of literary parasites is endowed with the rudiments of a family, a daughter—born, appropriately enough, in the kitchen

---

32. TO: sed eccum parasitum quoius mihi auxiliost opus.
    simulabo quasi non uideam: ita adliciam uirum.
    curate istic uos atque adproperate ocius,
    ne mihi morae sit quicquam ubi ego intro aduenero.
    commisce mulsum, struthea coluteaque appara,
    bene ut in scutris concaleat, et calamum inice.
    iam pol ille hic aderit, credo, congerro meus.
    SAT: me dicit, eugae! TO: lautum credo e balineis
    iam hic adfuturum. SAT: ut ordine omnem rem tenet!
    TO: collyrae facite ut madeant et colyphia,
    ne mihi incocta detis. SAT: rem loquitur meram.
    nihili sunt crudae nisi quas madidas gluttias;
    tum nisi cremore crassost ius collyricum
    nihilist macrum illud epicrocum pellucidum:
    quasi †iuueam† esse ius decet collyricum.
    nolo in uesicam quod eat, in uentrum uolo.
    TO: prope me hic nescioquis loquitur. SAT: o mi Iuppiter!
    terrestris te coepulonus compellat tuos.
    TO: O Saturio, opportune aduenisti mihi.

                                                    (*Persa* 83–101)

In 100 I follow Woytek in retaining *te*.

33. In treating Saturio as a parasite I am focusing on the Plautine play, in which he is labeled a parasite (*eccum parasitum,* 83). The character on whose help the lover relies in the Greek model may have been a sycophant rather than a parasite (Chiarini 1979; cf. Lowe 1989b), but the matter is far from clear. If he was a *sycophanta impudens,* how was he to be compensated for his services? Tricky slaves are promised manumission (see n. 26 in this chapter), and tricky parasites look forward to a feeding, but how would a tricky sycophant be paid? All of the money that was extracted from the *leno* by the Arab-captive ruse was paid back to the *leno* to buy Toxilus' beloved.

(631).[34] Hitherto he had brought her up properly (127–28), and she has (however improbably) turned out extremely well, being pretty, obedient, clever, and unswervingly honest.[35] But Toxilus now asks Saturio, who had been his *parasitus* for some time—he is on familiar terms with the leftovers at Toxilus' house (77–79)—to sell her to a brothel keeper.

TO: You are capable of procuring that money for me.

SAT: I'd like to, certainly.

TO: Then let me sell her.

SAT: You'll sell her, you say?

TO: Well actually I'll get somebody else to do the selling, someone who can claim that he has come from abroad. This *leno* came here from Megara just six months ago.

SAT: Those leftovers are spoiling. This business can wait until later.

TO: It can, can it? Believe you me, not a bite will you eat today until you promise that you'll do as I ask. And unless you bring your daughter over as quick as quick can be, I'll revoke your membership in the dining club. Well, what will it be? Why don't you tell me what you plan to do?

SAT: Sell me, too, if you like, so long as you sell me with a full belly!

TO: Well, get going if you're going to help.

SAT: I'm going to do just what you want.[36]

---

34. The parasite is usually bereft of material possessions (e.g., see Ter. *Eun.* 243: *omnia habeo neque quicquam habeo*) and relatives. According to Pollux (4.119), in Menander's *Sicyonius* the parasite Theron wears white because he is about to get married, but we do not know if he does in fact take a bride in the course of the play. Phormio, of course, claims that he is about to marry, but only as an aid to the stratagem. It comes to nothing. The lament at Pomponius 34 Ribbeck may be that of a parasite: vix nunc quod edim invenio; quid nam fiet, si quam duxero? The reference to parasites as home owners in the prologue of the *Menaechmi* (76) is anomalous.

35. *Persa* 130, 378–79, 521, 546–48, 564, 622–23, 635, 639, 645; cf. 382: necessitate me mala ut fiam faces. On the *virgo*'s part, see the recent discussion by Lowe (1989b).

36.   TO: hoc tu mi reperire argentum potes.
   SAT: cupio hercle. TO: tum tu me sine illam uendere.
   SAT: tun illam uendas? TO: immo alium adlegauero
   qui uendat, qui esse se peregrinum praedicet.
   sicut istic leno non sex menses Megaribus
   huc est quom commigrauit. SAT: pereunt reliquiae.
   posterius istuc tamen potest. TO: scin quam potest?

Saturio is understandably reluctant, but he finally capitulates when Toxilus threatens to cut off supplies. Threaten his belly, in fact, and he will agree to anything, to selling his daughter (it is worth noting that he agrees to the plan at lines 145–47, i.e., before he learns that the trick will allow him to rescue the girl before the worst consequences of the sale occur), and even to selling himself, provided he goes with a full belly.[37] The girl realizes that her name might as well be Lucris ("Profit"), for all she means to her father (624). The parasite of a demanding patron like Toxilus cannot afford to have scruples about paternal obligations or anything else.

Public opinion, for example, has long ceased to trouble Saturio. He expresses his contempt for it in vigorous terms: "Let them say what they like. To hell with them! All the hostility in the world doesn't worry me as much as the prospect of an empty table before me."[38] And in the course of the play Saturio is forced to abandon the props for his self-respect as well.[39]

In his entrance monologue we see him advancing the argument that there are worse villains than himself abroad, namely, the "legal experts" (*quadruplatores*) who press charges in cases that do not concern them in the hopes of profiting either from the court-ordained rewards for successful prosecution or from bribes from potential victims.

> numquam hercle hodie hic prius edis, ne frustra sis,
> quam te hoc facturum quod rogo adfirmas mihi;
> atque nisi gnatam tecum huc iam quantum potest
> adducis, exigam hercle ego te ex hac decuria.
> quid nunc? quid est? quin dicis quid facturu' sis?
> SAT: quaeso hercle me quoque etiam uende, si lubet,
> dum saturum uendas. TO: hoc, si facturu's, face.
> SAT: faciam equidem quae uis.

(Persa 133–47)

37. Voluntary self-sale is attested in the real world as well, though somewhat later (Ramin and Veyne 1981).

38.   ferant [sc. inimici] eantque maxumam malam crucem;
      non ego inimicitias omnis plure existumo
      quam mensa inanis nunc si apponatur mihi.

(Persa 352–54; cf. 371–74)

Saturio's daughter reveals what that "public opinion" would be: her father will be thought to have ruined himself (*quod habuit perdidit*, 644).

39. On the contrast between Saturio's boasts and his actions see Chiarini 1979, 88–92.

A long-standing and ancient profession have I, one handed down by my ancestors. I stick to it and practice it quite diligently. Not one of my ancestors but fed his belly by playing the parasite. Father, grandfather, great-grandfather, and back three generations further, all of them always ate other men's food (like rodents they were). And no one was ever able to outdo them at eating— they were called "Hardheads," after all. From them I get my profession and rank. I wouldn't dream of becoming a prosecutor: it's not right to go after other men's goods at no risk to oneself, and I don't approve of those who do so.[40]

---

40. ueterem atque antiquom quaestum maiorum meum
    seruo atque optineo et magna cum cura colo.
    nam numquam quisquam meorum maiorum fuit
    quin parasitando pauerint uentris suos:
    pater, auos, proauos, abauos, atauos, tritauos
    quasi mures semper edere alienum cibum,
    neque edacitate eos quisquam poterat uincere,
    namque is cognomentum erat duris Capitonibus.
    unde ego hunc quaestum optineo et maiorum locum.
    neque quadrupulari me uolo, neque enim decet
    sine meo periclo ire aliena ereptum bona
    neque illi qui faciunt mihi placent.

                                                              (*Persa* 53–64)

On this passage as a whole, see Woytek 1982, ad loc., as well as his 1973 article. In line 60 I read *namque* with Pius and Bergk for the *neque* offered by the manuscripts. The alteration is easy, palaeographically speaking, and is required by the sense. Leo and others have preferred *atque*, but this leaves the line, as Woytek points out, a non sequitur. To be sure, voracity and indifference to abuse are both well-established parasitical characteristics, but Saturio is not producing a sampler of features; he is focusing his attention on his ancestors' ability to fill their bellies at other men's expense. The ability to accept physical insult is causally connected to this idea: his ancestors ate as much as they did precisely because their heads were hard; unlike Gnatho's wretched friend (*Eun.* 244–45), they did not mind being *plagipatidae*. Like Marti (1984, 395) I am not persuaded by Woytek's *neque is cognomentum erat viris capitonibus*. Though Woytek objects to Leo's "Texteingriff," his own is more radical. I would agree with Marti (398) in saying that Plautus is expecting rather much of his audience's translating powers, and I add that it is not as easy a translation as κέ-φαλος/*capito* (as Woytek might lead one to believe). For as his own examples show, the comic name for the fish in passages relevant to parasites is inevitably κεστρεύς (see chap. 1 n. 3). And as Woytek admits, the νῆστις κεστρεύς was not remarked on by Romans. Furthermore, some reference to physical abuse here is necessary to explain Saturio's expression *sine meo periclo* in line 63,

Leaving aside the vexed question of the reality of the despised
quadrupulator, let us look at how this monologue functions in the
play.[41] Saturio professes the deepest scorn for these legal experts, but
he in fact behaves in much the same way that they do, for Toxilus' plan
requires Saturio to use legal pressure to get money from the pimp (*age
ambula in ius, leno*, etc., 745–52). And since Saturio is bound to win his
suit when he asserts that his daughter is freeborn, his attack on the
leno—who acquired the girl without guarantees (i.e., *suo periclo*, 665,
715)—involves no risk to himself. In this matter, then, as well as in the
sale of his daughter, it is clear that for a parasite nothing, whether personal independence, paternal duty, or self-respect, takes precedence
over the demands of the belly.

In the *Curculio* we saw that Curculio/"Leaky" used different techniques for different patrons: service for the *adulescens* and flattery for
the *miles*. Saturio, too, knows two approaches. The action of the *Persa*
displays him helpful to the point of servility, but dinner-party amusement in the form of jokes or submission to physical abuse had been his
meal ticket in the past. As "Hardheads," he and his forebears could suffer blows without being put off their feed (57–60). And as for the jokes,
Saturio has a whole sackful of first-quality joke books. He assures his
daughter that she will never be in want if she has these at hand.

> VIRGO: You're forcing me to spoil my good character, you know.
> You ought to watch out that the report of this business doesn't
> cause prospective husbands to cancel arrangements when you
> want to marry me off.
>
> SAT: Quiet, silly. Don't you see how things are today, how easy it

---

where he objects that the *quadruplatores* take other men's money without any
risk to themselves. Parasites, then, must "earn" their keep by exposing their
persons to the βέλος γελωτοποιόν.

41. Real element in Greek society: Leo 1912, 123–25; Paoli 1954. Ahistorical
blend of Greek and Roman: Woytek 1982, ad loc.; but see Marti 1984, 397. Plautine addition derived from the Roman sphere: Bettini 1977; Danek 1988.
Danek's essay, the most recent study of the passage, does take the persona of
the speaker into consideration, arguing that the scene contains an amusing and
very Plautine piercing of the dramatic illusion when the parasite, a purely
Greek figure, begins to comment on the *quadruplator*, a type at home in Rome as
well as Athens (231–32). But his premise, that the parasite resembled nothing in
Roman society, is undefended (and, I argue, indefensible).

is to find a husband even if one's reputation is not of the best?
As long as there's a dowry, faults don't get in the way.
VI: I hope you bear in mind the fact that I have no dowry?
SAT: Watch your tongue! For the love of the gods and our ancestors, don't you say you are dowerless when you've a perfectly
good dowry at home! Why, I've got a whole sackful of books. If
you carry out this job that we're on cleverly, you'll get six hundred jokes from my supply as a dowry—Attic jokes, all of 'em,
not a Sicilian in the bunch. With this dowry you'll be able to
marry even a . . . beggar.[42]

The past success of these jokes is attested by Saturio's daughter: when
the *leno* inquires about her father's standing, she replies (with scrupu-
lous attention to the truth): "No one was more popular. Slaves and free
men alike were fond of him" (648–49; cf. 645). Just at present, however,
the jester's approach does not seem to suffice. Toxilus requires service,
and service he gets. In the eyes of the *virgo*, however, Saturio goes too
far with his helpfulness. His efforts to secure a place at his patron's
table render himself and his daughter wretched: "Why should I mention who he was in time past? At present the only name we need is Misery" (*quid illum miserum memorem qui fuit? nunc et illum Miserum et me
Miseram aequom est nominarier*, 646–47).

Saturio's baseness contributes largely to the very Saturnalian atmosphere of a play in which the slaves display the habits and virtues of
wealthy and wellborn *adulescentes*, the young girl is a model of filial

---

42.   VI: uerum uideto, me ubi uoles nuptum dare,
        ne haec fama faciat repudiosas nuptias.
        SAT: tace, stulta. non tu nunc hominum mores uides,
        quoiiu' modi hic cum mala fama facile nubitur?
        dum dos sit, nullum uitium uitio uortitur.
        VI: ergo istuc facito ut ueniat in mentem tibi
        me esse indotatam. SAT: caue sis tu istuc dixeris.
        pol deum uirtute dicam et maiorum meum,
        ne te indotatam dicas quoi dos sit domi:
        librorum eccillum habeo plenum soracum.
        si hoc adcurassis lepide, quoi rei operam damus,
        dabuntur dotis tibi inde sescenti logei
        atque Attici omnes; nullum Siculum acceperis:
        cum hac dote poteris uel mendico nubere.

                                                        (*Persa* 383–96)

obedience, social respectability, and moral uprightness, while of the free men one is a brothel keeper and the other a particularly obsequious parasite. That there ought to be a connection between status and behavior is suggested near the end of the play when the slave Toxilus instructs his recently freed beloved about the behavior appropriate to her new status.

> You really ought to do as I say. If I wasn't around to look after you, this fellow would make a streetwalker out of you before long. Part of being an ex-slave is that if you don't oppose your former owner in something, you don't feel really free or respectable or honorable. You have to oppose him, criticize him, or show that gratitude only goes so far.[43]

Saturio's gratitude for his feed, however, knows no bounds.

Unlike Saturio, who shows no real reluctance to humble himself, the parasite of the *Menaechmi*, Peniculus ("Sponge"), chafes at his position in life.[44] When we first meet him, however, he seems to be an extraor-

---

43. te mihi dicto audientem esse addecet, nam hercle apsque me
    foret et meo praesidio, hic faceret te prostibilem propediem.
    sed ita pars libertinorum est: nisi patrono qui aduorsatust,
    nec sati' liber sibi uidetur nic sati' frugi nec sat honestus,
    ni id ecfecit, ni ei male dixit, ni grato ingratus repertust.

    (Persa 836–40)

44. Gratwick (1993, *ad* 77–78) glosses Peniculus' name with "Tail, Appendage," citing the equivalence "*penis = cauda*" given at Fest. 230 Müller [M], and suggesting that the name has a sexual connotation that the explanation given here ("because when I eat I wipe the tables clean," *Iuuentus nomen fecit Peniculo mihi / ideo quia—mensam quando edo, detergeo,* 77–78) deliberately disappoints. The diminutives of *penis, peniculus* and *penicillus,* frequent in discussions of art, medicine, and building construction, are used of "wipes" ranging in type from brushes, to sponges, to swabs (*TLL* s.vv.). In the *Menaechmi* Peniculus' name, besides being "explained," is the subject of two mistaken-identity jokes: at line 286 a *peniculus* is something carried in a sack while traveling (*eccum in uidulo saluom fero*); at 391 it is a device for cleaning shoes (*qui extergentur baxeae*). Both "tail" (i.e., "brush") and "sponge" would suit in all three passages, but "Sponge" (which is what *peniculus* clearly means at *Rudens* 1008–9) seems to me the better name for a parasite, as sponges were a regular item of convivial apparatus, appearing, for example, in banqueting type-scenes in the *Odyssey* (1.111–12, 20.151–52, 22.438–39). Parasites had little time for accessory pleasures, such as sex.

dinarily fortunate parasite, for he has a wealthy and generous young patron, of whom he can say:

> Menaechmus doesn't just feed folks, you see, he raises and revives them. There is no better healer than he. It's his way; at dinner he provides with a generous hand, Ceres-fashion. He loads the tables so, heaps the platters so high, that you have to stand up on the couch to serve yourself from the top.[45]

But of late there has been a worrisome and expensive absence of invitations, owing to the jealous watchfulness of his patron's wife, and Peniculus comes onstage complaining.

> Binding captives with chains and putting shackles on runaways are pointless measures, as I see it. For a wretched man faced with one evil on top of another is all the more eager to escape or to take some desperate action. One way or another he'll get free of his bonds. The ones in fetters apply the file to the ring or smash the lock with a stone, trivial tasks. But if you really want to keep someone close by and prevent him from escaping, you ought to use food and drink to bind him. Fasten his beak to a well-spread mess. As long as you provide him with food and drink—as much as he wants and every day—never ever will he run away. Even if he's due to lose his head, you'll keep him near if you use bonds like this. Food-fetters bend, they don't break, and the more you stretch them the tighter they pinch. I myself am on my way to Menaechmus' house. I was made over to him a long time ago. I'm just hoping he's got some fetters for me.[46]

---

45. nam illic homo homines non alit uerum educat
     recreatque: nullus melius medicinam facit.
     ita est adulescens ipsus; escae maxumae,
     Cerealis cenas dat, ita mensas extruit,
     tantas struices concinnat patinarias:
     standumst in lecto si quid de summo petas.
                    (*Men.* 98–103; the text is from Gratwick 1993)
Medicina is an unusual metaphor for the support of parasites, but cf. Timocles 13: ὡς δ᾽ ἦν ἡρμένη / βίου τιθήνη, πολεμία λιμοῦ, φύλαξ / φιλίας, ἰατρός ἐκλύτου βουλιμίας, / τράπεζα.
  46. homines captiuos qui catenis uinciunt
       et qui fugitiuis seruis indunt compedes
       nimis stulte faciunt mea quidem sententia.

A patron's generosity was a feeding trough (*praesepes*) for Curculio and a dining club (*decuria*) for Saturio, but to Peniculus it feels more like a fetter. Still, when resources run out at home (104–7), he shows up early in the day to remind Menaechmus of his existence and try for an invitation.

Obtaining an invitation is crucial for the success of parasites in Roman comedy. We saw earlier that the parasite of Greek comedy was customarily ἄκλητος, "uninvited," but we hear very little about uninvited guests in Rome.[47] The closest equivalents are the *umbrae* mentioned by Horace, but even these would seem to have been included in a blanket invitation issued to their sponsor.[48] There are no *umbrae* in comedy. In fact, parasites are frequently found complaining when their patrons intend to dine out without them. Thus when Menaechmus taunts his wife with "Because you insist on keeping an eye on me, I'll make your spying worthwhile today. I'll get me a girl and arrange a meal out somewhere," Peniculus finds cause for lament on his own account: "It may look like the fellow is hurting his wife with his talk, but really it's me. If he eats out I'm the one who pays the penalty, not

---

> nam homini misero si ad malum accedit malum,
> maior lubido est fugere et facere nequiter.
> nam se ex catenis eximunt aliquo modo,
> tum compediti anum lima praeterunt
> aut lapide excutiunt clauom. nugae sunt eae.
> quem tu adseruare recte ne aufugiat uoles
> esca atque potione uinciri decet.
> apud mensam plenam homini rostrum deliges;
> dum tu illi quod edit et quod potet praebeas,
> suo arbitratu, ad fatim, cottidie,
> numquam edepol fugiet, tametsi capital fecerit.
> facile adseruabis, dum eo uinclo uincies:
> ita istaec nimis lenta uincla sunt escaria,
> quam magis extendas, tanto adstringunt artius.
> nam ego ad Menaechmum hunc eo, quo iam diu
> sum iudicatus; ultro eo ut me uinciat.

(*Men.* 79–97)

47. In the *Captivi* Ergasilus says that he is generally *inuocatus . . . in conuiuio* (70), but in fact he receives an invitation to that day's dinner at line 176 and one *in perpetuum* later on (897). In the *Eunuchus* it is clear that Gnatho is asking for a special favor when he stipulates that the price of his services is *ut mihi tua domus / te praesente absente pateat, invocato ut sit locus semper* (1058–60).

48. On *umbrae* see *Sat.* 2.8.22, *Epist.* 1.5.28; cf. Plut. *Mor.* 707a and chap. 4 n. 26.

his wife."[49] In Roman comedy, as in Roman society, an invitation was necessary to get in the door.[50]

A hopeful Peniculus, then, is paying a very Roman visit to his patron: the morning *salutatio* was often the time at which invitations were issued.[51] Before he can make his call, however, Menaechmus himself emerges from the house.

> MENAECHMUS: Success at last! . . . I carried off booty from the enemy; my allies are safe and sound.
>
> PENICULUS: Hoy there, young fella! Is there anything in that booty for me?
>
> MEN: Help, an ambush!
>
> PEN: No, you're safe among your own, don't worry.
>
> MEN: Who is it?
>
> PEN: It's me.
>
> MEN: Greetings, friend Fit, friend Timely.
>
> PEN: Greetings.
>
> MEN: What are you up to?
>
> PEN: I'm holding my guardian angel by the hand.
>
> MEN: You couldn't have come at a better time.
>
> PEN: That's my way. I know all the ins and outs of fitting in.[52]

---

49. atque adeo, ne me nequiquam serues, ob eam industriam / hodie ducam scortum atque aliquo ad cenam condicam foras (*Men.* 123–24); illic homo se uxori simulat male loqui, loquitur mihi; / nam si foris cenat, profecto me, haud uxorem, ulciscitur (*Men.* 125–26). Cf. *Stich.* 190, 469–97, 596–613, *Capt.* 172–75.

50. We do not find parasites who are ἀσύμβολος in Roman comedy either, except at Ter. *Eun.* 339. The relationship between patron and parasite tended to last longer in Rome. Peniculus, for example, considers himself a member of Menaechmus' *familia* (*Men.* 667; cf. *Curc.* 146–50).

51. The details of parasite etiquette are less important than the evidence that authors writing for the Roman stage adapted the stock type to fit conditions with which their audience was familiar.

52. MEN: euax! . . .
    auorti praedam ab hostibus, nostrum salute socium
    PEN: heus adulescens, ecqua in istac pars inest praeda mihi?
    MEN: perii, in insidias deueni. PEN: immo in praesidium, ne time.
    MEN: quis homo est? PEN: ego sum. MEN: o mea Commoditas, o mea Opportunitas,
    salue. PEN: salue. MEN: quid agis? PEN: teneo dext<e>ra genium meum.
    MEN: non potuisti magis per tempus mihi aduenire quam aduenis.
    PEN: ita ego soleo; Commoditatis omnis articulos scio.
                                                    (*Men.* 127–40)

Peniculus receives a warm greeting (*o mea Commoditas, o mea Opportunitas*, 137) and provides Menaechmus with an audience to whom to display his thievish daring. The parasite takes his cue from a Menaechmus who is temporarily as puffed up with his recent victory over his wife as any *miles gloriosus:* when Menaechmus speaks of booty, Peniculus speaks of booty too. With a patron in this military frame of mind, flattery is in order, of course, and Peniculus obliges. He does so rather reluctantly, however, since he is preoccupied by the domestic contretemps that he overheard at the door.

> MEN: Tell me, have you ever seen a scene in a wall painting with
>   the eagle carrying off Ganymede? Or Venus Adonis?
> PEN: Often. But what do those scenes have to do with me?
> MEN: Well, look at me. Don't I remind you of something?
> PEN: What's that getup of yours?
> MEN: Tell me I'm a wit.
> PEN: When do we eat?
> MEN: But say what I told you to.
> PEN: Okay, you're a wit.
> MEN: Can't you add anything to that?
> PEN: A very funny one.
> MEN: Go on, go on.
> PEN: Not unless I know what's in it for me. You've had a fight with
>   your wife, so I'm wary of getting too close to you.[53]

An invitation to the naughty dinner party with which Menaechmus planned to celebrate his success is eventually forthcoming (152–53), but even after the invitation Peniculus is a strangely reluctant parasite. Menaechmus has to reprimand him twice, in fact. When Peniculus urges him to hurry up and make arrangements for the promised party, Menaechmus is rather curt: "You yourself get in the way of what you

---

53. MEN: dic mihi, <e>numquam tu uidisti tabulam pictam in pariete,
    ubi aquila Catamitum raperet aub ubi Venus Adoneum?
    PEN: saepe; sed quid istae picturae ad me attinent? MEN: age, me aspice.
    ecquid adsimulo similiter? PEN: qui istic †est ornatus tuos?
    MEN: dic hominem lepidissimum esse me<d>. PEN: ubi essuri sumus?
    MEN: dic modo hoc quod ego te iubeo. PEN: dico: homo lepidissime.
    MEN: ecquid audes de tuo istuc addere? PEN: atque hilarissime.
    MEN: perge, <perge, PEN:> non pergo hercle, nisi scio qua gratia.
    litigium tibist cum uxor<e>, eo mihi abs te caueo cautius.
                                                      (*Men.* 143–51)

want when you talk back to me" (156). Peniculus does apply his nose to the stolen cloak when asked to do so (he is supposed to use his keen sense of smell to figure out Menaechmus' intentions for the day), but even here he makes it clear that he doesn't much enjoy the job, for Menaechmus teases him with "You're very funny when you turn up your nose like that" (169).[54]

Peniculus is clearly no Saturio. In fact, his tolerance for abuse reaches its limit just halfway through the play, when he learns that owing to a mishap in the forum, he has missed the meal he had taken such trouble to get invited to. This latest disappointment drives him to break one of the cardinal rules of parasite behavior. He becomes angry with his patron and shows it: "You'll pay for insulting me, and I'll make sure that the dinner you ate up does not go unavenged."[55] A reluctant, angry parasite is appropriate in a comedy so unconventional as to end in a divorce rather than a betrothal, and Peniculus' final act is as peculiar as the rest of his behavior: he attempts to ally himself with the well-dowered wife against her husband.[56] But a *matrona* is not at all the right sort of patroness for a parasite. When he asks what the reward for his information about the theft of the cloak is to be, for example, she promises to return the favor when something has been stolen from him. This promise is of course of no use at all to him (664–65), and Peniculus takes himself back to the forum in a huff: "Husband and wife, be damned to you both. I can see that I've lost my place in this household."[57]

Peniculus severs his ties with his benefactor Menaechmus out of a momentary pique, not because Menaechmus had changed his Ceres-like policy of generous provisions. But midway through the play, Menaechmus shows that he is as reluctant a patron to an unnamed man (*cliens quidam*, 568) as Peniculus is a parasite. To appreciate the significance of the appearance of both parasite and *cliens* in this play, we need to look at Menaechmus' patronal lament.

---

54. On the animal qualities of parasites see chap. 1 n. 16 .

55. omnes in te istaec recident contumeliae. / faxo haud inultus prandium comederis (*Men.* 520–21).

56. The parasites in the *Asinaria* and the *Phormio* take the side of the *matrona* against her husband, but on behalf of their own patrons, not in the hope of appending themselves to the woman.

57. cum uiro cum uxore, di uos perdant. properabo ad forum, / nam ex hac familia me plane excidisse intellego (*Men.* 666–67).

Menaechmus sets off for the forum in the company of Peniculus but returns complaining about a client who has delayed his return to Erotium's house. Menaechmus prefaces his specific complaints about *cliens quidam* with some general remarks on the behavior of contemporary patrons.

> Everyone wants to have hordes of *clientes*, but they don't consider in the least whether their *clientes* are good men or bad. Money counts more in a *cliens* than a reputation for reliability. A man who has character but no cash is worthless as a *cliens*. Rich and dishonest, he's considered "a good sort." Break the laws and defraud your fellow, and you'll have patrons zealous on your behalf.[58]

He would seem to subscribe to the contemporary view himself, since he performs a service for *cliens quidam* at some inconvenience.

> When the trial date is set for *clientes*, it's set for their patrons as well; the case comes before the people or the praetor or into the aedile's court. That's how a client of mine kept me detained in court today—couldn't do what I wanted or keep the company I wanted. I took his case before the aediles, made up a defense for all his many awful acts. I drew up terms that were tricky, hard to follow. I said neither more nor less than what was needed to get an agreement down. And then he up and names me as his backer![59]

---

58. clientes sibi omnes uolunt esse multos:
    bonine an mali sint, id haud quaeritant;
    res magis quaeritur quam clientum fides
    cuius modi clueat.
    si est pauper atque haud malus, nequam habetur;
    sin diues malust, is cliens frugi habetur.
    qui nec leges neque aequom bonum usquam colunt,
    sollicitos patronos habent.

    (*Men.* 574–79)

59. †lisuirist ubi dicitur dies, simul patronis dicitur,
    quippe qui pro illis loquantur quae male fecerint.
    aut ad populum aut in iure aut apud aedilem res est.
    sicut me hodie nimis sollicitum cliens quidam habuit neque quod uolui
    agere <2/3> quicquam licitumst, ita me attinuit, ita detinuit.

It is a commonplace in both ancient and modern descriptions of patron-age that from the very beginning of the institution it was incumbent on *patroni* to defend their *clientes* in court. By saying that it is rich *clientes* (i.e., those who have something to pay with) and *clientes* involved in dubious business practices (i.e., those who have something to pay for) who have diligent patrons, Menaechmus suggests that the legal repre-sentation incumbent on patrons had its compensations. Indeed, he speaks of competition among potential patrons for *clientes*, particularly for wealthy *clientes*, no matter how dubious their character. In this situ-ation we see a relationship between patron and client in which the ini-tiative for establishing a relationship comes at least as much from above as from below. Menaechmus may resent the exertions involved in maintaining his own social position, but he exerts himself nonetheless.

The identity of his *cliens* is left obscure in the play; he is just *cliens quidam*.[60] Yet there is clearly a connection of some sort between Penicu-

---

> apud aediles pro eius factis plurumisque pessumisque
> dixi causam, condiciones tetuli tortas, confragosas.
> <h>aut plus , <h>aut minus quam opus fuerat dicto dixeram,
>   controuersiam†
> ut sponsio fieret. quid ille †qui praedem dedit?

(*Men.* 585–93)

For a discussion, see Fraenkel 1960, 152–54.

60. Gratwick (1993, 196) calls him "a shadowy second Peniculus" and sug-gests that in the Greek original the person to whose aid Menaechmus came in the forum was Peniculus himself. Such an identification would, he claims, pro-vide a better motivation for both Peniculus' morning visit to Menaechmus (he would be coming to ask for legal or business help, not an invitation to dinner) and Menaechmus' trip to the forum (for business, not drinking; cf. 213–14). But the identification is not necessary. Looking for an invitation is perfectly appro-priate parasite business, and drinking in the forum is a perfectly good excuse for an exit that the plot requires (the Epidamnian Menaechmus, Peniculus' patron, has to be cleared away before his Syracusan twin can appear). And the identification creates as many problems as it solves. If the Greek equivalent of Menaechmus was defending a Peniculus, how did the two get separated? And would the original Peniculus be upset about the loss of a dinner if he had just received so substantial a benefit as a legal defense from his patron? In the Greek original the recipient of Menaechmus' patronal attentions is more likely to have been someone like the relative who delayed Lysidamas with legal business at *Casina* 563–73 or the *amici* whom the young Lesbonicus is urged to aid (in pref-erence to his *amica*) at *Trinummus* 651. It is *amici* to whom Menaechmus looks for counsel when circumstances render him *exclusissimus* ("shut out absolutely everywhere," 698): neque domi neque apud amicam mihi iam quicquam cre-

lus and *cliens quidam:* both are dependents of the wealthy and generous Menaechmus. For the parasite, dependence on Menaechmus is a fetter, it compels him to do things he resents doing (such as flattering a foolish patron and using his nose like a bloodhound). *Cliens quidam,* however, though he has no voice, is presumably grateful for Menaechmus' defense. For of that pair it is Menaechmus who complains about the burden the relationship places on him. Patronal obligations get in the way of his fun. The complaints of Peniculus (about the fetter) and Menaechmus (about the inconvenience of clients) come from very different worlds. The plight of the parasite reflects a system in which the initiative for the relationship comes more from below than from above. Such a situation promotes parasitical behavior: obsequiousness to the point of servility, toleration of insult and injury, and so on. When the initiative is more from above than from below, however, as in the picture that Menaechmus gives, it is the patron's turn to complain. Whether the preponderant initiative comes from below or from above depends on historical circumstances; the "balance of power" between patron and *cliens* is different at different times. The juxtaposition of Peniculus and *cliens quidam* in this play is a useful indication of the variety of experience possible in relationships that would fit the definition of patronage.

To illustrate the sorts of behavior that arise when the subordinate is more eager to establish and exploit patronage ties than the patron is, we may turn to Plautus' *Stichus.* The parasite of this play, Gelasimus ("Mr. Funny"), is more wretched than any of his Plautine peers. He has a prominent part—roughly 140 lines or parts of lines out of 775—but this only means that he is more thoroughly abused than any other Roman parasite. His sorry plight stems directly from not having an active patron. Epignomus and Pamphilippus, young brothers who had been generous hosts in the past, have been away on business for upwards of two years when the play opens (137). Gelasimus comes on stage complaining about the paucity of opportunities elsewhere.

There's one sort of speech that men have utterly lost the habit of.
A great shame, this, since it was, to my mind anyway, a most

---

ditur. / ibo et consulam hanc rem amicos, quid faciendum censeant (*Men.* 699–700). On *sunegoroi* in Roman comedy see Rosivach 1983.

worthwhile and clever sort. They used to say: "Come to dinner at such and such a place. You should do it. Say you will. Don't say no. Can you make it? I want it to happen, you know, and I won't stop asking till you come." For this they've now found a substitute, a low cheapskate phrase, "I'd invite you to dinner if I weren't dining out myself."[61]

Not finding any invitations in contemporary "Athens," Gelasimus turns to the Romans in the audience and tries to interest them in the entertainment he can provide.

I've now decided to hold an auction. I've got to sell off everything I have. Step right up, won't you; everyone's a winner here. I'm selling my jokes. Come on, make a bid. Who'll say a dinner? Anyone give me a lunch? Hercules will smile on you. A lunch? A dinner, you say? Was that a nod? You won't find better jokes anywhere.[62]

But no invitations are forthcoming, for only the concealed maidservant Crocotium is amused, and she has no dinners to offer.[63] She does, however, have a commission for Gelasimus from his former patron's wife, Panegyris. Though Panegyris has never once asked him to dinner—she

---

61. oratio una interiit hominum pessume,
     atque optima hercle meo animo et scitissuma,
     qua ante utebantur: 'ueni illo ad cenam, sic face,
     promitte uero, ne grauare. est commodum?
     uolo inquam fieri, non amittam quin eas.'
     nunc reppererunt iam ei uerbo uicarium
     (nihili quidem hercle uerbumst ac uilissumum):
     'uocem te ad cenam nisi egomet cenem foris.'

                                                        (*Stich.* 183–90)

62. nunc auctionem facere decretumst mihi:
     foras necessumst quidquid habeo uendere.
     adeste sultis, praeda erit praesentium.
     logos ridiculos uendo. age licemini.
     qui cena poscit? ecqui poscit prandio?
     (Hercules te amabit)—prandio, cena tibi.
     ehem, adnuistin? nemo meliores dabit.

                                                        (*Stich.* 218–24)

63. *Stich.* 243; eu ecastor, risi ted hodie multum. Cf. 217: ridiculus aeque nullus est, quando essurit.

is characterized as a dutiful wife and daughter and a good manager—
Gelasimus is happy to go to the port for her.[64] And later he joins in a
flurry of housecleaning when ordered to do so by her peremptory slave
Pinacium.

> PINACIUM: I want this house clean! Bring some brooms and some
>   reeds out here so I can undo all that the spiders have done—
>   those shameful webs—and get rid of what they've woven.
> GELASIMUS: They'll be awfully cold afterward.
> PI: What? Do you think that like you they have just the one shirt?
>   Grab those brooms.
> GE: I'll do it.
> PI: I'll sweep here. You do over there.
> GE: I'll get it done.
> PI: Will somebody please bring me a bucket of water?
> GE: This guy's made himself aedile here, though nobody elected
>   him.
> PI: Hurry up. Wipe the floor. Clean in front of the door.
> GE: I'll do it.
> PI: It ought to be done already.[65]

When Pinacium finally divulges the extraordinarily good news that lies
behind this extraordinary behavior—his master, Epignomus, has
returned at last—Epignomus' parasite is as pleased as his fond wife is.
Epignomus' return makes Gelasimus hope for an end to his laments
over dead meals, dead drinking bouts, and dead lunches (211–13); his
patron is his *vita* (372). When he hears from Pinacium about the signs of
Epignomus' newly acquired wealth—gold, silver, expensive fabrics,

---

64. Penelope is the model Panegyris cites in her opening address (1a). On the
characterizations of Antipho's daughters see Arnott 1972, 54–64.

65. PI: munditias uolo fieri. ecferte huc scopas simulque harundinem,
       ut operam omnem araneorum perdam et texturam inprobem
       deiciamque eorum omnis telas. GE: miseri algebunt postea.
       PI: quid? illos itidemne esse censes quasi te cum ueste unica?
       cape illas scopas. GE: capiam. PI: hoc egomet, tu hoc conuorre.
        GE: ego fecero.
       PI: ecquis huc ecfert nassiternam cum aqua? GE: sine suffragio
       populi tamen aedilitatem hicquidem gerit. PI: age tu ocius
       pinge humum, consperge ante aedis. GE: faciam. PI: factum oportuit.
                                                        (*Stich.* 347–54)

and a luxurious dining apparatus; lyre-girls, flute-girls, and harp-girls (all exceptionally attractive); and perfumes of all sorts—he revises his plans for the future: "I won't be selling my jokes after all. No more auction for me. I've come into an inheritance!"[66] But Gelasimus is not destined to be happy for long. Pinacium knows just what will spoil the occasion for him and mentions one final item: "He had parasites with him, too, . . . really funny ones."[67]

Threatened competition combines with a scarcity of patrons to send the parasite scurrying off to buff up his wares: "I'll go inside to my books and learn off some of my better jokes. If I don't oust those jokers I've had it."[68] When he reemerges some fifty lines later, he hopes he can talk himself into Epignomus' good graces (*deleniam dictis*, 457). An inventory of the *logi ridiculi* he has at his disposal was provided in the auction scene: "I've got Greek jokes to use at the baths for sale, and naughty ones to pass with the after-dinner drinks. Quips, dollops of flattery, a parasite's little lies."[69] But Gelasimus' exchanges with Epig-

---

66. non uendo logos. / iam <iam> non facio auctionem, mi optigit hereditas (*Stich.* 383–84). The description of Epignomus' wealth is paraphrased from lines 374–83.

67. poste autem aduexit parasitos secum . . . ridiculissimos (*Stich.* 388–89). Pinacium appended this item to the list of luxuries simply to tease Gelasimus. Epignomus will do the same when he mentions Ambraciot *legati* at line 490–91—these are created out of thin air to frustrate the parasite's hopes of entering into his *hereditas*. For when Epignomus tells his slave Stichus to take "the women that I brought with me" into the house (*hasce . . . quas mecum adduxi*, 418; cf. 435) there is no mention of male companions, parasitical or ambassadorial. The audience will have seen that there were none such in Epignomus' train.

68. ibo intro ad libros et discam de dictis melioribus; / nam ni illos homines expello, ego occidi planissume (*Stich.* 400–401; cf. 454–57).

69.   uel iunctiones Graecas sudatorias
      uendo uel alias malacas, crapularias;
      cauillationes, adsentatiunculas
      ac peiieratiunculas parasiticas.

                                                        (*Stich.* 226–29)

Some editors read *unctiones* in line 226, following manuscript P; Petersmann (1973, ad loc.) explains this text with the suggestion that Gelasimus is offering to perform the slave's task of massage. This reading is inferior to manuscript A's *iunctiones*. Although many servile tasks performed by parasites can be cataloged from Greek and Roman comedy, nothing comparable to *unctiones* ever appears. (The fragments of Old and Middle Comedy emphasize degrading— but not sexual—tasks and a fairly standard set of jobs promoting sympotic and

nomus in lines 465–96 and with both of the brothers later (lines 579–631) are remarkably dull. They reveal none of the *dicta* with which he plans to entice them (457), none of the clever quips that ought to earn him a month of dinners (cf. *Capt.* 483), and not much flattery either.[70] In fact, Epignomus is the one who provides the fun, by willfully misunderstanding the purpose of Gelasimus' invitation.

> EPIGNOMUS: Me have dinner at your house? GE: Since you've come home safe.
> EP: I'm afraid I'm booked. But I thank you all the same.
> . . . .
> GE: Why don't you say you'll come? EP: I would if I could.
> GE: I'll promise you this: if you ask me, *I* won't say no.
> EP: Good-bye. GE: Sure? EP: Sure. I'm having dinner at home.
> GE: Well, since I got exactly nowhere by this route, I'll try another tack. I'll speak plainly. Since you won't come to my house, shall I come to yours?[71]

---

amatory pleasure.) And the end of a drinking bout is not a likely time for massage. Manuscript Λ's *iunctiones* would be a specific category of the *logi ridiculi* that Gelasimus advertised at the start of his auction (221); *cavillationes, adsentatiunculae,* and *peiieratiunculae* are other types (228–29). In line 230 he moves on to his material properties. *Unctio,* as a service, would sit awkwardly among the verbal possessions. There must, of course, be a contrast between *iunctiones graecae sudatoriae* and [*iunctiones*] *malacae crapulariae,* and more particularly between *sudatoriae* and *crapulariae.* The contrast might focus on the time of day relative to the *cena,* with *sudatoriae* representing the predinner bath and *crapulariae* the drinking bout that concluded the festivities. Or it might focus on the mode of production employed for the *iunctiones—sudatoriae* being the clever (*Graecas*; cf. the premium put on Attic wit at *Persa* 395) ones that require hard work, *crapulariae* the naughty (*malacas*) ones that occur to a parasite who has been drinking. For parasites at the baths see *Persa* 90–91, Martial 2.11.13, 12.82, Alciphron 3.2.1, 3.40.2–3; for parasites working hard see Anaxandrides 10 (καίτοι πολλοί γε πονοῦμεν. / τὸν ἀσύμβολον εὗρε γέλοια λέγειν Ῥαδάμανθυς καὶ Παλαμήδης). The translation in the text is based on the less extravagant trope.

70. Corbett (1986, 25) suggests that this reticence is to be explained by the fact that the *logi* Gelasimus and others speak of were professional secrets. Yet the auction scene was surely no less "professional" a performance, and there are plenty of examples of parasitical wit in the plays.

71. EP: Cenem illi apud te? GE: Quoniam salvos advenis.
  EP: Locatast opera nunc quidem; tam gratiast.
  . . . .

Gelasimus is disappointed here and once again in his attempt to find a welcome with Pamphilippus (582–624). The two brothers tease the parasite separately and in concert (*ludificemur hominem*, 578), moving him to displays of ever greater self-abasement. He says he would not need a place on a dining couch; a bench would do for him (*scis tu med esse unisubselli uirum*, 489). Later he says he would be content with the place where the dog sleeps (620). When Epignomus insists that the only place the parasite will find room to dine that day is the prison, Gelasimus says he is ready to go (624–25). "Great gods in heaven!" exclaims Epignomus, saying, "For a lunch or a dinner this fellow would endure any torment you might name!" The young men, eyes opened to the cost of associating with parasites, have decided to supply the jokes themselves (they have given ample evidence of their aptitude for joking) and to entertain one another.

> EP: My brother and I shattered our substance when you were our parasite.
> GE: When I was at your house didn't I . . .
> EP: I had a quite good enough look at that "good cheer" of yours. I've no intention of promoting you from "Mr. Funny" to "Mr. Ridiculous" today. [*exeunt brothers*]
> GE: Are they gone? Gelasimus, it's time to think "what next?" Me? Yes, you. About myself? Yes, about yourself. You see how high the cost of living is, don't you? Generosity and good fellowship

---

> GE: Quin tu promittis? EP: Non graver, si possiem.
> GE: Unum quidem hercle certo promitto tibi:
> Libens accipiam certo, si promiseris.
> EP: Valeas. GE: Certumne est? EP: Certum. Cenabo domi.
> GE: Sed—quoniam nil processit hac, ego iero
> apertiore magis via; ita plane loquar:
> Quando quidem tu ad me non vis promittere,
> vin ad te ad cenam veniam?

(Stich. 471–72, 479–86)

The text here is from Petersmann 1973. The principal difference between this text and Lindsay's here is the lacuna after line 469, which alters the speakers for lines 470–71.

Cf. *Capt.* 172–76, where the parasite Ergasilus uses a similar ploy more directly.

have quite vanished. Do you see how they consider funny men worthless and are dining with each other?[72]

When he leaves the stage for the last time, suicide seems the only solution (638–40). Earlier in the play he had been afraid this might happen: "It's my opinion, Gelasimus, that your situation is quite hopeless if neither the one who is here [Epignomus] nor the one who's on his way [Pamphilippus] does anything for you."[73] His livelihood is gone—he had used the phrase *mea vita* to refer to each of the brothers (372, 583) and life might as well go too.

Gelasimus does not appear in the final act of the play, the lively party with which the brothers' slaves Stichus and Sangarinus celebrate their own return. But Gelasimus' misery sounds a *basso continuo* under their revelry, for the contrasting lot of slave and parasite is an important theme in this play. Gelasimus had left the stage lamenting the extinction of "good fellowship" in his world (*prothymiae*, 636). But good fellowship abounded in the slaves' party (659).[74] The difference is that at that party all participants are of like status and share expenses. In fact, before they indulge too deeply in the wine—Stichus' contribution to the festivities—Stichus and Sangarinus between them give quite a little disquisition on proper party etiquette.

---

72. EP: dum parasitus mihi atque fratri fuisti, rem confregimus.
   GE: non ego isti apud te— EP: sati' spectatast mihi iam tua felicitas;
   nunc ego nolo ex Gelasimo mihi fieri te Catagelasimum.
   GE: iamne abierunt? Gelasime, uide, nunc consilio capto opust.
   egone? tune. mihine? tibine. uides ut annonast grauis.
   uiden? benignitates hominum periere et prothymiae.
   uiden ridiculos nihili fieri atque ipsos parasitarier?
   (*Stich.* 628–37)
The parasite Ergasilus assumes that potential hosts prefer a guest who can return the favor (*Capt.* 473). Pamphilus and Antipho could do so for Epignomus (*Stich.* 514–16).

73. enim uero, Gelasime, opinor prouenisti futtile, / si neque ille adest neque hic qui uenit quicquam subuenit (*Stich.* 398–99).

74. "Good fellowship" existed as an ideal in Rome (e.g., Cic. *Fam.* 9.24.3, *Sen.* 46 [with Powell's note ad loc.], and Plut. *Cat. mai.* 25.2: τὴν δὲ τράπεζαν ἐν τοῖς μάλιστα φιλοποιὸν ἡγεῖτο) but is very little evident in extant descriptions of Roman dinner parties, in which the care taken to preserve hierarchical distinctions is clearly documented (D'Arms 1990).

SANGARINUS: Go ahead on out. Lead the parade! I put you in
   charge of the wine jug, Stichus. We plan to try out all senses of
   the expression "living together" today. We find a charming
   welcome, I promise you, when we are received here. I want all
   passersby to be invited in to join us in our revelry.
STICHUS: Fine by me, so long as whoever comes brings his own
   wine with him. This little feast is being given for us and us
   alone. You serve me and I'll serve you.
SAN: Our party features an adequate supply of nuts, small beans,
   figlets, oil, food props, a modicum of bread (our means are limited, you know).
ST: A slave ought to spend moderately, not lavishly. Different
   things suit different levels. For those with money in the bank,
   boat-shaped cups and tankards to drink from. We use our
   cheap Samiaware cups. Still, we drink; we do our duty as best
   we can.[75]

One could hardly find a greater contrast with the kind of hospitality on
which Gelasimus relies. The *subsellium* on which Gelasimus said he
would be willing to sit also appears at Stichus' party (703; cf. 489),[76] as
does the weasel omen (672; cf. 461). And there were a number of para-
site/slave analogies earlier in the play. Gelasimus and the slave

---

75. SAN: Agite ite foras: ferte pompam. cado te praeficio, Stiche.
      omnibu' modis temptare certumst nostrum hodie conuiuium.
      ita me di ament, lepide accipimur quom hoc recipimur in loco.
      quisqui' praetereat, comissatum uolo uocari. ST: conuenit,
      dum quidem hercle quisque ueniet ueniat cum uino suo.
      nam hinc quidem hodie polluctura praeter nos datur nemini.
      nosmet inter nos ministremus monotropi. SAN: hoc conuiuiumst
      pro opibus nostris sati' commodule nucibus, fabulis, ficulis,
      oleae †intripillo†, lupillo, comminuto crustulo.
      ST: sat est seruo homini modeste facere sumptum quam ampliter.
      suom quoique decet: quibu' diuitiae domi sunt, scaphio et cantharis,
      batiocis bibunt, at nos nostro Samiolo poterio:
      tamen bibimus nos, tamen ecficimus pro opibus nostra moenia.
                                                          (*Stich.* 683–95)

76. Concern for appropriate seating was a motif introduced in the opening
act of the play: PAMPHILA: adside hic, pater. / ANTIPHO: non sedeo isti, uos
sedete; ego sedero in subsellio. / PANEGYRIS: mane, puluinum . . . ANTIPHO: bene
procuras. mihi sati' sic fultumst. sede (*Stich.* 92–94).

Pinacium were both sent to the port to inquire after Panegyris' husband. When they arrive together at her door, she scolds Gelasimus for Pinacium's overly vigorous knocking (326; cf. *Men.* 176 for a parasite offering to knock). The two of them sweep out the cobwebs side by side. Later Epignomus teases Gelasimus with an invitation—to wash the dishes (595). So when Gelasimus offers to supervise the rest of the welcome-home housecleaning, it is no accident that Panegyris' response is a dismissive "I've got enough slaves at home" (*sat servorum habeo domi*, 397).[77]

Scholarly appraisal of Gelasimus' role in the *Stichus* is varied. Was he brought on merely "to raise derisive laughter"?[78] Or do we feel pity at his discomfiture, seeing that his misery is pointedly contrasted with the revelry of the slaves and that he seems to care about what people will think of his distress (a curious trait in a parasite)?[79] On the whole, I do not think we do feel sorry for him. Sympathy is aroused not by piling up details of characterization, as Arnott suggests, but by giving recognizably human (and humane) traits to a character who is traditionally a figure of ridicule, such as the love-struck *miles* Polemon in Menander's *Perikeiromene*, the generous hetaera of the *Samia*, or the maternal one of the *Epitrepontes*. Gelasimus has no good traits, and he is teased and bullied and insulted by every character with whom he comes into contact (Crocotium at 244–62,[80] Pinacium at 319–89, Panegyris at 326–27, Epig-

---

77. If the free parasite is made to look servile, the slave is elevated *pari passu*. Pinacium, the self-elected "aedile" of the sweeping scene, is concerned about behaving as befits a man and maintaining his dignity (*Stich.* 297), and he mentions his *maiores* repeatedly (282, 303, 455). There is also a word that creates an analogy between parasite, slave, and wife: all three have *reges* (133, 287, 455).

78. Webster 1950, 112.

79. This view is Arnott's (1972). Gelasimus complains about the *curiosi* at 198–208 (cf. 386) and leaves the play with the following words: nam mihi iam intus potione iuncea onerabo gulam/ neque ego hoc committam ut me esse homines mortuum dicant fame (*Stich.* 639–40; cf. 581).

80. Is Crocotium's threat in line 262 a response to an obscene gesture made by the parasite with the "tongue of his belly?" If so, the exchange reveals an uncommon side of the parasite, who is usually too busy acquiring food and drink to worry about sex. Lindsay (1922, 253) suggests that Gelasimus' gesture consisted in sticking out his tongue. But *venter* = parasite is, as we have seen, a common metonymy; in this play Gelasimus' *venter* has, in addition to the "tongue" mentioned here, *medullae* (341) and clothing (376).

nomus and Pamphilus at 472 ff. and 592 ff.; cf. 578).[81] Even a weasel
finds sustenance in this play (*vita*, 462, recalling 372), but Gelasimus
does not. The name he earns should be not Miccotrogus ("Nibble Noth-
ing-much," 242) but, as Epignomus predicts when he washes his hands
of him, Catagelasimus ("Mr. Ridiculous," 630–31). If Epignomus and
Pamphilippus intend to entertain one another henceforth, the reciprocity that characterizes all effective patron/client relationships will no
longer exist, and the parasite will have nothing left to hope for.[82]

Gelasimus is unable to make himself welcome because he offers no
quid pro quo. His former patrons no longer value his brand of wit, and
the services he offers are better done by slaves. The parasite of the *Captivi*, Ergasilus, begins that play in similar straits due to the temporary
absence of his patron, Philopolemus.

   Philopolemus is a prisoner of war, and his father, Hegio, is spending
his available cash on prisoners for exchange rather than on sumptuous
dinners. So Ergasilus is looking to other potential patrons for something better than the scanty fare that awaits him at Hegio's house (*cena
aspera*, 497; cf. 189, 855)—with little success. His first words contain a
Latin pun based on a parasite characteristic prevalent in the fragments
of Greek comedy: he is called Scortum ("Lady-love"), he says, because
a parasite, like a courtesan, is *invocatus* (either "invoked" or "uninvited," punning on two different senses of the prefix *in-*) at young
men's dinner parties.[83] Ergasilus complains further that parasites go

---

   81. Though I would agree with Arnott that Gelasimus is considerably better
integrated into the play than scholars have generally recognized. See the preceding notes for some verbal and thematic echoes. Other evidence of integra-
tion includes the fact that Gelasimus' opening words (*Famem ego fuisse suspicor
matrem mihi, / nam postquam natus sum satur numquam fui, Stich.* 155–56) connect
with the unnamed sister's distress: hae res vitae me, soror, saturant (18). His
expressions of ingratitude to his mother *Fames* (157–60) contrast with the loyalty of Antiphon's daughters to their deceased mother (109–10). Also, the first
act as a whole is much concerned with techniques of persuasion, and nobody in
the play has less success than Gelasimus in persuading his interlocutors (*equidem hercle orator sum, sed procedit parum*, 495).

   82. Fraenkel (1960, 270 n. 1) goes beyond the evidence of the play, I think,
when he claims that Epignomus and Pamphilippus intend to live soberly
henceforth. After all, Epignomus brought home a crowd of musicians.

   83.   Iuuentus nomen indidit 'Scorto' mihi,
         eo quia inuocatus soleo esse in conuiuio.
         scio apsurde dictum hoc derisores dicere,

hungry when legal business is in a recess and potential hosts have withdrawn to the country (78–84). Parasites are a burden to their patrons (*odiossicique et incommodestici*, 87), he says, and have to expect abuse (88–90; cf. 472). Modern young men have no use for a parasite, for in their eyes Ergasilus is as superfluous as Gelasimus was in the *Stichus*.

> To hell with the parasitical profession! The young fellows keep their distance from us witty (and penniless) types. They don't look twice at spartan lads who make do with a bench, who take punches well and are flush with words (if not comestibles or cash). Instead, they want to invite someone who can easily return the favor at his own house. They do the shopping themselves (which used to be a parasite's job), and they march from forum to whorehouse quite openly, as openly as if they were passing judgment on crooks in a tribal court. They don't give a damn about funny men, since they're all wrapped up in one another.[84]

Ergasilus' solicitation scene in the forum meets with a distinctly chilly reception: no one so much as cracks a smile (585–93).

Unlike Gelasimus, however, Ergasilus was used to better treatment. He was not *invocatus*, since he received an invitation from Hegio to that day's dinner at line 176 and one *in perpetuum* later on (897).[85] And Ergasilus had been associated with Hegio's family for a very long time. He can comment on Hegio's habits as a *puer* (867) and recognize Sta-

---

at ego aio recte. nam scortum in conuiuio
sibi amator, talos quom iacit, scortum inuocat.

(*Capt.* 69–73)

84. ilicet parasiticae arti maxumam malam crucem,
ita iuuentus iam ridiculos inopesque ab se segregat.
nil morantur iam Lacones unisubselli uiros,
plagipatidas, quibu' sunt uerba sine penu et pecunia:
eos requirunt qui lubenter, quom ederint, reddant domi;
ipsi opsonant, quae parasitorum ante erat prouincia,
ipsi de foro tam aperto capite ad lenones eunt
quam in tribu sontes aperto capite condemnant reos.
neque ridiculos iam terrunci faciunt, sese omnes amant.

(*Capt.* 469–77)

85. The joke that precedes the invitation at line 176 is very similar to one that failed when the luckless Gelasimus tried it (*Stich.* 470–71).

lagmus, the slave who fled with a four-year-old Tyndarus nearly twenty years before the play's "present" (875, 980). If Ergasilus has been around the family for decades, it is likely that Hegio was the parasite's patron before his son took over. Both Hegio and his son, Philopolemus, do in fact appear to be of a character to enjoy Ergasilus' company: "[Philopolemus] was a young man with old-fashioned ways. If ever I provided amusement, I went away well rewarded. His father's manner is much the same. I'll go see him now. But there's the door opening, the door through which I often departed quite drunk with the pleasure of being full."[86] Philopolemus and his parasite never appear on stage together, so we have to take Ergasilus' word about the way he is treated by the son, but we can see for ourselves that Hegio enjoys a good verbal tussle with the parasite.

> ERGASILUS: If I'm blue, it's because the army of eating has been discharged.
> HEGIO: And in the meantime you haven't found anyone to take charge of that army?
> ER: Would you believe it? Everyone who has been offered that command since your son was captured runs away.
> HE: It's no wonder that they run. For that job you'd need lots of soldiers and all kinds of them. Bakersmen, first of all—there are several types. You'd need Breadmen and Cakemen too, then Birdmen—two sorts—and all the troops of the sea.[87]

---

86. ill' demum antiquis est adulescens moribus,
quoius numquam uoltum tranquillaui gratiis.
condigne pater est eius moratus moribus.
nunc ad eum pergam. sed aperitur ostium
und' saturitate saepe ego exii ebrius.

(Capt. 105–109)

87. ER: eheu, huic illud dolet,—
quia nunc remissus est edendi exercitus.
HE: nullumne interea nactu's, qui posset tibi
remissum quem dixti imperare exercitum?
ER: quid credis? fugitant omnes hanc prouinciam,
quoi optigerat postquam captust Philopolemus tuos.
HE: non pol mirandum est fugitare hanc prouinciam.
multis et multigeneribus opus est tibi
militibus: primumdum opus est Pistorensibus:
eorum sunt aliquot genera Pistorensium:

Ergasilus terms the son his *rex* (92) and his *genius* (879), but in Philopolemus' absence he successfully turns to the like-natured father for sustenance (if not luxury). These two patrons do not appear to find Ergasilus either *odiossicus* (irritating) or *incommodesticus* (highly inconvenient). Nor do they abuse him. Hegio does not even appear to be planning to curb his son's extravagance in this area; he encourages Ergasilus to look forward to more generous fare when the young man returns (167–71). And when Ergasilus brings the news that Hegio most wants to hear—that his son has returned—Hegio offers the parasite an equally welcome recompense.

HE: Tell me, on your honor, are you speaking the truth?

ER: On my honor.

HE: Great gods! I'm alive again, if what you say is true!

ER: Can it be that you still doubt me, when I've sworn by all that's holy? Well then, Hegio, if oaths carry no credit, go take a look at the port.

HE: I plan to. You take care of what needs to be done inside. Get what you need, ask the servants, decant whatever you like from the cellar. I'm putting you in charge of supplies.

ER: If my predictions prove false you can clean me up with a cudgel.

HE: I'll feast you forever, if what you say is true.

ER: Who's paying?

HE: Myself and my son.

ER: Promise?

HE: I promise.[88]

---

opu' Panicis est, opu' Placentinis quoque;
opu' Turdetanis, opust Ficedulensibus;
iam maritumi omnes milites opu' sunt tibi.

(*Capt.* 152–64)

88. HE: dic, bonan fide tu mihi istaec uerba dixisti? ER: bona.
HE: di inmortales, iterum gnatus uideor, si uera autumas.
ER: ain tu? dubium habebis etiam, sancte quom ego iurem tibi?
postremo, Hegio, si parua iuri iurandost fides,
uise ad portum. HE: facere certumst. tu intus cura quod opus est.
sume, posce, prome quiduis. te facio cellarium.
ER: nam hercle, nisi mantiscinatus probe ero, fusti pectito.
HE: aeternum tibi dapinabo uictum, si uera autumas.
ER: unde id? HE: a me meoque gnato. ER: sponden tu istuc? HE: spondeo.

(*Capt.* 890–98)

Free access to the wine cellar, feasts in perpetuity—what more could a parasite ask for? Ergasilus is not slow to take advantage of the freedom that Hegio grants him here, for a slave soon appears on stage decrying Ergasilus' depredations (911–18).

Yet one of the features that distinguishes Hegio from other comic fathers is his levelheadedness about money. For example, he has the uncommonly good sense to say, "I am rich enough, thanks to the gods and my ancestors."[89] If he spends large sums purchasing prisoners of war, he does it without being either wasteful or heedless (192–93). His tolerance of a parasite in his household—usually a sign of extravagance and/or conspicuous consumption—is therefore rather remarkable. Particularly since Hegio is clearly sensitive about his reputation: he hates knowing that one of the consequences of the trick Tyndarus played on him is that people will say, "there's the clever old coot who got swindled" (787). Ergasilus' opportunism must fall into a different category from Tyndarus' trick, however, for Hegio does not consider that he and his son are the dupes of Ergasilus. He is even willing to admit the parasite to the status of *amicus*.

> HE: Who's talking there?
> ER: I am, a man who is pained by your pain, who grows thin, grows old, pines away, feels wretched. Skin and bones I am with unhappy—thinness. The food I eat at home does me no good at all, and what I put to my lips at other folk's houses helps me just as little.
> HE: Ergasilus, hello.
> ER: Bless you, Hegio.
> HE: No crying now.
> ER: Shall I not weep for him, not weep for a young man with his qualities?
> HE: I've always felt that you were a friend to my son and known that he was a friend to you.[90]

---

89. ego uirtute deum et maiorum nostrum diues sum satis (*Capt.* 324).
90.   HE: quis hic loquitur? ER: ego, qui tuo maerore maceror,
      macesco, consenesco et tabesco miser;
      ossa atque pellis sum misera—macritudine;
      neque umquam quicquam me iuuat quod edo domi:
      foris aliquantillum etiam quod gusto id beat.
      HE: Ergasile, salue. ER: di te bene ament, Hegio.

No other Plautine parasite is so honored. Even if Hegio is speaking with full cognizance of the self-interested springs of this "friendship" (as seems to me likely, since this is a comedy, not a morality play), he does not resent the pretense.[91]

Ergasilus' role has often been described as "inorganic": he has two long monologues to himself (69–109, 461–97), but much less interaction with other characters than does Curculio, Gelasimus, or even Saturio. His only real contribution to the plot is to announce Philopolemus' arrival.[92] A slave could have done that (as the fact that Ergasilus dons the character of a *servus currens* for the scene suggests). But a slave would not have served as well to reveal the magnanimity of Hegio and (by extension) his son.

The manifold art of the parasite is well illustrated in these plays of Plautus, with Ergasilus' wit, the fine psychological insights of the parasite of the *Asinaria*, the flattery of Artotrogus and Peniculus, the servility shown by Gelasimus, and the variously substantial services of Saturio and Curculio. These texts provide a sense of just how many ways there were to make oneself welcome. Whether one succeeded or not depended on the fit between what the parasite offered and what the patron wanted. In the case of the unnamed parasite who makes a cameo appearance at lines 575–605 of the *Bacchides*, the fit was just about perfect. His patron, the soldier Cleomachus, is the rival of one of the *adulescentes* in the play. The parasite is sent to take possession of the girl for his patron. When asked his identity at the door, he gives not a name but a description: "I am the covering that protects him" (*illius sum integumentum corporis*, 601). Not all of Plautus' parasites were able (or willing) to adapt their own shapes to their patron's mold. Peniculus, for one, refused. But Terence's two parasites, as we shall see, are quite remarkably good at trimming themselves to fit.

HE: ne fle. ER: egone illum non defleam? egon non defleam
talem adulescentem? HE: semper sensi filio
meo te esse amicum et illum intellexi tibi.

(*Capt*. 133–42)

91. "To be magnanimous is necessarily to liberate oneself from the oppressive fear of being deceived and—which is more important, for an intelligent man who chooses to be magnanimous may know very well what is going on— from the fear of being seen or thought to be deceived" (Dover 1974, 194).

92. Prescott 1920; Hough 1942. Contra this reading see Viljoen 1963; Leach 1969; Konstan 1983, 67 n. 17.

3

Terence's Parasites

He is ready for all employment, but especially before dinner, for
his courage and his stomach go together.
—Thomas Overbury "The Flatterer," in *Characters or Witty
Descriptions of the Properties of Sundry Persons*

The parasite of Terence's *Eunuchus,* Gnatho ("The Jaw") has a fine
blend of traits and perhaps the best claim to the title "all-around parasite." The fullness of his characterization may be due to Menander,
from one of whose plays Terence transposed Gnatho and his soldier
patron Thraso ("Swashbuckle"), but the success of the transposition
(*Eunuchus* was Terence's most successful play) is due, at least in part, to
the contrast that Terence effected between the parasite and another
dependent in the play, Thais.[1]

Gnatho is as witty and eager to get to dinner as any Ergasilus (*Eun.*
459, 1057–60, 1081–82), and he performs a variety of services for Thraso:
delivering a present to the courtesan Thais (229), shopping for food
(255–58), conveying an invitation to dinner (266). At line 494 he is told
to stay and escort the courtesan to the party, at 499–500 to see that the
house is ready for the party. He leads the front ranks in the siege of
Thais' house (781–88),[2] and finds a way for Thraso to keep a part of the
courtesan's services for himself even after defeat.[3]

1. The prominence that Plautus allowed his parasites brought him a good
deal of critical reproach. Terence's importation of the *miles/parasitus* pair into
the *Eunuchus,* however, has tended to win approval. See, e.g., Gilmartin 1976
and Goldberg 1986, 105–22. The *Eunuchus* is one of the few plays for which we
have information about its (favorable) reception in antiquity (*Vita Ter.* 2), which
may incline critics toward a positive assessment. Terence has in fact worked the
miles and his *kolax* so well into the play that it is difficult to imagine a Menandrian Εὐνοῦχος without them. See, e.g., the reconstructions of Webster (1950,
71–72) and Ludwig (1959). Contra this reading see Lowe 1983.

2. THRASO: tu hosce instrue; ego hic ero post principia: inde omnibus signum
dabo (*Eun.* 781; the text of Terence is from Kauer-Lindsay 1926).

3. The services performed by the helpful parasite are mirrored by those of
the slave Parmeno. Parmeno's readiness to help his master's sons in affairs of
the heart was of long standing (*Eun.* 308–10; cf. *o Parmeno mi, o mearum volupta-
tum omnium / inventor inceptor perfector,* 1034–35). In the past he had been

Gnatho is also an expert flatterer. Like many of his fellows, he boasts of his expertise as soon as he comes on stage. At line 232 he appears shaking his head at an acquaintance's supine acceptance of misfortune and recounts the scolding he had given him.

"Did you lose your sense along with your property? Look at me. I started where you did. Look at my color, my glow, my garb, at how well set up I am. I've got it all, yet I don't own a thing. I've got nothing but lack nothing either." "But my wretched state is such that I can't play the fool or take a beating." "What!" I said. "Do you think that's how I got where I am? You're off the track completely. Men like that made a living a generation ago, but now there's a new method for catching your dinner. I was the first to find the way. Folks who think they're first-class in everything but aren't—those are the types I chase. I don't let them laugh at me; I laugh at them. The creatures are quite remarkable. I praise whatever they say; if they turn around and say the opposite, I praise that too. If someone says no, I say no; if he says yes, I do too. In sum, I've given myself orders to agree with everything. It's a very good way to make a living these days."[4]

Later in the play Gnatho gives a sampling of his wares. A number of techniques are in evidence. The parasite likes to amplify what the *miles*

---

rewarded with parasitical perquisites, edible goodies (310). We have seen the slave/parasite parallel in another play based on a Menandrean original, the *Stichus*. Since Terence added the parasite to Menander's Εὐνοῦχος, the parallelism here, it would seem, is to be credited to Terence.

4. "simul consilium cum re amisti? viden me ex eodem ortum loco?
qui color nitor vestitu', quae habitudost corporis!
omnia habeo neque quicquam habeo; nil quom est, nil defit tamen."
"at ego infelix neque ridiculus esse neque plagas pati
possum." "quid? tu his rebu' credi' fieri? tota erras via.
olim isti fuit generi quondam quaestus apud saeclum prius:
hoc novomst aucupium; ego adeo hanc primus inveni viam.
est genus hominum qui esse primos se omnium rerum volunt
nec sunt: hos consector; hisce ego non paro me ut rideant,
sed eis ultro adrideo et eorum ingenia admiror simul.
quidquid dicunt laudo; id rursum si negant, laudo id quoque;
negat quis: nego; ait: aio; postremo imperavi egomet mihi
omnia adsentari. is quaestu' nunc est multo uberrimus."
(*Eun.* 241–54)

says, for example: "THRASO: Was Thais very grateful to me? GNATHO: Exceedingly grateful. THR: She was pleased, you say? GN: Positively triumphant, not so much with the gift itself, but because it came from you."[5] Likewise, when the soldier estimates the cost of his rival's gift to the courtesan at three minas—a paltry sum in the circumstances—his parasite adds "barely."[6] Besides amplification, he employs bland agreement. When the soldier makes one of his outrageous claims, the parasite dutifully concurs: "THR: Somehow I am able to make whatever I do turn out well for me. GN: I've noticed."[7] Gnatho can also produce praise for the style of a boast and eager requests for more of the story.

> THR: Everyone is jealous of me—they snipe at me behind my back.
>   I couldn't care less. They are wretchedly envious though—one
>   fellow especially, the one in charge of the Indian elephants.
>   When he gets really annoying, I say, "Tell me, Strato, do you
>   get your ferocity from commanding beasts?"
> GN: Nicely put, indeed, and cleverly, too. Well! You certainly
>   throttled that one. What did he do then?
> THR: He shut up immediately.
> GN: How could he help it?[8]

---

5.   THR: Magnas vero agere gratias Thais mihi?
     GN: ingentis. THR: ain tu, laetast? GN: non tam ipso quidem
     dono quam abs te datum esse: id vero serio
     triumphat.

(*Eun.* 391–94)

6. *Eun.* 471–72. Cf. the exchange at 1042–43: THR: numquid, Gnatho, tu dubitas quin ego nunc perpetuo perierim? / GN: sine dubio opinor. The same technique is visible in fragment 2 (Sandbach) of Menander's Κόλαξ—the play from which Terence extracted his *miles/parasitus* pair—though Terence did not reproduce the passage's content in the *Eunuchus*. In commenting on the Κόλαξ passage Plutarch says that the flatterer is "dancing a jig on the soldier's stupidity" (κατορχούμενος τῆς ἀναισθησίας αὐτοῦ, *Mor.* 57e).

7. THR: est istuc datum / profecto ut grata mihi sint quae facio omnia. / GN: advorti hercle animum (*Eun.* 395–97). Cf. *mirum* (403), *haud iniuria* (433), *recte, probe* (773), *pulchre* (774), *sine dubio opinor* (1044).

8.   THR: invidere omnes mihi,
     mordere clanculum: ego non flocci pendere:
     illi invidere misere; verum unus tamen
     impense, elephantis quem Indicis praefecerat.
     is ubi molestu' magis est, "quaeso" inquam "Strato,
     eon es ferox quia habes imperium in beluas?"

When the occasion warrants, he speaks up in defense of his *miles*. He warns Chremes against insulting Thraso, for example, and gets Phaedria to retract the haughty dismissal he issues on seeing the humbled soldier (799–803, 1067–68).

Even more striking than Gnatho's verbal technique is the subject matter of the discussion in the flattery scene.[9] A Pyrgopolynices or Therapontigonus will come on blustering about his military prowess, but in this play the subject of *triumphat* is the hetaera Thais, not the soldier (394). Thraso does his wounding and killing with words alone.

THR: What about the story of how I twitted that Rhodian fellow at a party? Have I ever told you that one?

GN: Never. But please, tell me now. (I've heard it more than a thousand times already.)

THR: There was this fellow at a party with me, a young guy from Rhodes. I happened to have a girl with me. He began to joke with her and make fun of me. "What's this?" I say, "You have a lot of nerve! Do rabbits look for juicy bits of flesh?"

GN: Ha ha ha!

THR: Well?

GN: [*gasping*] Clever, charming, elegant, nothing more so. But tell me, is the joke yours? I thought it was an old one?

THR: You've heard it before?

GN: Often. It's considered one of the best.

THR: It's mine.

GN: Well, you certainly gave that fellow—a free man, too—a drubbing he didn't expect.[10]

GN: pulchre mehercle dictum et sapienter. papae
iugularas hominem. quid ille? THR: mutus ilico.
GN: quidni esset?

(*Eun.* 410–19)

9. Fabia 1895, 31–33, Barsby 1991, 40–41. The consequences for the text of Menander's Κόλαξ have been examined by Brown 1992.

10. THR: quid illud, Gnatho,
quo pacto Rhodium tetigerim in convivio,
numquam tibi dixi? GN: numquam; sed narra obsecro.
(plus miliens audivi.) THR: una in convivio
erat hic, quem dico, Rhodius adulescentulus.
forte habui scortum ; coepit ad id adludere
et me inridere. "quid ais" inquam homini "inpudens?

The exaggerations of a *miles gloriosus* are usually recognized as just that, exaggerations, but Gnatho devotes his efforts here to making Thraso preen himself on something he has none of, namely, wit.[11] Thraso is so dull-witted that he can hardly finish his sentences. When he wants to find a slightly elevated expression for his comparative clause at line 406, he gets Gnatho to do it for him: "THR: When [the king] is tired of company and fed up with his work, when he wants to relax, as if. . . . You know what I mean? GN: I know. As if he wanted to banish unhappiness from his mind. THR: That's it."[12] And when the soldier cannot figure out how to put a stop to Thais' annoying references to his rival Phaedria, Gnatho takes up the slack again, providing counseling about elementary amatory skirmishing tactics (434–51). Yet even with such unpromising material Gnatho succeeds in diverting Thraso's boasting from his amatory and military exploits to his witty coups against the elephant driver Strato and the Rhodian "rabbit." It is a very unusual *miles* who feels flattered by an explanation for his preferment like that found at 399–401: "With words alone a clever fellow can often transfer to his own account the glory that someone else worked hard to acquire. And clever you are." But Thraso does feel flattered: "My sentiments exactly."[13]

Concentrating Gnatho's flattery on Thraso's wit rather than his prowess was not simply a virtuoso variation on a stale theme, however, for it allows an emphatic display of Gnatho's scorn for the stupidity of

---

> lepu' tute's, pulpamentum quaeris?" GN: Hahahae.
> THR: quid est? GN: facete lepide laute nil supra.
> tuomne, obsecro te, hoc dictum erat? vetu' credidi.
> THR: audieras? GN: saepe, et fertur in primis. THR: meumst.
> GN: dolet dictum inprudenti adulescenti et libero.
>
> (*Eun.* 419–30)

11. *Eun.* 401; cf. *sapienter* at 416 and 452–53, *quantist sapere* at 791, and the phrase *exemplum placet* in 1027. For other auditors Thraso plainly produces more ordinary fare (482–83, 741).

12. THR: tum sicubi eum satietas
hominum aut negoti siquando odium ceperat,
requiescere ubi volebat, quasi . . nostin? GN: scio:
quasi ubi illam exspueret miseriam ex animo. THR: tenes.

> (*Eun.* 403–6)

13. GN: labore alieno magno partam gloriam
verbis saepe in se transmovet qui habet salem;
quod in test. THR: habes

> (*Eun.* 399–401).

his victim. Gnatho summarizes his (low) opinion of Thraso's intellect near the end of the play: "He's a fool, a dolt, a clod; he snores night and day."[14] And there was another reason to emphasize the soldier's verbal "successes" over his military ones.

Thraso displayed his attempts at wit at a king's court. Placing him there allows the author, whether Terence or Menander, to suggest that, vis-à-vis his *rex*, Thraso himself has parasitical attributes.[15] Like Gnatho in the siege scene, Thraso is entrusted with the conduct of campaigns (*omnem exercitum, consilia*, 402 3). He prides himself on convivial wit. His jokes are of the aggressive variety, but members of the company find amusement in him: after the quip about the Rhodian "rabbit," "everyone present about died laughing" (*risu omnes qui aderant emoriri*, 432). Although as a dinner companion he is agreeable to his host (403–7), his privileged position wins him hidden envy and open criticism from other guests (410–11, 424–25).[16] But like many another parasite, he has no interest in winning a favorable public opinion (411). There is in fact a ladder of parasites, with Thraso preying on the king, and Gnatho (much more successfully, it seems) on him.[17]

A pyramid might be a more accurate image, however, for Thraso is not the only closet parasite in the *Eunuchus*. Near the end of the play, Gnatho persuades Phaedria and Chaerea, *adulescentes* who are typically hard up for cash, to remain on good terms with the *miles*, who has money to burn.

> GN: [*to Phaedria and Chaerea, after telling Thraso to move out of earshot*] First of all, I hope you both will believe that the business I do for him I do most of all for my own sake. And if the same policy can be of service to you, too, it would be foolish of you not to do as I do.
>
> PHAEDRIA: What do you mean?
>
> GN: My recommendation is that you keep the soldier around as a rival.

14. fatuos est, insulsu' tardu', stertit noctes et dies (*Eun.* 1079).

15. Thraso's *rex: Eun.* 397, 401, 408. In this case, of course, *rex* refers primarily to a Hellenistic monarch, but it is convenient for the Latin playwright that it could also be used of a parasite's patron.

16. Skutsch (1985, ad loc.) correctly adduced lines 403–7 as a parallel for the picture of the good companion in Ennius.

17. Brown 1992, 102–3.

PHA: Keep him around, you say?

GN: Think about it. You are indulging yourself in Thais' company, Phaedria, (something you do eagerly and often), but you have only small resources for giving, while she needs to receive quite a lot. If you want to supply your love with all these things at no cost to yourself, you'll find no one more suited to your needs than Thraso. First, he has plenty to give, and no one gives more lavishly. He's a fool, a dolt, and a clod; he snores night and day. You won't need to worry that the woman will fall for him. You'd be able to give him the boot whenever you pleased.

CHAEREA: What are we waiting for?

GN: Then there's this, which to me seems of the first importance: nobody entertains more readily or more lavishly. He throws the best party around.

CH: I'd be surprised if we couldn't find a use for him.

PHA: I agree.

GN: A good decision.[18]

The *miles* had asked him to make an arrangement of this sort, of course, but the parasite, as he openly avows, is thinking of himself here. And Gnatho's intention is not that an amicable equality replace the rivalry

---

18.   GN: principio ego vos ambos credere hoc mihi vehementer velim,
        me huiu' quidquid facio id facere maxume causa mea;
        verum si idem vobis prodest, vos non facere inscitiast.
        PHA: quid id est ? GN: militem rivalem ego recipiundum censeo. PHA:
        hem
        recipiundum? GN: cogita modo: tu hercle cum illa, Phaedria,
        ut lubenter vivis (etenim bene lubenter victitas),
        quod des paullumst et necessest multum accipere Thaidem.
        ut tuo amori suppeditare possit sine sumptu tuo ad
        omnia haec, magis opportunu' nec magis ex usu tuo
        nemost. principio et habet quod det et dat nemo largius,
        fatuos est, insulsu' tardu', stertit noctes et dies:
        neque istum metuas ne amet mulier: facile pellas ubi velis.
        CH: quid agimus ? GN: praeterea hoc etiam, quod ego vel primum puto,
        accipit homo nemo meliu' prorsu' neque prolixius.
        CH: mirum ni illoc homine quoquo pacto opust. PHA: idem ego arbitror.
        GN: recte facitis.

                                                    (*Eun.* 1069–84)

for Thais' attentions that had existed before but that Phaedria and Chaerea join him in preying on Thraso.

> GN: There's just one thing I ask, that you include me in your crowd. I've been pushing that boulder long enough.
> PHA: Agreed.
> CH: And welcome.
> GN: Well then, I offer him to you for eating up and laughing down.[19]

The young men accept and join the conspiracy of scorn for their dupe (1087–93).

The characterization of Gnatho gives us a very unappealing picture of the parasitical profession. Gnatho takes knowing advantage of fools, and according to the slave Parmeno—who thinks Gnatho is the lowest of the low (*infra infimos*, 489)—he deprives these stupid men of what little sense they initially had. Antisthenes' much imitated pun "Better to be served up to the crows than to flatterers" is a warning against associating with men like Gnatho.[20] As *clientes*, Gnatho and his like are worse than worthless: lacking *fides*, they are positively dangerous. When Gnatho betrays the *miles* to his new buddies Phaedria and Chaerea, we see just how dangerous.[21] Gnatho's faults are made the clearer by the contrasting presentation of another client's behavior.

The Rhodian courtesan Thais declares early on in the play her desire to establish herself in Athens by making friends there: "I'm all alone here, Phaedria, with no friends and no relatives either. That's why I want to make myself some friends by doing something for them."[22] By

---

19. GN: unum etiam hoc vos oro, ut me in vostrum gregem
recipiati': sati' diu hoc iam saxum vorso. PHA: recipimus.
CH: ac lubenter. GN: at ego pro istoc, Phaedria et tu Chaerea,
hunc comedendum vobis propino et deridendum.
(*Eun.* 1084–87)

20. αἱρετώτερον εἰς κόρακας ἐμπεσεῖν ἢ εἰς κόλακας· οἱ μὲν γὰρ ἀπο-θανόντας τὸ σῶμα, οἱ δὲ ζῶντος τὴν ψυχὴν λυμαίνονται (Stob. 14.17; see further Ribbeck 1883, 103).

21. On the destructiveness of parasites see chap. 1 n. 43.

22. TH: sola sum; habeo hic neminem
neque amicum neque cognatum: quam ob rem, Phaedria,
cupio aliquos parere amicos beneficio meo.
(*Eun.* 147–49; cf. 870–71)
On the theme see Ludwig 1959, 23.

"friends" she means not admirers (she is speaking to an admirer when she says this) but rather protectors, patrons. In fact, she risks offending both of her current young men in attempting to put herself in a position to render a *beneficium* to a potential "friend."[23] Chremes is the man she has her eye on. She hopes to earn his gratitude by returning to him his long-lost sister Pamphila.

> THAIS: O Chremes, I was hoping you'd be here. Do you realize that you were the cause of that fight? And that the entire matter touches you closely?
> CHREMES: Me? How? You don't mean . . .
> TH: What I mean is that because I was trying to return and restore your sister to you, this mess and much more of the same came my way.
> CHR: Where is she?
> TH: At my house.
> CHR: Hmmm.
> TH: What's the matter? Her upbringing was what you and she both deserve.
> CHR: Are you telling me . . .
> TH: I'm telling you the truth. I give her over to you. I don't ask for any reward on her account.
> CHR: But you both deserve and have my gratitude, Thais, and I will repay the favor.[24]

This is just the sort of reward Thais had been hoping for. As it turns out, however, Chremes is a rather weak prop. Thais watches in dismay as he scurries off to the forum on hearing of Thraso's wrathful approach:

---

23. She annoys Phaedria at *Eun.* 150–74, Thraso at 743–46.
24.   TH: o mi Chreme, te ipsum exspectabam.
    scin tu turbam hanc propter te esse factam? et adeo ad te attinere hanc
    omnem rem? CH: ad me? qui? quasi istuc . . . TH: quia, dum tibi sororem
      studeo
    reddere ac restituere, haec atque huiusmodi sum multa passa.
    CH: ubi east? TH: domi apud me. CH: hem. TH: quid est?
    educta ita uti teque illaque dignumst. CH: quid ais? TH: id quod res est.
    hanc tibi dono do neque repeto pro illa quicquam abs te preti.
    CH: et habetur et referetur, Thais, ita uti merita's gratia.
                                                      (*Eun.* 743–50)

"I'm ruined. I got myself a protector, but he needs protection him-self."[25] Even Chremes, however, is a match for Thraso, and he emerges victorious from their verbal jousting (783–816). But not every opponent would be so easily overcome, so it is no surprise to hear that Thais finds herself additional support elsewhere. Near the end of the play, the father of Phaedria and Chaerea returns from the country. Chaerea (who is enamoured of Pamphila) begs Thais to help him persuade his father to let him marry the girl: "Please help me in this matter. I put myself in your hands. I make you my patron, Thais, please? I'll die if I can't marry her."[26] She speaks his case offstage—very successfully, to judge by Chaerea's jubilant reappearance soon thereafter. Pamphila is to be his, and what is more, he says, "I have cause to rejoice that my brother's love affair seems to be sailing smooth. Harmony reigns at home. Thais commended herself to my father; she has entered our care and *clien-tela*."[27] Without betraying or discarding Chremes, Thais has secured herself three more "friends." She is "the benefactress of our entire fam-ily," says Chaerea (*nostrae omnis fautrix familiae*, 1052).[28] The language that Charea uses here—Thais is simultaneously benefactress/patron and *cliens*—reveals clearly the reciprocity and mutually advantageous nature of the new relationship. The contrast with the exploitative and perfidious Gnatho, who is about to hand his *miles* over to the impecu-nious young men for eating up and laughing down, is striking.

I conclude the discussion of the parasites of Roman comedy as I began it, with a parasite skilled in legal maneuvers who supplies his services to an *adulescens* in love. But Phormio has a far more prominent role in

---

25. perii, huic ipsist opu' patrono, quem defensorem paro (*Eun.* 770).

26.   CH: nunc ego te in hac re mi oro ut adiutrix sies,
      ego me tuae commendo et committo fide,
      te mihi patronam capio, Thai', te obsecro:
      emoriar si non hanc uxorem duxero.

                                                    (*Eun.* 885–88)

27.   tum autem Phaedriae
      meo fratri gaudeo esse amorem omnem in tranquillo: unast domus;
      Thais patri se commendavit, in clientelam et fidem
      nobis dedit se.

                                                    (*Eun.* 1037–40)

28. At the beginning of the play, by contrast, Thais was called *nostri fundi calamitas* (*Eun.* 79).

the play named for him than Diabolus' parasite in the *Asinaria* did.[29]
And the *Phormio* is a suitable play to set at the boundary between parts
1 and 2 of this book, because in the material that Terence used for
reworking the character of Phormio, we find the first signs of the parasite's subsequent career in satire and beyond.

Both of the young men in the *Phormio* benefit from the parasite's
attentions. To help Antipho, Phormio devises a plan that exploits the
Athenian law of inheritance to "force" Antipho to marry the girl he
loves (157; cf. 125–32). In so doing, Phormio earned himself a fight with
Antipho's father, but so long as he had the young men's favor, he was
satisfied (133; cf. 427, 596–98, 885, 1052–53). I say the young *men's* favor,
for when Phaedria's amatory difficulties are placed before the master-
mind, he shows himself eager to help here too (829–30), and he comes
to Phaedria's financial aid in the third trick of the play. Phormio's helpfulness even prompts a number of characters to credit him with the status of "friend" (*amicus*, 324, 562, 598, 1049; cf. 688–89).

The question of who helps whom is of major thematic importance in
this play: slave helps slave (Davus, Geta: 55–56),[30] cousin helps cousin
(Phaedria, Antipho: 87, 218–303, 475–76, 502, 836), brother helps
brother (Demipho, Chremes: 581, 590, 966, 1001–2, 1014–35). Old slaves
also help their young charges (87, 188–89, 733–34), and the *matrona*
Nausistrata helps her brother-in-law (785; cf. 803). The *amici* that
Demipho assembles to advise him, however, are singularly worthless:
a "ridicula advocatio" Donatus calls them (*ad* 312).[31] The group of buddies (*amici aequales*) from whom Phaedria hopes to get a loan seems an
equally weak reed. He has to plead with them to get even the promise
of a loan (*supplex*, 887), and he waits a dangerously long time for the
cash (513, 703). The *leno* Dorio is even worse: he hasn't a helpful bone in
his body. His policy, as Donatus remarks, is to prefer the bird in the

---

29. The meaning of Phormio's name (which Terence took unchanged from
his Greek model) is disputed; see Austin 1922, 34–37.

30. Davus opens the play proper with the words *amicu' summu' meus* . . .
Geta (*Phorm.* 35).

31. Demipho announces his intention of gathering friends *ut ne inparatu' sim
si veniat Phormio* (*Phorm.* 314). The advising scene is 441–59. Cf. also 624–25,
where Geta has to pretend that Demipho's friends gave him coherent advice.
Geta is willing to help his master's nephew but similarly inadequate to the task
(534 ff.).

hand, cash down rather than gratitude.[32] "ANTIPHO: [Phaedria's] not asking for much time, Dorio. Let him have what he wants. If you do something nice for him, he'll return the favor double. DORIO: Promises, promises."[33] The only kind of profit that interests Dorio has a clink to it, so he will never say what Phaedria naively hopes he will at line 493, "That good deed paid off nicely."[34]

Phormio has a different philosophy: he concentrates on building up a supply of *gratia* (337). Geta praises him for being "energetic in this matter [sc. Antipho's predicament] as in others" (*strenuum hominem in hac re ut in aliis*, 476), and Phaedria is confident that Phormio will help him as well: "GETA: [*to Phaedria*] You'll get what you want. But I'll have to have Phormio to help me out. PHAEDRIA: You'll get him. Whatever task you charge him with, he'll do it with dash. There is no better friend in need."[35] That Phaedria's confidence was justified can be seen in Geta's description of his meeting with the parasite.

If there's anyone cleverer than Phormio, I've never met him! I went to tell him that we needed money and how I thought we might get it. Before I'd said half my piece he got the picture. He loved my idea and said so. He asked where the old man was and gave thanks to the gods that an opportunity had come his way for showing that he was as much a friend to Phaedria as to Antipho.[36]

---

32. Semper commodum prius est quam fides (Donatus *ad* 532).

33. AN: haud longumst id quod orat: Dorio, exoret sine.
idem hoc tibi, quod boni promeritu' fueris, conduplicaverit.
DO: verba istaec sunt.

(*Phorm.* 515–17)

34. PHA: feneratum istuc beneficium pulchre tibi dices. DO: logi! (*Phorm.* 493).
To Dorio words like *cognatus, parens,* and *amicus* are so much hot air: PHA: tu
mihi cognatu', tu parens, tu amicu', tu . . . DO: garri modo (*Phorm.* 496).

35. GE: iam feres:
sed opus est mihi Phormionem ad hanc rem adiutorem dari.
PHA: praestost: audacissime oneri' quidvis inpone, ecferet;
solus est homo amico amicus.

(*Phorm.* 559–62)

36. Ego hominem callidiorem vidi neminem
quam Phormionem, venio ad hominem ut dicerem
argentum opus esse, et id quo pacto fieret.
vixdum dimidium dixeram, intellexerat:

We saw in the *Asinaria* that the *rex* who was dissatisfied with his love life was of no use to a parasite (918–19); this may explain why Phormio was so eager to help Phaedria get his girl. Phormio's motives are most clearly visible at line 1036, where he intervenes in Demipho's attempts to ease Nausistrata's sense of injury over Chremes' bigamy. Phormio wants to make sure that any tolerance Nausistrata is going to show to her husband is available to her son as well: "Before she can say she forgives him, I'll do something for Phaedria and for myself as well" (*enimvero priu' quam haec dat veniam, mihi prospiciam et Phaedriae*). If Phaedria is well set up for self-indulgence, so is his parasite.

One of the qualities that allows Phormio to be so helpful to his friends is his parasitical talent for pretense. He adopts different roles and attitudes quite deliberately: "Just now I need to take up a new stance and a new look" (*nunc gestu' mihi voltusque est capiundus novos*, 890). When the *adulescens* Antipho tries a similar tactic—though feeling guilty and fearful, he wants to present a frank and confident face to his father—he is so unsuccessful that he hides himself away instead (210–18). But Phormio's fictions are completely successful. He pretends to be a longtime friend of Phanium's family (*paternum amicum me adsimulabo virginis*, 128); he gives circumstantial details at 350–74; the jury seems to have believed him (135; cf. 129, 275). Later he pretends to be on the verge of an unwanted marriage, and both Demipho and Chremes are taken in by this pretense (650–78). Phormio's final coup is pretending to be angry at being deprived of the girl he pretended he had wanted to marry all along (915–50). Convincing Demipho and Chremes of this is what renders permanent the transfer of funds from the older generation to the younger and completes the resolution of the young men's amatory difficulties.

Phormio's most successful fiction, however, is his sycophant act.[37]

> gaudebat, me laudabat, quaerebat senem,
> dis gratias agebat tempu' sibi dari
> ubi Phaedriae esse ostenderet nihilo minus
> amicum sese quam Antiphoni.

(Phorm. 591–98)

In this respect he resembles Menander's parasite Chaireas, who always aimed to leave his friends with a μνεία of how well he managed their affairs (*Dysc.* 66–68). For Chaireas as a parasite see chap. 1 n. 34.

37. On the aims and tactics of sycophants, see Osborne 1990; Harvey 1990; Christ 1992. The standard older work is Lofberg 1917. Lofberg's monograph musters evidence from the orators and from Old Comedy. For developments in

Chremes does not know about the conspiracy behind Antipho's marriage arrangements until line 756, when Phanium's nurse explains the plot to him. Demipho remains unenlightened longer, until he has an offstage conversation with his brother between lines 819 and 894. In the beginning, therefore, the two fathers naturally suppose that Phormio had battened on Antipho's inexperience as a source of gain and amusement for himself: "DEMIPHO: Have you ever heard of a more insulting injury?"[38] Their initial reading of the situation—one strongly promoted by the conspirators—is that Phormio is a *sycophanta* who instigated a fraudulent suit in the hopes of being bought off by a victim who was anxious to stay away from the mudslinging of the courts.

> DE: It's our own fault that scoundrels do so well these days. We are too eager for people to think us generous and good. Run if you must, but hide if you can, as the saying goes. Surely it was quite enough to let him get the better of us [sc. in court]. Do we have to pay him off, too, so that he can live to cook up something else?[39]

The sycophant impersonation was in fact necessary to prevent Demipho from suspecting a plot.[40] A similar (though less formal) syco-

New Comedy see his 1920 article. Lofberg goes too far in downplaying Phormio's parasitism, as do Segal and Moulton (1978): "the hero is a lawyer" (276). Arnott (1970), following Donatus' lead (see, e.g., *ad* 318, 327), gives proper emphasis to the verbal showmanship that aligns Phormio with his fellow parasites. The comment at Dziatzko 1898, 70 n. 1 ("halb Parasit, halb Sykophant"), is balanced but imprecise.

38. DE: Enumquam quoiquam contumeliosius / audisti' factam iniuriam quam haec est mihi? (*Phorm.* 348–49).

39.   DE: Nostrapte culpa facimus ut malis expediat esse,
       dum nimium dici nos bonos studemus et benignos.
       ita fugias ne praeter casam, quod aiunt. nonne id sat erat,
       accipere ab illo iniuriam? etiam argentumst ultro obiectum,
       ut sit qui vivat dum aliud aliquid flagiti conficiat.
                                                          (*Phorm.* 766–70)
The sycophant's favorite victim was the ἀπράγμων (cf. 623, where Demipho is described as *liberalis et fugitans litium*). On ἀπράγμονες see Osborne 1990, 94–102, and Lofberg 1917, 33–34.

40. Some scholars argue that the original Phormio was a sycophant and that Terence added a parasitical interest in food and drink to him to produce his own *Phormio parasitus* (27–28). See, e.g, Nencini 1891, 35; Lefèvre 1978, 48. See also Barsby 1991, 98–100. Support for this view is found in Donatus' statement that Terence adapted part of Phormio's most parasitical speech from a source

phant simulation was undertaken by the parasite in the *Asinaria,* who informed Demaenetus' wife about her husband's disreputable activities (820–26, especially 826, *litis concias,* "stir up lawsuits"). He too wanted to conceal a conspiracy, to make her think that he was looking out for her interests (and his own), not those of Diabolus: "We don't want her to think that it is your love rather than her predicament that makes this so upsetting to you" (Plautus *Asin.* 821–23). Phaedria draws on the same predatory busybody stereotype in making excuses to Demipho for Antipho's failure in court: "But if a scoundrel lays a trap for our youthful inexperience and wins his case, are we to blame?"[41] Phaedria's fellow-plotter Geta reinforces this characterization of Phormio when he taunts Phormio with being a "blackmailer who twists the law" (*bonorum extortor, legum contortor,* 374). The picture is most fully developed in Geta's account of a (fictitious) conversation with the parasite.

> GETA: I decided to sound the man out. I got him alone and said, "Phormio, don't you think it would be preferable to settle things with good feelings all around rather than with hard ones? My master's a generous man and he prefers to avoid the courts, but his friends all advised him just now to throw the girl out."
>
> ANTIPHO: [*eavesdropping*] What is he up to, and how will it all turn out, I wonder?

---

other than Apollodorus (*ad* 339). On this speech, see chap. 4 n. 3. The biggest obstacle to crediting Terence with all of the parasite material is that if the Greek Phormio was not a parasite he had nothing to gain by helping the young men (as is observed in Dziatzko 1898, 70 n. 1, and Lofberg 1929). He cannot have been a helpfully tricky slave, since the plot requires him to use the courts and to be an eligible husband for an Athenian girl. An independent sycophant would want some of the profit from the deception to end up in his own hands (cf. 633–34), but the sum extracted from Chremes goes straight to the pimp. For a parasite, however, the prospect of preying on self-indulgent young men like Antipho and Phaedria would be sufficient to motivate any degree of exertion.

41.   sed siqui' forte malitia fretus sua
      insidias nostrae fecit adulescentiae
      ac vicit, nostra culpa east?

(Phorm. 273–75)

Harvey 1990, 110–12; Lofberg 1917, 15–16.

GE: "Perhaps you'll say that the courts will make him pay if he throws her out? He's thought of that. You'll have yourself uphill work if you start something with someone who speaks as well as he does, I can tell you that. But suppose he loses; it'll just mean a fine, nothing stiffer." My words were having an effect, I could tell. The man was softening. "It's just the two of us here," I say. "Tell me what we'd have to pay to get rid of the girl without going to court, and to keep you from making trouble?"[42]

Phormio may impersonate a sycophant to facilitate Antipho's marriage to Phanium, but he is a full-fledged parasite. The bird metaphor is not inappropriate, for one of Phormio's parasitical features is the analogy that is drawn between him and that segment of the animal world. He boasts to Geta that although he has "beaten down innumerable folk, foreigners and citizens alike," he is safe from prosecution for injury.

GE: Why do you say that?
PHORMIO: Because nobody spreads a net to catch hawks or kites, the birds that are actually harmful. The nets are there to catch perfectly innocent birds, because they're the ones that can make you a profit. The game is worthwhile with them. You're

---

42. GE: visumst mihi ut eiu' temptarem sententiam.
prendo hominem solum: "quor non," inquam "Phormio,
vides inter nos sic haec potiu' cum bona
ut componamu' gratia quam cum mala?
eru' liberalis est et fugitans litium;
nam ceteri quidem hercle amici omnes modo
uno ore auctores fuere ut praecipitem hanc daret."
AN: quid hic coeptat aut quo evadet hodie? GE: "an legibus
daturum poenas dices si illam eiecerit?
iam id exploratumst: heia sudabis satis
si cum illo inceptas homine: ea eloquentiast.
verum pone esse victum eum; at tandem tamen
non capitis eius res agitur sed pecuniae."
postquam hominem his verbis sentio mollirier.
"soli sumu' nunc hic" inquam: "eho quid vis dari
tibi in manum, ut erus his desistat litibus,
haec hinc facessat, tu molestu' ne sies?"
(*Phorm.* 619–35)

only in danger if something can be squeezed out of you. They
know there's nothing to be had from me.[43]

Also parasitical is, of course, Phormio's interest in comestibles. Like
Saturio (son of "Hunger") he boasts of his *edacitas*.[44] He doesn't fear
prosecution, he says, because he has nothing to lose.

> PHO: You say they'll take me off in chains; they won't. They don't
> want to have a hungry fellow like me to fill up. Very sensibly
> they balk at doing what would be the greatest possible service
> in return for an injury.
> GE: [Antipho] will never be able to show his thanks enough.
> PHO: On the contrary, no one can thank a generous host suffi-
> ciently. When you come in from the baths washed and suitably
> anointed, without anything to offer, without a care, he's all
> worn out with the worry and the expense. He grimaces but sets
> out what will please. You laugh. You're the first to drink and
> first to approach the table. A puzzle-meal is put before you.
> GE: What in the world is a puzzle-meal?
> PHO: When you have to puzzle over what's best to choose. All you
> have to think about is what will taste best and what cost the
> most. Who wouldn't consider the fellow who provides all this
> a veritable god on earth?[45]

---

43. PHO: quot me censes homines iam deverberasse usque ad necem,
     hospites, tum civis? . . .
     GE: qui istuc? PHO: quia non rete accipitri tennitur neque miluo,
     qui male faciunt nobis: illis qui nil faciunt tennitur,
     quia enim in illis fructus est, in illis opera luditur.
     aliis aliundest periclum unde aliquid abradi potest:
     mihi sciunt nil esse.

                                                    (*Phorm.* 327–34)

44. According to Donatus, the first actor to play Phormio did so blatantly
potus et satur (*ad* 315). The author approved.

45. PHO: dices "ducent damnatum domum":
     alere nolunt hominem edacem et sapiunt mea sententia,
     pro maleficio si beneficium summum nolunt reddere.
     GE: non potest sati' pro merito ab illo tibi referri gratia.
     PHO: immo enim nemo sati' pro merito gratiam regi refert.
     ten asymbolum venire unctum atque lautum e balineis,
     otiosum ab animo, quom ille et cura et sumptu absumitur!
     dum tibi fit quod placeat, ille ringitur: tu rideas,

He likes liquid refreshment, too: during a lull in the intrigue, his one thought is to engineer a drinking bout with Phaedria (830). The final reward for all of his help is, appropriately enough, an invitation to dinner (1052–54). Food intrudes itself into a foreign context for this parasite, as for others: the exhortation "you've got to gobble it all down" in line 319 refers to facing the forthcoming conflict with Demipho, not to dinner-table exertions (*tute hoc intristi: tibi omnest comedendum*).[46]

Donatus detected near the end of the play a parasite metaphor that we have seen before. Demipho tries to keep Phormio from summoning Nausistrata by threatening him with a beating: "if he doesn't come away, apply your fists to the belly" (*nisi sequitur, pugnos in ventrem ingere*, 988). "A clever remark," says Donatus, explaining that "It practically equates 'belly' and 'parasite'" (*ad* 988). Phormio's helpfulness, particularly his role as facilitator of amatory affairs, is another mark of a parasite (not a sycophant).[47] Other characters, notably slaves, are called on for this service as well, but only a parasite could be imagined doing what Demipho accuses Phormio of planning to do at line 934. At this point in the play Demipho is aware of the conspiracy that brought about Antipho's unwanted marriage. The assumption that his adversary is a sycophant no longer fits the case. What then prompts Phormio's offer to marry Phanium himself? Demipho concludes, "You'd marry her so that my son could have access to her at your house; that's what the two of you were planning."[48] This kind of service would require the parasite to stoop even lower than Saturio did in lending his daughter to a plot in the *Persa*, but it is one that we will find in later developments of the parasite type.[49]

Whatever the character of the original Phormio, Terence's Phormio

---

prior bibas, prior decumbas; cena dubia apponitur.
GE: quid istuc verbist? PHO: ubi tu dubites quid sumas potissimum.
haec quom rationem ineas quam sint suavia et quam cara sint,
ea qui praebet, non tu hunc habeas plane praesentem deum?
                                                                    (*Phorm.* 334–45)

46. Arnott 1970, 36–37.

47. See n. 3 in this chapter.

48. ut filius / cum illa habitet apud te, hoc vostrum consilium fuit (*Phorm.* 933–34).

49. Hor. *Sat.* 2.3.237–38; cf. 2.5.75–76. A philosopher-parasite is accused of being the μαστροπός of his own wife at Lucian *Symp.* 32. A similar tactic later backfired on Otho, husband of Poppaea and dining companion of Nero (Tac. *Ann.* 13.45–46).

is a parasite. And it is clear that Terence added parasite material to whatever he found in his original, for Donatus tells us that a little scene from Ennius' *Satires* was reworked by Terence to make Phormio's speech about a parasite's gratitude to his host (338–42, quoted earlier; see further the discussion in chap. 4). This addition is a small but concrete example of a point Donatus makes more generally, that Terence paid particular attention to Phormio's parasitism.[50] As for his predecessor Plautus, so for Terence the character of the parasite was not something to be adopted unexamined and unmodified from his Greek models but a type to adapt and promote.[51]

The use of type characters is one of the distinctive features of Greek New Comedy and the Roman comedy that was modeled on it. Taken as a group, the parasites that Plautus and Terence adopted, adapted, and promoted in the ten plays I have discussed demonstrate something of the value of this particular type as a compositional device. The parasite can be sketched with a few essential traits: he ranks food as his summum bonum, he is unable (through situation or temperament) to provide it for himself but is clever enough to extract it from others, and he lacks the pride and principles that ought to characterize a man of his free status. From this simple beginning, development proceeded in a number of different directions.

Presenting the essential traits afresh each time was one challenge. We saw examples of the resultant innovations in language, image, and trope in all three chapters of part 1. The parasite appeared with significant names and nicknames ("The Jaw," "Mr. Funny," "Sponge,"

---

50. In hac scaena de parasitis vilioribus Terentius proponit imaginem vitae, ut in Eunucho de potioribus; animadvertendum autem huiusmodi genus hominum magis a Terentio lacerari (*ad* 315; cf. *ad* 327, 344, 348, 385). Donatus labels Phormio a sycophant in six places (*ad* 133, 279, 319, 348, 352, 356 [*calumniator*]), a parasite in twenty-five (including *scurra ad* 384). He also comments on Terence's implementation of parasite themes on several occasions (*ad* 315, 317, 321, 334, 1052), never on sycophant themes. On 317, for example, he says the following: ideo velut expergefactus ad has causas accedit Phormio, quia non diu sollicitum convenit esse parasitum nec quicquam aliud nisi de convivio vel propter convivium cogitare. Cicero gives Phormio's two personae equal weight, referring once to his sycophant side (*nec minus niger nec minus confidens quam ille Terentianus est Phormio, Caec.* 28; cf. Ter. *Ph.* 73, *homo confidens*), and once to his parasite side (*Phil.* 2.15, quoted in my introduction).

51. Fraenkel 1960, 123–27, 237–39, etc.

"Dory") or in different guises: as a fasting mullet, as a belly creeping along on its teeth, or as his patron's skin. Artotrogus drank in his soldier's boasting to keep his stomach full, Ergasilus gets drunk with the pleasure of being full, Peniculus was fettered by food and drink, Phormio has to gobble down a plan. The combination of hunger, dependency, and spinelessness proved a fertile one, spawning not only innovative descriptions but also some entirely new traits, such as the parasite's exertions in the production of jokes and his connoisseurship, his hardheaded physique, and his professional pose.

A further possibility, and one better documented in chapters 2 and 3, was the development of behaviors that revealed the parasite's essential traits. His subordination of pride to the demands of his belly, for instance, is well documented in the numerous flattery scenes. The cost to his pride was the higher if he knew the man he flattered to be a fool (as was the case for Artotrogus and Gnatho). Equally demeaning was the necessity of adapting his own character to circumstances, a behavior memorably developed in the extended impersonations of Curculio and Phormio. The shape-shifter Proteus was well chosen as an emblem for the man who employs flattery: "The flatterer really does seem to be the sort of thing that Proteus is. For he has all sorts of shapes, and it is not just his shape that changes but his manner of speaking, too. He is a man with a tongue of many tunes."[52] Beyond flattery was service, and the services required of a parasite were designedly humiliating, both the substantive ones, as when Saturio sells his daughter to aid an amatory plot or when Gelasimus sweeps away cobwebs with a slave, and the simply degrading ones (e.g., Peniculus applying his nose to the stolen cloak). Further pride swallowing is illustrated when the parasite tolerates insults: the nicknames, the teasing (the way the banker treated "Leaky" in the *Curculio*, Epignomus toying with "Mr. Funny" in the *Stichus*), the bad food (Curculio's leftover leftovers), the humble seating (Gelasimus' stool). And just how much pride a parasite had to swallow is made evident by the brazen claims to professional credentials he makes when his patron is out of earshot.

Beyond traits and behaviors were the possibilities of development along thematic lines. The relative prominence of the parasite's basic traits could be adjusted to suit various themes. Emphasize the importance of food, as Plautus does in the *Persa*—remember the bait-laying

---

52. Clearchus of Soli (c. 340–250), *FHG* 2.312.

scene—and you have a memorable demonstration of a free man's servility. Increase the parasite's cleverness vis-à-vis his benefactor, and
you get a flatterer who takes advantage of a fool; that is, you get someone like Artotrogus or Gnatho. Make him a helpless dependent like
Ergasilus, however, and you reveal a generous patron in a Hegio.

The parasite's lack of principle was perhaps the most fruitful source
of thematic development; there were so many principles that he lacked.
His relationship with his *rex* ought to have been a reciprocal exchange
of services involving a mutual sense of obligation and goodwill, but the
parasite knows nothing of the ethical or spiritual dimensions of the
relationship; his only thought is for his own self-interest. He will
encourage his *rex* in extravagant living, for instance, so as to skim off
some extravagance for himself (as do the parasite in the *Asinaria*, Curculio, Gelasimus before his young patrons went abroad, Peniculus,
Gnatho, Phormio). Curculio and Gnatho (at the very least) ought to
have known better, since each had ruined his own inheritance by the
very lifestyle that he encouraged in his patron. But no thought of his
benefactor's financial or moral well-being ever governs a parasite's
behavior. In fact, the more his "friend" is blind to his own faults, the
more success the parasite will have in turning those faults to his own
advantage. Flattery succeeds, says Aristotle, with those who love themselves.[53] Furthermore, the parasite has no loyalty to his benefactor. Curculio, for example, was ready to transfer his attentions to a new patron
(Therapontigonus) when it looked like the old one had exhausted his
resources.

Thematic development was also possible via contrast. The relationship between parasite and *rex* could be set in parallel with a relationship closer to ideal: the mutually beneficial *clientela* that Thais estab-
lishes with Chaerea's family in the *Eunuchus*, for example, or the
equality and good fellowship enjoyed by the slaves in the final act of
the *Stichus*. In this area the Romanness of the Roman plays becomes
most apparent. When Plautus creates a confusion in the *Curculio*
between the roles of parasite and *libertus*, he adds a Roman twist to the
parasite/slave analogy that is well attested in the Greek fragments and
seems to have been exploited with particular enthusiasm by Menander.
The *libertus*-as-parasite theme did not prosper, however, perhaps
because the legal and moral bonds between former master and freed-

---

53. φιλοκόλακες are φίλαυτοί (*Rhet.* 1371b22–23; cf. *EN* 1159a12–17).

man were not matched by anything in the parasite/*rex* relationship. Plautus' juxtaposition of the parasite Peniculus and the annoying *cliens quidam* in the *Menaechmi* ventures into a territory more fully developed in the pyramid of parasites in the *Eunuchus* and in the contrast between Phormio and Thais in the Phormio. This analogy succeeded.

The variety of compositional opportunities offered by the parasite clearly made him welcome to the authors of comedy, particularly of Roman comedy, where his role seems to have increased in prominence. As the parasite moved out into other genres of Latin literature, he took with him the traits and behaviors that we have seen deployed and developed in part 1. In satire and forensic oratory we will find the now familiar figure in different settings, most of them recognizably Roman. For Cicero and for Horace, Martial, and Juvenal, the parasite's potential lay in his ability to serve as an emblem of the *cliens.* As we shall see in parts 2 and 3, the type was put to use in caricaturing many different types of dependents; the gap between the parasite/*rex* relationship and the socially and ethically sanctioned relationship of *cliens* to patron offered a wide field for invective and social commentary.

Part 2: Satire

4

The Parasite in Horace

Nor can I crouch, and writhe my fawning tayle
to some great Patron, for my best availe.
Such hunger-starven Trencher-poetry;
or let it never live, or timely dye.
　　　　—Joseph Hall *Virgidemiarum* 1.1.11–14

The scene of Horace's *Satire* 2.3 is the Sabine farm, the season December. Horace has retired to the country to get some writing done. But things are not going well, and he receives a scolding: "What was the point of packing Menander in next to Plato, Eupolis, Archilochus? Why did you take along such distinguished companions?"[1] Horace's reading list is an acknowledgment of generic affiliation: the social criticism and personal invective of Eupolis and Archilochus were important constituents in the works of Horace's immediate predecessor in the genre, Lucilius. And in *Satires* 2 Horace himself owes a large debt both to the ethical categories and dialectic form of the Socratic tradition (represented on the list by Plato) and to the character typologies so familiar from New Comedy (Menander).[2] One particular borrowing will concern us: from Greek New Comedy and its Latin adaptations Horace drew the parasites who people his *Satires* and *Epistles.*

But Horace was not the first satirist to see that the mask of the parasite had potential for use outside of drama, as a parasite is present even in the earliest and most fragmentary collection of satires that has come down to us, the *Satires* of Ennius. The sole surviving fragment of book 6 of Ennius' *Satires* is part of a tirade on the asymmetric relationship

---

1. quorsum pertinuit stipare Platona Menandro, / Eupolin, Archilochum, comites educere tantos? (Hor. *Sat.* 2.3.11–12; the text is from Shackleton Bailey 1985).

2. New Comedy is not mentioned in other programmatic statements about satire. Yet scholars have identified more than one vignette adapted from New Comedy for satire. Hor. *Sat.* 1.2.20–22 draws on Terence's *Hautontimorumenos*, *Sat.* 2.3.259–71 is very close to Ter. *Eun.* 46–63, and Persius *Sat.* 5.161–74 is based on Menander's original *Eunuchus.* See Leach 1971; Freudenburg 1993, 107–8.

between guest and host, a relationship in which the guest has all the advantages and the host all the worries.

> You show up happy, without a care—you've bathed, your jaws are set to attack, your arm is free for action, bright-eyed you are and standing tall, poised like a wolf to pounce—you lick your way through somebody else's fortune, and how do you think your host feels then? Miserable, by the gods! As he tries to safe-guard his supplies, you swallow them down with a grin.[3]

We know nothing about the context of this complaint (even the book number is uncertain), but it is clear nevertheless that the person to whom these lines are addressed is a parasite drawn on the comic model: he is aggressively hungry, expensive, unwilling to provide for his own wants, and lacking in consideration for others. He has the comic parasite's animal-like appetite and attracts an eating metaphor ("you lick your way through somebody else's fortune") comparable to those we have seen employed in connection with Artotrogus, Peniculus, and Phormio. "You show up" (*advenis*) probably indicates that the satirist's parasite, unlike most of his confreres in Roman comedy, is uninvited (ἄκλητος); the picture of the host carefully husbanding supplies contributes to the idea that he has an unexpected mouth (a doughty one) to feed. Another regular attribute of the Greek comic parasite—his failure to contribute materially to the meal (the word for which is ἀσύμβολος)—may lie behind the expression "your arm is free for action" (*expedito bracchio*): a parasite's arm would be free for action,

---

3.　quippe sine cura laetus lautus cum aduenis,
　　　infestis malis, expedito bracchio,
　　　alacer celsus, lupino expectans impetu,
　　　mox alterius abligurris cum bona,
　　　quid censes domino[s] esse animi? pro diuum fidem,
　　　ill' tristist dum cibum seruat, tu ridens uoras.
　　　　　　　　　(Enn. 14–19 Vahlen; the text is from Courtney 1993, 12)
According to Donatus, these lines were the source of Terence *Phormio* 339–42 (*ad* 339, see discussion in text). The author's name is lost in a textual corruption. Arnott (1970, 37 n. 2) argues for a dramatic original: Cen<tauro τοῦ δεῖνα>. But Reeve (1979, 316) vindicates the reading *sed e sexto satirarum Ennii*.
　　For "poised like a wolf to pounce," cf. Plautus' wolflike parasites, Ergasilus (*quasi lupus esuriens metui ne in me faceret impetum, Capt.* 912) and Gelasimus (*Stich.* 577).

unencumbered by any offering. Terence, in his adaptation of this speech (see the following quotation), uses the adjective *asymbolus* to render this part of the description. Both of these traits—being uninvited and contributing nothing—are, as we have seen, more characteristic of the parasite of Greek comedy than his Roman counterpart, so Ennius may have taken his parasite directly from a Greek model rather than from a Roman play. Still, the representation of the type is so faithful to its comic origin that the speech can be taken back into comedy: these lines of Ennius survive because an ancient scholar saw that Terence had used them to supplement the principal text from which he created the *Phormio* in a speech by the parasite Phormio.

> When you come in from the baths washed and suitably anointed, without anything to offer, without a care, the host is all worn out with the worry and the expense. He grimaces but sets out what will please.[4]

Terence has altered the tone of the passage by putting the words in the mouth of an utterly complacent parasite, but this change only makes the Ennian moralist's criticism of the selfishness of the type more vivid.

That Ennius used the figure of the parasite in his new genre of satire, then, is certain; how he used it cannot now be determined. Not knowing the degree to which Ennius' satire was a model for Horace—Ennius is not mentioned in any of the passages in which Horace defines and defends his genre—adds a further element of uncertainty about the connection between Ennius' parasite and those we will meet in Horace. The situation is not greatly improved when we turn to the *Satires* of Horace's avowed model, Lucilius. Finding parasites in Lucilius is a difficult business. His fragments are brief and poorly attested, and there is rarely enough context to permit one to feel confident that one actually has hold of a parasite. Even the one indisputable Lucilian reference to parasites is little more than a tease:[5] "A cook doesn't care that a [sc. pea-

---

4. ten asymbolum venire unctum atque lautum e balineis, / otiosum ab animo, quom ille et cura et sumptu absumitur! / dum tibi fit quod placeat, ille ringitur: tu rideas (Ter. *Eun.* 340–42). The term *asymbolus* refers to a dining custom more Greek than Roman and occurs nowhere else in Roman comedy.

5. We will encounter another possibly Lucilian parasite in the discussion of Horace's *Satire* 2.1; other potential parasite references are treated briefly in appendix 2.

cock's] tail looks nice, so long as it is well fatted. Likewise, friends look
to the state of your character; those who are concerned with your property and the state of your finances are parasites."[6] The comic origin of
these parasites is evident from the label that is applied to them, *parasiti*,
and from their behavior, their self-interested simulation of friendship,
their concern with their host's external advantages, not his character.
But again we are unable to discern the use to which the poet puts them,
for the contrast of friend and parasite is a commonplace. The most one
can say is that *parasite* seems to be a negative label for a kind of behavior here, not a description of any real individuals. The fragment supplies a wealthy man with a touchstone on which to test the behavior of
his associates: Are they friends or parasites?

Not until we turn to Horace's satirical works do we begin to see
what the satirists saw in the comic parasite. The parasites who frequent
Horace's *Satires* and *Epistles* are a varied bunch. Some of them retain
their comic markings without perceptible alteration (except, as we shall
see, in the label applied to them). Others, on contact with the more thoroughly Roman world of satire, have undergone metamorphosis. These
retain enough of their original type to be recognizable but have traits
and behaviors not found in any of their comic counterparts. Still other
parasites figure in Horace's representations of the particular social
nexus of which he was a part, as illustrations of a role that he either did
or did not play (depending on the poem) or that was (or was not) recommended to his friends. For in Horace's day, as in that of the seven-
teenth-century satirist Joseph Hall (some of whose lines on this subject
appear in the epigraph to this chapter), the poet who benefited from a
patron's favor was liable to incur the charge of playing the parasite:
"For in this smoothing age who durst indite, Hath made his pen an
hyred Parasite, To claw the back of him that beastly lives, And pranck
base men in proud Superlatives" (*Virgidemiarum* 1.praef.9–12).

Horace assigns to a number of his creations the characteristics of the parasites of comedy. Their literary heritage allowed for rapid sketching.
Thus the attributes of Mulvius in *Satire* 2.7 are blocked in with two quick
lines: he is "a lightweight who does what his belly orders, who leans

---

6. cocus non curat caudam insignem esse illam, dum pinguis siet; / sic amici
quaerunt animum, rem parasiti ac ditias (Lucil. 716–17 Marx). Horace's adaptation of these lines focuses on the culinary (*Sat.* 2.2.23–30).

way back to raise his nose to the scent of cooking," who is, in short, "a
weak and idle glutton."[7] The comic parasite is recognizable in Mulvius'
obedience to his *venter*, his search for savory smoke, his inability to provide for his own wants, and his prodigious consumption.

Different but equally parasitical traits are to be found in the guest
occupying the lowest couch of a hypothetical dinner in *Epistle* 1.18. This
man plies both the obsequiousness and the petulant wit of the comic
parasite and appears in the appropriate convivial setting. He would
have done Terence's Gnatho proud as a graduate of his academy for
parasites in training: he "watches out for the wealthy man's nod, echoes
his words, and carries the conversation when the other falters."[8] "You
would think," says Horace, "that he was a boy repeating his lessons for
a heavy-handed schoolmaster, or a mime actor playing the supporting
role."[9] "Playing the supporting role" is precisely what made Gnatho
famous: the exchange between Gnatho and Thraso in which the parasite
amplifies each of the soldier's words (Ter. *Eun.* 391–94) is the passage
that Cicero selects to illustrate a flatterer's technique (*Amic.* 98). Horace
does not use a comic label for his flatterer, however: the man is called
neither *parasitus* nor *kolax* but *scurra* (*Epist.* 1.18.4).[10]

The term *scurra* had a history.[11] In the plays of Plautus the *scurra* was

---

7. 'etenim fateor me' dixerit ille / 'duci ventre levem, nasum nidore
supinor, / imbecillus, iners, si quid vis, adde, popino' (*Sat.* 2.7.37–39).

8. alter in obsequium plus aequo pronus et imi / derisor lecti . . . nutum
divitis horret / . . . iterat voces et verba cadentia tollit (*Epist.* 1.18.10–12). On
the disciples of Gnatho see Terence *Eun.* 262–64.

9. ut puerum saevo credas dictata magistro / reddere vel partis mimum
tractare secundas (*Epist.* 1.18.13–14).

10. Horace's avoidance of the term *parasitus* itself is probably to be ascribed
to his indirect method of acknowledging his debt to New Comedy. He says he
is following Lucilius, who modeled his work on Old Comedy, but he himself
has a distinct preference for the types and topics of New Comedy. Horace does
not acknowledge his allusions to New Comedy explicitly, however, except in
the "reading list" at the beginning of *Sat.* 2.3. When he draws a father very similar to the father Demea in Terence's *Adelphoe*, for instance, he says that it is his
own real father he is describing. Given its distribution (see appendix 1), the
term *parasitus* would have been an explicit reference to New Comedy.

11. The various meanings of *scurra* have been discussed by Corbett (1986).
Note, however, the reservations expressed in the brief review by Rudd (1987)
and in Fowler 1987, 90; Fowler refers to Corbett's discussion as "almost a model
of how not to go about an investigation of this kind." A better treatment is Lejay
1911, 551–53.

a rich but unreliable gossip (with, perhaps, a penchant for passive homosexual relations).[12] Catullus' *scurra* Suffenus gets a more favorable billing: he is a paragon of taste in all fields but the writing of poetry and is *dicax et venustus*, "witty and good company," to boot.[13] He is rich, too, if one may judge by the quality of the book rolls to which he consigns so many horrid verses (22.5–8).[14] Cicero, in contrast, seems to associate the *scurra* with poverty, not wealth, though he, too, credits him with wit (*de Or.* 2.247). In the *pro Quinctio*, for example, he maintains that not even in the unlikely event that property should come his way would the *scurra* show himself a good head of household: "it's an old saying that 'a *scurra* will sooner become rich than responsible'" (*Quinct.* 55). Elsewhere Cicero supplies the epithet *locuples*, "wealthy," to the label *scurra* to show that the men to whom he is thereby referring ("patrons" of Clodius: *Har.* 42, *Sest.* 39) were not ordinary poor *scurrae*. It is not possible to pinpoint the financial status of the *scurra* who appears in a sample speech quoted in a treatise written while Cicero was still a young man, the *Rhetorica ad Herennium*, but one can say that his aggressive language was the sort of talk associated with some scruffy parts of Rome, "the Sundial, backstage, and places of that sort."[15] This *scurra*, the speaker avers, had the advantage over the modest youth he accosted, because he knew that his reputation could not get any worse; he could behave as he liked at no cost to himself.

Already in the early part of the first century B.C., *scurra* was plainly a label that could cover a collection of negative traits, but Horace appears to have been the first to use *scurra* in a sense approaching that of *parasitus*. We have met the *scurra* of *Epistle* 1.18; the same heavily comic typology of that description is also apparent in some of Horace's other

12. *urbani adsidui cives quos scurras vocant . . . qui omnia se simulant scire neque quicquam sciunt* (Plaut. *Trin.* 202–5); for the hint of passive homosexual relations see *Poen.* 612.

13. *qui modo scurra / aut si quid hac re scitius videbatur* (Catull. *Carm.* 22.12–13); *homo est venustus et dicax et urbanus* (2).

14. Later complimentary descriptions may be found in Phaedrus (5.5: *notus urbano sale*) and Seneca (*Contr.* 1.7.3–18: another *scurra* who is *venustus* and *dicax*). But *scurra* also became a standard element in disapproving descriptions of an emperor's entourage (Juv. 4.31, Suet. *Tib.* 57.2, Tac. *Hist.* 2.87, *Ann.* 12.49, etc.). On still later occurrences of the term, see Baldwin 1986. For the type (though not the term) in Martial see Saggese 1994.

15. *Rhet. Her.* 4.10.14. For "the Sundial" cf. Cic. *Quinct.* 59.

scurrae.[16] There is Maenius, the "*scurra* on the prowl" (*vagus*) of *Epistle* 1.15, for example. Maenius was a man who had no reliable food trough (*praesepe*), who was an abyss capable of engulfing the contents of an entire marketplace, and who deposited all profits directly into his belly.[17] In short, he was a hungry parasite akin to Mulvius of *Sat.* 2.7 (who either is a *scurra* or associates with them: *Mulvius et scurrae . . . discedunt*, 36). Aristippus, in contrast, the courtier-philosopher and *scurra* of *Epistle* 1.17, has the comic parasite's professional pride: "I play the *scurra* for my own benefit—to have a horse to carry me and a patron to feed me, I do a job of work" (*scurror ipse mihi . . . equus ut me portet, alat rex, / officium facio*, 13–15). And the *scurrae* of *Satire* 2.3 are the familiar predatory types who flock to a young heir eager to squander his newly acquired wealth. They are summoned, appropriately enough, together with other aids to gastronomical delight: "The specialty chef [came] along with the *scurrae*; along with the fancy-goods district came the whole marketplace."[18]

Scurra may, however, have been adapted to parasitical uses by Horace's predecessor and model, Lucilius. One of Horace's *scurrae*, at least, the significantly named Pantolabus ("Take-all") of *Satires* 1.8 and 2.1, is in all probability based on a Lucilian model. Pantolabus' appearance in *Satire* 2.1 is part of a programmatic passage about the proper subject of satire. Horace's interlocutor here, Trebatius, urges Horace to take the praise of famous men as his subject (10–17) and understands

---

16. The two Horatian *scurrae* who are not endowed with the traits of the comic parasite are Sarmentus, who is not (as far as the poem tells us, anyway) particularly hungry (*Sat.* 1.5.52–70), and Volanerius, whose passion is gambling (*Sat.* 2.7.15–20). Still, Juvenal found Sarmentus more parasitical than the bare bones of *Satire* 1.5 indicate, for Sarmentus is an exemplum of parasitism in the opening paragraph of *Satire* 5—perhaps Juvenal knew what his scholiast did, that Sarmentus was Maecenas' freedman and was accompanying him on the trip.

17. *Epist.* 1.15.26–35, quoted later in this chapter; see n. 58 for the text.

18. cum scurris fartor, cum Velabro omne macellum (*Sat.* 2.3.229; cf. Terence *Eun.* 256–57 and my chap. 1 n. 38). Apuleius, too, associates parasites and heirs. His stepson, an heir apparent, seems to have had his own collection of opportunisitic *parasiti*. Apuleius maintained that the real beneficiaries of his wife's will would be her son's cronies: "it was not you, her son, that she made her heir, but the future of Aemilianus, the marriage of Rufinus, that wine-soaked crowd of your parasites" (*sed Aemiliani spes et Rufini nuptias, set temulentum illud collegium parasitos tuos, Apol.* 100).

Horace's response to mean that Horace intends to do so as soon as an opportunity presents itself. He commends Horace's good sense: "A much better idea than writing depressing stuff attacking Pantolabus the *scurra* and the spendthrift Nomentanus!"[19] Trebatius has of course misread the evasive response he received, for Horace proceeds to declare his loyalty to Lucilius' satiric genre (28–29). Pantolabus himself does not appear in the extant fragments of Lucilius, and the extravagant Nomentanus with whom Horace twice pairs him does so only by dint of emendations to Lucilius' text.[20] Nevertheless, Pantolabus' significant name, the repetition of the phrase *Pantolabum scurram Nomentanumque nepotem* (a quotation or paraphrase of a line of Lucilius?), and the fact that so many of Horace's *scurrae* are parasitical *scurrae* (and thus very different from the *scurrae* of Plautus and Catullus) suggest that there was a parasitical *scurra* named Pantolabus in the *Satires* of Lucilius. There is no unambiguously parasitical *scurra* of any name in what we have of Lucilius, but there is a *scurra*, the ball-playing Coelius, and he has more than a soupçon of the parasitical about him (see appendix 2).

The Horatian *scurrae* that we have met so far have been types, quickly sketched but recognizable because of their comic heritage. Maenius is practically pure comedy; Aristippus belonged to the court of Dionysius II of Syracuse, the predators of *Satire* 2.3 to the timeless tradition of extravagant heirs; only Mulvius, the would-be guest at Horace's table, is unambiguously Roman. Horace's other Roman parasites get more space, for instead of applying the label *scurra*, he lets them act out their characters.

There are fully four active parasites in that most convivial of *Satires*, "Nasidienus' Dinner Party" (*Sat.* 2.8). The host, Nasidienus, has two parasites in attendance on his own account. The first of these is a funny fellow named Porcius ("The Porker"), whose party trick is said to be

---

19. Quanto rectius hoc quam tristi laedere versu / Pantolabum scurram Nomentanumque nepotem (*Sat.* 2.1.21–22).

20. Fragments 56 and 59–60 Marx have been emended by some scholars to contain the name Nomentanus (Rudd 1966, 142). Even if one were to accept these emendations (neither Marx nor the most recent editor of Lucilius, F. Charpin, does), there is nothing to declare Nomentanus a spendthrift in the passages in question, so they do not provide a link to the Nomentanus of Horace.

stuffing whole cakes into his mouth at once (*ridiculus totas semel absorbere placentas*, 24). Since this dinner fails to get beyond the fish course, he does not really get a chance to show his stuff. His contribution to the party is modest: the excessive wine intake of some of the guests worries Nasidienus, so Porcius and his companions on the lowest couch—Nasidienus himself and his other parasite, a helpful fellow named Nomentanus—drink sparingly (*imi / convivae lecti nihilum nocuere lagoenis*, 40–41).

His couch-mate Nomentanus outshines Porcius. Placed just beneath the most important guest, Maecenas, he appoints himself subdocent of Nasidienus' ambitious meal, making sure that the guests notice their host's luxurious touches (*qui, si quid forte lateret, / indice monstraret digito*, 25–26).[21] We have met the name *Nomentanus* before; Nomentanus was the name of the spendthrift sidekick of Pantolabus the *scurra*. Is there a connection between that extravagant fellow and Nasidienus' helpful guest? Nomentanus the *nepos* was already proverbial as a self-indulgent gourmand in Horace's day (*Sat.* 1.1.102, 2.3.175, 2.3.224).[22] One might think it unlikely that Horace would set such a character at a table with real named contemporaries. But *Nomentanus* need not be the real name of the guest described in *Satire* 2.8 any more than the significant name *Porcius* is.[23] The culinary expertise that the paradigmatic Nomentanus gained as a self-indulgent gourmand is transferred to the character to whom Horace gives his name; precisely this quality makes him useful to his host, Nasidienus. The transformation of *nepos* to parasite was neither difficult nor unusual. The fellow who has squandered his property on parties and other pleasures often resorts to preying on fools who follow his example. Plautus' Curculio was one such fallen star, Terence's Gnatho was another, and Gnatho had a friend in similar straits: "I bumped into a fellow of my own station and rank today, a bloke with style who had licked clean the plate of his inheritance."[24] Maenius, the *scurra* of *Epistle* 1.15, is yet another spendthrift turned par-

---

21. Cf. *vel continuo patuit* at 29 and *post hoc me docuit* at 31.

22. Cf. Sen. *Vit. Beat.* 11.4: aspice Nomentanum et Apicium, terrarum ac maris, ut isti vocant, bona conquaerentis et super mensam recognoscentis omnium gentium animalia.

23. See Rudd 1966, 144.

24. conveni hodie adveniens quendam mei loci hinc atque ordinis, / hominem haud impurum, itidem patria qui abligurrierat bona (Ter. *Eun.* 234–35; cf. 241).

asite: "Maenius first earned the character of an amusing fellow after he'd manfully finished off all that he had inherited from his mother's side and his father's."[25]

Familiarity with the finer points of extravagant cuisine is not Nomentanus' only recommendation. Like the Protean parasites of comedy, he can change his spots. After a dusty tapestry falls and ruins the course in progress, for example, leaving Nasidienus immobile and practically inconsolable, Nomentanus plays the *sapiens* in an attempt to retrieve the situation: "O Fortune, who of the gods is more cruel to us than you? How you delight in toying with human affairs!" (61–63). One of the guests, the self-sufficient Varius, finds Nomentanus' quick change funny ("Varius had difficulty hiding his laughter behind his napkin," 63–64), but Nomentanus' fellow dependent Servilius Balatro ("The Babbler") picks up the conversational ball and runs with it for some distance (64–74).

Balatro and another fellow named Vibidius had come to the party in Maecenas' train, as his "shadows" (*umbrae,* 22).[26] They were the guests whose capacity for drink had worried Nasidienus: "Said Vibidius to Balatro: 'If we don't make a dent on the drink supply, we'll have missed our chance for revenge.' Whereon he asks for bigger cups."[27] But they did their best to earn their drinks. Balatro, as we have seen, follows Nomentanus' lead in consoling Nasidienus. He achieves a double success, gratifying his host—Nasidienus says, "You're a good man and a charming guest" (*ita vir bonus es convivaque comis!* 76)—and amusing the other guests (77–78). When the newly enheartened Nasidienus leaves the room to see to matters in the kitchen, Vibidius and Balatro team up to provide the entertainment.

> Meanwhile Vibidius asks the slaves if the wine pot has been broken, too, seeing that he isn't being given the drinks he asked for.

---

25. Maenius, ut rebus maternis atque paternis / fortiter absumptis urbanus coepit haberi (*Epist.* 1.15.26–27).

26. *Umbra* is not attested with this particular metaphorical sense earlier (but cf. *Epist.* 1.5.28). A passage in Plautus' *Casina* reveals its probable origins: quia certum est mihi, quasi umbra, quoquo tu ibis, te semper sequi (92). It is difficult to believe, however, that the *Satire* passage contains its earliest occurrence, since Horace offers neither apology for nor explanation of the metaphor.

27. tum Vibidius Balatroni: / 'nos nisi damnose bibimus moriemur inulti,' / et calices poscit maiores (*Sat.* 2.8.33–35; cf. 39–40).

Everyone laughs at what he comes up with, and Balatro keeps it
going.[28]

Nasidienus and the parasites manage the meal between them, in fact;
the other guests are passive except for the occasional snicker.

The combination of officiousness and amusement is highly parasitical, of course, so it is not surprising that Balatro's speech of consolation
had several generations of parasitical antecedents. Balatro claims that
Nasidienus' guests (or he himself, at the very least) recognize the
efforts he has made on their behalf, regardless of the mishap to their
dinner.

> In order that I might be given an elegant entertainment you've got
> worries on all sides: lest the servants bring out bread that is
> burned or a sauce that is ill seasoned, lest they themselves be
> insufficiently well dressed and groomed. Add to these dangers
> the possibility that the tapestry may come down (as it just did) or
> that the boy may lose his footing and break a dish.[29]

We have encountered this speech before, once in Terence's *Phormio*, and
once in the *Satires* of Ennius, and we saw that Ennius probably derived
his sketch from a parasite scene in Greek New Comedy. Balatro adds a
chaser of praise to his Phormian gesture, likening the good host to a
commander in the military: "As with a general, so too with a host, mis-
fortunes reveal his talent, while good fortune keeps it hidden" (*sed con-
vivatoris uti ducis ingenium res / adversae nudare solent, celare secundae*,
73–74). The raison d'être of comic parasites, according to Cicero, was to
puff up the martial pretensions of boastful soldiers; here, employing

---

28. Vibidius dum
    quaerit de pueris num sit quoque fracta lagoena,
    quod sibi poscenti non dantur pocula, dumque
    ridetur fictis rerum, Balatrone secundo.

    (*Sat.* 2.8.80–83)

29. tene, ut ego accipiar laute, torquerier omni
    sollicitudine districtum, ne panis adustus,
    ne male conditum ius apponatur, ut omnes
    praecincti recte pueri comptique ministrent?
    adde hos praeterea casus, aulaea ruant si,
    ut modo, si patinam pede lapsus frangat agaso.

    (*Sat.* 2.8.67–72)

the tactic of ironic praise of which Artotrogus was so much the master, we see four Roman parasites puffing the pretensions (culinary and other) of a boastful host. The world of comedy is very close to the surface. Indeed, the man to whom the account is told feels that he has missed a play—"I'd rather have watched these shows than any others" (*nullos his mallem ludos spectasse*, 79)—*ludi*,"shows," being the name for the public festivals at which plays were performed (among other entertainments, to be sure). And the "play" could hardly have been given a more appropriate narrator, for Fundanius, who recounts the whole amusing dinner to Horace, is a comic poet (19; cf. *Sat.* 1.10.40–42).[30]

In *Satire* 2.8 parasitical behavior was ascribed to two types of *cliens:* the sort who fill up the lowest couch at their patron's dinner party (Nomentanus and Porcius) and the sort who swell the retinue of an important Roman going visiting (Vibidius and Servilius Balatro). In other *Satires* Horace uses the figure of the parasite to interpret quite different social types. In *Satire* 1.2, for example, we find some elements of a *matrona*'s entourage described as *parasitae*, "female parasites."

To direct a young man's sexual interests away from well-born, well-bred Roman matrons, the satirist ticks off the obstacles in the way of courting such a woman.

> If you will go after what is forbidden and what is surrounded by defenses (this is what drives you mad, I know), you'll find many things blocking your way: guardians, a sedan chair, hairdressers, hangers-on [*parasitae*], a dress that goes down to her ankles, and on top a shawl all around her.[31]

---

30. In *Sat.* 1.10 Horace pronounces himself disinclined to vie with the talented Fundanius, but Horace's fondness for combining a *recusatio* with some verses in the manner of the rejected genre is well known. Freudenburg (1993, 232–33) argues that there is a fifth parasite in *Satire* 2.8, namely, Horace himself, who was not invited to the party and is thus a "hungry parasite who experiences the meal vicariously through the comic descriptions of his friend Fundanius." But the essence of the uninvited parasite is showing up uninvited and wangling a meal anyway, not staying home hungry.

31.   si interdicta petes, vallo circumdata (nam te
          hoc facit insanum), multae tibi tum officient res;
          custodes, lectica, ciniflones, parasitae,
          ad talos stola demissa et circum addita palla.

                                                        (*Sat.* 1.2.96–98)

The *parasitae* here are just one entry in an argument about the difficulties of an adulterous relationship, but the label is nevertheless a striking novelty. Elsewhere we hear very little about parasites (of either gender) preying on women.[32] Peniculus, for example, failed utterly in his attempt to transfer his attentions to Menaechmus' wife.

The context of *Satire* 1.2 does not give us much information about these *parasitae,* and one is inclined to suspect that they merited the uncomplimentary label simply because they would be an annoyance to the prospective lover. The "moralist" (the speaker of the *Satire*), who is trying to make the *matrona* as unappealing as possible as an object of sexual pursuit, sees an opportunity to make a clever and rhetorically effective identification, and the female friends with whom the woman surrounds herself (for companionship and to have visible indicators of her standing) are reduced to "hangers-on," self-interested and tenacious types who are not at all inclined to move aside for a lover.

That the term *parasitae* is an interpretation of this particular type of relationship rather than an objective description of it is to be expected, given the rhetorical situation; that this actually is the case is suggested by the fact that one can find different interpretations elsewhere. Juvenal, for example, offers a mercenary explanation for what must be a similar entourage: a woman wishing to make a splash in public will, according to Juvenal, surround herself with ". . . companions, a sedan chair, a cushion, girlfriends, a nurse, and a blond maid to whom she is always giving orders."[33] If display is the motive for this woman—she is going to a show—money (not clout) is the means, for her *comites* and *amicae* are hired (*conducit*).

Juvenal's mercenary picture is even more negative than Horace's, but one can also find approving descriptions of relationships between women of unequal rank. For example, in the preface to the first poem of the fifth book of Statius' *Silvae,* Statius claims that the (deceased) wife of his addressee had been fond of his own wife Claudia.

---

32. Clearchus of Soli (a pupil of Aristotle's) does, however, mention some Greek and Macedonian women of rank who received the attentions of female flatterers called "ladder women" (κλιμακίδες), so-called from the fact that they let their patronesses climb into conveyances by mounting on their backs (Ath. 6.256d; cf. Plut. *Mor.* 50d). See further my discussion of Caesennia in chap. 7.

33. ut spectet ludos, conducit Ogulnia vestem, / conducit comites, sellam, cervical, amicas, / nutricem et flavam cui det mandata puellam (Juv. *Sat.* 6.352–54).

I leapt to the task [sc. of writing a *consolatio*] not as an unknown from the crowd or to flaunt my services. For your wife was very fond of my wife and, by loving her, increased my own sense of her worth. So I would be positively ungrateful if I were to neglect your tears.[34]

The connection between the two women gave Statius the entrée he needed to offer his consolatory services to a powerful imperial freedman. Ovid's wife, too, had connections with the great. She had done what she could to earn the patronage of Paullus Fabius Maximus' wife Marcia ("Marcia approved of and loved her from an early age; she counted her among her companions"),[35] and Marcia's husband is repeatedly asked to use his influence with Augustus on Ovid's behalf. Since both Statius and Ovid refer to their wives' connections in addressing client services or requests for service to the husband of the wife's friend, they naturally paint a favorable picture of the relationship between women of unequal rank.

Horace's *parasitae* had no direct descendants, but in another case Horace's creative adaptation of the type was very fruitful indeed. The *captator* (inheritance-hunter), first fully described in the conversation between the seer Tiresias and the desperate-for-cash Ulysses in *Satire* 2.5, is a parasite gone modern.[36]

The points of contact between *captator* and parasite are numerous. There is an *ars* to the inheritance-hunting business, as there is to that of the parasite, and Ulysses is urged to adopt it to restore his fortunes. The inheritance-hunter's art consists, in part, in steeling himself to provide services as demeaning as those offered by his comic prototype.[37] The good *captator* is a considerate walking companion, for example: "No

---

34. ego tamen huic operi non ut unus e turba nec tantum quasi officiosus adsilui. amauit enim uxorem meam Priscilla et amando fecit mihi illam probatiorem; post hoc ingratus sum si lacrimas tuas transeo (*Silv.* 5.praef.5–7).

35. hanc probat et primo dilectam semper ab aevo / est inter comites Marcia censa suas (*Pont.* 1.2.137–38; cf. 3.1.77–78). She had also been a familiar of Marcia's mother (and Augustus' maternal aunt) Atia (*inque suis, Pont.* 1.2.139–40).

36. Both Ribbeck (1883, 29) and Rudd (1966, 303 n. 17) note the parasitical origins of the typology. Champlin (1991, 92) calls *captatores* "extraneous parasites" but does not develop the image.

37. *Ars: Sat.* 2.5.3, 26.

matter if the fellow tells lies in court, or is low born, or spattered with a brother's blood, or a runaway; if he asks you to walk with him, go along, and keep on the street side of him, too."[38] There are all sorts of attentions to busy oneself with: one can attract notice with inexpensive gifts (birds for the table, apples, 10–14)[39] or curry favor with praise ("Does he insist on hearing praise? Well then let him have it. Fill up that swelling head of his with your gushing speeches. Keep it up until he lifts his hands to the sky and says, "Enough, already!").[40] A pretense of intimacy is effective ("'Quintus,' suppose you say, or 'Publius'—tender little ears love those first names"),[41] as is a display of concern for one's victim's well-being: "Pretend it is him you are thinking of when you make your move. If it's getting windy out, urge him to protect his precious head with a hat; use your shoulders to get him out of a crowd."[42] Or one can offer the more substantial service of a legal representative (27–41). And when the business of the day has been completed, the *captator* will attend to his target's sexual needs, too, or offer up his wife, if that is what will suit (75–76).[43]

Even less intimate forms of service than these last two require a certain swallowing of pride: "Shall I play escort to filthy Dama? That was not my way at Troy," says Ulysses (18–19). Indeed, the *captator* must resign himself to using the sort of tactics available to such undignified creatures as a "cunning woman" (*mulier dolosa*) and a freedman (70–72). But occasionally the *captator* submits to treatment that is even more painful than that: the wealthy prey of inheritance-hunters, like the

38. qui quamvis periurus erit, sine gente, cruentus / sanguine fraterno, fugitivus, ne tamen illi / tu comes exterior si postulet ire recuses (*Sat.* 2.5.15–17).

39. Gift giving is not a behavior attested among the parasites of comedy proper, but it is present in Theophrastus' κόλαξ (*Char.* 2.6). On the ties between the *Characters* and comedy see Ussher 1960, 46; on *hamata munera*, Pliny *Ep.* 9.30.2.

40. importunus amat laudari? donec "ohe, iam!" / ad caelum manibus sublatis dixerit, urge, / crescentem tumidis infla sermonibus utrem (*Sat.* 2.5.96–98).

41. "Quinte," puta, aut "Publi" (gaudent praenomine molles / auriculae) (*Sat.* 2.5.32–33).

42. obsequio grassare; mone, si increbruit aura, / cautus uti velet carum caput; extrahe turba / oppositis umeris (*Sat.* 2.5.93–95). At lines 37–41 it is recommended that the *captator* safeguard his victim's health even at the cost of his own: ire domum atque / pelliculam curare iube. fi cognitor ipse; / persta atque obdura, seu rubra Canicula findet / infantis statuas seu pingui tentus omaso / Furius hibernas cana nive conspuet Alpis.

43. See chap. 3 n. 49.

patrons of parasites, were in a position to toy with those who hoped to profit from their wealth.[44] We have seen how in Plautus' *Stichus* Pamphilippus and Epignomus amused themselves by teasing the ever hopeful Gelasimus; Horace offers an anecdote about the duping of a *captator* in the story of Nasica and Coranus (55–69). Tiresias had warned the captatorial Ulysses not to be discouraged by the occasional failure (24–26). Indeed, damage suffered at the hands of a potential legator is not necessarily a dead loss. For example, if in serving the object of his hope as a legal representative the inheritance-hunter is party to a bad or fraudulent case, the damage he does to others and to his own self-respect need not concern him, as long as he makes himself a name for utility: "'You can see, can't you,' someone will say as he gives the man next to him a nudge with his elbow, 'how much he [sc. the *captator*] puts up with, how well he shapes himself to his friends, how energetic he is?' Many fine fish will swim up to swell your fishpond's population."[45] In other words, if the current fish fails to bite, another might.

The "friendship" mentioned in the passage just quoted and elsewhere in the poem (*comes*, 17; *amicum*, 33; *sodalis*, 101) is patently self-serving and insincere (33–34, 101–4). Insincerity is in fact a desirable trait in a *captator*, since an important part of his art consists in adapting himself to the character of the target of the moment: one type of behavior will suit the patron who writes poems (74–75), another the man who likes female companionship (75–76); a lively line in chatter will not suit one patron at all but might be just the ticket for another (90–91); and so on. The *captator*, like the parasite, needs to make himself into a kind of second skin for his victim.

A compact statement of the *captator*'s art is given in lines 47–48: "Worm your way into expectations by being helpful" (*in spem / adrepe officiosus*). So helpful, in fact, and so lacking in pride is the ideal *captator* that his profession, like that of the parasite, can be labeled "slavery" (*servitium*, 99).[46]

---

44. The sport of the *captator*'s prey is also the subject, much later, of Ben Jonson's play *Volpone*, a comedy with numerous inheritance-hunters and one fine parasite, Mosca ("The Fly").

45. 'nonne vides' aliquis cubito stantem prope tangens / inquiet, 'ut patiens, ut amicis aptus, ut acer?' / plures annabunt thynni et cetaria crescent (*Sat.* 2.5.42–44).

46. Cf. the analogy between *captator* and comic slave at lines 91–92: Davus sis comicus.

The *captator* made only incidental appearances in Latin literature before Horace, with one reference in Plautus (*M.g.* 705–15) and a handful in Cicero (*Off.* 3.74, *Parad.* 39, 43). But Horace, with the help of the comic parasite, defined the type for subsequent generations: the *captator* is parasitical in Seneca, Petronius, Pliny, Martial, Juvenal, Plutarch, and Lucian (to name just the most extensive treatments).[47] The crowning touch to the picture of the parasitical *captator* was supplied by Petronius. Near the end of what we have of the *Satyricon*, the poet Eumolpus finds himself beset by *captatores*. He takes a malicious pleasure in putting into his will a clause that will expose the true nature of his tormentors: those who wish to take up the monetary legacies he leaves them will have to consume his physical remains first (*corpus consumant*, 141.4).[48] "Your stomach will do as you tell it," he says, adding, "Just cover your eyes and pretend that you are eating a hundred thousand sesterces rather than human flesh."[49]

The parasitical origin of Horace's *captator* is fairly easy to discern. Both types "consume" their hosts, but whereas the parasite needs his ration daily, the *captator* can afford to wait for his prize.[50] With the pest of *Satire* 1.9 the metamorphosis has gone further, for he is not ostensibly concerned with food, real or metaphorical, at all; he wants connections. And yet the fate foretold for Horace (as he reports it in this *Satire*, anyway) puts his relationship with the pest into the same comestible context as that of Eumolpus and his *captatores*.

"Neither deadly poison nor hostile sword will take him off, not an internal ailment, not a cough, not slow-killing gout. A chattering fellow will gobble him up one day [*consumet*]; if he's got any

---

47. For a fuller set of references to passages on *captatio* see in Champlin 1991, appendix 4.

48. omnes qui in testamento meo legata habent praeter libertos meos hac condicione percipient quae dedi, si corpus meum in partes conciderint et astante populo comederint . . . his admoneo amicos meos ne recusent quae iubeo, sed quibus animis devoverint spiritum meum, eisdem etiam corpus consumant (Petron. *Sat.* 141.2–4).

49. sequetur imperium [sc. stomachus tuus] . . . operi modo oculos et finge te non humana viscera sed centies sestertium comesse. (Petron. *Sat.* 141.6–7).

50. The *captator* was not the only "professional" for whom the model of the parasite was adapted at this period; for an ample discussion of the parallels between the tactics of the parasite and the elegiac lover see Labate 1984.

sense, he'll avoid those talkative types, especially when he's come
to manhood."[51]

Appropriately enough, then, the skills that the talkative type of *Satire*
1.9 advertises are skills that would be displayed in a convivial setting:
"Who could write more verses more quickly? Who could dance more
naughtily? Even Hermogenes would envy the songs that I sing."[52]

This pest has the parasite's boldness in introducing himself to a
potential patron, seizing the hand of a man who professes to know him
by name only and dousing him with warm familiarity: "How *are* you,
you sweet thing, you?"[53] And the pest's plan C for meeting Maecenas—
plan A was an introduction from Horace, plan B is bribing the servants
to admit him—likewise involves accosting a patron in the street: "I'll
pick a good time, bump into him at the intersection, make myself his
escort" (*tempora quaeram; / occurram in triviis; deducam*, 58–59).

We have seen that the art of drawing attention to oneself was crucial
to parasitical success, but striking up a conversation in the street was
only half of the job: one had to keep hold of one's victim to arrive at the
desired invitation (for a parasite) or introduction (for a pest). The pest's
plans A and C both involve escorting patrons, and he shows himself
considerably more tenacious than, for example, the parasite Peniculus
in the *Menaechmi*, who, though he knows the appropriate game plan
("I'm going to keep hold and follow you about. You couldn't pay me all
the money in heaven to get me to let you out of my sight today,"
216–17), loses contact with his patron amid the distractions of the
forum. The pest, too, declares that he will hold on as long as it takes
(*usque tenebo*, 15; cf. *deducam*, 59; *assectaretur*, 6; *prosequar*, 16; *sequar*, 19)
and shows himself willing to do so even at some cost to himself: his

---

51. hunc neque dira venena nec hosticus auferet ensis
       nec laterum dolor aut tussis nec tarda podagra:
       garrulus hunc quando consumet cumque; loquaces,
       si sapiat, vitet, simul atque adoleverit aetas.

(*Sat.* 1.9.31–34)

52. nam quis me scribere pluris / aut citius possit versus? quis membra
movere / mollius? invideat quod et Hermogenes ego canto (*Sat.* 1.9.23–25).

53. accurrit quidam notus mihi nomine tantum / arreptaque manu 'quid
agis, dulcissime rerum?' (*Sat.* 1.9.3–4). Cf. the familiarities broached by the *captator* in *Sat.* 2.5.32–33 and the scenes of accosting in comedy (e.g., Plaut. *Capt.*
478–86, *Curc.* 337–38, *Stich.* 218–24).

question "Shall I let go of you or forfeit my case?" (40–41) is decided in favor of holding on to what he has caught (namely, Horace). It took a legal summons to pry him loose (77–79).

The pest, like Gelasimus, is well aware of the competitive nature of his pursuit. He attempts to win Horace's interest by offering to second Horace's own putative efforts: "I'd be a big help to you, if you'd only get me in. I'd be supporting actor to your lead."[54] We have met parasites in the supporting role before: the guest in *Epistle* 1.18 and the master flatterer Gnatho. The pest refuses to believe Horace's assertion that there is no jockeying for position in Maecenas' circle, and with a single word he reveals both the insincerity of his offer to play Horace's second and his own ultimate aim: what he wants is not simply a place for himself at Maecenas' table but the best place: "you just make me more eager to get as close as possible to him" (*proximus*, 53–54).

The parasites of comedy were much more modest in their seating aspirations. They were perfectly satisfied to be on the lowest couch or even on a stool in the corner. There are other touches in *Satire* 1.9 that show that the pest is not simply a comic parasite transplanted: no comic parasite has legal business of his own to attend to, and parasites do not bribe slaves for admittance.[55] In fact, in this *Satire* the figure of the parasite has been adapted to serve as a caricature for the ambitious *cliens* in first-century B.C. Rome.

As we saw in the case of the *parasitae*, one's point of view has a great deal to do with the way one describes a relationship. The satirist finds the pest annoyingly parasitical: he is a shameless outsider and potential rival who aims to break into the happy circle gathered around Maecenas' table. But what the pest was asking for was not ipso facto untoward, as can be seen in two poems not too distant in date from Horace's *Satires* in which a poet unabashedly requests regular hospitality from a patron and presents the credentials that he thinks will make his plea persuasive.

---

54. haberes / magnum adiutorem, posset qui ferre secundas, / hunc hominem velles si tradere (*Sat.* 1.9.45–47). Cf. the cooperative entertainment provided by Vibidius and Balatro at Nasidienus' party (esp. *Sat.* 2.8.83: *Balatrone secundo*) and the conspiracy of parasites at the conclusion of the *Eunuchus* (1069–87).

55. This practice was learned from the lovers of comedy (cf. Ter. *Haut.* 300–301) and became a topos in both elegy and satire.

The *Panegyricus Messallae*, from about 31 B.C., is the earlier of the two. Its author (whose identity is unknown) aims to become the *laudator* of M. Valerius Messalla Corvinus.

> Writers will crowd around, eager to put praise of you on record. Some will be singers with fixed measure; others will write prose. There will be a competition to see who is best. May I be winner over all, so that I may inscribe my name onto your great accomplishments![56]

The *Panegyricus* is the author's competition piece: "I hope this small effort gives you pleasure, and that hereafter I may show my gratitude by writing more poems for you."[57] The author, like the pest, makes no bones about his need. Formerly a wealthy man, he has now become another of Fortuna's victims (181–89) and as such must say to Messalla, proleptically, "I am all yours" (*sum quodcumque tuum est*, 197). The author of the *Laus Pisonis* is similarly frank: "My sole aim is to make you see fit to open your home to me."[58] In neither of these poems does the description of the hoped-for relationship between poet and patron have anything specifically parasitical about it, for the view taken is positive, not negative. But the relationship itself is clearly not very different from what the pest of *Satire* 1.9 was aiming at; how one interprets

---

56. convenientque tuas cupidi componere laudes
    undique quique canent vincto pede quique soluto.
    quis potior, certamen erit: sim victor in illis,
    ut nostrum tantis inscribam nomen in actis.

                                              ([Tib.] 4.1.35–38)

Cf. the *Graeculi* jostling for the job of writing a Greek history of Cicero's consulship (*Att.* 2.1.2).

57. hic quoque sit gratus parvus labor, ut tibi possim / inde alios aliosque memor componere versus ([Tib.] 4.1.16–17; cf. 203–11). It has recently been argued that a rival bid, or, more accurately, a response to the challenge presented by this poem, is extant. Both Schoonhoven (1983) and Papke (1986) see *Catalepton* 9 as an essentially Callimachean critique of the *Panegyricus*. It would be pleasant to think that what might have amounted to a battle for a poet's livelihood could be conducted on such a purely literary plane, but given the frailty of the arguments for changing the date of the *Panegyricus* from about 31 (cf. Momigliano 1950) to nearer the time of Messalla's triumph in 27 (an event celebrated in *Cat.* 9), I remain unconvinced that there is any evidence of rivalry.

58. dignare tuos aperire Penates, / hoc solum petimus (*Laus Pis.* 218–19). Much the same point is made by the echo of 81–82 in 109–11.

the behavior used to initiate and maintain such a relationship depends on one's point of view.

In the poems we have examined so far, the parasite has proven his utility as a type for the negative characterization of the *cliens* in several of his social manifestations: eager-to-please dinner guest, escort, female companion, inheritance-hunter, and connection-seeker. The largest set of Horatian parasite references—and in many ways the most surprising one—consists of passages in which parasite and poet (our poet) are juxtaposed.

Consider Maenius, the *scurra vagus* of *Epistle* 1.15. He is equipped with a full set of parasite traits.

> Maenius first earned the character of an amusing fellow after he'd manfully finished off all that he had inherited from his mother's side and his father's. He was considered a *scurra* on the prowl, without any fixed place to feed. Unfed, he wouldn't discriminate between fellow citizen and enemy, they thought: he had a ferocious way of making up just about anything disreputable about just about anyone. A pestilence he was, a storm, a bottomless pit into which one might upend the marketplace. Anything he acquired he presented as a gift to his greedy gullet. When he had extracted nothing (or just a little) from those who cheered on his bad behavior or the timid types, he would dine on cheap foods, but plattersful, enough for three bears.[59]

---

59. Maenius, ut rebus maternis atque paternis
     fortiter absumptis urbanus coepit haberi:
     scurra vagus, non qui certum praesepe teneret,
     impransus non qui civem dinosceret hoste,
     quaelibet in quemvis opprobria fingere saevus.
     pernicies et tempestas barathrumque macelli,
     quidquid quaesierat ventri donabat avaro.
     hic ubi nequitiae fautoribus et timidis nil
     aut paulum abstulerat, patinas cenabat omasi
     vilis et agninae, tribus ursis quod satis esset.
                    (*Epist.* 1.15.26–35, with punctuation lightly
                       altered from Shackleton Bailey's edition)
     Cf. the appetite of the parasite in Antiphanes 82 Kassel-Austin [K-A]: καταβε-
     βρωκὼς σιτία ἴσως ἐλεφάντων τεττάρων.

Maenius is another of the character names adopted from Lucilius, but Horace has gone back to comedy for details of language and imagery.[60] We have seen a parasite's food trough (*praesepe*) in Plautus' *Curculio* (228). Storm words or terms indicative of destruction were frequently applied to parasites, as in the nicknames "Thunder" and "Lightning." Maenius has the parasite's insatiable hunger (*barathrum macelli*, 31; cf. 35), and his *venter* is referred to as an entity almost independent of his body (*ventri . . . avaro*, 32; cf. 36–37). Finally, it is typical of a parasite to define the summum bonum as good feeding: "The same man, whenever he'd bagged a bigger prize, promptly rendered it smoke and ashes, saying, 'I quite understand how men can eat their way through their fortunes, since there's nothing better than a fat thrush, nothing more attractive than a stuffed paunch.'"[61] Maenius, then, is a quintessential parasite. Yet despite the assemblage of negative traits, Horace adopts Maenius as an emblem of himself in the very next line: "I'm only too much like him" (*nimirum hic ego sum*, 42).

The juxtaposition produces a pleasant little piece of self-depreciation (*Epistle* 1.15 is, on the whole, the most modest of the *Epistles*). In the lines that follow, Horace defines more precisely the grounds for the analogy between himself and Maenius, highlighting Maenius' apparently proverbial inconsistency. When Maenius' takings are small, he eats cheaply (though still a lot) and castigates the spendthrift's luxurious fare, but when he can afford to treat himself, he does so unabashedly. In the same way, Horace tolerates modest circumstances, but when someone invites him to share more affluent surroundings for a time, he proves capable of appreciating them.

> When funds have run dry, I can face humble circumstances bravely enough, but when something better and more luxurious comes my way I say that you and yours have got good taste and that the only folks who know how to live well are those whose solid wealth manifests itself in the form of splendid villas.[62]

---

60. Rudd 1966, 140.

61. 'non hercule miror,' / aiebat, 'siqui comedunt bona, cum sit obeso / nil melius turdo, nil volva pulchrius ampla' (*Epist.* 1.15.38–41).

62. cum res deficiunt, satis inter vilia fortis;
  verum ubi quid melius contingit et unctius, idem
  vos sapere et solos aio bene vivere, quorum
  conspicitur nitidis fundata pecunia villis.

(*Epist.* 1.15.42–46)

His moral ballast, so to speak, has a distressing tendency to shift. But inconsistency is not the only thing he and Maenius share, for it is clear that he, like Maenius, is dependent on others for his access to luxury. The villa so elegantly appointed is not his own but one to which someone like Vala (the addressee of the letter) might invite him.

At an earlier period Horace was not quite so ready to don (if only momentarily) a parasite mask. Yet we will see that some of his contemporaries might have thought it perfectly fitting, for Horace seems to have been accused, repeatedly, of preying on Maecenas. Augustus, in a letter to Maecenas preserved by Suetonius, puts the charge most concisely: "Tell him he should leave that parasitical table of yours and come to my kingly table" (*veniet ergo ab ista parasitica mensa ad hanc regiam et nos in epistuli scribendis iuvabit*, Suet. *Vit. Hor.*). The wording here deserves more attention that it has hitherto received. It is not enough to say that the adjective *regia*, "kingly," plays on the standard comic term for a parasite's patron, *rex*. The *parasitus/rex* collocation is indeed common, as we have seen, but what did Augustus mean when he called Maecenas' table *parasitica*? It is usually assumed that he was identifying the table as one at which Horace was a parasite. What does *regia mensa* mean in this context then? Is Augustus offering himself as Horace's new *rex*? If this is true, it involves an awkward deviation from the parallelism usually preserved between two modifiers of a single noun, since *parasitica* refers to Horace's position at one table, and *regia* to Augustus' at another. Moreover, "He will come from the table at which he is a parasite to the one at which I am a *rex*" is not the neat turn of phrase that this is obviously meant to be. Augusto Rostagni explains the change of referent by saying that Horace would not be a parasite at Augustus' table (in the terms of the joke, of course), because he would have a proper job as Augustus' secretary.[63] But if Horace is not a parasite, Augustus is not a parasite's patron. According to Rostagni's reasoning, the adjective *regia* is stripped of the comic flavor that alone makes it palatable.

An alternative interpretation is available. Suppose Maecenas, the addressee, is the parasite in question. Augustus is then Maecenas' *rex* (Augustus is speaking in jest, remember), and Horace is a sort of subparasite.[64] One may compare the multilayered arrangements proposed

---

63. Rostagni 1956, ad loc.
64. Augustus and Maecenas were on those terms. Maecenas' luxurious softness is the object of an imperial tease preserved by Macrobius: Cilniorum

by the pest in *Satire* 1.9.45–48 and by Gnatho in Terence's *Eunuchus* when he invites two young men to join him in "eating up and laughing down" the *miles* Thraso.[65] Suetonius' more complimentary analysis puts the sequencing in chronological, rather than hierarchical, terms, but the result is much the same: "[Horace was] introduced first to Maecenas and soon thereafter to Augustus" (*primo Maecenati, mox Augusto insinuatus, Vit. Hor.*; cf. *TLL* s.v. insinuo, 1915.41–49).

Suetonius had another bit of what purported to be documentary evidence about the relationship between Horace and Maecenas, a prose letter of self-recommendation from Horace (*epistula prosa oratione quasi commendantis se Maecenati*, presumably a functional equivalent of the *Panegyricus Messallae* and the *Laus Pisonis*). Suetonius considered it a forgery on stylistic grounds (the prose was obscure); the "letter" was probably an exercise in rhetorical prosopopoeia, such as the *Commentariolum petitionis* from someone writing as Quintus Cicero to his brother or the *invectiva in Sallustium* of someone playing Cicero himself. A forgery can tell us nothing about the real relationship between poet and patron, but it can tell us about the terms in which outside observers viewed the relationship. The unknown wit who undertook to compose a letter in which "Horace" recommended himself to Maecenas obviously found Horace's connection with Maecenas easy to interpret in everyday client/patron terms.[66]

To Augustus the analogy between clients and parasites, patrons and *reges*, was, as far as we can determine, raw material for a joke. Horace, understandably enough, could not always achieve the same degree of detachment, for some of his contemporaries were only too ready to view his cultivation of Maecenas in precisely these terms.

Maecenas was the most visible source of the good fortune that led Horace to be called *Fortunae filius*,"Fortune's son," as early as the second book of *Satires* (30–29 B.C., *Sat.* 2.6.49). Success has a tendency to attract negative comment. The criticisms that Horace lets us hear about

smaragde, iaspi Iguvinorum, berulle Porsennae, carbunculum Hadriae, ἵνα συντέμω πάντα, μάλαγμα moecharum (Macrob. *Sat.* 2.4.12).

65. *Eun.* 1087. Cf. also Hor. *Sat.* 2.7.37–42, where the *scurra* Horace has his own *scurrae*.

66. venerunt in manus meas et elegi sub titulo eius et epistula prosa oratione quasi commendantis se Maecenati, sed utraque falsa puto; nam elegi volgares, epistula etiam obscura, quo vitio minime tenebatur (Suet. *Vit. Hor.*).

concern his relationship with Maecenas. The speaker of the *Satires* and *Epistles* made repeated efforts both to record these criticisms (they were, after all, a sure sign of success) and to produce defenses against them.[67]

In *Satire* 1.6, for example, Horace reports reproaches old and new: people had been making envious remarks about the fact that he, the son of an ex-slave, was so freely entertained at the house of Maecenas.

> Now I come back to myself, son of a freedman father, about which son of a freedman father everyone has something nasty to say. Now, Maecenas, they talk because I am so freely entertained at your house; awhile back it was because I was a tribune with a Roman legion under my command.[68]

Horace demonstrates his lack of presumption by admitting that the older criticism was understandable—on the grounds that military office was the prerogative of a class not his own (*quoniam in propria non pelle quiessem*, 22)—and concentrates his forces on the current charge, the fact that he was a regular guest at Maecenas' dinner table (*quia sim tibi, Maecenas, convictor*, 47).

Since our source of information on this charge is Horace himself, no expression comparable to Augustus' *parasitica mensa* appears. In fact, the term *convictor* that Horace puts in the mouth of his critics is (as we can see from its usage elsewhere) part of his defense; detractors would not have been so gentle. In *Satire* 1.4 Horace gives the term to a dependent describing his position vis-à-vis a generous patron: "I've been the *convictor* and friend of Capitolinus since I was a boy. He has often acted on my behalf when I asked him to."[69] In this passage *convictor* is a term applied by a *cliens* to himself, so it is not here an uncomplimentary label. *Convictor* can also be used in a positive sense of a dependent by a

---

67. One of the excuses he offers for his dangerous habit of writing satire is that he uses it in self-defense rather than for gratuitous attack (*Sat.* 2.1.74–78).

68. nunc ad me redeo libertino patre natum
   quem rodunt omnes libertino patre natum,
   nunc quia sim tibi, Maecenas, convictor, at olim
   quod mihi pareret legio Romana tribuno.

   (*Sat.* 1.6.45–48)

69. me Capitolinus convictore usus amicoque / a puero est causaque mea permulta rogatus / fecit (*Sat.* 1.4.96–98).

patron. Cicero's son, for example, uses the term of some Greek philosophy instructors that he spent time with in Athens (Cic. *Fam.* 16.21.4); the context makes it clear that the young Roman played host to these men. Cicero Junior must mean *convictor* to be a flattering description, not a demeaning one, for the letter (addressed to Tiro) is an attempt by this young scapegrace to paint his companions in the best light possible to a suspicious surrogate parent. To give one further instance, a well-meaning Augustus uses the term in addressing someone whom he would have liked to have made his dependent (Horace, in fact): "Don't stand on ceremony with me, but act as you would if you were my *convictor.* Such behavior would be entirely proper (not a bit presumptuous), since I wanted us to have that degree of familiarity if your health had permitted."[70]

Convictor is a positive rephrasing of what critics said, then, and addresses the outrage and envy provoked by Horace's social success. But outrage at and envy for Horace's status as Maecenas' dinner guest were not the only possible responses. The view from the top down, for example—that is to say, the perspective of a satisfied patron—is very different. We get a glimpse from that point of view in what Seneca says about his correspondent Lucilius Iunior.

The same combination of literary talent and influential friendships that had fueled Horace's success lay behind that of Seneca's friend, who rose from obscure beginnings to hold several important procuratorial posts. Seneca says to his friend, "The force of your talent, the elegance of your writings, the friendships you have made among the eminent and well-born, these have all contributed to your present prominence."[71] Seneca was himself one of Lucilius' influential friends, and the view he takes of the man's career is positive; there is no name-calling here. Indeed, Seneca even composes a boast for the man he names, at one place, "my poet" (*poeta meus*).

Say, "I devoted myself to the liberal arts (although my scanty resources urged other pursuits on me) and I turned my talent away from the fields in which studies bring immediate rewards. I

70. sume tibi aliquid iuris apud me, tamquam si convictor mihi fueris; recte enim et non temere feceris, quoniam id usus mihi tecum esse volui, si per valitudinem tuam fieri possit (Suet. *Vit. Hor.*).

71. in medium te protulit ingenii vigor, scriptorum elegantia, clarae et nobiles amicitiae (Sen. *Ep.* 19.3).

devoted myself to writing poems that no one paid for and took up the healthful study of philosophy. I showed that virtue can turn up in anyone, and that I had been rated not by my luck but by my character, and that I had escaped the narrow expectations of my birth and now stand equal to the highest."[72]

The compliment is very nice, but one should perhaps not assume that everyone looked with Seneca's complacent eye on the man's rise; those of "the highest" with whom he eventually rubbed shoulders might not have refrained from calling him Seneca's *convictor* (or worse).

Two points emerge from our examination of *Satire* 1.6: first, that the connection between a literary *cliens* and his patron looks different from different points of view; second, that the hospitality Maecenas extended to Horace served as a shorthand emblem of what was objectionable about the connection (*quia sim tibi, Maecenas, convictor*). Conviviality was not an inevitable focus for criticism of such a relationship, however. Martial, for instance, produces a whole litany of irritations that his success had caused in others: his poems are read, passersby point him out in a crowd, the emperor gave him the rights of a father of three, he has a suburban property and a small town house as well, his friends like him, and he has many a dinner invitation (9.97). Hospitality shown to the poet is only one item (the last) on this list. In book 2 of the *Satires*, Horace himself associates envy with other aspects of his relationship with Maecenas: "For nearly eight years now yours truly has been exposed to envy, more every day and hour. Suppose he's watched a show with me or played ball in the Campus Martius: 'Fortune's son!' they all cry."[73] One might argue, I suppose, that at the time of the first book of the *Satires* Horace had received no other visible benefit than hospitality from Maecenas, but even supposing this were true (we simply do not know), that argument loses much of its force when we see that in *Odes* 2.20, written when Horace was in possession of the

---

72. dic "liberalibus me studiis tradidi, quamquam paupertas alia suaderet, et ingenium eo abduceret ubi praesens studii pretium est. ad gratuita carmina deflexi me, et ad salutare philosophiae contuli studium. ostendi in omne pectus cadere virtutem nec sorte me sed animo mensus et eluctatus natalium angustias par maximis steti" (*QNat.* 4.praef.4).

73. per totum hoc tempus subiectior in diem et horam / invidiae noster. ludos spectaverat una, / luserat in campo: 'Fortunae filius!' omnes (*Sat.* 2.6.47–49).

Sabine farm (to mention only the most obvious *beneficium*), Horace himself chooses Maecenas' dinners as the symbol of their connection. When he wants to enhance his proud boast of immortality by making his mortal state as humble as possible, he starts with his lowly parentage but reinforces his point by mentioning Maecenas' dinners: "The offspring of poor parents am I, and a man whom you, dear Maecenas, summon to dinner, but I will not perish, nor will the river Styx keep me captive."[74] The man whom Maecenas summons to dinner is the lowly mortal incarnation of the weird and wonderful immortal swan. Being fed by one's patron seems to have been a particularly humbling *beneficium* for the *cliens*.

Commensality remains the emblem of choice for the patron/client relationship in the seventh *Satire* of Book 2. In this poem a Saturnalia-emboldened Davus charges Horace with inconsistency in professing contentment with a modest dinner at home but rushing eagerly off the minute an invitation from Maecenas arrives.

> "If you happen to be without a dinner invitation one evening, you praise the worry-free dinner of plain garden fare. You say you are well-off and fond of yourself, too, if you don't have to go out drinking anywhere—as if you only go out under compulsion! But suppose Maecenas gives you a last-minute summons to dinner when the lights are just beginning to be lit: 'Won't you hurry up with the oil,' you shout. 'Can't anybody hear me?' And off you run."[75]

The fundamental problem addressed in this *Satire* is the difficulty of seeing one's own faults, the hump on one's own back (to use Catullus'

---

74. non ego, pauperum / sanguis parentum, non ego quem vocas, / dilecte Maecenas, obibo, / nec Stygia cohibebor unda (*Carm.* 2.20.5–8).

75.   si nusquam es forte vocatus
      ad cenam, laudas securum holus ac, velut usquam
      vinctus eas, ita te felicem dicis amasque
      quod nusquam tibi sit potandum. iusserit ad se
      Maecenas serum sub lumina prima venire
      convivam: 'nemon oleum fert ocius? ecquis
      audit?' cum magno blateras clamore fugisque.

                                                    (*Sat.* 2.7.29–35)

memorable formulation, from *Carm.* 22.21). Davus is trying to hold up a mirror—a risky proposition, as he discovers at the end of the poem (116–18). In this scene, after showing how superficial his master's devotion to the "dinner of plain garden fare" is, he gives the lie to the "plain" part of the phrase, too. Present at the dinner of this would-be *rusticus* (28) were *scurrae*, urban, urbane creatures if ever there were any, the sort of guests whose presence betokened not only extravagance but extravagance on display.[76] When their host receives an invitation of his own, they, of course, are out of luck (Maecenas' invitation came late in the day, and there is no mention of *umbrae*).[77]

Most of what the *scurrae* mutter as they file out unfed is, it seems, unprintable (*tibi non referenda precati*, 36), but Davus puts a few home truths into the mouth of one of them, Mulvius by name. We have met Mulvius, before, of course: it was he who was so efficiently characterized as a parasite. "I am a lightweight who does what my belly orders, who leans way back to raise my nose to the scent of cooking. I am, in short, a weak and idle glutton."[78] But this is only half of what Mulvius has to say. The mask that he applies to himself he passes deftly along to his host as well: "But you, who are just what I am (or perhaps even worse), should you act superior and criticize me, when all the while you're covering up your own faults with fine words?"[79] The charge of parasite behavior is renewed by Davus himself later in the poem, as part of his demonstration of his master's servile subjugation to his own desires.

---

76. On conspicuous extravagance see chap. 1 n. 20. The contrast with the wished-for rustic dinner of the preceding poem, with its vegetable dishes (*faba* and *holuscula*), its happy, well-fed, homegrown slaves, its relaxed etiquette, and its pleasantly improving conversation (*Sat.* 2.6.63–76), must be deliberate.

77. The timing of an invitation is not a comic motif. It is obviously connected with the Roman custom of issuing dinner invitations at the morning *salutatio* (Hor. *Epist.* 1.5.56–57, Martial 2.18, Juv. 5.14–23, Lucian *Gall.* 9, *Symp.* 24, etc.); it could not be humiliating to receive an invitation late in the day until it became the custom to issue them early. The picture of Horace as the parasite of Maecenas in *Satire* 2.7 is composed of elements that may or may not be real but that are indubitably comic in flavor, spiced up, so to speak, with a dash of contemporary Rome.

78. 'etenim fateor me' dixerit ille / 'duci ventre levem, nasum nidore supinor, / imbecillus, iners, si quid vis, adde, popino' (*Sat.* 2.7.37–39).

79. tu cum sis quod ego et fortassis nequior, ultro / insectere velut melior verbisque decoris/ obvolvas vitium? (*Sat.* 2.7.40–42).

"Worthless you say I am if I am drawn to a cake still steaming from the oven. Do your masses of virtue and character say 'no' to luxurious dinners? Why then does obedience to my belly bring worse trouble to me? If I get a beating, how is it that you go scot-free when you chase after foods that can't even be acquired cheaply? To be sure, you'll eventually regret those dinners you were always after, when your feet stumble beneath you and refuse to carry your ruined body."[80]

Obedience to his belly is the leading characteristic of a parasite, as we have seen, and the image is made even clearer by the hunting metaphors in "chase after" (*captas*) and "dinners that you were . . . after" (*epulae . . . petitae*). According to Davus, Horace does not just say "yes" when Maecenas asks him (the gravamen of lines 29–35) but actually pursues such invitations (lines 102–8). Of course, only a very biographically minded reading of the *Satires* would impute all of "Horace's" faults to the real Horace, but the allusion to Maecenas' invitation at lines 32–34 cannot help but evoke the historical Horace. An author may create any persona he likes in his own name, but it is not clear that Horace, at any rate, took the same liberties with contemporaries. Whenever "Horace" comes into contact with Maecenas in these poems, he risks losing his status as only a character.

In the *Epistles*, written some ten years after the second book of the *Satires*, we see in Horace a new frankness, even an exaggeration, in the acknowledgment of his debt to Maecenas. In *Epistle* 1.1, for example, he is no longer the companion (*sodalis*) of the *Satires* (1.6.62, 2.6.41–42) but a self-confessed dependent: "You watch out for all my affairs, you get annoyed at an ill-cut fingernail on the friend who depends on you and looks up to you, too" (*rerum tutela mearum / cum sis et prave sectum sto-*

---

80. Nil<i> ego, si ducor libo fumante: tibi ingens
     virtus atque animus cenis responsat opimis?
     obsequium ventris mihi perniciosius est. cur?
     tergo plector enim. qui tu impunitior illa
     quae parvo sumi nequeunt obsonia captas?
     nempe inamarescunt epulae sine fine petitae
     illusique pedes vitiosum ferre recusant
     corpus.

                                                        (*Sat.* 2.7.102–8)

macheris ob unguem / de te pendentis, te respicientis amici, 101–5). The new terms in which the relationship is to be presented are made visible early in this *Epistle*. Horace begins with a *recusatio:* "why do you ask me to write more poems, Maecenas, when I am no longer up to it?" (a paraphrase of lines 2–9). Maecenas' "request" may or may not be historical (again, we do not know), but in the poem it functions as a peg on which Horace hangs the defense of his new pursuit of moral reflection. Of more consequence to us is the fact that the rhetorical strategy he employs causes him to sketch a relationship in which Maecenas has the authority to make such a request. In the seventh *Epistle* Horace goes even further in describing the extent of his dependence. When he says, "You've often praised my unassuming self, and I've called you 'patron' [*rex*] and 'father' (nor am I any less generous with my gratitude when you are not there to hear),"[81] he is donning the parasite mask as easily as Mulvius did in *Satire* 2.7. The reference is unmistakable, for only a parasite calls his patron *rex*. Like the one-line description of Horace as a dependent friend in *Epistle* 1.1 (*de te pendentis, te respicientis amici,* 105), this two-line assertion of Horace's active gratitude serves to buttress Horace's claim that he has done enough to requite what Maecenas had done for him. And in both poems this claim is used to justify Horace's plans for the future, his intention of withdrawing himself from *regia Roma* ("Rome with its great patrons [or kings—the term follows the description of Menelaus' lavish generosity to Telemachus]," *Epist.* 1.7.44) and the demands of city life (*Epist.* 1.7.8–9; cf. *Epist.* 1.1.23–26).[82]

By the time of the first book of the *Epistles*, then, Horace was quite frank about the possibility of caricaturing his own client behavior with the figure of the parasite. The passages we have examined so far are fairly brief and contribute directly to Horace's arguments. In *Epistle* 1.17, however, parasite and *cliens* jostle for position throughout the poem. Horace's own experience as a *cliens* is still relevant to the discussion, but it is much less prominent than it was in *Epistles* 1.1 and 1.7—it

---

81. saepe verecundum laudasti, rexque paterque / audisti coram, nec verbo parcius absens (*Epist.* 1.7.37–38). In this same poem he refers to himself as "Maecenas' bard" (*vates tuus*, 11). Note too that the qualities that Horace says Maecenas will need to renew in him if he wants his companionship at Rome (25–28) are not simply those of youth but those of a pleasant dinner companion (*dulce loqui, ridere decorum et / inter vina fugam Cinarae maerere protervae*).

82. Lyne 1995, 143–55.

serves as a kind of backdrop against which the livelier antics of Aristippus and other assorted *clientes* are displayed.

The subject of *Epistle* 1.17 purports to be "the right way to keep company with men more important than oneself" (*quo . . . pacto deceat maioribus uti, Epist.* 1.17.2). Horace would appear to have both a continuing interest in the question (*docendus adhuc . . . amiculus,* 3) and a certain amount of experience on which to base the advice he offers.

The first issue that he tackles is not, however, the right way to keep company with prominent men but whether or not there is a right way (not *quo pacto decet?* but *decetne?*). He illustrates the alternative responses with Aristippus (yes) and Diogenes (no). Aristippus makes himself useful to his patron and happily reaps the rewards; Diogenes bites the hand that feeds him but requires feeding nonetheless. The argument would seem to be straightforward—Aristippus' "decet" is the approved answer. What follows ought therefore to be practical advice on the details of how to go about the job in a seemly fashion (*quo pacto decet*). But scholarly opinion is divided regarding the content of Horace's message in *Epistle* 1.17. Are the sanction given to Aristippus (11–42) and the precepts of lines 43–62 supposed to offer information of practical use to Scaeva and other potential *clientes* among Horace's readership (i.e., to answer the question about cliental decorum)?[83] Or is the puzzling and self-destructive whole designed as a deterrent, with "what Horace really believes in" lurking just below the paraenetic surface?[84] A more careful examination of the terms of the advice offered in the poem will clarify the picture.

The dispute between Aristippus and Diogenes, as Horace has framed it anyway, centers on food. "'If Aristippus could tolerate vegetable dinners, he wouldn't want to keep company with kings.' 'If my critic knew how to keep company with kings, he would turn up his nose at vegetables.'"[85] More precisely, it centers on the connection

---

83. Noirfalise 1952; Maurach 1968, 114; McGann 1969, 75–77; Macleod 1979, 18–19; Kilpatrick 1986, 43–48.

84. The quoted phrase belongs to Fraenkel (1957, 321), a scholar whose open dislike for this *Epistle* leads him to treat it only "in passing." As this quotation shows, however, he is to be numbered among those who deny that Horace is offering sincere advice based on long experience here. Cf. also Perret 1964, 104, and Williams 1968, 14–17. Rohdich's long 1972 essay, which regards the subject of the poem as the difficulty of maintaining individual freedom in Roman society, is sui generis.

85. 'si pranderet holus patienter, regibus uti / nollet Aristippus.' 'si sciret regibus uti, / fastidiret holus qui me notat' (*Epist.* 1.17.13–15).

between what one eats and how one interacts with *reges*. Are these *reges* kings or patrons? What we know about the historical Aristippus supports reading them as the former (he lived for a time in the court of Dionysius II of Syracuse, who, though not a king, was certainly a head of state), but the context of the passage makes the latter meaning at least as prominent. Consider the services Aristippus offers. His wit, like that of the parasite, amuses his *rex* and so brings benefit to himself: "I play the wit for my own advantage" (*scurror ego ipse mihi*, 19). Consider, too, the form that the benefits take: a horse to ride and a seat at his patron's table.[86] The combination of these two goods was proverbial as a definition of a satisfying life, and a lesser parasite than Aristippus might have been content with the second element alone, for "in order that my patron may feed me" (*ut me . . . alat rex*) is a superbly efficient expression of the parasite's highest good. And the parasitical equation of food and patronal *beneficia* runs throughout the poem. The whining *cliens* of lines 46–49, for example, though he appears to be talking about the needs of his family and the inadequacy of his property to provide for them, is really saying to his patron (to his *rex*, in fact: *coram rege*, 43), "Feed me!" (*victum date*, 48). Food also features in Horace's description of the *beneficia* that the patron provided: "The loaf will be split, a little help will go to each" (*dividuo findetur munere quadra*, 49).[87] It likewise figures in the exemplum of the crow. By drawing attention to the benefits he has received, the noisy crow alerts other claimants to the presence of a generous patron and so gets less of the feast for himself: "If the crow were able to feed in silence, he'd end up with more of the food and less squabbling, less envy."[88] Competitive rivalry and envy are the seasoning for many a parasite's meal, as we have seen.

Parasite and *cliens* would appear to be obverse and reverse of the same coin in *Epistle* 1.17. Jacques Perret was not very far from the mark when he called the poem an *ars parasitandi* (a handbook for parasites).[89] And the presence of the parasite makes it easier to assess the tone of the poem, for we have seen that outside of comedy the parasite attracts a very negative press.

---

86. equos ut me portet, alat rex / officium facio (*Epist.* 1.17.20–21).

87. Other metaphors were available. In *Epist.* 1.18.31–36, e.g., clothing, rather than food, represents a patron's *beneficia*.

88. sed tacitus pasci si posset corvus, haberet / plus dapis et rixae multo minus invidiaeque (*Epist.* 1.17.50–51).

89. Perret 1959, 132.

The impact of the use of parasite as an equivalent for *cliens* in this poem is most jarring in the transition from the Aristippus exemplum to the practical pointers with which the *Epistle* concludes.

> One man shudders at a burden too heavy for his small spirit and frame; another takes it up and carries it to the end. Either virtue is an empty word, or the man who makes the attempt is justified in seeking a reward and fee. Those who keep quiet about their poverty in the presence of their patron will often go off with more than the one who demands assistance; there is a difference between taking something modestly and snatching it. And going off with more is what this business is all about, where it all starts.[90]

In this passage we move from "the man who makes the attempt" (*experiens vir*, line 42), whose service to a patron is a kind of *virtus*, to the *cliens*-parasite (identified as such by the word *rege* in line 43), who would seem to constitute the grim reality behind the proud posing of the *vir*. Precisely at this point in the poem, Horace forces the reader to decide which is the more accurate picture, the comic mask or the self-deceiving *vir*: "What we seek [i.e., a model for seemly client behavior, *quo pacto decet*] is either here or nowhere" (*hic est aut nusquam, quod quaerimus*, 38–39). *Virtus*, "manly behavior," is not a quality often (ever?) attributed to parasites; they tend, in fact, to attract the label "servile." Perhaps, then, one ought to answer, "Then it is nowhere."

A reader who concludes that *virtus* is an empty word when applied to a *cliens* will be confirmed in that belief by *Epistle* 1.18, a poem closely linked to its predecessor by theme and image. The figure of the parasite

---

90. hic onus horret
       ut parvis animis et parvo corpore maius:
       hic subit et perfert. aut virtus nomen inane est,
       aut decus et pretium recte petit experiens vir.
          coram rege sua de paupertate tacentes
       plus poscente ferent (distat sumasne pudenter
       an rapias); atqui rerum caput hoc erat, hic fons.

(Epist. 1.17.39–45)

Shackleton Bailey marks the awkwardness of the juxtaposition by beginning a new paragraph at line 43.

is one of the links between the two and helps Horace articulate his argument.[91] The verb *scurror* (meaning "I play the *scurra*"), which Aristippus applied to himself in *Epistle* 1.17, occurs at the outset of *Epistle* 1.18: "If I know you well, Lollius, being the most independent of men, you will be afraid to show the colors of a *scurra* when you've called yourself a friend" (*si bene te novi, metues, liberrime Lolli, / scurrantis speciem praebere, professus amicum*, 1–2). The *scurra* is here characterized as treacherous (*infido*, 4); that his infidelity lies in his inability to speak truthfully to his friend is shown by the contrast between the *scurra* and the companion who is impossibly frank (5–8).[92] And the immediate sequel identifies the offender as a parasitical *scurra*, offering a dining room in which he plys his obsequious ways. We have met this *scurra* before.

> This one stoops too low in making himself agreeable. As the wit on the humblest couch, he snaps to attention at the rich man's nod. He parrots the man's words and carries the conversation. You'd think he was a boy repeating his lesson for a heavy-handed schoolmaster, or a mime actor playing the supporting role."[93]

This opening would seem to betoken a poem concerned with finding a behavior midway between flattery and rudeness. But the argument has shifted by the end of the poem, where the poet desires solitude, with books his only companions.

> What do you think my feelings are, what, my friend, my prayers?
> May I keep what I have now (or even less), and may I live for

---

91. Another link is the designing *meretrix*, who is an exemplum of (improper) scurrile behavior in 1.17 (55–57) and reappears in the third line of 1.18: ut matrona meretrici dispar erit atque / discolor, infido scurrae distabit amicus. For further discussion see McGann 1969, 78–79.

92. The ease of sketching a preexisting type is particularly apparent here, as the label *scurra infidus* (4) needs a counterweight of three lines (6–8) on the too-frank friend, who lacks a comic model.

93. alter in obsequium plus aequo pronus et imi
     derisor lecti sic nutum divitis horret,
     sic iterat voces et verba cadentia tollit,
     ut puerum saevo credas dictata magistro
     reddere vel partis mimum tractare secundas.

(*Epist.* 1.18.10–14)

myself in what remains of my life, if the gods are willing that there should be some remainder. May I have a good store of books, and food for the coming year, and may I not slip along clinging to the hope of an hour that may never come.[94]

At the end of this pair of *Epistles,* as at the beginning, the "hidden way, the life without spectators," not success as a dependent, enjoys positive billing (*secretum iter et fallentis semita vitae,* 1.18.103; cf. 1.17.10). Careful attention to the precepts of lines 21–95 may make a man a successful companion to a *dives* or *potens amicus,* says Horace, but it will leave him no good friend to himself (101). As in *Epistle* 1.17, here Horace has little positive to say about the life of a dependent friend.

The reappearance of the parasite in the middle section of the poem reveals how the argument has shifted. At the outset of *Epistle* 1.18 the parasitical *scurra* represents one of the extremes of behavior to be avoided, but the behavior of the man who makes his own interests coincide with those of his patron ("when He wants to go hunting, don't you be jotting down poems," *nec cum venari volet ille, poemata panges,* 40) is distressingly like that of the *scurra,* particularly given the short-term reward that Horace specifies: "Give in to your powerful friend's gentle commands," says Horace. "That way, you'll get a dinner" (*cenes,* 48). The accommodations prudent in this friend are perilously close to those practiced by the parasites of comedy.

Epistle 1.18, then, would seem to supplement the argument of *Epistle* 1.17 by showing in more detail the difficulty of finding *virtus* in the role of a dependent friend. The two poems harmonize with the other passages of the *Epistles* that we have examined in which friendship with the great is used as a foil for contemplative withdrawal. Given that contemplative withdrawal is what Horace was trying to clear a space for in the *Epistles,* the foil to it is naturally drawn in the most negative terms. For this, Horace plainly found the figure of the parasite very useful.

That the comic parasite might be relevant to critical descriptions of Roman society is evident from his presence, however scantily attested,

---

94. quid sentire putas? quid credis, amice, precari?
   sit mihi quod nunc est, etiam minus, et mihi vivam
   quod superest aevi, si quid superesse volunt di;
   sit bona librorum et provisae frugis in annum
   copia, neu fluitem dubiae spe pendulus horae.

(Epist. 1.18.106–10)

in the *Satires* of Ennius and Lucilius, but the uses to which the type might be put are best seen in the *scurrae* of the *Satires* and *Epistles* of Horace.

The *scurra*—the parasite's comic name did not get transferred along with his characteristics—could be quickly sketched for use in an argument, often as one element in a list of objectionable behaviors: Pantolabus and Nomentanus are yokemates twice, the too-obsequious parasite of *Epistle* 1.18 is set against the friend who is too frank, a parasitical Aristippus is contrasted with an overly independent Diogenes (*Epist.* 1.17.13–32), the parasitical *scurrae* of *Satire* 2.3 are just a small segment of the crowd of predators fastening onto the new heir, and so on. The parasites of *Satire* 2.8, however, team up to reveal several varieties of parasite behavior. More interesting still are the passages in which the bundle of negative traits that was the parasite is repackaged to represent some other objectional element in Roman society (objectionable not in an absolute sense, of course, but simply in the eyes of the speaker who creates the picture or assigns the label). Thus a woman's female friends are an obstacle to a potential lover, an ambitious would-be *cliens* is an annoyance to those above him, and an inheritance-hunter is an annoyance to those who object to seeing someone angling to get a good that he has no ordinary title to. In all these cases the mask of the parasite was applied as an efficient and effective vehicle for negative characterization.

The neophyte inheritance-hunter of *Satire* 2.5 has a fictional name, while the *parasitae* of 1.2 and the pest of 1.9 are nameless (the latter pointedly so: while Horace says he knew the man by name only—*nomine tantum*—Horace's readers know him by character only, for he remains an anonymous *quidam, Sat.* 1.9.3), but the utility of the type was not limited to general cases like these; individuals could find themselves looking out through the eyes of a parasite mask as well. We have seen how Horace works at creating a more flattering front for himself in *Satire* 1.6 (his "real character," he calls it: *quod eram, Sat.* 1.6.60) and how he makes it serve his argument in later poems (*Sat.* 2.7; *Epist.* 1.1, 1.7, 1.15, 1.17, 1.18). The fact that the parasite mask could be made to fit a dependent poet was not lost on later satirists: Persius, Martial (properly an epigrammatist, but manifestly concerned with many of the same social and moral ills that provide material for satire), and Juvenal all, in their turn, experiment with the picture of the poet as producer of "Trencher-poetry" (see the epigraph to this chapter). And Juvenal, as we shall see in chapter 6 of this book, went well beyond Horace in adapting the type to fit new categories of objectionable contemporaries.

I began this chapter with Horace's predecessors and end with a glance at a successor in the genre whose debt to Horace in matters parasitical is direct. Persius opens his collection of *Satires* with a poem about the production of poetry by men in a social position much like his own. Well-educated men of leisure wanted to display their literary culture: "What point is there in having an education if this ferment and the wild fig tree that has taken root inside me can't burst the confines of my liver and emerge?"[95] Providing such authors with an appreciative audience was a service that a helpful *cliens* could offer. The dangers inherent in such an arrangement give the satirist material for a lively vignette in *Satire* 1. Persius conjures up the latter end of a dinner party: some well-fed sons of Romulus, with their after-dinner drinks in front of them, are looking for a reason to start the recitation (30–31). Up gets a fellow in a fancy purple cloak and gives a reading of a tear-jerking classic, the Phyllises and Hypsipyles of some dead poet or other. The company approves (*adsensere viri . . . laudant convivae*, 36–38), but an interlocutor breaks into Persius' narrative, objecting to the disdain evident in the satirist's description of the posthumous kudos won by the author of those Phyllises and Hypsipyles. A justification (naturally) follows.

> Your "wow!" and "swell!" are not the last word in what's right, in my opinion. Let's shake out that "swell!" of yours. What doesn't it have inside? Doesn't it have the *Iliad* of Attius, a poem steeped in the medicine they give to madmen? The little elegies that drunken lords have given forth? The stuff that gets written on those fancy citrus-wood dinner tables? You serve a nice warm sow's udder and do it well, you give a shivering friend a cast-off cloak, and then you say, "Please, tell me the truth about myself, the truth, mind you." How can he?[96]

---

95. quo didicisse, nisi hoc fermentum et quae semel intus / innata est rupto iecore exierit caprificus?' (Pers. *Sat.* 1.24–25; the text is from Clausen 1992).

96.   sed recti finemque extremumque esse recuso
       'euge' tuum et 'belle.' nam 'belle' hoc excute totum:
       quid non intus habet? non hic est Ilias Atti
       ebria ueratro? non siqua elegidia crudi
       dictarunt proceres? non quidquid denique lectis

In this passage Persius is making simultaneous allusion to two bits of Horace. The first is a passage of the *Ars poetica* in which Horace lists the patronal *beneficia* that will prevent a wealthy poet from getting helpful literary advice (i.e., criticism) from a *cliens*: "I'd be surprised if a well-off fellow who can set a nice rich table, guarantee a poor man's loans, and disentangle him from legal difficulties could tell the difference between a liar and a true friend."[97] Feeding is only one of the *beneficia* Horace mentions, so his *cliens* is not particularly parasite-like. Persius changes that by setting the dependent at his patron's dinner table. He also adds parasitical material to the other passage to which he is alluding here. In *Epistle* 1.19.35–41 Horace explains why his works have not won publicly expressed favor: it is because he has not bestirred himself to "buy" an outward demonstration of appreciation for his verse; that is, he hasn't courted the support of the loudmouthed populace by going to the expense of dinners and by giving away gifts of (old) clothing.[98] Persius uses this same combination of *munera*—food and clothing—in his passage, but his scene has more of the parasite about it because the beneficiary is an individual rather than the Roman plebs en masse, and because he needs just what the patron provides: Persius' guest is shivering, and what he gets is warm food and warm clothing (used clothing, to be sure, as in *Epistle* 1.19, but better than anything the *cliens* has been able to provide for himself). The parasite in Plautus' *Menaechmi* knew just how effective the first of these *beneficia* was: "If you really want to keep someone close by and prevent him from escaping, you ought to use food and drink to bind him" (87–88). And we shall see that clothing keeps Juvenal's parasite Trebius under control, too ("There are a great many things one daren't say when one wears a worn-out cloak," *Sat.* 5.130–31).

---

scribitur in citreis? calidum scis ponere sumen,
scis comitem horridulum trita donare lacerna,
et 'uerum' inquis 'amo, uerum mihi dicite de me.'
qui pote?

(Sat. 1.48–56)

97. si vero est unctum qui recte ponere possit
et spondere levi pro paupere et eripere artis
litibus implicitum, mirabor si sciet inter-
noscere mendacem verumque beatus amicum.

(Hor. Ars 422–25)

98. non ego ventosae plebis suffragia venor / impensis cenarum et tritae munere vestis (Hor. *Epist.* 1.19.37–38).

Persius has taken two passages about inadequate audiences from Horace and added a dash or two of the parasite to them to come up with a negative picture of his own. Brief and isolated as this sketch is— it is Persius' only evocation of the parasite—it is not just a passing hit, for the evaluation of various audiences is the principal theme of *Satire* 1, and the parasite is held up as the representative of a type of auditor that was becoming ever more prevalent as wealthy and important men devoted more and more of their energy to literary pursuits. The guest in Persius' passage produces praise that is bound to be insincere, for his needs, like those of Plautus' Peniculus or Juvenal's Trebius, prevent him from speaking freely. He cannot afford to take his patron literally when he says, "Please, tell me the truth about myself, the truth, mind you." That would be to put his host's advantage above his own, something a parasite would never do. Persius' interest, of course, is in the morals of the host, not the plight of the too-eager-to-please guest. His little skit is meant to open the host's eyes to the potential falsity of the praise that comes from someone who has reason both to feel grateful to him and to hope for the continuation of a relationship that has brought welcome comfort to a previously needy existence. Persius was able to portray the *cliens* as a parasite because this type had a long history of bringing destruction to his patron. "Don't let flatterers fool you" is advice given in the patron's interest, as we saw in the case of Lucilius' touchstone; the dependent's interests (both material and ethical) are beside the point. In the boast that Seneca composed for "his poet," we had a complacent view, from the top down, of the dynamics of patronage. In Persius' little sketch, we have a less sanguine (or more fearful) analysis from the same vantage point.

The curtain comes down on the dinner-party scene at line 55, as Persius moves on to other types of audience, but in one of those curious shifts that make Persius' *Satires* such a challenge and delight to read, the parasite's insincere praise reappears near the end of the poem (*euge, bene, mirae res*, 111).

"What is the point of scraping tender ears with biting truths? You want to be careful the thresholds of powerful men don't freeze you out; I hear the growling now." Okay, then, let everything henceforth be white. I don't care. Congratulations, everybody! Well done, all! You'll all be marvels! Do you like that? You say, 'I forbid anyone to take a shit here.' Paint two snakes: 'Boys, this is hallowed ground. Go pee elsewhere.' And away I go.[99]

In this passage Persius gives a little debate on the advisability of writing satires, much as Horace did (less pungently) in *Satire* 1.4. Satire does not please the great, the argument goes; watch out lest you lose your welcome into their homes. Okay, says the poet, I will be all sweetness and light; you are all great, terrific, wonderful folks, every one of you. Here we find the parasite's *euge* and *bene* in the mouth of a poet who wants to make sure of his welcome in the houses of the great. "Away I go," says Persius when the forbidden ground is pointed out to him. Persius is trying on a role here and finds it does not suit him: whitewashing was not what his predecessors in the genre did (Lucilius and Horace are the ones he mentions), and whitewashing is not in his plans either. As a wealthy young man, Persius can afford to brush off the advice his interlocutor supplies him, and as a satirist he must do so, but not every poet could (or did). "The belly," says Persius in the prologue to his little book, "teaches you skills and puts your ingenuity to work" (*magister artis ingenique largitor / uenter, Prol.* 10–11). The belly teaches the *cliens* at dinner to conceal unpleasant truths, and it teaches the poet on the doorstep to sing his patron's praises, to produce "hunger-starven Trencher-poetry" (see the epigraph to this chapter). Persius does not need to haunt anybody's doorstep, and he rejects the role of parasite-poet for himself, but we shall see in chapter 5 that it is a role that Martial, in the next generation, found all too prevalent in the world around him.

---

99. 'sed quid opus teneras mordaci radere uero
     auriculas? uide sis ne maiorum tibi forte
     limina frigescant : sonat hic de nare canina littera.'
     per me equidem sint omnia protinus alba;
     nil moror. euge omnes, omnes bene, mirae eritis res.
     hoc iuuat? 'hic' inquis 'ueto quisquam faxit oletum.'
     pinge duos anguis: 'pueri, sacer est locus, extra
     meiite.' discedo.

                                        (*Sat.* 1.107–14)

5

Martial, "Like parcel, parasite and satyr"?

An epigrammatist is a port of small wares, whose muse is short-winded and quickly out of breath. She flies like a goose, that is no sooner on the wing, but down again. . . . His wit is like fire in a flint, that is nothing while it is in, and nothing again as soon as it is out. He treats of all things and persons that come in his way, but like one that draws in little, much less than the life.
> His bus'ness is t'inveigh and flatter,
> Like parcel, parasite and satyr.
> —Samuel Butler *Characters*

Whereas Persius uses the parasite to embody the dangerous dependent who threatens his patron's ability to know himself (to give, in other words, a negative view from above), Martial uses the same type from right in the middle of the fray to depict the miseries of client life. Given the brief compass of his chosen form, he often evokes the parasite by a single trait (hunger, tolerance of abuse, leftovers, etc.), but his interest in the type was such that he devised wider scenes for them to play on, too. By this I mean not only long epigrams—some of his longer and wittier ones are about parasites—but also the epigram cycle that takes the parasitical Selius as its center. Selius and his brethren in suffering busy themselves with all the ordinary cliental *munera* (attendance at the morning *salutatio*, escorting their patron about town, issuing audible praise, etc.), but of particular interest (and prominence) in Martial's collection are the parasitical *clientes* who are also poets. These are interesting not so much because they represent Martial's own experience—the conventions of the genre make it prudent to dissociate the *ego*-voice of an epigram from that of its author—but because Martial's twelve books of epigrams comprise an important collection of the special *munera* that dependent poets had to offer, namely, occasional poems. By looking at some of these, we will see what made the mask of the parasite particularly well suited to the dependent poet.

Tucked into the middle of book 6 is a little four-line epigram that neatly captures the nature of the epigrammatist's engagement with social criticism.

My books are praised and loved and read out in Rome. Every pocket, every hand has got a copy. Look, someone's blushing, or someone's turning pale; this one is stunned, that one gapes, another hates me. This is what I want; now my poems please *me*.[1]

In his satirical *Epigrams* Martial describes the faults of individual people, but not of specific individuals, for any old *quidam* can recognize himself in them. His satirical strategy is to show how a problem manifests itself in a person, not to treat it, say, as a systemic evil. Martial (fortunately) does not give us thoughtful analyses of impersonal causes and effects for systemic problems like the decline of upper-class freedom under the principate, the availability of the dole for residents of Rome, the growing number of citizens with origins outside of Italy, and so on; rather, he offers descriptions of current Roman failings so accurate and so vivid as to make any possessor of those failings "recognize" himself (or herself) and react accordingly. But Martial's method must not be taken as an indication of a lack of interest on his part in the larger problems of contemporary Rome. The gap between the ideal of Roman patronage and the way the system worked in his own day is a topic to which Martial returns again and again in his collection. The misery of the *cliens* and the arrogance of the patron are favorite themes, as are the competition for patronal favors and the calculating self-interest with which those favors were dispensed. This gap between ideal and reality was a problem that Martial presented from many different angles: we hear not only the voice of the miserable *cliens* but also that of the patron and those of various observers.

In the real world, patron/client relationships clearly involved a range of degrees of dependency: some *clientes* were beholden to their patrons for food and/or lodging, others looked to a patron for legal protection or career advancement, and still others simply kept up the

---

1. Laudat, amat, cantat nostros mea Roma libellos,
    meque sinus omnes, me manus omnis habet.
  ecce rubet quidam, pallet, stupet, oscitat, odit.
    hoc volo: nunc nobis carmina nostra placent.
                (*Ep.* 6.60; the text is from Shackleton Bailey 1990)

connection in case it might prove useful some day. A satirist seeking to portray client misery naturally focuses on the relationship with the greatest degree of dependency, that in which a client gets his food from his patron, and for this the prefabricated persona of the parasite proved itself extremely useful.

One hungry *cliens* is Philo, a kind of latter-day Gelasimus (the parasite in Plautus' *Stichus*; see discussion in chap. 2) who lacks the where-withal to feed himself: "Philo swears that he has never dined at home—it's quite true, for he doesn't eat dinner at all if he's not invited out."[2] Another is the addressee of *Epigram* 8.67, Caecilianus, who is the sort of parasite who shows up very early for dinner—before the fifth hour, in fact, when dinner is served at the ninth or tenth. The kitchen ovens are not even alight when Caecilianus arrives: "It would be better to come early, Caecilianus; . . . you've come too late for breakfast."[3] A third hungry guest dressed in comic colors is the addressee of *Epigram* 5.50, Charopinus ("Bright-Eyes"), who keeps watch on the chimney and kitchen of a potential host's house to learn when a dinner party is in preparation. The surveillance provokes the host to protest, "Your belly's got to be the most shameful thing on earth! Please, stop keeping watch on my kitchen; let my cook give you the slip now and then."[4] This plaint is fairly feeble; one suspects that if Charopinus and his belly show up on a dinner day again, the speaker will bite his tongue and invite him in.

In contrast, the addressee of *Epigram* 6.51 has stopped inviting his parasite to dinner.

> You often have a dinner without me, Lupercus, but I've found a way to make you smart. I'm angry, I am. Go ahead and invite me, send me a message, ask me to come. "What will you do?" you ask. What will I do? I'll come.[5]

---

2. Numquam se cenasse domi Philo iurat et hoc est: / non cenat quotiens nemo vocavit eum (*Ep.* 5.47).

3. mane veni potius . . . / ut iantes, sero, Caeciliane, venis (*Ep.* 8.67.9–10).

4. improbius nihil est hac, Charopine, gula. / desine iam nostram, precor, observare culinam, / atque aliquando meus det tibi verba cocus (*Ep.* 5.50.6–8).

5.   Quod convivaris sine me tam saepe, Luperce,
          inveni noceam qua ratione tibi.
      irascor: licet usque voces mittasque rogesque—
      'quid facies?' inquis. quid faciam? veniam.

                                                          (*Ep.* 6.51)

My translation, "You often have a dinner without me," does not really succeed in rendering the nuances of the Latin phrase *convivaris sine me* in English. *Convivari* means "to get together with people," but in this poem there are no "people" to be seen. Lupercus' "get-together" is not so much *with* other people as *without* the speaker. And for this outrage the speaker intends to get revenge. The joke of the epigram, of course, lies precisely in the form of the revenge implied in *noceam*, "I'll make you smart." Up until the last word of the poem one takes *noceam* to indicate the speaker's preemptive refusal of future invitations—he will punish the host who has been neglecting him by ignoring his advances in the future. After the surprise ending "I'll come," we can see that *noceam* designates a quite different form of revenge; in a relationship as cold as this one seems to be, showing up for dinner (and, no doubt, eating heartily) will be as satisfying a form of revenge as staying away in proud disdain. It will be more satisfying, really; pride is an expensive luxury for this hungry *cliens*. It is for any other as well, according to the advice provided to Cantharus ("Wine-Bowl") in *Epigram* 9.9. "You like to dine at other men's houses, Cantharus, but you shout and curse and threaten. My advice to you is this: put aside your stiff-necked ways. You can't be both free-spoken and attentive to your belly."[6]

For *clientes* like Cantharus, Charopinus, and Philo, who sacrifice their pride to their belly, the edible portion of the *cena* is what matters, but Roman dinners were as much about talk as about eating, and Martial uses a parasitical figure in describing the verbal side of dinners as well. In *Epigram* 6.44 there is a fellow named Calliodorus who thinks he has something to contribute to this phase of the party.

> You believe your jokes amusing, Calliodorus. You think that you alone are steeped in wit that's really salty. You laugh at everybody; you've got a *mot* for everyone. You think that this can make you a guest who pleases.[7]

---

6. Cenes, Canthare, cum foris libenter,
   clamas et maledicis et minaris.
   deponas animos truces monemus:
   liber non potes et gulosus esse.

   (*Ep.* 9.9)

7. Festive credis te, Calliodore, iocari
   et solum multo permaduisse sale.
   omnis irrides, dicteria dicis in omnis;
   sic te convivam posse placere putas.

   (*Ep.* 6.44.1–4)

To be a "guest who pleases" is the aim of every parasite, but the speaker is not sanguine about Calliodorus' chances of success. He predicts, "Nobody, Calliodorus, will drink your health."[8] This prediction is not quite so dire as it might be—he might have forecast a dearth of invitations, after all—but it indicates clearly enough that the petulant wit on which Calliodorus (like many bold parasites before him) prided himself may not have the appeal it once did; more than two centuries earlier, Terence's Gnatho had already discovered that obsequiousness was more to most patrons' tastes (*Eun.* 244–53).

Not all of Martial's brief parasite sketches take the dependent as their target. As we saw in the plays that we looked at earlier in this book, the target that an author has in mind when creating a parasite is sometimes the parasite's prey. Martial uses the same indirect technique in *Epigram* 9.14.

> Your table, your dinners, have won you a friend, but do you think what he feels is loyal friendship? It's your boar he loves and your mullet, your sow's udder and your oysters, not you. If I provided dinners as nice as yours, he'd be my friend, too.[9]

Persius, as we have seen, had already drawn the connection between a *sumen*, "sow's udder" (his was nicely warmed), and a friend one could not count on.[10]

The superficiality of the sort of friendship that one can buy with a dinner is the subject of *Epigram* 2.19 as well, but the perspective is different again. Whereas in *Epigram* 9.14 the speaker is an observer who

---

8. nemo propinabit, Calliodore, tibi (*Ep.* 6.44.6).

9. Hunc quem mensa tibi, quem cena paravit amicum
       esse putas fidae pectus amicitiae?
    aprum amat et mullos et sumen et ostrea, non te.
       tam bene si cenem, noster amicus erit.

(Ep. 9.14)

10. The theme of the guest who was *captus . . . unctiore mensa* is treated again in *Epigram* 5.44, from the point of view of the host whose lesser table (the mere *ossa cenae*) has been abandoned. That of flattery proffered by *clientes* (a *turba togata*) hoping for a dinner appears in *Ep.* 6.48, addressed to a declaimer whose speeches were praised: non tu, Pomponi, cena diserta tua est (*Ep.* 6.48.2).

identifies problems in a system that he looks at from a distance, the speaker of 2.19 is the untrustworthy friend himself (and proud of it): "Do you think I am rendered happy by a dinner, Zoilus? By *your* dinner, Zoilus? Someone who is made happy by your dinner, Zoilus, must have been a guest on the hill at Aricia [a regular haunt of beggars]."[11] This speaker, who vents his annoyance at the triviality of the services for which he is expected to show gratitude, is in much the same position as the guest of Horace's Calabrian host who offers unwanted pears (*Epist.* 1.7.14–21). Like the Calabrian host, Zoilus thinks that a trivial *beneficium* (a meager dinner; a gift of pears that will otherwise be fed to the pigs) ought to produce real obligation in a *cliens*.[12] This version of the reciprocal exchange that was supposed to characterize the patron/client relationship is clearly lopsided; the reluctant speaker would seem to have a measure of justice on his side. A person whom a dinner did render a "friend" would be not the speaker of 2.19 (who seems to have some standards, anyway) but the parasite that we met a moment ago in *Epigram* 9.14.

There is another disgruntled guest (or would-be guest) in the poem immediately preceding the one addressed to Zoilus, *Epigram* 2.18. The dissatisfaction of this speaker is such that he breaks off his connection with his patron. His new independence gives him the distance he needs to look back on what he had been doing before and to see that his behavior had been that of a parasite.

> I'm in pursuit of dinner *chez vous*, Maximus. I'm embarrassed to admit it, but a dinner is what I'm after. But you are in pursuit of a dinner at somebody else's house—on this count we're equals. When I show up early at your levee, they tell me you're already out at someone else's—on this count we're equals. I keep you company, precede my fatheaded *rex* everywhere. You keep someone else company—on this count we're equals. It is bad enough to

---

11.   Felicem fieri credis me, Zoile, cena?
           felicem, cena, Zoile, deinde tua?
       debet Aricino conviva recumbere clivo,
           quem tua felicem, Zoile, cena facit.

(Ep. 2.19)

On the *clivus Aricinus* see Martial 12.32 and Juvenal 4.117.

12.   A thoroughly unpleasant dinner hosted by Zoilus is described at some length in *Ep.* 3.82.

be a slave; I won't stand for being a slave's slave any longer. The man who wants to be a *rex*, Maximus, shouldn't have a *rex* of his own.[13]

From the vantage point of after-the-fact, this speaker can see that an arrangement in which cliental *munera*—showing up for *salutationes*, swelling a patron's retinue, listening to his boasts—are exchanged for a meal is a poor relation of Roman *patrocinium*, a situation suitably displayed in the colors of the comic pair of parasite and *rex*.[14]

Epigrams such as those we have seen so far have a strong flavor of social criticism about them: something is rotten in the (people of the) state of Denmark, and the poet is going to point it out for all to see; perhaps they will be shamed or shocked into improving themselves.[15] But some of Martial's parasite epigrams are (happily) more frivolous, showing the epigrammatist's delight in the sheer power of words.

A good example is *Epigram* 7.20.

There is nothing so miserable and so greedy as Santra. He positively runs to where he's invited to a proper dinner (something he's been in quest of for many days and nights together). He asks

---

13. Capto tuam, pudet heu, sed capto, Maxime, cenam,
        tu captas aliam: iam sumus ergo pares.
     mane salutatum venio, tu diceris isse
        ante salutatum: iam sumus ergo pares.
     sum comes ipse tuus tumidique anteambulo regis,
        tu comes alterius: iam sumus ergo pares.
     esse sat est servum, iam nolo vicarius esse.
        qui rex est regem, Maxime, non habeat.

                                                           (*Ep.* 2.18)

14. A less venturesome soul appears at *Epigram* 5.57 with a wry comment on his servitude: Cum voco te dominum, noli tibi, Cinna, placere: / saepe etiam servum sic resaluto tuum.

15. In *Ep.* 10.33 Martial says that his policy is to spare individuals but attack vices (*parcere personis, dicere de vitiis*, 10). This needs a little glossing: he does spare real people, but the vices he attacks are not vices in the abstract (infidelity, greed, fellatio, etc.) but actions and habits that one sees in the people around one. Martial depicts adulterers, gluttons, fellators, and, of course, parasites.

for three servings of boar's lights, four of the thigh, both haunches of the hare, and the two forelegs, too.[16]

The list of what Santra is served goes on and on. He not only fills himself up but packs all he can in a napkin to take home. "He's not ashamed to reach his right hand way out to pick up scraps that even the sweepers and the dogs had left behind."[17] One might say of Santra what Horace said of Maenius, that he is an abyss into which one could upend the marketplace (*Epist.* 1.15.31). But it turns out that the supplies in the napkin are not destined for Santra's belly (his *gula*, 18) after all. Rather than eating up the marketplace, in fact, he is going there to sell his booty. Once again the final line of the poem changes the picture dramatically. In lines 1–21 we are presented with a parasitical Santra: he chases invitations, runs eagerly to dinner, stuffs himself disgracefully, and shows no shame about any of it. One would have thought this a quite sufficiently negative portrait, but Martial can make it worse: Santra is not just a parasite with a parasite's old familiar faults—one can laugh at the parasite's appetite, but after all it is just an exaggerated form of something very human. What makes Santra worse is that he is mercenary to boot. He is not going to eat all of the food that he got (quite illegitimately) from his host; rather, he is going to *sell* it. This is not really social criticism satire but pure epigrammatic pleasure in painting a very ugly picture in twenty lines or so and then making it many times worse with one final stroke. The parasite is the raw material with which Martial began.

The parasite of *Epigram* 12.82, Menogenes, is described at nearly equal length, but the surprise denouement takes even less space than that of 7.20—the last word suffices.

---

16. Nihil est miserius neque gulosius Santra.
     rectam vocatus cum cucurrit ad cenam,
     quam tot diebus noctibusque captavit,
     ter poscit apri glandulas, quater lumbum,
     et utramque coxam leporis et duos armos.

                                                                    (*Ep.* 7.20.1–5)

17. colligere longa turpe nec putat dextra
     analecta quidquid et canes reliquerunt.

                                                                    (*Ep.* 7.20.16–17)

Try what you may, you won't escape from Menogenes at the baths, neither in the sauna nor around the pool. He will grab for the warm [?] ball with right hand and left, so that you get the points he makes your opponent miss. He will gather up the loose ball from the dust and bring it back to you, even if he's already had his bath, already got his dinner shoes on. If you pick up some towels, he'll say he's never seen whiter ones (even if they are filthier than a child's shirt). Suppose you are combing your hair: it's getting thin these days, but he'll say you have arranged the locks of an Achilles. He doesn't mind drinking from the lees of smoky wine, and he'll even towel your face dry. He will praise everything, admire everything, until finally, when you've suffered through a thousand forms of tiresomeness, you say, "Come."[18]

Bubbling over with (insincere) praise, eager to serve in any capacity (indeed, inventive in finding new ways to be officious), dinner shoes at the ready, Menogenes is everything that Plautus' Gelasimus was, only more successful. The parasite was clearly still able to provide comic relief as well as to serve as a focus for comment of a more serious sort.

We have now seen parasites in short epigrams and in longer ones, in (fairly) serious poems and in witty ones. All of these epigrams, whatever their length, are self-sufficient: Martial creates a voice and a point of view in a few quick strokes, says what he has to say, and moves on to the next epigram. Prefabricated types like the parasite

---

18. Effugere in thermis et circa balnea non est
    Menogenen, omni tu licet arte velis.
captabit tepidum dextra laevaque trigonem,
    imputet exceptas ut tibi saepe pilas.
colliget et referet laxum de pulvere follem,
    etsi iam lotus, iam soleatus erit.
lintea si sumes, nive candidiora loquetur
    sint licet infantis sordidiora sinu.
exiguos secto comentem dente capillos
    dicet Achilleas disposuisse comas.
fumosae feret ipse propin de faece lagonae
    frontis et umore colliget usque tuae.
omnis laudabit, mirabitur omnia, donec
    perpessus dicas taedia mille 'veni!'

(*Ep.* 12.82)

contribute not a little to his ability to achieve epigrammatic brevity. But the individual poem is not the only format found in the collection. There are a number of paired poems, a form in which the second poem is connected to the first by a common name (Postumus, 2.22–23) or subject (the grant of the privileges of a father of three, 2.91–92), or where the second poem comments on (i.e., defends) a striking feature of its predecessor (length, 1.109–110, 3.82–83; meter, 6.64–65; obscenity, 1.34–35; flattery, 1.39–40, 10.44–45). Not all of the pairs are adjacent: the one-eyed Thais of 3.8 returns after a brief respite in 3.11, and there is an even larger gap between the poem that complains about Zoilus' crummy meal (2.19, quoted earlier in this chapter) and a poem that describes that meal in detail (3.82). A still more generous format is the cycle of epigrams, and one such cycle is devoted to a parasitical fellow named Selius.[19]

Selius is introduced in *Epigram* 2.1.

Selius has got a gloomy face, Rufus; late in the day he's still wearing away the portico with his walking. His grim expression is keeping back something mournful, it seems; his nose—none too clean—is practically dragging on the ground, his right hand beats his breast and plucks at his hair. It's not the death of a friend he's mourning, however, or of a brother; both of his boys are still alive (I pray that they may stay that way), his wife is fine, and so are his belongings and his slaves. No tenant of his or bailiff has lost him any money. What, then, is the cause of all this grief? He has to have dinner at home.[20]

---

19. On epigram cycles see Sullivan 1991, 11 n. 24, with the bibliography there cited.

20.   Quod fronte Selium nubila vides, Rufe,
       quod ambulator porticum terit seram,
       lugubre quiddam quod tacet piger vultus,
       quod paene terram nasus indecens tangit,
       quod dextra pectus pulsat et comam vellit:
       non ille amici fata luget aut fratris,
       uterque natus vivit et precor vivat,
       salva est et uxor sarcinaeque servique,
       nihil colonus vilicusque decoxit.
       maeroris igitur causa quae? domi cenat.

(*Ep.* 2.11)

Selius, it appears, is something of a paradox: despite evidence of his material substance (family, belongings, slaves, at least one tenant, and a bailiff), he is distraught at having to dine at his own expense. His plight is not quite as desperate as that of Philo, but he is apparently no less eager than Philo must have been to dine at someone else's expense.

The next poem in the cycle, *Epigram* 2.14, elaborates on the picture with which *Epigram* 2.11 began, that of Selius wearing away a portico with his walking late in the day. It turns out that Selius was not taking a walk to relieve his depression (as one might have concluded in 2.11); rather, he is out looking for something quite specific, for the invitation that will save him from the dire fate of dining at home.

> If Selius sees he'll have to dine at home, there's just nothing he doesn't try, nothing he won't attempt. He runs to the temple of Europa (and to you, Paulinus—he praises your "feet of Achilles"; there's no stopping him). If Europa can't do anything for him, off he goes to the Saepta, to see if the son of Philyra [Chiron] has anything for him, or Aeson's son [Jason]. Disappointed here, too, he hangs about the temple of Isis; he plops himself down, sad heifer, by your seats. Then he goes to the building whose roof rests on fully a hundred columns. After that, to the theater Pompey built and the twin groves [of the Caesars]. He doesn't miss the baths of Fortunatus, or those of Faustus either, or the dark baths of Gryllus, or the drafty ones of Lupus. He visits each of the baths again (and bathes again). And when he's had his bath (again), back he goes to the grove of warm Europa, in case a friend might be taking a late walk there. I pray to you, lusty traveler, and to your girl: please, O bull, please invite Selius to dinner.[21]

---

21. Nil intemptatum Selius, nil linquit inausum,
    cenandum quotiens iam videt esse domi.
currit ad Europen et te, Pauline, tuosque
    laudat Achilleos, sed sine fine, pedes.
si nihil Europe fecit, tunc Saepta petuntur,
    si quid Phillyrides praestet et Aesonides.
hic quoque deceptus Memphitica templa frequentat,
    assidet et cathedris, maesta iuvenca, tuis.
inde petit centum pendentia tecta columnis,
    illinc Pompei dona nemusque duplex.
nec Fortunati spernit nec balnea Fausti,
    ne Grylli tenebras Aeoliamque Lupi:

Selius prowls about the lounging spots of a Rome teeming with people and finds (for the most part) only the divine or heroic figures represented in the decorative schemes of famous monuments. His Rome is as deficient in people as Lupercus' *convivium* was.

He did, however, meet one person from whom an invitation might have been forthcoming, namely, Paulinus, with his feet of Achilles (Paulinus was probably walking quickly in an attempt to shed Selius).[22] The flattery that Selius only just broaches in 2.14 comes into its own as the subject of the next poem in the cycle, *Epigram* 2.27.

> Suppose you are giving a reading or making a speech for the defense; here's Selius spreading his nets for dinner: "A masterpiece! How impressive! Lively! Naughty! Well done! Divine! Just the ticket!" "Okay, okay, you've got yourself a dinner. Now keep quiet!"[23]

The addressee of this poem obviously could not take to his heels as Paulinus did. He could only turn off the fulsome flow by giving Selius what he wanted. Thus both Selius and Menogenes get their dinners by being tiresomely helpful. And the hunting metaphor that we saw applied to the ex-parasite speaker of 2.18 (*Capto tuam, pudet heu, sed capto, Maxime, cenam*, 2.18.1) is apparent here as well.

Now that Selius has his invitation, his activities cease to be of interest, but Martial does not abandon him quite yet. Having created in Selius a figure with a fine range of parasitical traits, he uses him as an exemplum a bit later in book 2, in a poem about dining out.

> nam thermis iterum ternis iterumque lavatur.
>   omnia cum fecit, sed renuente deo,
> lotus ad Europes tepidae buxeta recurrit,
>   si quis ibi serum carpat amicus iter.
> per te perque tuam, vector lascive, puellam,
>   ad cenam Selius tu, rogo, taure, voca.

(*Ep.* 2.14)

22. In one of Alexis' plays there was a scene in which a host was running away from a tenacious parasite (fr. 205 K-A).

23.   Laudantem Selium, cenae cum retia tendit,
          accipe, sive legas sive patronus agas:
      'effecte! graviter! cito! nequiter! euge! beate!
          hoc volui!' 'facta est iam tibi cena, tace.'

(*Ep.* 2.27)

You say you hate to go out to eat, Classicus. Hanged if you're not a liar. Apicius himself enjoyed going to a dinner and was rather less happy when he dined at home. If you hate venturing out, Classicus, why do you go? "I have to," you say. Well, so does Selius "have to." Suppose Melior invites you to a full-dress dinner, Classicus: where are those empty words of yours now? If you are a man, Classicus, let's see you say no.[24]

The utility of the parasite for making visible the gap between *virtus*, "manly behavior," and dependency is familiar to us from Horace's *Epistle* 1.17. Classicus is probably no more likely to say no than was the speaker of *Epigram* 6.51 or his forebear, the Horace of *Satire* 2.7. And now, having been exploited to the full, Selius disappears from the collection.

Selius' techniques ("nets," *retia*) for getting the invitation that would save him from dining at his own expense seem to have been flattery (2.14.3–4, 2.27) and being in the right place at the right time (2.14 passim). One of the right places was clearly the baths—Selius visited no fewer than four bathing establishments, and Menogenes, too, spent his efforts at the baths. Cadging an invitation at the baths is also the subject of *Epigram* 1.23, but the point of view is new: the dinner-seeker himself is the *ego* of this poem.

Only men with whom you have bathed get an invitation to dinner from you, Cotta; the baths provide you with all of your guests. I used to wonder why you never invited me, Cotta. I gather that in the buff I don't appeal to you.[25]

---

24.   Invitum cenare foris te, Classice, dicis:
          si non mentiris, Classice, dispeream.
      ipse quoque ad cenam gaudebat Apicius ire:
          cum cenaret, erat tristior ille, domi.
      si tamen invitus vadis, cur, Classice, vadis?
          'cogor' ais: verum est; cogitur et Selius.
      en rogat ad cenam Melior te, Classice, rectam:
          grandia verba ubi sunt? si vir es, ecce, nega.

                                                          (*Ep.* 2.69)

25.   Invitas nullum nisi cum quo, Cotta, lavaris
          et dant convivam balnea sola tibi.

Here, as in a number of the other epigrams that we have looked at already (e.g., 6.51, 2.18, 2.19), the speaker is someone who acts in ways that are in other poems labeled parasitical: the speaker of 1.23 obviously has much in common with Selius and Menogenes. In discussing the parasitical speakers we have encountered so far, I have concentrated on the rhetorical strategy of the presentation, avoiding (I hope) any suggestion that the *ego* was to be identified with the historical individual M. Valerius Martialis.

Negotiating between Martial the author and the *ego* of the poems is one of the most difficult tasks for anyone working on this vast collection. Epigram convention allows for a wide variety of *ego* voices in close proximity: the inscribed object (whether real or imagined) may speak, the voice may be that of the dedicator, or the poem may be the reaction of an onlooker whose relation to the epigram subject is quite unspecified. Frequently the author offers what looks like his own persona as mouthpiece, but there may be a multiplicity of these "authorial" personae within the corpus. In Martial's collection one finds a married speaker in 11.43 and 11.104, for example, and a determined bachelor in 11.23,[26] a well-endowed *ego* in 7.35 and a speaker with a less impressive physique in 7.55.[27] Yet there are a great many epigrams where the situation of the *ego* bears a strong resemblance to what we think we know about the situation of the real Martial. The complaints about the misery of client life, for example, given that Martial must have spent some time dancing attendance on, say, Regulus (a patron to whom he refers in fourteen epigrams) or Pliny the Younger (who himself mentions the verses Martial wrote for him and the recompense—traveling money for Martial's retirement to Spain—that he provided).[28]

The problem of distinguishing between *ego* and author is particularly acute in the poems that have a poet as *ego*—that is, that have an *ego*

---

    mirabar quare numquam me, Cotta, vocasses:
    iam scio me nudum displicuisse tibi.

(Ep. 1.23)

26. This inconcinnity has given rise, not surprisingly, to a series of arguments about Martial's marital status. See, most recently, Sullivan 1991, 25–26.

27. The different penis sizes are pointed out in Howell 1993.

28. In the epigram that Pliny quotes in one of his letters, Martial "addresses a Muse and tells her to seek Pliny's house on the Palatine, to approach it with all due respect" (Plin. *Ep.* 3.21.5; in Martial's collection the verses are *Ep.* 10.20[19].12–21). The verses themselves show familiarity with Pliny's household routine.

who refers to his compositions in the course of the poem, not just an *ego*
who happens to be speaking in elegiac couplets, hendecasyllables, or
scazons. Consider *Epigram* 11.24, where a poet protests to his patron
that his cliental duties—escorting him about town, listening to chat,
praising everything he says or does (1–3)—are so time-consuming as to
prevent the poet from producing the very works that make him a valuable *cliens:* "Who can tolerate this? Shall my books be fewer in number
so that you can have more togaed attendants about you?"[29] Of course,
he himself had tolerated the arrangement in the past, because there was
a tangible (or edible, anyway) reward to be had: "In nearly thirty days
a single page is all I've been able to produce. This is what happens
when a poet is unwilling to eat dinner at his own house."[30] The *ego* of
this poem is a popular author—his works were read by Romans and by
visitors to Rome, by knights and senators, by lawyers and other poets
(6–8)—as was Martial (*Ep.* 6.60). He was also a *cliens* who performed
certain services for a patron in exchange for *beneficia,* as did Martial. Yet
the *ego* of 11.24 uses the figure of the parasite, that of the man who will
tolerate any kind of inconvenience or injury to get a dinner, to characterize (negatively) the position he himself is in. Was Martial willing for
that same type to be applied to himself?

One feature of 11.24 gets in the way of an easy transfer. Like the
great majority of the satirical epigrams, this poem has a fictional
addressee, Labullus.[31] While a poet who evokes a connection between
a real individual and an *ego* voice must be willing to have the *ego* identified with his own historical self (this is precisely the rhetorical situation in Martial's very numerous occasional epigrams), a poem
addressed to no one in particular, to a fictional Labullus, can more easily take the voice of no one in particular.[32] If the addressee is "Labul-

---

29. hoc quisquam ferat? ut tibi tuorum / sit maior numerus togatulorum, /
librorum mihi sit minor meorum? (*Ep.* 11.24.10–12).

30. triginta prope iam diebus una est / nobis pagina vix peracta. sic fit / cum
cenare domi poeta non vult (*Ep.* 11.24.14–15).

31. Labullus is addressed in only one other poem, a complaint about his
stingy gifts (*non es, crede mihi, bonus, Ep.* 12.36.6); his female counterpart Labulla
gets two epigrams about her sexual appetite (4.9, 12.93).

32. Most of the addressees of the poems we have examined so far—e.g., Caecilianus, Charopinus, Lupercus, Zoilus, and so on—have been fictional. In the
case of Maximus (the addressee of 2.18) and Rufus (the addressee of 2.11) the
issue is less clear, because Martial addresses both occasional and satirical
poems to people with these common cognomens (see the *Index nominum* in

lus," not Regulus, or Pliny, or Stella, the *ego* can be "Martial," not Martial. The relevance of the nature of the addressee to determining the connection between the *ego* of a poem and the poet Martial is perhaps best revealed by looking at two poems that have much the same subject as 11.24—poet as *cliens*—but that are addressed to real individuals.

Epigram 1.70 is a poem written to the attention of one C. Julius Proculus, a man who also receives Martial's congratulations on his recovery from a dangerous illness (*Ep.* 11.36). Martial sends a book to Proculus' *salutatio* instead of going himself: "Go make my early morning greeting for me, dutiful book. Your orders are to go to the elegant house of Proculus."[33] It is clear that Martial is not planning to attend a *salutatio* at which he was expected to make an appearance. He substitutes the sort of *officium* that only a poet could provide (a book of poems) for the personal attendance that any old *cliens* might offer. The poem is an apology (of sorts), but it is not a cringing one. Proculus is (or ought to be) a connoisseur of poetry ("he is as close to me as Apollo and the Muses are," 15), and it is this taste of his to which Martial appeals in framing his excuses: "If he [sc. Proculus] asks, 'Why didn't the writer come in person?' you may give him the following excuse: 'Because someone who goes to *salutationes* can't write the sort of poems that get read.'"[34] The difference between the self-confident *ego* of 1.70 and the put-on and parasitical *ego* of 11.24 is accentuated by the absence (in 1.70) of any mention of the reward that the poet expects for his services. The speaker of 11.24 wants a dinner and will do a great deal to obtain it, but services worth only a dinner are not worth much. By specifying the reward that the poet of 11.24 has in view, Martial trivializes the value of the services he provides. No such "price tag" brings down the value of

---

Shackleton Bailey's 1990 edition). The question is perhaps of limited interest in 2.11, because Rufus is a casual addressee in a poem whose barb is aimed at Selius. But Maximus is the butt of 2.18; can he be a real person? I think not, seeing that when Martial refers to a real Maximus he takes care to mention *nomen* and *cognomen* in the first line of the poem (*Maximus . . . Caesonius*, 7.44.1 [this is the first line of a pair of poems about Caesonius Maximus]; *Vibi Maxime*, 11.106.1). See also n. 49 in this chapter.

33. Vade salutatum pro me, liber: ire iuberis / ad Proculi nitidos, officiose, lares (*Ep.* 1.70.1–2). Epigram 9.99 is another poem addressed to a real patron in which a book is sent in the poet's stead: tu qui longa potes dispendia ferre viarum, / i, liber, absentis pignus amicitiae (5–6).

34. si dicet 'quare non tamen ipse venit? / sic licet excuses: 'quia qualiacumque leguntur / ista, salutator scribere non potuit (*Ep.* 1.70.16–18).

the "dutiful book" (*liber officiosus*) that Martial himself offers instead of a visit.

The nature of Martial's *officia* to another real patron, the consular Sex. Julius Frontinus, is the subject of another apology poem, *Epigram* 10.58: "It is not only those who hover at your doorstep day and night who love you, Frontinus; it doesn't become a bard to waste his time that way. By all that's holy to my Muses and by all the gods above I swear, Frontinus: I am your friend even if I don't perform the regular *officia*" (*et non officiosus amo*, *Ep*. 10.58.14).[35] The ordinary duties of a *cliens*, what Martial calls elsewhere "the work that one does in a toga" (*opera togata*, *Ep*. 3.46.1), are not becoming, it seems, to the sort of *cliens* that Martial makes himself out to be.[36] What Martial offers instead is a testimonial to Frontinus' literary taste and to his pleasant piece of real estate in Anxur ("at your country place we had time to keep company with the Muses together," 5–6).[37] One may infer from this passage that Martial had been a guest at Frontinus' country estate—poets, especially occasional poets, were frequently treated to this sort of hospitality—but Martial is not so crude as to say that his poems earned him his country vacation or, even worse, that he wrote his poems with an eye to procuring an invitation to Anxur. That is the sort of stuff satire is made of, not poems addressed to people from whom you expect a liberal return.

---

35. Pace White (1975, 295 n. 41), who argues that the "Frontinus" of *Ep*. 10.58 is not to be identified with the consul of 98 (by whom Martial dates the dinner party of *Ep*. 10.48).

36. Another apology for remiss cliental behavior occurs in the preface to book 12: Scio me patrocinium debere contumacissimae trienni desidiae; quo absolvenda non esset inter illas quoque urbicas occupationes, quibus facilius consequimur ut molesti potius quam ut officiosi esse videamur. His shortfall is made good in dedicating book 12 to his addressee, Terentius Priscus.

37. *Epigram* 10.58 may have a companion piece in 10.51, which assembles a similar list of the delights of Anxur and shares with 10.58 both its complaint about the tedium of the *negotia* necessary in Rome and its address to Quirinus (51.15–16, 58.10). Anxur is not praised elsewhere by Martial except in passing. The addressee of 10.51, according to the manuscripts and their editors, is Faustinus, but Faustinus liked to hear about the advantages of Baiae and Tibur, not Anxur (3.58, 4.57, 5.71). Faustinus receives no other poem after book 8 (dated to 93), though he had been a very frequent addressee in the first eight books (1.25, 114; 3.2, 25, 39, 47, 58; 4.10, 57; 5.32, 36, 71; 6.7, 53; 7.12, 80; 8.41). Palaeographically speaking, it is simple to correct 10.51.5 to *Frontine*, and the existence of an error in this part of the line may have had something to do with the corruption still troubling the end of the line.

The contrast between these two poems and 11.24 is significant, because the two sets are in fact representatives of categories that do not overlap. *Epigram* 11.24 is one of a number of poems in which a poet-*ego* complains about the miseries of cliental *officia* that are both time-consuming and ill rewarded. These poems all have fictional addressees: 3.4 is addressed to the book of epigrams it was meant to accompany, for example, 3.46 to "Candidus," 10.74 to Rome, 12.68 to "an early-morning client" (*matutine cliens*). When Martial addresses real people (as in 1.70 and 10.58), he does not mention ordinary client *officia* (except, as we have seen, to apologize for—or vaunt—his failure to perform them); these are not the aspects of relationships with his patrons that Martial puts on record in his occasional poetry.[38]

What we do find in poems addressed to real people are verses that have a job to do: consoling the bereaved; congratulating newlyweds; issuing birthday greetings, get-wells, farewells, and welcomes-back; and so on. These messages are accompanied by very little in the way of biographical context. There is a poem celebrating the opening of Claudius Etruscus' bathhouse, for example (*Epigram* 6.42), which contains nineteen lines of description—of the water, the atmosphere, the lighting, the decor, the warmth, and so on—but no information whatsoever about why Martial is writing the poem or what he expects to get in return. This is by no means an extreme case, either. In *Epigram* 3.58 there are fully forty-four lines describing the farm of someone named Faustinus, but there is no indication of what Martial's connection with Faustinus is. Faustinus is the addressee of some twenty epigrams (see n. 37 in this chapter), so there must have been a connection.

Perhaps the most striking poem in this regard is *Epigram* 4.64, on the

---

38. Ovid is more forthright about his production of occasional poems (*ille ego sum, qui te colui, quem festa solebat / inter convivas mensa videre tuos? / ille ego, qui duxi vestros Hymenaeon ad ignes, / et cecini fausto carmina digna toro, Pont.* 1.2.129–32), because he is asking a favor of his addressee (intercession with Augustus). Martial does not connect his compositions and the rewards he received in any kind of neat equation. *Epigram* 9.89 might seem to be an exception. This little poem is addressed to a patron, L. Arruntius Stella, who receives a number of very flattering poems from Martial's pen: "A harsh decree, Stella, to compel your guest to produce verses. 'Well, I didn't say they had to be good ones.'" But even here we do not find a simple *munus*/dinner exchange such as that which defines the parasite of 11.24. The poet is a *conviva* when the poem begins, and verses are simply called for in the course of dinner (as Trimalchio calls for stories from two of his guests in Petron. *Sat.* 60.2, 64.2).

estate of Julius Martialis. Again we are presented with a substantial chunk of description (thirty lines) and nothing about the relationship between the property owner and the poet, though Martialis is the recipient of some of Martial's warmest addresses: he is "dear" in 5.20 (*care Martialis*, 1), "especially dear" in 6.1 (*in primis mihi care Martialis*, 2; book 6 is dedicated to him), "most delightful" in 10.47 (*iucundissime Martialis*, 2), and so on.[39] As this list of expressions of affection shows, Martial is not always quite so reticent as he is in 6.42 and 3.58; the genre of these two poems (property description) might make a relatively high degree of reticence acceptable, since readers would naturally assume that the poet had been a guest at the property described.

But even in the poems where Martial allows himself a presence on the occasion described, he is quite chary of details. Sometimes he is only one among a crowd of well-wishers: all Rome mourns for the Glaucias whose death is commemorated in *Epigram* 6.28, for example (Martial presumably among the rest); in *Epigram* 10.87 he is immersed in a crowd of *clientes* who celebrate the birthday of someone named Restitutus (*natalem colimus*, 4).[40] In other poems Martial expresses a more individual interest, as in the convalescence of the addressee of 11.68; he is "restored" to Martial, who had been praying for him (*votis redditus ecce meis*, 2).[41] Warmer, but still very uninformative, is the form of address used in *Epigram* 4.13, a wedding poem for "my friend Pudens" (*meo . . . Pudenti*, 1).[42] With poems like *Epigram* 8.45, which shows the poet making preparations for a welcome-home party for his friend Flaccus, or 9.42, where Martial is making vows on Stella's behalf, we begin to see some of the rhetorical strategies that make Horace's *Odes* such testimonials to friendship. But poems such as these, which tempt us to make inferences about the nature of Martial's relationships with his addressees, are really the exception rather than the rule. One must set against them the very numerous poems in which weddings and birthdays are feted, voyagers are sped on their way, career mile-

39. Martialis is also the addressee of some of the more serious and impressive poems in the collection (1.15, 9.97, 10.47, 12.34).

40. Group feelings are also evoked in 1.12 (*nostras . . . querelas*, 9), 6.68 (*Flete . . . Naides*, 1–2), and 9.86 (*cum grege Pierio maestus Phoeboque querebar*, 3).

41. A similar sentiment occurs in another *soteria*: redderis—heu, quanto fatorum munere—nobis (*Ep.* 7.47.3).

42. Cf. 7.97 (*Auli . . . mei Pudentis*, 3), 8.63 (*meus Aulus*, 4), 3.58 (*nostri . . . Faustini*, 1), 9.39 (*mei . . . Rufi*, 3), 9.60 (*nostro . . . Sabino*, 5), etc.

stones are commemorated, people or things are described and/or praised, and deaths are lamented with no indication whatsoever about the relationship of which the poem is a momentary instantiation.[43] And in none of his occasional poems—neutral or affectionate—does Martial mention material rewards hoped for in return for his poetic *munera*, though it is clear that he was a well-rewarded poet.[44]

In fact, there is a distinct difference between the way Martial portrays the *cliens* who is also a poet in the satirical epigrams (defined very minimally as poems with fictional addressees) and the way he portrays the same figure in poems with real addressees: the one is an ill-rewarded wretch whose resource deficiency imposes social obligations on him that no self-respecting (self-supporting) poet would tolerate for a moment. The other is a protégé of the Muses whose poems enhance events and people and objects of personal and social significance to his patrons and thereby confer immortality on them; what he gets in return for his services is—as far as these poems are concerned—immaterial.[45] Only in the satirical poems addressed to no one in particular is the figure of the parasite used to crystallize one of the varieties of client misery that a poet might experience. The *ego* of poems like 11.24 in which poet and parasite are aligned, then, has just as little of the real Martial in him as do the parasitical speakers of 6.51, 2.18, and 2.19.

There are two more poet-parasites to be considered before we move on to the question of why Martial found the comic mask a fitting bit of

---

43. Weddings, 6.21, 7.74, 11.78; birthdays, 3.6, 7.21–23, 10.23; voyages, 9.56, 12.98; career milestones, 4.54, 8.32; praise, 1.31, 1.48, 1.50[49], 5.48, 6.38, 7.15, 7.50, 7.29, 7.63, 8.66, 9.43; deaths, 6.18, 6.29, 6.52, 7.40, 7.96, 10.26, 10.71, 11.13. This list is only a sampling.

44. A few poems are essentially thank-you notes for material benefits received: a dinner (9.72), a cup (8.50), a toga (8.28, 10.73), roof tiles (7.36), a carriage (12.24), property in Spain (2.31). But Martial gives no indication of what he had done to earn these tokens of esteem. On Martial's thank-you notes see Damon 1992. On the importance of gifts to Martial's finances see Saller 1983.

45. I mean *immaterial* in both senses of the word: the *beneficia* that Martial does solicit from his patrons (generally when he offers them a collection of poems, a *libellus*), that is, things like editorial advice (4.10, 4.86, 5.80, 6.1, 7.11), publicity (2.6, 7.52, 7.97.13: *uni mitteris, omnibus legeris*), and defense against detractors and plagiarists (1.57, 7.26, 10.33), go well beyond the material goods like roof tiles, cloaks, and country vacations for which he thanks his patrons, but what Martial receives from his patrons is also immaterial in that it is not relevant (at least not overtly relevant) to the poem that Martial offers.

outerwear for dependent poets. What distinguishes these fellows from
the speaker of *Epigram* 11.24 and his like is the fact that they both aim to
exchange a poet's *munera,* poems, for a dinner. No more *salutationes* for
them!

The speaker of *Epigram* 1.108 is an old poet who lives a weary distance from a patron who expects to see him at his morning levee. The
poet sends his book to the *salutatio* instead of going himself, as Martial
did in *Epigram* 1.70, but this poet promises to show up for dinner in
person.

> To get to your house in the morning, Gallus, I'd have to move my
> own. Even if you lived further off, though, it would be worth it.
> Still, it doesn't much matter to you if I make one more togaed
> attendant for you, and it matters a great deal to me if I take that
> one away from myself. I'll come as often as you like at the tenth
> hour, Gallus, but in the morning my book will salute you for
> me.[46]

The speaker is as frank about his desire for a dinner as was the *ego* of
11.24, but the sacrifice entailed in earning it is greater (*migrandum est*),
so he has decided to take a chance and try substituting one form of service (the *liber*) for another (personal attendance).[47] One suspects, however, that this hungry fellow would not be at all pleased to find that his
host, Gallus, had substituted for the dinner the sort of favor that Martial solicits from those to whom he addresses collections of his poems
(*libelli*), namely things like editorial advice, publicity, and defense
against detractors and plagiarists.[48] Who is this Gallus? Is he real or fictional? Martial addresses (or refers to) a Gallus in eight poems (and to

---

46. migrandum est, ut mane domi te, Galle, salutem:
         est tanti, vel si longius illa [sc. domus] foret.
     sed tibi non multum est, unum si praesto togatum:
         multum est hunc unum si mihi, Galle, nego.
     ipse salutabo decima te saepius hora:
         mane tibi pro me dicet havere liber.

                                                    (*Ep.* 1.108.5–10)

47. Cf. *Ep.* 3.46, where the poet-speaker plans to send a freedman of his to a
salutatio instead of going himself. The freedman, he maintains, can do all of the
chores of a client—following a sedan chair, clearing a path in a crowd, flattering, defending a patron against annoyances—better than he can himself
(except, of course, writing poetry).

48. For references, see n. 45 in this chapter; for discussion see White 1974.

his feminine counterpart Galla in sixteen). In only one of these poems (10.33) is the tone polite, and in that one poem the addressee has a nomen (Munatius, 1) that suffices to distinguish him from the Galli toward whom Martial permits himself varying degrees of rudeness.[49] It would seem, then, that the Gallus of 1.108 is as fictional as the Gallus of 2.86, whose wife, Martial implies, traded sex for sesterces; the Gallus of 4.16, who sleeps with his stepmother; and, of course, the Labullus of 11.24.[50]

In the other poem in which a poet's poetical services are rewarded (at least in anticipation) with a dinner and are therefore characterized as parasitical, Martial distances the type from himself not by providing a fictional addressee but by attacking the parasitical poet. His victim in *Epigram* 9.19 is a (fictional) poet named Sabellus: "In three hundred verses, Sabellus, you praise the baths of Ponticus, a man who gives good dinners. It's a dinner you want, Sabellus, not a bath."[51]

---

49. On the problem of epigrams that are openly abusive of "people" with names that also belong to patrons praised in the collection see n. 32 in this chapter. Details of nomenclature are also used to differentiate Caecilius Secundus (7.84), Secundus (5.80), and Plinius (10.19) from the "Caecilius" abused at 1.41, 2.72, and 11.31. Similarly, the cognomen of his son (Urbicus) distinguishes the bereaved father Bassus from the "Bassus" of many a satirical epigram. But there remain cases in which neither this solution to the problem nor any other is adopted. The possibility of a mistaken reference is perhaps most striking in the poems addressed to "Polla." It is clear that the praiseworthy Polla of 7.21, 7.23, and 10.64 is the widow of the poet Lucan, but in close proximity to the last of these, we find epigrams abusing "Polla" roundly (10.40, 10.69, 10.91; cf. also 3.42 and 11.89). It may be possible to explain away the problematic contemporaneity of praise and abuse in book 10 by supposing that the widow Polla was dead by then and that 10.64 was included in the book not to please her but because it had programmatic value. Other explanations can be found for other cases: a large gap in time between laudatory and abusive epigrams and/or a low profile for the abused "individual" mitigates the problem for Calenus (abuse, 1.99; praise, 10.38), Celer (abuse, 1.63; praise, 7.52), Macer (abuse, 8.5; praise, 10.17, 10.78), and Pompeius Auctus (abuse, 8.6; praise, 7.51; incidental references, 9.21, 12.13). More difficult to understand is the mixture of praise and abuse in the epigrams addressed to Paulus and Lupus (though Kay 1985, *ad* 11.88, is useful for Lupus). The topic would benefit from a thorough examination.

50. Howell (1980, ad loc.) and Citroni (1975, ad loc.) are to different degrees undecided on the question of Gallus' identity, but Howell inclines toward a fictional Gallus, Citroni to a real one.

51. Laudas balnea versibus trecentis /cenantis bene Pontici, Sabelle, / vis cenare, Sabelle, non lavari (*Ep.* 9.19).

Both the speaker of *Epigram* 1.108 and Sabellus attract the satirist's attention because they want to use poems to get invitations to dinner. This calculating tit-for-tat sort of exchange is just what the reciprocal services of the ideal patron/client relationship were not supposed to be. The ideal was a much more fluid sort of give-and-take in which a poet's desire to support his patron's bid for visibility in, say, undertaking to build a fancy bathhouse ought to give rise to some nice quotable verses on said bathhouse, while the patron's gratitude for the verses ought to manifest itself in, say, an invitation to dinner. The net result might not be very different from that described in *Epigram* 9.19, but the attitudes of the parties involved would be. The relationship described in 9.19 in particular is stripped of all the personal elements (e.g., mutual interest in one another's well-being) that characterize the ideal. It might as well be a pay-as-you-go sort of arrangement.

Being an epigrammatist, Martial does not spend much time describing ideals. But his contemporary Statius shows in *Silvae* 4.6 what a positive depiction of the relationship Martial holds up to scorn in *Epigrams* 1.108 and 9.19 would look like. The focus of *Silvae* 4.6 is a work of art, a statuette of Hercules owned (newly acquired?) by the addressee of the poem, a soi-disant connoisseur of art named Novius Vindex. Statius saw it on the occasion of a dinner at Vindex' house. Praise of the miniature Hercules and of his patron occupies the bulk of the poem (lines 17–109), but Statius begins with a vignette that explains how he found himself at Vindex' table.

One day as I was whiling away some free time with a late afternoon stroll in the broad Saepta (I was taking a break from my studies and had cleared my breast of Apollo), the dinner of generous Vindex hurried me off. The good I got from that dinner remains with me still, stored up in the inmost chambers of my soul, for our fare was not treats for the belly or dishes provided by faraway lands or wine rivaling in age Rome's unbroken series of annual records. Ah, wretched folk, who take pleasure in knowing in what particulars the bird of Phasis [a kind of pheasant] differs from the wintry crane of Rhodope, or which sort of goose has the best innards, or why the Tuscan boar is more noble than the Umbrian, or on what beach the slippery shellfish are most comfortable. No, for us true love and conversation about the arts and lively wit persuaded us to stay up late that winter night and to drive soft sleep from our eyes, until Castor's brother peeped out from the underworld and the Tithonian maid [Aurora] laughed at yesterday's tables.[52]

This scene has a strong resemblance to the picture Martial gave of Selius (though Selius was not a poet) in *Epigram* 2.14, only with a positive twist in place of the satirist's more negative view. Statius was not looking for a dinner invitation, he was taking a break from his real work, composing weighty epics.[53] And the dinner itself carried him off. Apparently, no flattery and no services were required of him (though both are plentiful in lines 17–109 of the poem). And his pleasure in the dinner was not due, he says, to a full or well-fed belly but to the emotional and intellectual fare that kept him late at the table—the affection between host and guest as well as the conversation, both serious and frivolous. Within the space of about a decade, then—the Selius cycle comes from book 2, published in about 86, while *Silvae* 4 seems to have been published in 95—we get two very different views of what was essentially the same phenomenon, the exchange of an invitation to din-

---

52. Forte remittentem curas Phoeboque leuatum
      pectora, cum patulis tererem uagus otia Saeptis
      iam moriente die, rapuit me cena benigni
      Vindicis. haec imos animi perlapsa recessus
      inconsumpta manet; neque enim ludibria uentris
      hausimus aut epulas diuerso a sole petitas
      uinaque perpetuis aeuo certantia fastis.
      a miseri, quos nosse iuuat quid Phasidis ales
      distet ab hiberna Rhodopes grue, quis magis anser
      exta ferat, cur Tuscus aper generosior Vmbro,
      lubrica qua recubent conchylia mollius alga.
      nobis uerus amor medioque Helicone petitus
      sermo hilaresque ioci brumalem absumere noctem
      suaserunt mollemque oculis expellere somnum,
      donec ab Elysiis prospexit sedibus alter
      Castor et hesternas risit Tithonia mensas.
                    (*Silv.* 4.6.1–16; the text is from Courtney 1990)
53. According to Coleman (1988, ad loc.), Statius "absolves himself from the suspicion of waiting for an invitation since *cena* [sic] usually began before sunset," but Martial's Selius was looking for an invitation late in the day (*ambulator porticum terit seram, Ep.* 2.11.2; cf. *si quis ibi serum carpat amicus iter,* 2.14.16); it was a measure of his desperation.

ner for cliental services. To Martial it looks like the man who flattered his way into the dining room provided "services" that were valueless (indeed tiresome) and got in return something that he wanted a great deal. According to Statius, however, the host got something he wanted (namely, a presentable poem on a nice little piece in his art collection)—he sought the poet out, after all—while the guest got food that was not particularly luxurious and a pleasant (if rather long) evening. In the one view we have a parasite, in the other a useful fellow, a man you might recommend to your friends when they needed the sort of services he could provide. The value a person assigns to the goods and services exchanged is clearly crucial to the way the exchange appears to that person. And an outsider, like the satirist of the Selius cycle, is likely to rate them differently than do the participants in the exchange.

We have now looked at parasites in some twenty of Martial's epigrams. It is a nicely varied collection of hungry parasites and abject ones, predatory parasites who look for invitations on the streets of Rome and others who prefer the more confined spaces of a bathhouse, reformed ex-parasites and parasites whose "friendship" can still be bought with a dinner. Martial's various parasites have in common their ability to serve in the satirist's presentation of aspects of the patron/client relationship that depart from the ideal, relationships where there may be an exchange of *munera* but where the more personal elements of the connection—protection and gratitude, for example—have withered away. In such a relationship money might as well be the medium of exchange; in the convivial sphere of the time, dinner invitations were in fact giving way to baskets of food waiting in the entrance hall, which in turn were giving way to small sums of money.[54] What made this sort of development cry out to the satirist's pen is the fact that the language of the earlier, more personal, relationship was still used: "Suppose a slave comes up and says into your poor cold ear, 'Laetorius asks you to dine with him.' For twenty bits? No thanks."[55] When a Laetorius invites someone to a *cena*, meaning all the while to have a slave hand him a handful of coins, there is a gap between language and reality that is just waiting to be filled with satire. However welcome these coins may have

---

54. On the transformation of the *sportula* see Courtney 1980, *ad* 1.95
55. accedit gelidam servus ad auriculam, / et 'rogat ut secum cenes Laetorius' inquit. / viginti nummis? non ego (*Ep.* 12.26.12–14).

been—and *Epigram* 3.30 suggests that a *cliens* might well prefer coins to a free dinner, given that he needed not only to eat but also to clothe, lodge, bathe, and entertain himself—the relationship between provider and receiver has lost some of the elements that are present in the ideal of *patrocinium*.[56] The parasite, as we have seen, helps Martial point to (and shake his finger at) the difference.

One of the specific areas in which Martial points to a difference was the production of occasional verse. It is not a prominent theme in his collection—in fact, there is just a single epigram, that about Sabellus and his praise of Ponticus' baths (9.19), in which a poet is accused of proffering verses in hopes of a dinner—but we will see in chapter 7 that an author who was not himself a writer of versified compliments, namely, Cicero, was more free with the collocation of poet and parasite in his caricature of Philodemus, as "foreigner . . . flatterer . . . poet" (*Graeculus . . . adsentator . . . poeta, Pis.* 70). The ideal from which parasitical poets depart can best be seen in the *Silvae* of Statius, a poet who takes great care to present himself as someone with a personal relationship with his addressee—that is, as a friend or client. One does not necessarily need to believe what Statius says about himself to see the ideal to which he is appealing. It may well be that some occasional poems were essentially bought items or attempts at contact that failed to flourish into connections, but for centuries the Romans had been stretching the concepts of *amicitia* and *clientela* to fit situations for which they were not originally designed. There was a long-standing habit, from which both sides stood to gain, of labeling a relationship *clientela* or *amicitia* in the hopes that it would become assimilated to that model. Martial's parasitical Sabellus is a useful reminder of the gap that too often existed between the label and the reality underneath it.

---

56. sportula nulla datur; gratis conviva recumbis:
 dic mihi, quid Romae, Gargiliane, facis?
 unde tibi togula est et fuscae pensio cellae?
 unde datur quadrans? unde vir es Chiones?

(*Ep.* 3.30.1–4)

6

Parasites in the *Satires* of Juvenal

A Parasite is the image of iniquity; who for the gain of dross is
devoted to all villainy. He is a kind of thief in committing a bur-
glary when he breaks into houses with his tongue and picks pockets with his flattery. His face is brazen that he cannot blush and
his hands are limed to catch hold of what he can light on. . . . In
sum, he is a danger in a court, a cheater in a city, a jester in the
country and a jackanapes in all.
—Nicholas Breton *The Good and the Bad, &c.*

The parasite is as useful to Juvenal as he was to Horace and Martial.
Juvenal's parasites are perhaps less originally conceived than those of
Horace—there is nothing quite as striking as Horace's *parasitae* or as
productive of imitation as his parasitical *captator*—and Juvenal offers
no self-portraits in which the parasite lifts its ugly head, but his collection of parasites is worthy of examination nonetheless. Juvenal's originality lies in part in the way he links parasites across poems. The figure
of the parasite that the satirist summons up in *Satire* 1 is used by Umbricius in *Satire* 3 and Virro in *Satire* 5, for example, and the parasitical
Naevolus of *Satire* 9 is linked to Virro's parasite by his reference to an
archetypal patron named Virro. In connecting his parasites in this way
Juvenal creates a crescendo of evils not paralleled by anything in
Horace. But Juvenal's merit goes beyond this. For unlike any of his predecessors, he gives a perspective on the act of applying the label *parasitus* to a contemporary. In Juvenal's *Satires*, in fact, both the parasite
and the man who calls him parasite receive their due of criticism. The
poems are thus useful for showing that the label was chosen from
among other possible descriptions of the Roman *cliens,* and that the use
of the label reveals as much about the user as about the person so
labeled.

The client/parasite equation is present already in the programmatic
satire with which the collection begins. Topping off the catalog of
annoyances that have goaded the satirist into speaking his mind—the
wealthy ex-slave ex-barber, the informer, the inheritance-hunter, the

complaisant cuckold, the crazy driver, the female poisoner, and the consul in quest of a handout—we find *clientes* who have grown old hoping. At the end of a tedious day spent, Selius-like (see Martial *Epigram* 2.11, discussed in chap. 5), frequenting places where one might "bump into" potential hosts, the clients, disappointed in their hopes of an elegant (or at least free) dinner, go off to buy the supplies necessary for their own poor meal, while their patron eats his way through his patrimony by himself.

> Old and tired, the *clientes* leave the big front halls, stowing their hopes for the day (though dinners do keep a man hoping longer than anything else). The poor wretches have got to pick up a cabbage to eat and some fuel to cook it with. And all the while their patron [*rex horum*] will be devouring the best of forest and sea; he'll be reclining all by himself in a dining room full of couches.[1]

The necessary consequence when this scenario is repeated throughout the city and over time is that "Soon there won't be a parasite left" (*nullus iam parasitus erit*, 139).

The conditions of *clientela* being what they are, this host's disappointed friends will not allow themselves the luxury of open resentment—they probably have not yet given up hope for tomorrow's dinner (*longissima cenae / spes homini*, 133–34)—but when he dies the death he deserves, "his funeral proceeds to the sound of his angry friends' clapping" (*ducitur iratis plaudendum funus amicis*, 146). That Juvenal is here drawing on comedy for his caricature of the *clientes* is made evident both by the traits he saddles them with—their persistence in seeking an invitation, their refusal to get angry, the quick demise of their "friendship" when the wealthy man is no longer around for them to prey on—and more particularly by the terms he uses for both *cliens* and patron.

Parasitus and *rex* rarely appear outside of comic contexts.[2] We do not

---

1.   uestibulis abeunt ueteres lassique clientes
     uotaque deponunt, quamquam longissima cenae
     spes homini; caulis miseris atque ignis emendus.
     optima siluarum interea pelagique uorabit
     rex horum uacuisque toris tantum ipse iacebit.
                         (*Sat.* 1.132–36; the text is from Clausen 1992)

2. See appendix 1.

know what Ennius called the parasitical speaker of the lines that Terence had Phormio imitate, but Lucilius (it seems) and Horace (certainly) use *scurra*, not *parasitus*, when they want to label a dependent.
Horace uses a word like *parasitus*, namely, *parasitae*, only when the people so labeled are so different from the standard comic parasite that
vocabulary has to be pressed into service to secure the identification
desired. Juvenal, however, has none of Horace's reticence vis-à-vis
New Comedy and its characters. In fact, he relishes applying comic
labels to people whose claim to them is not obvious. He calls Messalina
"a whore-empress" (*meretrix Augusta, Sat.* 6.118), the goddess Isis a
"madam" (*Isiacae . . . lenae, Sat.* 6.489), and the complaisant husband of
an adulteress a "brothel keeper" (*leno, Sat.* 1.54). His use of *parasitus* as
an equivalent for the *cliens* who will become extinct if rich men insist on
dining alone is another application of this rhetorical device.

One might think that a behavior that resulted in the extinction of
parasites was not much to be regretted, but that is not the way the
satirist sees it. His gripe is with the *rex*: "Who could keep quiet about
riches so rotten? How big must that belly be that sits down alone to a
boar, an animal made for company dinners!" (*sed quis ferat istas / luxuriae sordes? quanta est gula quae sibi totos / ponit apros, animal propter
conuiuia natum!* 139–41). What exactly is so reprehensible about those
rotten riches (*luxuriae sordes*)? Is it that this selfish form of extravagance
involves all the luxury of a real Roman *cena* but none of the sociability
that was often evoked to excuse the expenditure? Or is it perhaps something less high-mindedly moral? Elsewhere in the poem, the satirist
couches his objections to what he sees around him in personal terms:
the wordly success of Crispinus is an affront to the man—the satirist—
who used to be shaved by him, for instance (24–30).[3] And the satirist
gives the impression that he is jostled in the streets by objectionable
types and crowded by them on the thresholds of important men
(99–101 [esp. *nobiscum*, 101], 117–26). His protest about the success of
such criminals as the man who forges a will or the woman who poisons
her husband is not so much a critique of society as a peevish expression
of resentment at his own failure to have done so well for himself: "If
you want to be somebody, you've got to dare to do things that ought to
get you banished to tiny Gyara or sent to prison. Upright behavior gets

---

3. The classic study of the less-than-admirable satirist in Juvenal's *Satires* is
Anderson 1964.

praise, and it shivers" (*aude aliquid breuibus Gyaris et carcere dignum, / si uis esse aliquid. probitas laudatur et alget, Sat.* 1.74–75). So speaks one who fancies himself both upright and unfairly neglected in the distribution of worldly rewards. That the satirist's irritation at the solitary diner's voluptuary self-indulgence has some of the same springs of personal grievance will become clearer when, after looking at Umbricius' plaint in *Satire* 3, we turn to *Satire* 5.

In *Satire* 1 the comic *parasitus* emerged as a figure with an intimate connection to themes of major importance in Juvenal's *Satires*, namely, friendship, dependence, and that peculiarly Juvenalian target, parsimonious extravagance. The latter two themes dominate Umbricius' long, drawn-out Parthian shot in *Satire* 3, and the parasite duly appears.

Umbricius is leaving Rome, it seems, because he lacks the characteristics necessary to succeed there. He cannot make money himself (29–40), nor can he make himself useful to someone who already has money.

> What am I to do in Rome? I don't know how to lie, so if a book is bad I can't praise it and ask [sc. to hear more]. I don't know the movements of the stars; I don't want to promise that somebody's father will die, nor have I the ability to do so. I have never taken a reading from the innards of a frog. Other folks know how to execute commissions for an adulterer, carrying gifts and messages to [somebody else's] bride. No one will have my aid in stealing, which is why I don't go out to the provinces with anyone. That's how deficient I am; a man with a lifeless right hand, a useless bod.[4]

The services in this list will win the attention and/or gratitude of a not-very-upright patron. If these are the abilities one must have to succeed

---

4. quid Romae faciam? mentiri nescio; librum,
   si malus est, nequeo laudare et poscere; motus
   astrorum ignoro; funus promittere patris
   nec uolo nec possum; ranarum uiscera numquam
   inspexi; ferre ad nuptam quae mittit adulter,
   quae mandat, norunt alii; me nemo ministro
   fur erit, atque ideo nulli comes exeo tamquam
   mancus et extinctae, corpus non utile, dextrae.

                                                        (*Sat.* 3.41–48)

in Rome (Umbricius implies they are), it is clear that one gets ahead by preying on the faults of men above one: a rich author's vanity, an heir's impatience for his father's demise, an adulterer's involvement with other men's women, and the rapacity of public officials.

Umbricius' inability to succeed in such a Rome is not due to any innate virtue. The problem, as he sees it, is that there are too many men who are good at playing the parasite in Rome these days. He makes a connection between the helpful but unscrupulous *cliens* and the comic parasite in the next section of the poem. There has been, he complains, a huge influx of Greeks: "One man comes from lofty Sicyon, another from Amydon, this one from Andros, that one from Samos, another from Tralles or Alabanda. They all seek the Esquiline and the hill named for withes [sc. the Viminalis]; they are the vital organs (*viscera*, literally "innards") of great houses, and soon they'll be the masters."[5] He realizes, of course, that Greeks had been a presence in Rome for a long time, for so long, in fact, that even the quintessentially Roman *rusticus* had adopted their "ways of speaking and doing" (*lingua et mores*, 63): "Your salt-of-the-earth Roman, Quirinus, wears dinner slippers now and has athletic trophies hung about his well-anointed neck" (*rusticus ille tuus sumit trechedipna, Quirine, / et ceromatico fert niceteria collo*, 67–68). The Greek word *trechedipna* in particular (literally "shoes for running off to dinner in") carries in it a whole range of parasitical associations: hunger, impatience for the arrival of the dinner hour, lack of concern about showing undue eagerness, absence of prior engagements.[6] Still, Umbricius is not worried about this laughably anomalous rustic, because he considers the talented and versatile *Graeculus esuriens* ("hungry little Greek," or, in Samuel Johnson's unforgettable rendering, "fasting Monsieur") so much more of a threat: "He brings over within himself any character you like—teacher of literature, rhetoric, or

---

5. hic alta Sicyone, ast hic Amydone relicta,
    hic Andro, ille Samo, hic Trallibus aut Alabandis,
    Esquilias dictumque petunt a uimine collem,
    uiscera magnarum domuum dominique futuri.

(Sat. 3.69–72)

6. The scholiast calls them *vestimenta parasitica*. *Niceteria*, "athletic trophies," are not displayed by the parasites we have seen so far, but at Anaxippus 3 K-A a parasite is encountered leaving the palaestra, and Pollux indicates that the parasite mask attested diligent attendance at the palaestra (good hunting grounds for spendthrift youth, after all): κόλαξ δὲ καὶ παράσιτος μέλανες, οὐ μὴν ἔξω παλαίστρας (4.148).

geometry; painter; trainer; seer; tightrope walker; doctor; magician—
the hungry little Greek knows everything. Bid him go to heaven; to
heaven he'll go."[7]

The *Graeculus esuriens* is a useful type. And for the little Greek, as for
Persius' poet-crows and poetess-magpies, hunger is what drives him to
display his shape-shifting talents. It is only to be expected, therefore,
despite Umbricius' chagrin, that one setting in which the Greekling's
utility finds its reward is the *cena:* "Is he going to place his seal on documents before I do and prop himself on a better cushion at dinner?" (*me
prior ille / signabit fultusque toro meliore recumbet?* 81–82). The digestive
organ metaphor that Umbricius had used for the first phase of the parasite's social success (*viscera magnarum domuum,* 72) was well chosen.

Beyond the practical skills that are so useful in a *cliens,* Umbricius
credits the newcomers with a remarkable aptitude for flattery (*adulandi
gens prudentissima,* 80). This facility (he says rather smugly) a Roman
cannot hope to equal (92–93). The newcomers are like the comic actors
who are so good at their jobs that they persuade you that the illusion
they create is somehow real: "Is the man any less talented than the actor
who plays the *meretrix* Thais or the wife in a comedy or even the maidservant Doris (who wears nothing but a shift)? For in the play it looks
as though it really is a woman speaking, not a male actor with a mask."[8]
The successful *clientes* that stand in Umbricius' way put their mimetic
abilities to work not onstage, however, but in the company of the great
men (owners of golden chamber pots) of Rome.

> If you laugh, he rocks with laughter; if his friend has tears in his
> eyes, he doesn't just cry, he weeps. If you call for a bit of fire in the
> winter, he puts on a sweater. If you say, "I'm hot," he starts sweat-
> ing. We are not equals, he and I. He's got the advantage, since he

---

7. quemuis hominem secum attulit ad nos:
   grammaticus, rhetor, geometres, pictor, aliptes,
   augur, schoenobates, medicus, magus, omnia nouit
   Graeculus esuriens: in caelum iusseris, ibit.

   (*Sat.* 3.75–78)

8. an melior cum Thaida sustinet aut cum
   uxorem comeodus agit uel Dorida nullo
   cultam palliolo? mulier nempe ipsa uidetur,
   non persona, loqui.

   (*Sat.* 3.93–96)

can always, any time of the night or day, find a countenance in somebody else's face. Why, he can toss up his hands (praise at the ready) if someone issues a real good belch or pees straight, or if the bottom of the golden chamber pot returns a satisfying thud.[9]

The little Greek's ability to read his patron is just as misleading as a female mask on a male actor, for hidden here is a man who will hop into bed with any old member of his friend's household: with his wife, his virgin daughter, her downy fiancé, the *filius familias*, or even, if desperate, with Granny (109–12). A paradox such as this might easily give rise (in a moralist or a satirist) to a rational exposé of or a diatribe against the dangers of flattery. Cicero and Plutarch, for example, provide the first of these, and Persius, as we have seen, provided the second.[10] But Umbricius is neither a moralist nor a satirist, so he gets quickly to the heart of the matter as far as he is concerned.

There is no place in Rome for a Roman now; Protogenes (it may be) is king now, or Diphilus, or Hermarchus, and they've all got their national fault of never sharing out a friend. Once he's dripped a little of his Greek poison into a patron's unsuspecting

---

9. rides, maiore cachinno
    concutitur; flet, si lacrimas conspexit amici,
    nec dolet; igniculum brumae si tempore poscas,
    accipit endromidem; si dixeris "aestuo," sudat.
    non sumus ergo pares: melior, qui semper et omni
    nocte dieque potest aliena sumere uultum
    a facie, iactare manus laudare paratus,
    si bene ructauit, si rectum minxit amicus,
    si trulla inuerso crepitum dedit aurea fundo.

                                                    (*Sat.* 3.100–108)

For the final image see Nisbet 1991.

10. Flexibility like that shown by Umbricius' Greekling comes in for treatment in Cicero's treatise on friendship, for example: cum autem omnium rerum simulatio vitiosa est—tollit enim iudicium veri idque adulterat—tum amicitiae repugnat maxime; delet enim veritatem, sine qua nomen amicitiae valere non potest. nam cum amicitiae vis sit in eo ut unus quasi animus fiat ex pluribus, qui idem fieri poterit si ne in uno quidem quoque unus animus erit idemque semper, sed varius commutabilis multiplex? (*Amic.* 92). Plutarch, like Clearchus, equates the κόλαξ and Proteus (*Mor.* 96e; on his flexibility see *Mor.* 52a–f).

ear, I can't get a foot in the door any more, and all my years of service [slaving] have gone to waste.[11]

What Umbricius objects to is not the corrosive effect of flattery in the unsuspecting ear but the fact that he has been supplanted. Umbricius stands forth as the best and fullest illustration of the envious Roman who uses the comic type of the parasite to shape and adorn his version of the man whose position in society he objects to. For him the parasite model is essentially a belittling device; his is the view from below. Depicting his rivals as parasites allows him to feel superior despite his manifest inferiority on many practical counts.

Umbricius, then, laments (and simultaneously boasts of) his own inability to achieve worldly success as a parasite. He bills it not as a personal failure but as a consequence of his birth and a childhood "fed on the Sabine berry" (*baca nutrita Sabina*, 85), just as the success of the Greeks is their national heritage (*gens*, 58, 86; *gentis vitio*, 121; *veneno patriae*, 123).[12] Juvenal does not allow this self-serving generalization to stand for long, however, for in *Satire* 5 we get another look at the parasite.

If you are not yet ashamed of what you've set out to do, and intend to keep on as you are—thinking that the highest good is feeding at someone else's expense [literally, "living on somebody else's loaf"]—if you can put up with treatment worse than anything Sarmentus or that crummy Gabba took at the status-conscious table of Caesar, then I'd be afraid to believe you when you

---

11. non est Romano cuiquam locus hic, ubi regnat
     Protogenes aliquis uel Diphilus aut Hermarchus,
     qui gentis uitio numquam partitur amicum,
     solus habet. nam cum facilem stillauit in aurem
     exiguum de naturae patriaeque ueneno,
     limine summoueor, perierunt tempora longi
     seruitii.

(Sat. 3.119–25)

12. Even within *Satire* 3 Juvenal exposes the sour-grapes mentality, for he makes Umbricius complain, quite unabashedly, that in one of the services he could and would offer—serving as a (presumably false) witness on behalf of his patron—he has been ousted by richer *clientes* who were more valuable in court (*Sat.* 3.126–46).

give evidence, even on oath. I don't know anything cheaper to fill than a belly, but suppose you don't have even enough to buy what will satisfy a hollow gut, can't you find a free bit of wall somewhere, a bridge and a scrap of beggar's matting? Are the injuries you suffer for dinner and the hunger you feel even there so great a boon? You'd be a better man shivering on a bridge and chewing away at the barley bran they feed to dogs.[13]

This is the beginning of the *Satire:* we have eleven lines of characterization before we even learn the name of the person so described. The definition of the greatest good as "living on somebody else's loaf" and the references to suffering in a convivial context, to previous professionals (Sarmentus and Gabba), to bellies (*ventre, alvo,* 6–7), and to self-degradation combine to produce a highly efficient first paragraph characterizing the addressee as a parasite.[14]

In the next paragraph we hear a little more: for example, that the addressee's place at the table is a "tangible return" (*merces solida*) for a long series of *officia* (12–13). In the best Juvenalian style, this sentiment is repeated in the following line with new and more striking terms for the goods exchanged: food, *cibus,* is the fruit of a friendship with one of the great (*fructus amicitiae magnae,* 14), a revealingly paltry return.[15]

---

13. si te propositi nondum pudet atque eadem est mens,
   ut bona summa putes aliena uiuere quadra,
   si potes illa pati quae nec Sarmentus iniquas
   Caesaris ad mensas nec uilis Gabba tulisset,
   quamuis iurato metuam tibi credere testi.
   uentre nihil noui frugalius; hoc tamen ipsum
   defecisse puta, quod inani sufficit aluo:
   nulla crepido uacat? nusquam pons et tegetis pars
   dimidia breuior? tantine iniuria cenae,
   tam ieiuna fames, cum posset honestius illic
   et tremere et sordes farris mordere canini?

(*Sat.* 5.1–11)

14. See Horace *Epist.* 1.17.49 for another loaf (*quadra*). On Sarmentus see chap. 4 n. 16; for Gabba's convivial wit see Quintilian *I.O.* 6.3.27, 6.3.90. For the parasite as an unreliable witness, cf. the exchange at Plaut. *Capt.* 890–98, where Hegio distrusts the good news brought to him by the parasite Ergasilus.

15. Cf. 108, 134. Note the emphasis in all these places on the relative degrees of the "friends": amicitiae *magnae* (14), *modicis . . .* amicis (108), *quantus . . .* amicus (134). It is no accident, I think, that when *amicus* appears for the final time in both poem and book it is paired with an adjective of quality, not quantity: his epulis et *tali* dignus amico (*Sat.* 5.173).

The addressee's "great friend" is drawn into the comic sphere, too: he is the parasite's alter ego, his *rex* (14).

This *rex* is as uninterested in being a real patron to his *cliens* as the *cliens* of lines 1–11 (whose sole objective is a meal) is in being a real *cliens* to his patron.

> The *rex* reckons up the cost of the food; even if he doesn't play the host very often, still he calculates the cost. Suppose he wants to invite his *cliens*—two months have gone by since he last remembered his existence, and anyway he doesn't want the third cushion to be wasted, the couch empty. "Why don't you join me?" he says. What more could one want? Now Trebius has that for which he cuts short his dreams and hurries out without taking time to fasten up his sandals, in case the whole crowd of morning visitors completes its round while you can still just about see the stars and the chilly Wain of slow-to-set Bootes.[16]

Trebius (as we finally discover the addressee to be named) trades morning calls for dinners. The "relationship" between patron and *cliens* has been reduced to a minimal sort of exchange, the sort of thing that we saw satirized in some of Martial's epigrams, only a small step away from a commercial connection.[17]

There is nothing particularly Greek about the parasite at Virro's dinner table in *Satire* 5. His nomen, Trebius, is a perfectly good Roman one. In line 127 Trebius reaches for the bread baskets "as if he were a citizen" (*tamquam habeas tria nomina*), which might suggest that he did not have

---

16. inputat hunc rex,
    et quamuis rarum tamen imputat. ergo duos post
    si libuit menses neglectum adhibere clientem,
    tertia ne uacuo cessaret culcita lecto,
    'una simus' ait. uotorum summa. quid ultra
    quaeris? habet Trebius propter quod rumpere somnum
    debeat et ligulas dimittere, sollicitus ne
    tota salutatrix iam turba peregerit orbem
    sideribus dubiis aut illo tempore quo se
    frigida circumagunt pigri serraca Bootae.
    (*Sat.* 5.14–23)
For Trebius' objective see 166: spes bene cenandi uos decipit.

17. See lines 76–79 for more morning calls—despite the grand sound of *vetera officia* (13), attendance at the *salutatio* is the only *officium* mentioned in the poem.

Roman citizenship. But perhaps the joke is that Trebius does have the citizenship that the *tria nomina* are a mark of but is not allowed by his domineering *rex* (or by his own obsequiousness) to behave accordingly.[18] Trebius is not as invidiously successful as Umbricius' Greeklings either, which is perhaps another of the satirist's corrections. At the meal to which Trebius is invited (*votorum summa!*), wealthy guests and poor ones are served different dishes, which is humiliating, but poor food is the least distressing facet of the evening. There are fights in which Trebius can expect to be bloodied (*iurgia*, 26), and there are suspicious, supercilious, downright insulting slaves to put up with, too (40–41, 59–65, 74–75).

That Trebius does put up with them is due to his poverty: "There are a great many things one daren't say when one wears a worn-out cloak" (*plurima sunt quae / non audent homines pertusa dicere laena*, 130–31). One simply keeps quiet at dinner, with one's bread at the ready (*stricto pane quietus*, 169). To illustrate the power of money in this relationship, the satirist sketches a fantasy in which Trebius has acquired the four hundred thousand sesterces that would raise him to equestrian status. Automatically Virro's intimate friend (*amicus*, 134; *frater*, 135, 137), Trebius can aspire to the status of *dominus*, at least, and even, if his wife does not encumber him with offspring (140–42), to that of *rex* (137). Trebius' hypothetical wealth would make a *captator*-like Virro play the parasite to him, in fact. But this is only a fantasy. Trebius' real situation is such that, should he father a child, he would only provoke his patron to sneer at the "parasite child" (*parasitus infans*, 143). That this was the light in which Virro regarded the father as well is suggested by the poem's final paragraph, where we learn that the humiliating dinner was a comic scene that Virro staged for his own amusement.

> Perhaps you think that Virro is trying to keep the expense down? You're wrong—he's doing it to cause you pain. For what comedy, what mime, is better than a grieving belly? For your information, everything that happens here is meant to wring tears of vexation from you, to make you grate and grind your teeth. You think that

---

18. For the battle described in lines 26–29—a battle between Trebius and a *cohors* of freedmen—to have its full (demeaning) impact, Trebius has to be of a higher status than his opponents. Note also that what the satirist recommends in place of behavior like Virro's is "treating your guests like fellow citizens" (*solum / poscimus ut cenes civiliter*, Sat. 5.111–12).

you are a free man; he thinks you're caught by the fragrance of his kitchen. He's quite right, you know.[19]

So Virro does see his longtime *cliens* as the typical parasite of comedy, a grieving belly with a nose well up into the air to catch the smell of cooking.

When Umbricius looks from below, then, and Virro from above, both see as a parasite a *cliens* whose behavior vis-à-vis his patron is, for one reason or another, displeasing to him. Neither Umbricius nor Virro is himself a wholly estimable figure, of course: Umbricius' sneer may be credited to jealousy, Virro's to a kind of cruel arrogance that is very far from the ideal attitude of patron to client. As the final lines of the *Satire* show, however, the satirist is inclined to agree with Virro's assessment of Trebius: "The man who treats you this way has got good sense. If you can put up with anything, you deserve to put up with anything. If you will stick your smooth-shaven head out for a pummeling, if you will stand up bravely to hard blows, then you are worthy of meals like this and of this sort of friend."[20] The satirist looks at Trebius and sees someone who looks very much like the parasite in the *Persa* who boasted that he and his forebears owed their ability to feed themselves (at someone else's expense, of course) to their hard heads (*Pers.*

---

19. forsitan inpensae Virronem parcere credas:
     hoc agit, ut doleas; nam quae comoedia, mimus
     quis melior plorante gula? ergo omnia fiunt,
     si nescis, ut per lacrimas effundere bilem
     cogaris pressoque diu stridere molari.
     tu tibi liber homo et regis conuiua uideris:
     captum te nidore suae putat ille culinae,
     nec male coniectat.

                                                      (*Sat.* 5.156–63)
Note the other comic motifs concentrated in this passage: the parasite reduced to his essential organ (*plorante gula*), the impossibility of expressing anger (*per lacrimas effundere bilem*), the term *rex*, and the shamelessness (*tu tibi liber homo . . . uideris*). These are supplemented a few lines later by the reference to physical abuse, and the picture of the *stupidus* in 171 (on which see Courtney 1980, ad loc.).

20. ille sapit, qui te sic utitur. omnia ferre
     si potes, et debes. pulsandum uertice raso
     praebebis quandoque caput nec dura timebis
     flagra pati, his epulis et tali dignus amico.

                                                      (*Sat.* 5.170–73)

57–60). Hardly model client behavior, Trebius' supineness brings out the worst in Virro. And Virro's worst is something that the satirist shows himself to have an interest in discouraging.

> I'd like to say a few words to Virro himself, if he'll lend me a tolerant ear. No one asks you to give out the sort of things that Seneca, say, that worthy Piso, or Cotta gave to the friends they had in the middling rank. For in those days the glory of giving was greater than the glory that came with honors and command. All we ask is that you be a civil host at dinner [literally, "that you act like our fellow citizen," *civis* (and, by implication, not like a *rex*)].[21]

The satirist gives his assent to Virro's description of Trebius as a parasite because it suits him to make Virro look like a *rex*. The worse the picture of the relationship between patron and client is, the stronger is his case for replacing it with something more to his taste. The speaker of *Satire* 5 has improved on (i.e., made uglier) the picture that was drawn in *Satire* 1, by bringing the solitary self-indulgent patron and the needy self-abasing *cliens* into the dining room together while keeping their relationship as cold and calculating as ever. In *Satire* 9 he will go one step further, putting patron and parasite into the same bed.

Satire 9 opens with a catalog of the visible manifestations of the misery of the addressee, one Naevolus ("Warty").

> I should like to know, Naevolus, why so many times when I've bumped into you lately you've been looking as glum as a Marsyas who's about to be flayed? Why do you have the same expression as Ravola had when he was caught rubbing away at Rhodope's crotch with a wet beard? I don't imagine that Crepereius Pollio looks any more wretched than you do, though he goes around

---

21.   ipsi pauca uelim, facilem si praebeat aurem.
       nemo petit, modicis quae mittebantur amicis
       a Seneca, quae Piso bonus, quae Cotta solebat
       largiri; namque et titulis et fascibus olim
       maior habebatur donandi gloria. solum
       poscimus ut cenes ciuiliter.

                                                   (*Sat.* 5.107–12)

looking for a loan at three times the going rate and even then can't find anybody witless enough to lend to him. Where did all those wrinkles come from?[22]

Self-prompted, the satirist begins speculating about the reasons for Naevolus' misery: "It seems to me that you have changed your ways, and that your life is very different from what it was before" (*igitur flexisse uideris / propositum et uitae contrarius ire priori*, 20–21; cf. the satirist's words to Trebius at the beginning of *Satire* 5, "If you are not yet ashamed of what you've set out to do, and intend to keep on as you are . . ." quoted earlier in this chapter).

What is said about Naevolus' (former) ways? It seems that a significant portion of Naevolus' activity had been conducted at the dinner table: "I know you used to be a homegrown *eques*, content with modest means, an amusing guest (*conviva*) with a knack for biting fun, a man whose lively jokes were of the finest made-in-Rome variety."[23] Petulant wit and modest expectations combine here with the dinner-party setting and the initial echo of *Satire* 5 to suggest that Naevolus was some kind of parasite.[24] The outlines are not yet unmistakable, but we have been given a sketch to which further touches will be added.

The next thing we hear about Naevolus' manner of life is, coming after this beginning, a complete surprise.

------

22. scire uelim quare totiens mihi, Naeuole, tristis
     occurras fronte obducta ceu Marsya uictus.
     quid tibi cum uultu, qualem deprensus habebat
     Rauola dum Rhodopes uda terit inguina barba?
     non erit hac facie miserabilior Crepereius
     Pollio, qui triplicem usuram praestare paratus
     circumit et fatuos non inuenit. unde repente
     tot rugae?

                                                   (*Sat.* 9.1–9)

23. certe modico contentus agebas
     uernam equitem, conuiua ioco mordente facetus
     et salibus uehemens intra pomeria natis.

                                                   (*Sat.* 9.9–11)

24. As was seen by the author of the *titulus* to *Satire* 9 in the F group of manuscripts: LOQUITUR AD PARASITUM QUENDAM QUI SERVIERAT REGIBUS. The same view is implied by the *titulus* QUAERELA NAEVOLI DE REGE IMPUDICO, which is found in another group. See Knoche 1950 for details. The parasite model is noted, but not pursued, in Braund 1988, 170–71.

It wasn't long ago that you used to frequent the temple of Isis, the temple of Peace with its statue of Ganymede, the Palatine haunts of the Great Mother, the temple of Ceres—women make themselves available in front of every temple, don't they? A more notorious adulterer than Aufidius, you got around, and you used to have the husbands bend over for you, too, though you don't talk much about *that*.[25]

Naevolus tells us in his response (which starts just here) that in living this way he was only doing what was expected of him as a *cliens*: "What you describe is the way a lot of people make their living, but it was never worth my while. A greasy cloak, now and then, to go over my toga (and always of a harsh and clotted color, slackly woven by some weaver from Gaul)—that's what I'd get. That or a thin little bit of silver from a second-rate vein."[26] The connection between Naevolus' behavior and his client status is revealed by the form his "payment" took: clothing and plate are both standard items in the lists of goods donated to needy *clientes*.[27]

Sexual services have not heretofore appeared in the repertoire of the parasite (though the parasite-like *captator* of Horace's *Satire* 2.5 is certainly urged to offer them). Yet they are a logical extension of the *munera* that a parsimonious patron might require of a self-abasing *cliens*. In fact, it is not too much to say that *Satire* 9 as a whole presents

---

25.   nuper enim, ut repeto, fanum Isidis et Ganymedem
      Pacis et aduectae secreta Palatia matris
      et Cererem (nam quo non prostat femina templo?)
      notior Aufidio moechus celebrare solebas,
      quodque taces, ipsos etiam inclinare maritos.

      (*Sat.* 9.22–26)

26.   'utile et hoc multis uitae genus, at mihi nullum
      inde operae pretium. pingues aliquando lacernas,
      munimenta togae, duri crassique coloris
      et male percussas textoris pectine Galli
      accipimus, tenue argentum uenaeque secundae,

      (*Sat.* 9.27–31)

27. Clothing: Hor. *Sat.* 1.2.4–6, *Epist.* 1.19.38, Pers. 1.54, Martial 7.36, 8.28, 10.73, 12.36. Plate: Martial 8.33, 8.51, 8.71, 10.57, 12.36. Both were important for keeping up appearances. Cf. Juv. 3.168–70 (tableware and clothing) and 147–51 (clothing). This is the *ambitiosa* component of cliental *paupertas* (Juv. *Sat.* 3.182–83). At line 59 Naevolus asks for land, another common patronal *beneficium*.

a kind of *reductio ad absurdum* beginning where *Satire* 5 left off: the parasite metamorphoses into a gigolo while retaining (as so often in metamorphoses) significant features of his former self.

Naevolus himself draws an analogy between the iniquities of his patron and those of the *rex* of *Satire* 5, Virro.

> If the stars are against you it won't do you a bit of good to have a prick of unprecedented size, not even if a Virro sees you in the buff and starts to drool. Sure, he'll send you note after densely written note inviting you over (a pansy is naturally attracted to a man),[28] but what could be worse than a cheapskate fruit?[29]

Virro's calculating ways are to be found in the patron of whom Naevolus complains, too: "He counts up how much [sc. he has given you] and wants to get laid" (*computat et ceuet*, 40). Naevolus clearly has much in common with the parasitical Trebius of *Satire* 5, so it is not surprising that he is offered the remains of "yesterday's dinner" (*hesternae . . . cenae*), though in a state even less appealing than that hoped for by comic parasites: (*an facile et pronum est agere intra uiscera penem / legitimum atque illic hesternae occurrere cenae?* 43–44). And where Trebius had *officia* (*Sat.* 5.13), Naevolus is worse off with *labores* (*Sat.* 9.42). He is a humble, helpful hanger-on (*humili adseculae . . . cultori*, 48–49), on call for both his patron and his patron's wife, it seems: "If your wife is no longer a virgin, it's only because I was a devoted, dedicated *cliens*. Don't you think you owe me something for that?" (*quanto / metiris pretio quod, ni tibi deditus essem / deuotusque cliens, uxor tua uirgo maneret?* 70–72). It is no wonder that the man puts in a claim for a bit of land on which to rest his worn-out loins (59–60). And in *Satire* 9, as in *Satire* 5, the sugar coating of *amicitia*—the satirist labels the man who supports Naevolus a friend (*amicus*, 130)—is supposed to make the realities of his relationship with his host easier to swallow.

---

28. Juvenal plays on a tag from the Odyssey (αὐτὸς γὰρ ἐφέλκεται ἄνδρα σίδηρος, *Od.* 16.294, 19.13; see Courtney 1980, ad loc.).

29. nam si tibi sidera cessant,
     nil faciet longi mensura incognita nerui,
     quamuis te nudum spumanti Virro labello
     uiderit et blandae adsidue densaeque tabellae
     sollicitent, αὐτὸς γὰρ ἐφέλκεται ἄνδρα κίναιδος.
     quod tamen ulterius monstrum quam mollis auarus?

                                                    (*Sat.* 9.33–38)

The connection between parasite and gigolo is neatly summed up near the end of the poem: "I'm doing well if my prick gets my belly enough to eat."[30] This aspiration sounds modest enough, but Naevolus is no more sympathetic a figure than Trebius was. When he comes to list his requirements more precisely, it turns out that he wants an income of twenty thousand sesterces from his loans (well-secured ones), silver vessels of good quality (ten pounds worth at least), two big brutes from across the Danube to carry his sedan chair around town, a slave who knows how to do silver chasing, and another who paints (140–47; cf. 64–69, where he contemplates increasing the size of his domestic establishment). It is clear that he is by no means "content with modest means" (*modico contentus*, 9). His greed, acting together with the parsimony of his rich patron, produces the metamorphosis for the worse that the poem describes.

We have seen that the parasite was quite useful to Juvenal as a carica-ture of many aspects of the contemporary patron/client relationship. It is thus something of a surprise to find scarcely a hint of his presence in the one remaining satire in which patronage is a central theme.

In *Satire* 7 Juvenal takes up one of Martial's favorite questions, namely, how literary types (poets and others) support themselves. The picture Juvenal paints is considerably darker than Martial's: so nig-gardly are potential patrons these days, says Juvenal, that writers' only hope of support lay in patronage from Caesar (*et spes et ratio studiorum in Caesare tantum*, 1). But "Caesar" (probably Hadrian) had just come into power, and his patronage is only something to look forward to in the future: "hereafter no one will have to suffer treatment unworthy of his talents, no one, that is, who weaves melodious words with tuneful measures and chews the inspiration-making laurel."[31] In the past, how-ever, writers had had to look to lesser men for patronage, and the bulk of *Satire* 7 is a diatribe on their sufferings at the hands of the miserly rich (*dives avarus*, 30). The wealthy misers of *Satire* 7 are not, however,

---

30. at mea Clotho / et Lachesis gaudent, si pascitur inguine uenter (*Sat.* 9.136). Martial made the connection, too: ad cenam inuitant omnes te, Phoebe, cinaedi. / mentula quem pascit, non, puto, purus homo est (9.63, cf. 9.80).

31. nemo tamen studiis indignum ferre laborem / cogetur posthac, nectit quicumque canoris / eloquium uocale modis laurumque momordit (*Sat.* 7.17–19).

like Virro. For the literary types in this poem do not experience patronage based on familiar contacts or even a painful debasement of a relationship like this; rather, theirs is a hand-to-mouth existence based, for the most part, on cash transactions. The poem is full of references to money as the poet's aim: there is not a penny in the Pierian shade (8–9; cf. 59–61); you need money to buy yourself furniture (45–47), blankets (66–67), and food (87, 174–75); the play *Atreus* was sold for dishes and a cloak (73); Quintilian's fee was paid in cash (186–87; cf. 216, 218); and so on.[32] There is nothing here about dining with a patron or doing any of the cliental *munera* that came up so often in Martial's epigrams about the miseries of being a dependent poet.[33]

In fact, early on in the poem a poet is urged to refuse to provide one service of the sort that a patron might expect from a *cliens*, namely, serving as false witness at a trial.

> If there is not a penny to be seen in your Pierian shade, . . . you will sell everything that can be sold in the heat of an auction to the people who hang around them, your wine jug, your tripods, your bookcases and baskets, the *Alcithoe* of Paccius, the *Thebes* and *Tereus* of Faustus. Far better this than saying to the judge, "I saw it," when you didn't see it.[34]

---

32. *Quadrans* (8), *indulgentia* (21; cf. Tac. *Dial.* 9 for the equation of *indulgentia* and a cash award), *quanti* subsellia constant . . . (45–47), maesta paupertas atque aeris inops (60–61), mentis . . . de lodice *paranda* attonitae (66–67), Rubrenus Lappa . . . cuius et alueolos et laenam *pignerat* Atreus (73), esurit [sc. Statius], intactam Paridi nisi *uendit* Agauen (87), *summula* ne pereat qua uilis tessera *uenit* / frumenti (174–75), hos inter sumptus *sestertia* Quintiliano, / ut multum, *duo* sufficient (186–87), *quantum* grammaticus meruit labor (216), *merces* (228), etc.

33. Including a poem (*Ep.* 12.18) in which Martial says that Juvenal himself is sweating up and down the hills of Rome in a toga and standing on the thresholds of the houses of powerful men (*limina . . . potentiorum*, 4).

34. nam si Pieria quadrans tibi nullus in umbra
ostendatur, ames nomen uictumque Machaerae
et uendas potius commissa quod auctio uendi
stantibus, oenophorum, tripedes, armaria, cistas,
Alcithoen Pacci, Thebas et Terea Fausti.
hoc satius quam si dicas sub iudice 'uidi'
quod non uidisti.

(*Sat.* 7.8–14)

The satirist recommends leaving this sort of service to Umbricius' foes, the newly wealthy arrivals from the East (*equites Asiani*, 14), and to people who have been slaves (16). It was a service that Umbricius himself would have stooped to, if only he had had the proper credentials for plausibility (*Sat.* 3.137–46), but the writers whose part the satirist takes in *Satire* 7 are not to lower themselves in this way.[35] Given the patrons who people the world Juvenal creates, writing for cash was perhaps less damning than performing tasks "unworthy of their talents," that is, behaving like Trebius or, even worse, like Naevolus.[36] Juvenal was not as ready as Martial was to apply the mask of the parasite to the dependent poet who spent his time and energy (and self-respect) on services for a patron.[37]

Nicholas Breton's parasite, "who for the gain of dross is devoted to all villainy" (see the epigraph to this chapter), can stand nicely as a latter-day amalgamation of Juvenal's parasites. The particular form of "dross" aimed at by Juvenal's parasites—from the hungry *clientes* of *Satire* 1, to the men Umbricius calls the "innards of great houses," to the too-tolerant Trebius and Naevolus, with his "prick of unprecedented size"—was patronal support of the most material kind, namely, food. And the villainous pursuits with which they limed their hands ranged from the fairly innocuous (if rather tedious) practice of attending on a great man, through various degrees of encouraging a patron in vicious habits, to the positively criminal activities that Umbricius ascribes to his rivals. Like his generic predecessors, Juvenal uses the figure of the parasite to caricature the *cliens*.

Satire as a genre demanded of its authors reactions to real problems of some magnitude. Flogging dead, moribund, or insignificant individuals was prudent, but tilting at nonexistent social and moral failings

---

35. Cf. *Sat.* 5.5, where it is implied that Trebius, too, would be willing to perform this particular service.

36. Cf. Martial *Ep.* 10.58.11–12: sed non solus amat qui nocte dieque frequentat / limina nec vatem talia damna decent.

37. A Juvenalian parasite who hovers between these two areas is mentioned (no more) at 14.45–46 as someone a concerned parent ought to keep away from his children: procul, a procul inde puellae / lenonum et cantus pernoctantis parasiti. For his pursuits see Lucian *Merc. Cond.* 27 on resident intellectuals as reciters of ἐρωτικὰ ᾄσματα.

would have been absurd.[38] Satire does not provide sober and objective documentary of contemporary problems; attack, rather, is the mode, and pleasure and instruction the twin goals. So the prominence of parasites in the poems we have been considering in part 2 of this book is evidence not so much of the presence of men like Saturio and Curculio at the tables of wealthy Romans as of the fact that the type, with all his comic *apparatus* and his long history of abuse, could serve as a caricature in attacks on real social conditions. Juvenal was the first satirist to really problematize the use of the caricature. Horace constructed defenses against its application to himself, but his response is specific to his own case, not an all-purpose argument about the use of the caricature. By putting the caricaturists Umbricius and Virro into his poems alongside the caricatured *clientes*, Juvenal allows us to see that *parasitus* is a caricature, not an objective description of reality. As we have seen, Umbricius and Virro reveal as much about themselves as about the parasites they sneer at. Roman clients only look like parasites to those (like the jealous Umbricius and the miserly Virro) who are irritated by the way patronage works when it impinges on them. In chapter 7 we will see how Cicero exploits these irritations to the detriment of his clients' opponents in his forensic speeches.

---

38. The bibliography on realism in Roman satire is extensive and includes Levi 1955, 170–80; Marache 1961; Highet 1974; Gérard 1976; Bardon 1977; and, most recently, Marache 1989. But little or nothing is said about parasites in these works.

Part 3: Oratory

7

Parasites in the Speeches of Cicero

Chaque société donne cours à une monnaie langagière qu'on peut
échanger avantageusement pour l'estomac.
— Michel Serres *Le Parasite*

"It is my opinion," says Cicero, "that the characters of comedy were developed by the poets to make us see our own ways reproduced in others and to show us a picture of our daily life."[1] With these words Cicero defends a rhetorical strategy he has just employed in his speech on behalf of Sextus Roscius, that of drawing an analogy between a comic type, an *adulescens comicus*, and someone present in the court-room, in this case his own client, Roscius. Cicero's statement about the compositional practices of comic poets may or may not be true, but it is certainly true to say that he himself often used a ready-made type from comedy or tragedy to create a picture of contemporary life that served his own argument. In the *pro Caelio*, for example, he labels Clodia "a Palatine Medea" (among other things, 18) and depicts Caelius as another sympathetic comic *adulescens*, "addressed," in turn, by stern and accommodating fathers modeled on characters from Caecilius Statius and Terence (37–38).[2] The parasite was one of the characters Cicero found it useful to evoke, and he did so both quickly, as when he "renamed" one of Antony's associates—"Let's call him Phormio, or Gnatho, or even Ballio" (*Phil.* 2.15)—and in more detail, as in the speeches that we will consider in this chapter: the speeches on behalf of

---

1. Etenim haec conficta arbitror esse a poetis ut effictos nostros mores in alienis personis expressamque imaginem vitae cotidianae videremus (*pro Sex. Rosc.* 47). *Haec* is rendered with "the characters of comedy" because this sentence follows immediately on Cicero's justification for basing his argument here on a character, an *adulescens comicus*, rather than on a real contemporary: homines notos sumere odiosum est, cum et illud incertum sit velintne ei sese nominari, et nemo vobis magis notus futurus sit quam est hic Eutychus, et certe ad rem nihil intersit utrum hunc ego comicum adulescentem an aliquem ex agro Veienti nominem (47).

2. For the *pro Caelio* see Geffcken 1973; on Sextus Roscius see Vasaly 1993, 156–72.

Publius Quinctius and Aulus Caecina and the attacks on Gaius Verres and Lucius Piso.

We begin with Cicero's earliest extant speech, the *pro Quinctio*. The disputants in the case are P. Quinctius and Sex. Naevius. The connection between the two goes back some years before the trial. Naevius and the brother of Cicero's client, C. Quinctius, had been partners in the ownership and management of some property in Gaul. When the brother died, the partnership necessarily dissolved. Cicero's client, heir to his brother's estate, went out to Gaul, ostensibly to settle the affairs of the partnership. But he stayed there for a year, running the property with Naevius. At some point Naevius married into the family. But when the affairs of the first partnership were still entangled some two years after the death of C. Quinctius, Naevius seized some property of Gaius' heir, Publius. When the case reached a youthful Cicero (the date was 81 B.C.), Quinctius was trying to avoid the consequences, to both his reputation and his finances, of this action. By all accounts, he had very little on which to base his case.[3]

To make the best of a bad case against Naevius, Cicero had to enlist the sympathy of the judge for his client and prejudice him against their opponent. The picture he gives of Naevius' past life is one of several devices he used to this end.[4] It begins at the opening of the *narratio*.

> Naevius is a fine man, but his upbringing left him unacquainted with the rules of partnership and with the responsibilities of a real head of household. I'm not saying that he lacked talent, for no one ever judged Naevius an insufficiently clever wit [*scurra*] or a boorish crier [*praeco*]. What is it, then? Only that he put the best thing that nature had given him, his voice, out to work and used the one thing his father had left him, his freeborn status, to play the wit without fear of reprisal.[5]

---

3. For the difficulty of Quinctius' position see Long 1851–58, 2:1–8, and Kinsey 1971, 3–5.

4. For further discussion see May 1988, 14–21, and Hinard 1975.

5. uiro bono uerum tamen non ita instituto ut iura societatis et officia certi patris familias nosse posset. Non quo ei deesset ingenium; nam neque parum facetus scurra Sex. Naeuius neque inhumanus praeco umquam est existimatus. Quid ergo est? Cum ei natura nihil melius quam uocem dedisset, pater nihil praeter libertatem reliquisset, uocem in quaestum contulit, libertate usus est quo impunius dicax esset (*Quinct.* 11; the text is from Reeve 1992).

Naevius, it seems, had the advantage of free birth but had no liberal education, no paternal example to follow, and no other resource than his supple voice. Marketing this resource (note *venalis*, 13), he became a *praeco*, an auction crier.[6]

The *praeco*'s profession, what with the fees he charged and the tips he earned from grateful sellers whose wares needed a vigorous and none-too-scrupulous salesman, was profitable.[7] Gallonius, a *praeco* who featured in Lucilius' satires, is mentioned by both Cicero and Horace as a byword for extravagance (*sumptus*).[8] Another wealthy *praeco* in Lucilius was the witty Q. Granius, who played host to a senator.[9] And we hear of still other *praecones* who fathered men who met the equestrian property qualification.[10] Naevius, like the upstart *praecones* whom Lucilius mocks, was able to put together some capital in the auction halls. However, the profession was a hindrance to social aspirations. The disqualifications that the *praeco* shared with the personnel of funerals in the *lex Iulia municipalis*, for example—both groups were prohibited from seeking and holding municipal office as long as they were exercising their profession (Bruns 18.94–96)—may serve as small indicators of a far more widespread contempt for *praecones*.

One strike against Naevius, then, was his former profession. But closely tied to this in the passage just quoted is his wit, the characteristic that earned him the label *scurra*. Damning him with faint praise, Cicero concedes that no one ever judged Naevius "an insufficiently clever wit" (*parum facetus scurra*, 11). Cicero goes on with more of the picture.

---

6. On the profession see Rauh 1989 and Hinard 1976.

7. For attempts to regulate the *praeco*'s fee scale see Schneider 1953, col. 1199. For false guarantees made by a *praeco* on behalf of a seller see Cic. *Quinct.* 19, quod promisisset, non plus sua referre quam si, cum auctionem uenderet, domini iussu quippiam promisisset.

8. Lucil. 1134–35 and 1238–49 Marx, Cic. *Fin.* 2.24–25, 90, Hor. *Sat.* 2.2.46.

9. Lucil. 411–12, 1181–82 Marx, Cic. *Brut.* 160, *de Or.* 2.244, 2.254, 2.281–82, *Planc.* 33, *Fam.* 9.15.2. On Granius' status see Nicolet 1974, 2:905–6.

10. The equestrian L. Aelius Praeconinus Stilo was the son of a *praeco* (Suet. *Gram.* 3), the consular L. Piso the grandson of another (if we may believe Cicero's insults at *Pis.* fr. ix and 62). A very prosperous *praeco* of imperial date, Arruntius Euarestus, is mentioned by Josephus (*Ant. Iud.* 19.145). The Horatian *praeco* Volteius Mena (*Epist.* 1.7) achieved only a comfortable sufficiency (58), but then he was unusual in not being driven by *amor habendi* (85; cf. 57). When Petronius' character Echion intends to find his son a profitable profession (i.e., one that *habet panem*), the options he thinks of are *tonsor*, *praeco*, and *causidicus* (Petron. *Sat.* 46.7; cf. Martial 5.56.11–12 and 6.8).

As a potential partner he had nothing to recommend him, unless you wanted him to use your money to learn the benefits of having money to spend. Nevertheless, C. Quinctius, moved by his acquaintance with the man and his friendly feeling for him, made Naevius his partner in some property he was buying in Gaul, a substantial pastureage and a well-managed and productive farm. Plucked up from the Atria Licinia and the company of his fellow criers, Naevius is transferred to Gaul, right across the Alps.[11]

The crucial event in Naevius' career (as it pertains to this case anyway) was the invitation from C. Quinctius to join in a partnership. What prompted the invitation? Quinctius was apparently "moved by his acquaintance with the man and his friendly feeling for him" (*inductus consuetudine ac familiaritate,* 12). Naevius' qualifications (if any) as a property manager are unlikely to have been of interest to someone who, at least in Cicero's depiction of him, was not a particularly responsible manager himself, and who left behind a considerable debt when he died (15, 17, 73, 75, 76).

Achieving a position of *consuetudo* and *familiaritas* with C. Quinctius, then, was the basis of Naevius' success. How he achieved this intimacy becomes clear as the speech proceeds, and it is stated most explicitly in the peroration, where Cicero offers a tongue-in-cheek picture of P. Quinctius admitting his disadvantages vis-à-vis Naevius.

P. Quinctius doesn't try to compete with you in influence, or wealth, or resources. He has none of those talents that made you great—he confesses that he is no wit, that he can't trim his talk to the pleasure of his interlocutor, that he doesn't abandon a friend in trouble while hurrying to ally himself with a more prosperous one.[12]

---

11. Quare quod socium tibi eum uelles adiungere nihil erat nisi ut in tua pecunia condisceret qui pecuniae fructus esset. Tamen inductus consuetudine ac familiaritate Quinctius fecit ut dixi societatem earum rerum quae in Gallia comparabantur. Erat ei pecuaria res ampla et rustica sane bene culta et fructuosa. Tollitur ab atriis Liciniis atque a praeconum consessu in Galliam Naeuius et trans Alpis usque transfertur (*Quinct.* 12).

12. Non comparat se tecum gratia P. Quinctius, Sex. Naeui; non opibus, non facultate contendit. Omnes tuas artes quibus tu magnus es tibi concedit. Fatetur se non belle dicere, non ad uoluntatem loqui posse, non ab afflicta amicitia transfugere atque ad florentem aliam deuolare (*Quinct.* 93).

Quinctius' résumé of the talents that made Naevius great includes not only the *scurra*'s wit (*belle dicere*) but also obsequiousness (*ad voluntatem loqui*) and attention to a "friend's" property and financial stability (cf. *rem parasiti ac ditias*, Lucil. 717 Marx).[13] As befits their placement at the end of the speech (and immediately after Cicero's plea that the judge Aquilius give special consideration to the "personal histories" [*vitae rationes*] of the men before him in making his ruling, 92), each of these items is a reprise. Wit, the common denominator of all *scurrae*, was, as we have seen, prominent from the outset. Naevius' imitative ability was mentioned shortly thereafter, in section 16, where he was said to be "aping the speech of honorable men" and shown to be doing so insincerely: "Quinctius believed that the man who aped the speech of honorable men would also ape their deeds" (*credidit Quinctius eum qui orationem bonorum imitaretur facta quoque imitaturum*). Quinctius was wrong, of course, and suffered for his credulity when Naevius reneged on his offer to loan him the money with which to satisfy some creditors.

The emptiness of the various "friendships" in which Cicero shows Naevius involved is a more prominent theme, for Naevius—as Cicero tells the story—betrays each successive friend and patron. To begin with, Cicero alleges that Naevius defrauded his first partner, C. Quinctius.

> Of the partnership's property he took whatever he could into his own house. He was very diligent about this, as if he thought that the courts tended to rule against those who managed a partnership in good faith. . . . The partnership ran for some years. Quinctius had a number of suspicions about Naevius' management, and Naevius couldn't render a satisfactory account of the affairs he had been running with reference to his desires, not any rational policy. At this point Quinctius died in Gaul. Naevius was there, and Quinctius died suddenly.[14]

---

13. For *ad voluntatem loqui* see Cic. *Parad.* 39, where it is predicated of an inheritance-hunter: hereditatis spes quid iniquitatis in serviendo non suscipit? quem nutum locupletis orbi senis non observat? loquitur ad voluntatem; quicquid denuntiatumst facit; assectatur assidet muneratur. I have already noted the similarity of the techniques used by parasite and *captator* (see chap. 4).

14. Itaque hercule haud mediocriter de communi quodcumque poterat ad se in priuatam domum seuocabat; qua in re ita diligens erat quasi ei qui magna fide societatem gererent arbitrium pro socio condemnari solerent. . . . Cum annos iam compluris societas esset et cum saepe suspectus Quinctio Naeuius

Here we see not only fraud but also a hint of the inevitable accession of crime involved in covering up fraud: the juxtaposition of Quinctius' suspicions about Naevius' managerial policies and Quinctius' sudden death is no doubt meant to suggest that there was a causal connection (involving Naevius) between the two. Earlier we saw Naevius' failure to provide a promised loan to P. Quinctius, who was not only a friend and business partner but also an in-law. Cicero later gives Naevius' perfidy (*perfidia Sex. Naevi*, 75; cf. 94) a contemporary relevance by contrasting Naevius' opportunism with the loyalty of Quinctius' friend and agent Sex. Alfenus, who had used his connections to help Quinctius fend off Naevius' attacks. Alfenus lost his life in the political convulsions of the late 80s.

> If Alfenus' party affiliations made him powerful, Naevius' made him far more powerful. If Alfenus used his influence to ask for something unfair, Naevius used his to procure something far more unfair. I don't believe there was any difference in your enthusiasm for the cause, but you surpassed him in displaying it, thanks to your nature [*ingenio*] and your long-standing expertise [*artificio*]. I need only say this: whereas Alfenus perished by the side and on behalf of his friends, you, when your friends were unable to win, made friends with those who were winning.[15]

Opportunistic friendship was particularly common but also particularly reprehensible in a period of civil strife when the stakes were so

fuisset neque ita commode posset rationem reddere earum rerum quas libidine, non ratione gesserat, moritur in Gallia Quinctius, cum adesset Naeuius, et moritur repentino (*Quinct.* 13–14).

It sounds as though Naevius served as property manager (Naevius is running the show at 23 [*res gesserat*], and in section 38 we learn that some of the business was conducted by letter). The reference to Quinctius' growing suspicions about Naevius' managerial behavior suggests that Quinctius was not involved in the day-to-day business of running the property (14). On the mechanics of *societates* see Badian 1983, 67–76.

15. si propter partium studium potens erat Alfenus, potentissimus Naeuius; si fretus gratia postulabat aliquid iniquius Alfenus, multo iniquiora Naeuius impetrabat. Neque enim inter studium uestrum quicquam ut opinor interfuit: ingenio, uetustate, artificio tu facile uicisti. Ut alia omittam, hoc satis est: Alfenus cum eis et propter eos periit quos diligebat, tu postquam qui tibi erant amici non poterant uincere, ut amici tibi essent qui uincebant effecisti (*Quinct.* 70).

very high. Unlike the loyal Alfenus, Naevius succeeded in negotiating this troubled decade, thanks to his nature (*ingenium*), which was capable of persuasive simulation of enthusiasm for a cause, and to his professional approach to deploying it (*artificium*). These same strategies, writ small, would have been useful to him in procuring *consuetudo* and *familiaritas* with the prodigal C. Quinctius.

The sum of these traits would seem to go considerably beyond the labels *scurra* and *praeco* that Cicero applied to Naevius at the outset. It was not enough, it seems, to call Naevius a wit and an aggressive salesman. The disreputable facets of Naevius' "personal history" are revealed much more thoroughly via his relationships with those who helped him rise to his present position of strength. And for this Cicero used behaviors that, at the very least, mirror those of the successful parasites of comedy. That in so doing Cicero intended to evoke the comic type, to graft his traits onto those of the *scurra*, is harder to prove, but several items can be adduced to support such a claim.

To begin with, the world of drama would have been more easily evoked in the court in which Quinctius' case was heard than in most others, since Quinctius' most prominent backer, indeed the man who persuaded Cicero to speak on Quinctius' behalf, was Q. Roscius, an actor admired and respected by some of the leading men of his day (77). Among his admirers was the current consul and dictator, Sulla himself. Roscius had played in both tragedy and comedy—more successfully in the latter, it appears. And if one may believe a story told by the fourth-century grammarian Diomedes, Roscius' facial structure was particularly suited to the portrayal of parasites (1.489 Keil). Whatever one's verdict on this last point, in this speech, as in the festival-scheduled *pro Caelio*, circumstances fostered the evocation of the dramatic. And Cicero gives circumstances a nudge when he professes his reluctance to "act" (*agere*) in the presence of so great an actor as Roscius.

The comic potential established by Roscius' presence is focused on Naevius when Cicero applies to him language specifically associated with the parasites of comedy. The clearest instance of this is his reference to Naevius' pursuit of leftovers, *reliquiae*. At one point in this protracted dispute, Naevius seized some of Quinctius' property, an act Cicero likens to a funeral, "if you can call it a funeral when you have not friends coming to pay their respects but buyers who come like butchers to cut up and drag off the mortal remains [*reliquias vitae*]"

(50).[16] The "leftovers" that Naevius has in view are metaphorical left-overs, of course—it is property he wants, not food—but the phrase is striking. Not surprisingly, the notion of leftovers does not feature in other passages concerning the butchery of mortal remains, but we have seen a similarly gruesome combination of ideas in Petronius' description of the parasite-like inheritance-hunters who are to consume the corpse of their benefactor (*Sat.* 141).

Another metaphor reminiscent of the parasites of comedy lies in the verb that Cicero has Alfenus use of Naevius' plan for putting legal pressure on Quinctius. Alfenus, as Cicero tells the story, had argued that equity demanded that Naevius wait for Quinctius to return to Rome before proceeding, but he had said that he would represent Quinctius in court "if he [sc. Naevius] is unwilling to do this and has gulped down [*imbiberit*] the idea of forcing Quinctius to accept his terms."[17] "Gulped down" is used only rarely in this metaphorical sense (there are three other examples in *TLL* s.v.), but it conveys well the avidity that Cicero wishes to evoke in characterizing Naevius' action. The metaphorical use of the vocabulary of consumption was easy apropos of comic parasites, as we have seen.

A further item that Cicero takes from the parasite's bag of traits to apply to Naevius is unreliability as a witness. This appears in a throw-away line that Cicero addresses to Naevius when he professes to cite Naevius' evidence against himself: "Your evidence, though it would be insignificant [*leve*] if it pertained to anybody else's case, ought to be quite weighty when it pertains to your own case, since it is unfavorable to you."[18] To say he plans to convict Naevius out of his own mouth is bad enough, but the added slight, which sets Naevius on a par with the parasites who sought to make themselves useful (and welcome) by giving false evidence on their patron's behalf, makes the insult even worse.

---

16. si funus id habendum est quo non amici conueniunt ad exsequias cohonestandas sed bonorum emptores ut carnifices ad reliquias uitae lacerandas et distrahendas (*Quinct.* 50).

17. denuntiat sese procuratorem esse; istum aequum esse famae fortunisque P. Quincti consulere et aduentum eius exspectare; quod si facere nolit atque imbiberit eius modi rationibus illum ad suas condiciones perducere, sese nihil precari et si quid agere uelit paratum esse iudicio defendere (*Quinct.* 27).

18. Opinor tuum testimonium quod in aliena re leue esset, id in tua quoniam contra te est grauissimum debet esse (*Quinct.* 76).

In portraying Naevius' past life, then, Cicero supplements the labels *scurra* and *praeco* with information about Naevius' behavior vis-à-vis those who helped him get ahead and with a few small details evoking parasitical hunger and unreliability. We saw in chapter 4 that Horace, too, has parasitical *scurrae* and that the merging of the two types might have been a Lucilian innovation. The presence of parasite traits in a character labeled *scurra* in Cicero's *pro Quinctio* lends some support to that possibility, particularly since Cicero borrows heavily from Lucilius in this speech. For to aid him in his task of creating an objectionable character for Sex. Naevius, Cicero brought in—in addition to the *scurra*—two other figures familiar from the pages of Lucilius.

Gallonius, the ex-*praeco* who became a byword for extravagance, is the clearest of these. Gallonius was notorious for spending much (too much) on the fish course: "O Publius, O gut of Gallonius, unhappy man. You've never in your life dined well, though you spend your all on that prawn and on a prize sturgeon."[19] The *scurra* is the model for Naevius' younger self, but Naevius' present self, rich and well connected, is like this profligate Gallonius, at least in his wealth and wastefulness. His character, however, was worse: Naevius is one of "those who have turned their backs on virtue, who chose to follow Gallonius in making money and spending it, but who have gone beyond him in presumption and treachery."[20] Naevius' extravagance is detailed in Quinctius' review of the differences between himself and Naevius: "He [sc. Quinctius] doesn't live extravagantly, doesn't host lavish and showy parties, doesn't close his house to modesty and purity or leave the door open for greed and pleasures."[21] Naevius is the one charged with all these faults, and they are no more than one might expect from a *scurra* who finds himself possessed of wealth. For Cicero makes the

---

19. 'O Publi, o gurges Galloni, es homo miser,' inquit. / 'cenasti in uita numquam bene, cum omnia in ista consumis squilla atque acupensere cum decimano' (Lucil. 1238–40 Marx).

20. Ista superiora esse ac plurimum posse his moribus sentit. Quid ergo est?—non usque eo tamen ut in capite fortunisque hominum honestissimorum dominentur ei qui relicta uirorum bonorum disciplina et quaestum et sumptum Galloni sequi maluerunt atque etiam, quod in illo non fuit, cum audacia perfidiaque uixerunt (*Quinct.* 93–94).

21. non profusis sumptibus uiuere, non ornare magnifice splendideque conuiuium, non habere domum clausam pudori et sanctimoniae, patentem atque adeo expositam cupiditati et uoluptatibus (*Quinct.* 93).

connection between *scurra* and wastrel clear in a little monologue that he produces for Naevius in section 55.

> You can be sure that Naevius is amused by our foolishness in wanting from him an account of proper consideration for his connections and in looking for the policies of virtuous men in his life. "What," he asks, "do virtue and attention to duty have to do with me? Good men may feel that sort of behavior incumbent on them, but they ought to think differently about me. Not what I have now, but how I acquired it—that's what they ought to consider; *I* remember my birth and upbringing. It's an old saying that 'a *scurra* will sooner become rich than responsible.'"[22]

The Gallonius-like Naevius remains a *scurra* at heart, squandering his newfound wealth, a living confirmation of the truth of the old saying that it is easier for a *scurra* to become rich than responsible. And in section 40 Cicero likens Naevius to yet another Lucilian character, one who has been hiding, unnoticed hitherto, in the text of the *pro Quinctio*.

In section 40 Cicero insists that Quinctius' alleged debt to Naevius was a fiction, arguing that if money had been owed to him, the grasping Naevius would never have waited the two years that he did wait to make his claim. The "proof" of this proposition lies in Naevius' character. A delay in demanding payment would have been the act of a carefree spendthrift, but "would even the most thoroughly profligate wastrel, a spendthrift with plenty of cash still on hand, have been as remiss as was Sex. Naevius?"[23] Next Cicero says, "in saying his name, I think I make myself clear."[24] What is self-evident in Naevius' name?

---

22. Ridet scilicet nostram amentiam, qui in uita sua rationem summi offici desideremus et instituta uirorum bonorum requiramus. 'Quid mihi' inquit 'cum ista summa sanctimonia ac diligentia? Viderint' inquit 'ista officia uiri boni. De me autem ita considerent: non quid habeam sed quibus rebus inuenerim quaerant. Et quem ad modum natus et quo pacto educatus sim memini. Vetus est 'de scurra multo facilius diuitem quam patrem familias fieri posse' (*Quinct.* 55; cf. *neque . . . posset rationem reddere earum rerum quas libidine, non ratione, gesserat*, 14).

23. Quis tam perditus ac profusus nepos non adesa etiam pecunia sed abundanti sic dissolutus fuisset ut fuit Sex. Naeuius? (*Quinct.* 40).

24. Literally, "With his name, I seem to me to say enough" (*cum hominem nomino, satis mihi uideor dicere*, *Quinct.* 40).

Warts (*naevus* means "wart, blemish") are irrelevant to the context, so it is not an etymological joke. Rather, it is an allusion to a prior Naevius, one made famous by Lucilius. Horace cited Lucilius' Naevius as the type of miserliness: a decent man will be neither excessively harsh to his slaves, like old Albucius, says Ofellus in *Satire* 2.2, "nor imitate the unabashed cheapness of Naevius and welcome his guests with greasy water."[25] When Cicero names Naevius, then, he answers his own rhetorical question: no one named Naevius could have been as unconcerned about a debt as (our) Naevius would like to make us believe he was; therefore he is lying.

Naevius is like a Lucilian spendthrift, then, and like a Lucilian miser, and even more thoroughly like the *scurra* that Lucilius seems to have modeled on the comic parasite. These types are in effect a kind of shorthand. For Cicero's audience, the name or the label itself would evoke the appropriate context. In the case of the parasitical Lucilian *scurra*, the context explained, in a suitably negative way, the partnership that lay at the bottom of the whole case.[26] We cannot know the real reason why C. Quinctius took Naevius into partnership or why influential men in the year 81 considered him worth defending in a fairly lengthy process, but we can see that Cicero was willing to lay a substantial stake (his own nascent reputation as a speaker [96] and Quinctius' financial well-being and honor [6 and passim]) on the proposition that a witty, ingratiating type who betrayed his friends as the occasion demanded would be a plausible villain. The types do not of course mesh very well together (it might have required considerable ingenuity to reconcile the spendthrift and the miser, for example), but Cicero must have felt that the advantage of economy in using these types outweighed the disadvantage of inconcinnity.[27] James May labels Cicero's use of types as

---

25. 'nec sic ut simplex Naevius unctam / convivis praebebit aquam' (Hor. *Sat.* 2.2.68–69). The connection to Lucilius is provided by Porphyry (*ad Sat.* 1.1.101: *Naevius autem fuit in tantum parcus, ut sordidus merito haberetur, ut Lucilius ait* [Lucil. 1212 Marx]). Porphyry's text of Horace clearly named Naevius in *Sat.* 1.1 as well as in *Sat.* 2.2. A defense of the emendation *Maenius* that appears in Shackleton Bailey's text of *Sat.* 1.1.101 is found in Bentley's edition, *ad* 100.

26. In view of this, Kinsey (1971, 65) cannot be justified in saying of Naevius' character portrait that "it would probably be automatically discounted by his hearers and do his case neither harm nor good."

27. For a recent discussion of Cicero's preference for local effect over complete consistency see Gotoff 1993.

"only the most prosaic of his methods of expressing character."[28] Perhaps they are more prosaic than such devices as prosopopoeia. But the types are nonetheless precious indicators of social values—our understanding of ancient Rome would be much poorer without them. One would like to know, of course, whether the types were plausible because they reflected something real in Roman society or whether the plausibility lay in their presence in familiar works of literature. I will return to the question of plausibility after examining three more parasites in the speeches of Cicero: Sex. Aebutius, Q. Apronius, and Philodemus.

Cicero's first extant letter to his brother Quintus, then governor of Asia, contains a discussion of the practices that will allow Quintus to leave office with a clean record and a good reputation. In this discussion the management of associates is a matter of considerable importance. Cicero identifies four categories within the governor's staff. First, there are the legates and quaestors, "whom the state itself has provided for you as companions and helpers for matters of public business" (*quos tibi comites et adiutores negotiorum publicorum dedit ipsa res publica, Qfr.* 1.1.11). These men have their own reputations to worry about and can be held legally responsible for such misdeeds as extortion. One therefore need not scrutinize their activities too closely. At the other extreme are the governor's slaves. These, too, are fairly easy to manage—they must be kept entirely out of public business. And punishment for misbehavior in other matters was readily available.[29] In between, however, are two categories that can cause difficulties. The first is the *cohors*, "those whom you wished to have with you as live-in companions or as your personal staff" (*quos vero aut ex domesticis convictionibus aut in necessariis apparitionibus tecum esse voluisti*, 12). These men expect much from their friendship with the governor and can only be restrained by informal means: by example, by praise for proper conduct, by censure "when they are too little concerned about your reputation" (*minus consulentes existimationi tuae*, 12). The second intermediate category, the provincials and Roman citizens resident in the province who have insinuated themselves into the governor's circle of friends, is particularly dangerous: "You need to be most on your guard with these asso-

---

28. May 1988, 166.
29. *Qfr.* 1.1.17. Cf. 1.1.18 for the *familiae gravis et constans disciplina.*

ciates, since they have all kinds of moneymaking schemes and do everything for the sake of money. They won't be with you long, so they don't worry about your reputation at all."[30] Cicero knew very well how much damage a governor's friends could do to his reputation, since in his prosecution of C. Verres a decade earlier he had insisted on the governor's responsibility for the misdeeds done by his circle of intimates. The figure of the parasite proved extremely useful to him in that endeavor.

Cicero predicts that one of the central elements of Verres' defense in his trial for extortion will be that other men, not he, conducted the spoliation of the province (*fecisse alios, Ver.* 3.205).[31] He will claim, Cicero suggests, that the governor is not to be held responsible either for the illegal exactions of the businessmen who contracted with him to farm the taxes and to buy surplus grain for Rome or for the malicious prosecutions brought before his court by individuals with an eye to their own profit. Cicero cites an incident that shows Verres to have made use of this claim at least once already.

Some men from the town of Bidis had paid a sum of money as an advance on the reward the governor would get if he ruled in their favor in a case they intended to bring before him. When the bribe became public knowledge, Verres decided to scotch the gossip.

> The men from Bidis say they gave [sc. the money] to Volcatius. They don't add, "as Verres told us to do." Verres summons Volcatius, orders him to give the money back. Volcatius was perfectly content to bring forward the cash, since *he* wasn't losing anything. There was a large crowd watching when he gave it back. The men from Bidis go away with the money.[32]

---

30. nullum erit genus in familiaritate cavendum magis, propterea quod et omnes vias pecuniae norunt, et omnia pecuniae causa faciunt, et, quicum victuri non sunt, eius existimationi consulere non curant (*Qfr.* 1.1.15).

31. The prediction is made, though less succinctly, at *Ver.* 2.49, too: et tamen aiunt eum queri solere non numquam se miserum quod non suis, sed suorum peccatis et criminibus prematur. Cf. 2.26–27, 3.175. For the various categories of *alii* see Classen 1980.

32. Dicunt Bidini Volcatio se dedisse; illud non addunt, 'iussu istius.' Volcatium vocat, pecuniam referri imperat. Volcatius animo aequissimo nummos adfert, qui nihil amitteret, reddit inspectantibus multis; Bidini nummos auferunt (*Ver.* 2.56; the text is from Peterson 1917).

The bribers and Sicilian public opinion were apparently appeased, but Cicero insists that Volcatius took the blame for Verres' crime on himself as a service to his patron. His "proof" is the fact that relations between the two men were undisturbed by the case.

> Afterward, Volcatius behaves just the same as before toward you, though an *eques Romanus*, though terribly disgraced. For what is more disgraceful for a free man than to be compelled by a magistrate, in front of a huge crowd, to give back something he had stolen? If Volcatius had the spirit befitting not just an *eques Romanus* but any free man, he wouldn't have been able to look you in the face afterward. Once he had been humiliated, he would have been your opponent, your enemy, unless you and he were up to something and he were more careful of your reputation than his own.[33]

Cicero tries to preempt the *fecisse alios* defense at the trial in Rome by insisting that Volcatius and his like were agents of Verres. To make his point even more damning, he portrays them not as the legitimate agents of Verres the representative of Roman control but as personal connections of Verres the libertine.[34]

Verres' friends were, according to Cicero, active in both judicial and administrative affairs. In court, for example, this same Volcatius (who, with his lack of concern about his own reputation and his involvement in legal matters, looks very much like a latter-day Archedemus)[35] challenged the will of a wealthy Sicilian. Verres, as governor, was to make

---

33. Volcatius idem apud te postea fuit, eques Romanus, tanta accepta ignominia; nam quid est turpius ingenuo, quid minus libero dignum quam in conventu maximo cogi a magistratu furtum reddere: qui si eo animo esset quo non modo eques Romanus, sed quivis liber debet esse, aspicere te postea non potuisset; inimicus, hostis esset tanta contumelia accepta, nisi tecum tum conlusisset et tuae potius existimationi servisset quam suae (*Ver.* 2.58).

Contrast the more reputable behavior of another of Verres' legates, P. Tadius, who kept his distance: unus legatus P. Tadius qui erat reliquus non ita tecum multum fuit; qui si semper una fuisset, tamen summa cura cum tuae, tum multo etiam magis suae famae pepercisset (*Ver.* 2.49).

34. Cicero adduces the praiseworthy restraint of Scipio Africanus as a contrast: Africanus refused a prefecture in his province to someone who was a *vetus adsectator et ex numero amicorum* (*Ver.* 2.28).

35. For Socrates' parable about Archedemus see my introduction.

a ruling. The victims of this groundless suit, who had been in comfortable possession of their inheritance for upwards of twenty years, eventually won their case, but it cost them four hundred thousand sesterces: "They say they gave it to Volcatius. Did Volcatius have enough strength to strip two men of four hundred thousand sesterces?"[36] In fact, says Cicero, Volcatius was one of the many "hands" into which money destined for Verres could be paid (2.27, which will be discussed shortly).

Verres also used his friends to subvert the administrative safeguards established by law and tradition. When Verres auctioned off the job of collecting the tithe at Leontini, for example, he gave the contract to his "darling" (deliciae) Apronius, despite the fact that another bidder had been willing to pay more (3.147 50).[37] And it would seem that much the same thing happened at Herbita, where Verres' man outbid the purchaser put up by the locals but subsequently had his contract reduced (3.77). These are just a few instances from a plentiful supply of similar charges. But making allegations is one thing, and making them convincing is another. How does Cicero go about "proving" the objectionable connections between Verres and his agents?

Familial relationships (based on birth or marriage) were ready-made indicators of the potential for cooperation in wrongdoing. But few of Verres' relatives appear in the Verrines, and those who do were probably not much help to the governor.[38] When Verres tried to get his son-in-law to do what Volcatius had done, for example, the man "took thought for his own reputation, age, and character. He addressed the

---

36. Volcatio dicunt sese dedisse. Quae vis erat in Volcatio tanta ut HS CCCC milia duobus hominibus auferret? (Ver. 2.26). For other instances of calumniae that Cicero charges to Verres' account cf. 1.27, calumniatores ex sinu suo adposuit; 2.22, adponit qui petat . . . illam hereditatem. petit Naevius Turpio quidam, istius excursor et emissarius; 4.40, Apponit de suis canibus quendam qui dicat se Diodorum Melitensem rei capitalis reum velle facere; and 5.108, adponitur iis tamen accusator Naevius Turpio quidem . . . homo bene positus ad istius audaciam, quem iste in decumis, in rebus capitalibus, in omni calumnia praecursorem habere solebat et emissarium.

37. tuam rem illam et praedam fuisse; nam ni ita esset, cur tu Apronium malebas, quem omnes tuum procuratorem esse in decumis, tuum negotium agere loquebantur, quam Minucium decumas agri Leontini sumere? (Ver. 3.149). For another bid by an emissarius of Verres, Venuleius quidam, see 3.99.

38. Verres' son accompanied his father to Sicily (see, e.g., Ver. 3.23 and 5.30, 64, 81, 137) but is not credited with any misdeeds of his own.

senate of Syracuse, said the business was nothing to do with him."[39] Cicero takes particular delight in citing relatives as witnesses *against* Verres. Verres' brother-in-law P. Vettius Chilo, for instance, seems to have had no inclination to join forces with the governor—as far as we can gather from Cicero's account, he was intent on protecting the Roman state and his own business partners from Verres' financial shenanigans: "Vettius tells [sc. his partners] that he will be at your side keeping an eye on the accounts you submit to the treasury, so that if you fail to turn the interest over to the state, you will return it to the company."[40] Cicero uses the evidence of Q. Tadius—"a close friend of Verres' father, a blood relative of his mother (he even has the same name as she does)"[41]—to make a similarly damaging point.

Less close, but still close enough to be implicated ipso facto, are long-standing associates like Verres' useful friend Volcatius, his freedman-aide Timarchides, his *scriba* Maevius (who had followed him from Asia to Rome to Sicily, 3.187), and sundry other members of his entourage. After sketching an instance of Verres' *fecisse alios* defense in which the blame was to be transferred to some "businessmen" (*mancipes*), Cicero counters:

> If you plan to use this defense, it won't work. Volcatius, darling of you and yours, gets in the way of that word *manceps*. Timarchides, too, that pillar of your household, shuts off this defense to you. For one city made its contribution to both him and Volcatius. Finally, your scribe with that gold ring of his—the one he earned by just this sort of business—he won't let you use this defense either.[42]

---

39. habuit et dignitatis et aetatis et nobilitatis suae rationem; verba apud senatum fecit, docuit ad se nihil pertinere (*Ver.* 2.48). I am assuming that the *proximus, paene alter filius* mentioned here is the same man as the *gener, lectus adulescens* mentioned in 2.49. The name of Verres' son-in-law is not known.

40. Praesto se tibi ait futurum Vettius et observaturum quem ad modum rationes ad aerarium referas, ut, si hanc ex faenore pecuniam populo non rettuleris, reddas societati (*Ver.* 3.167).

41. homo familiarissimus patris istius, non alienus matris eius genere et nomine (*Ver.* 1.128).

42. hac ipsa [sc. defensione], si uti cupias, non licet; vetat te Volcatius, tuae tuorumque deliciae, mentionem mancipis facere; Timarchides autem, columen familiae vestrae, premit fauces defensionis tuae, cui simul et Volcatio pecunia a civitate numerata est; iam vero scriba tuus anulo aureo suo, quem ex his rebus invenit, ista te ratione uti non sinet (*Ver.* 3.176).

We have already seen Volcatius in action and remarked on his likeness to Archedemus; in the category of "sundry other members of his entourage" are some helpers that Cicero calls *canes*, recalling the dogs in Socrates' parable. The *canes* were two men from Cibyra, Tlepolemus and Hiero, whom Verres had met when a legate in the East. Both artists by trade, they attached themselves to the soi-disant connoisseur Verres after getting into trouble in their hometown.

> He kept them with him while he was in Asia, and he often used their help and advice in the plundering and thieving that he did as legate. He got to know them well, and they proved their usefulness in action [*bene cognitos et re probatos*], so he took them along with him to Sicily. Once there, they showed a marvelous ability at sniffing out and tracking down all things [i.e., all works of art]. One might call them hunting dogs, so many techniques did they have for finding where each piece was.[43]

Even members of the *cohors* without the professional qualifications of a Tlepolemus or a Hiero were able to make themselves useful to their patron. They could be appointed to hear complaints about the collection of taxes, for example, as happened when a Roman citizen with equestrian status asked the governor to initiate a legal investigation of the relationship between himself and Apronius. Verres offered to provide a board of *recuperatores* (adjustors) to hear the case, but he made it clear that the *recuperatores* would be chosen not from the general body of Roman citizens resident in the province but from his own *cohors* (3.135–36).[44] "And what sort of a hearing would it be," asks Cicero, "if three of the hangers-on of Verres' crowd of creeps and criminals were sitting there as judges, associates not handed down to him by his father

---

43. Habuit eos secum illo tempore et in legationis praedis atque furtis multum illorum opera consilioque usus est. . . . Eos iam bene cognitos et re probatos secum in Siciliam duxit. Quo posteaquam venerunt, mirandum in modum (canis venaticos diceres) ita odorabantur omnia et pervestigabant ut, ubi quidque esset, aliqua ratione invenirent (*Ver.* 4.30–31).

44. The normal procedure would have been to empanel Roman citizens resident in Sicily, the *conventus* (*conventus honestus Syracusis, multi equites Romani, viri primarii, ex qua copia recuperatores reici oportere, Ver.* 3.136; cf. 2.32). From these panels the *recuperatores* would then be chosen by the litigants. Cicero waxes sarcastic about Verres' new selection process: Quid praetor? iubet recuperatores reicere. 'Decurias scribamus.' Quas decurias? 'de cohorte mea reicies,' inquit (3.28).

but recommended to him by his woman?"[45] It would certainly not be a hearing in which the ruling would be based on an impartial consideration of the evidence, for these hangers-on (*adseculae*) were men without property of their own.[46] That such men as these and men in disgrace (e.g., Tlepolemus and Hiero) depended on their patron's pleasure will have been obvious to the Roman audience. The relationship is described with a vivid and unusual metaphor: "Those companions [*comites*] you chose were your hands. The prefects, the scribes, the aides, the doctors, the fortune-tellers, the criers—these were your hands. The closer anyone's connection, relationship, or intimacy with you was, the more he was considered to be one of your hands."[47]

The biggest "hand" of all, Q. Apronius, had no obvious ties to Verres. He did not arrive in Sicily in Verres' train as did the members of the *cohors*. But neither was he a native of Sicily (3.51). He was a businessman with Roman citizenship, a member, in fact, of the category of associates that Cicero, writing in 60 B.C., considered most dangerous to a governor's reputation: "Verres had sought out the most worthless men in the province and had brought with him to Sicily no small number of men of his own type, but the man he judged to be most like himself in worthlessness, extravagance, and audacity was Apronius."[48] Apronius

---

45. Etenim quod esset iudicium, cum ex Verris turpissimo flagitiosissimoque comitatu tres recuperatorum nomine adsedissent adseculae istius, non a patre ei traditi, sed a meretricula commendati? (*Ver.* 3.30).

46. *Ver.* 3.28. On the *cohors* and its members (including Valerius the *praeco*, Volusius the haruspex, and three Cornelii—*medicus, pictor,* and *lictor,* respectively) see 1.67; 2.33, 75; 3.28, 54, 66–70, 137. The Cornelii seem to have owed their Roman citizenship to Verres (Shackleton Bailey 1988, 98).

47. comites illi tui delecti manus erant tuae; praefecti, scribae, accensi, medici, haruspices, praecones manus erant tuae; ut quisque te maxime cognatione, affinitate, necessitudine aliqua attingebat, ita maxime manus tua putabatur (*Ver.* 2.27; the metaphor reappears in Umbricius' plaint *nulli comes exeo tamquam / mancus et extinctae corpus non utile dextrae,* Juv. 3.47–48). *Cognatio* and *affinitas* usually describe familial bonds of blood and marriage, of course, but none of the numerous *ministri* that Cicero names was related in either of these ways to Verres, so I have translated the terms more loosely. In this same speech, Cicero uses *affinitas* to describe the relationship between Verres and the husbands of his mistresses (2.36, .89).

48. Hic est Apronius quem in provincia tota Verres, cum undique nequissimos homines conquisisset, et cum ipse secum sui similis duxisset non parum multos, nequitia luxuria audacia sui simillimum iudicavit (*Ver.* 3.22).

seems to have been far more prominent than such citizens as Naevius Turpio and Venuleius (see notes 36–37 in this chapter). He is not introduced with the obscurity indicator *quidam;* rather, he is "that well-known Quintus Apronius" (*Q. ille Apronius*, 3.22). As collector of the tithe in many sections of Sicily, Apronius was the visible agent of much governmental rapacity, and most of the evidence concerning threats, seizures, and personal violence will have pointed to him, not Verres.[49] At least one attempt at charging him with wrongdoing on his own account had already been made; it proved unsuccessful due to Verres' influence with his successor in Sicily (3.152–53).[50] Apronius' status may have been such that he could not plausibly be reduced to a mere henchman. Cicero in fact quotes a letter in which Timarchides (that "pillar" of Verres' household) asks Apronius to use his influence and money on behalf of the ex-governor when Verres faces prosecution (3.154–57). In any case, Cicero does not try to so reduce Apronius: he calls him "chief of all the so-called tithe collectors" and "land-based pirate-captain"; he speaks of Apronius' influence in drafting praetorian edicts (3.36), of all Sicily handed over to him for mistreatment (3.24, 61), of his "kingship" (*regnum*, 3.58, 200) and "dominion" (*dominatio*, 3.31, 228).[51] Yet since Verres, not Apronius, was the defendant in the case, Cicero had to show that Apronius, however substantial in his own right, was at this period an agent of Verres.[52]

Some of the evidence helped: Apronius had made occasional use of armed attendants procurable only from the governor (the infamous *servi Venerii*).[53] An argument from probability, too, was advanced:

---

49. Q. ille Apronius . . . de cuius improbitate singulari gravissimarum legationum querimonias audivistis (*Ver.* 3.22).

50. Another attempt to get at Apronius may be reflected in the *sponsiones* about the business connection between Apronius and Verres (*Ver.* 3.131–40), but it is not clear which of the two was in fact the target here.

51. eorum omnium qui decumani vocabantur princeps (*Ver.* 3.22); terrestris archipirata (5.70). Cf. 2.108, where Cicero asserts that Apronius considered himself *non Timarchidi, sed ipsius Verris conlegam et socium.*

52. At *Ver.* 3.60, however, he threatens Apronius with a trial of his own after Verres' case is concluded.

53. Hoc quoque attendite, apparitores a praetore adsignatos habuisse decumanum, si hoc mediocre argumentum videri potest istum decumanorum nomine ad suos quaestus esse abusum (*Ver.* 3.36; cf. 50, 65). On the *Venerii* see Eppers and Heinen 1984–85.

would Verres have allowed Apronius to rampage as he did if he were not himself gaining by it?[54] What Cicero works hardest at, however, is depicting the personal relationship between the two men. Verres and Apronius, says Cicero, were "brought together not by any business concern or personal introduction but by the like sordidness of their pursuits."

> You know Verres' base and filthy habits; imagine for yourselves (if you can) someone who can match his unspeakable passion for crimes of all sorts: you've got friend Apronius here, a bottomless pit [vorago] and sinkhole [gurges] of all forms of vice and wickedness—you can see it not only in his way of life but also in his body and mouth. Verres put the fellow at the forefront in all things, in debauchery, in plundering temples, in dirty dinner parties. So powerful a bond was their likeness of character that Apronius, whom everyone else found a barely civilized bore, seemed to Verres companionable and clever [commodus ac disertus]. Everyone else hated the man and avoided even the sight of him; Verres couldn't be without him. Others wouldn't go to a party if Apronius was going to be there; Verres drank out of the same cup as Apronius. And finally, that odor that emanates from Apronius' body and throat—they say even animals cannot stand it—why, Verres finds it positively delightful. This is the man that the praetor kept beside him on his tribunal, alone with him in his bedroom, and above him at dinner. Apronius was never more the life of the party than when he began to prance naked about the dining room—despite the presence of the praetor's young son. This is the man to whom, as I started to say, Verres wanted to give the job of overturning and plundering the fortunes of Sicily's farmers.[55]

---

54. *Ver.* 3.65, 66, 72, 91, 107, 110, 115; cf. 130 and 176 for the same argument but different *ministri*.

55. itaque istos inter se perbrevi tempore non res, non ratio, non commendatio aliqua, sed studiorum turpitudo similitudoque coniunxit. Verris mores improbos impurosque nostis: fingite vobis si potestis, aliquem qui in omnibus isti rebus par ad omnium flagitiorum nefarias libidines esse possit; is erit Apronius ille qui, ut ipse non solum vita sed corpore atque ore significat, immensa aliqua vorago est aut gurges vitiorum turpitudinumque omnium. Hunc in omnibus stupris, hunc in fanorum expilationibus, hunc in impuris conviviis principem adhibebat; tantamque habet morum similitudo coniunctionem

An affectionate relationship based on a similarity of character and shared interests—is this not *amicitia*? It should not be considered such when the elements the two men have in common are vices rather than virtues. In fact, what Cicero describes here is a perversion of that ideal.[56] The objectionable elements in the alliance between Apronius and Verres (as Cicero presents it) are many.

To begin with, the origin of the connection was all wrong. Verres chose for himself an associate whose only recommendation was his viciousness. If only Apronius had had business interests to make himself profitable to Verres or an introduction to make himself noticeable; either of these, Cicero implies, would have been a proper criterion for choosing a subordinate.[57] But vices earn Apronius the status of *familiaris* (3.106) and even *deliciae praetoris* (3.72).

His vices were displayed to the greatest effect in Verres' dining room, it seems. A large appetite was one of them. Or it is at least one that Cicero wants his audience to attribute to Apronius: a natural result of this form of indulgence would be the girth to which Cicero seems to be pointing when he says, "a bottomless pit . . . you can see it . . . in his body."[58] We have seen applied to other parasites such eating

---

atque concordiam ut Apronius, qui aliis inhumanus ac barbarus, isti uni commodus ac disertus videretur; ut quem omnes odissent neque videre vellent, sine eo iste esse non posset ; ut cum alii ne conviviis quidem isdem quibus Apronius, hic isdem etiam poculis uteretur; postremo ut odor Aproni taeterrimus oris et corporis—quem, ut aiunt, ne bestiae quidem ferre possent—uni isti suavis et iucundus videretur. Ille erat in tribunali proximus, in cubiculo solus, in convivio dominus, ac tum maxime cum accubante praetextato praetoris filio saltare in convivio nudus coeperat. hunc, uti dicere institui, principem Verres ad fortunas aratorum vexandas diripiendasque esse voluit (*Ver.* 3.22–24).

56. Cf. the limits Cicero sets to helping one's friends at Cic. *Amic.* 61: si qua fortuna acciderit ut minus iustae amicorum voluntates adiuvandae sint . . . declinandum de via sit, *modo ne summa turpitudo sequatur* (cf. also *Amic.* 20, 27, 75).

57. Apronius is included among the subordinates labeled *ministri ac satellites cupiditatum* (*Ver.* 3.21; cf. *satelles istius Apronius*, 128), *procuratores istius* [sc. *Verris*] *quaestus et administri rapinarum* (3.50, *procurator* again in 3.149 and 178; *cognitor* in 137), and *emissarii* (3.91).

58. Cicero maintains the fiction of the courtroom throughout the second *actio* of the *Verrines,* though this was not delivered in court but published as a monograph after Verres left the country. He had "pointed Apronius out" to the judges earlier in this speech: aspicite, iudices, vultum hominis et aspectum (*Ver.* 3.22).

metaphors as *vorago* and *gurges* (both formed from roots meaning "to swallow"). Another convivial term, *corollarium*—which properly refers to a gift given to dinner guests (cf. *Ver.* 4.49)—is used of the sums that Verres allows Apronius to skim off the tithes he collects for "the government" (3.118). That Verres finds Apronius a clever conversationalist (*commodus ac disertus*) is in itself an indication of vice, since in the dining room Verres likes to hear dirty jokes and flattery.[59] Cicero credits Apronius not with real wit, of course—"everyone else found [him] a barely civilized bore"—but only with a talent for suiting the taste of his host (*isti uni commodus*).[60] And Apronius never succeeds better at this than when he dances around the dining room naked, not something that a self-respecting Roman would do.[61] It was a form of entertainment more commonly associated with slaves, in fact, and it is not long before Cicero calls Apronius just this, a *servus homo* (3.91).[62] Appetite, entertainment both verbal and physical, servility—these qualities defined the comic parasite.

But Apronius is not a parasite pure and simple, for, like Cicero's Naevius, Apronius plays the extravagant host as well.[63] *Luxuria* was in fact one of the qualities that he shared with his patron (3.22). And Apronius, too, uses his parties to cultivate "friends" who will serve his nefar-

---

59. Tantum apud te quaestus Aproni, tantum eius sermo inquinatissimus et blanditiae flagitiosae valuerunt ut numquam animum tuum cura tuarum fortunarum cogitatioque tangeret (*Ver.* 3.65; cf. *sermone impuro atque improbo,* 3.158)?

60. The phrase *isti uni commodus* (*Ver.* 3.23) is made more explicit later: Q. Apronio . . . ad Verris flagitia libidinesque accommodato (3.60).

61. Velleius, who gives a rather elaborate description of another convivial display of this sort, appends an unfavorable judgment on the dancer's character: the ex-consul and future censor L. Munatius Plancus, despite his pedigree and rank, is called *humillimus adsentator reginae et infra servos cliens* (2.83). On another ex-consul's dancing at Cic. *Pis.* 18, Nisbet suggests (1961, ad loc.) that "the charge may be the exaggeration of an isolated incident at a symposium." This is in all probability true of Apronius, too, but it is the nature of the charge that is of interest here, not its accuracy.

62. Nicolet (1966, 325), Treggiari (1969, 105 n. 1), and Classen (1980, 104) consider him *libertinus*. It is true that Cicero's generous repertory of insults for the man includes phrases like *homo vix liber* (*Ver.* 3.134) and *homo in dedecore natus* (3.60), but it is difficult to believe that Apronius was actually born a slave, for he is never once given a servile cognomen. Shackleton Bailey (1988, 18) thinks him freeborn.

63. Apronius' *convivia: Ver.* 3.28, 31, 61–62, 65, 105.

ious ends—to make friends of Verres' friends, for example. Cicero
amuses himself by imagining a scenario in which a hardworking Sicilian farmer brings a case against Apronius before the *recuperatores* that
Verres had appointed from his *cohors:* "the poor man would have to
oppose Apronius in front of judges who had not yet recovered from
their sousing at Apronius' party the night before."[64] Extravagance was
also one of the techniques that won Apronius Verres' affection.

> Apronius would not have been able to buy Metellus [Verres' suc-
> cessor as governor of Sicily] with money, as he did Verres, or with
> parties, or women, or filthy talk, though these were the means he
> used not to creep gradually into Verres' friendship but to take
> rapid possession of the entire man and his entire praetorship,
> too.[65]

Parasite and wastrel, then, are two of the images used to explain Apronius to the audience. There is one more.

The personal ties implicit in the last phrase of the paragraph just
quoted—Apronius took "possession of the entire man and his entire
praetorship, too" (*totum hominem totamque eius praeturam possederat*)—
are rather stronger than those between friends. Cicero, I think, would
have liked his audience to believe that Apronius and Verres had been
in bed together. There are unmistakable parallels between Verres' *deliciae* Apronius and his mistresses Chelidon, Pipa, and Tertia.[66] Like Chelidon, Apronius is said to have given Verres advice on how to formu-
late his edict so as to make it profitable for himself. At 3.36 Cicero asks,
"What sort of edicts did the fellow issue at the urging of Apronius?"
And in the speech recounting the misdeeds of the urban praetor, Cicero

---

64. Veniendum erat ad eos contra Apronium qui nondum Aproniani convivi
crapulam exhalassent (*Ver.* 3.28). There were no such cases, however (3.32). But
the related incidents described at 2.75, 3.54, 3.69, and 3.136 give Cicero the
material he needs to produce his fabrication.

65. Apronius ipsum Metellum non pretio, ut Verrem, non convivio, non
muliere, non sermone impuro atque improbo posset corrumpere, quibus rebus
non sensim atque moderate ad istius amicitiam adrepserat, sed brevi tempore
totum hominem totamque eius praeturam possederat (*Ver.* 3.158).

66. On Apronius qua love-object see *Ver.* 3.27: delicias ac vitam tuam. Cf.
3.72: Apronio, deliciis praetoris, lucelli aliquid iussi sunt dare. For Chelidon see
1.104, 106, 120, 136–40; 5.34, 38. For Pipa see 3.77–82; 5.31, 81. For Tertia see
3.78–83; 5.31, 40, 81.

adds large dollops of sarcasm to his assertion that one of the clauses in Verres' edict—one that barred women from being named as heirs to large estates—was inserted "lest the whole edict look as though it were written to suit Chelidon."[67] Pipa and Tertia, Verres' mistresses in Sicily, use their *arbitrium* and *auctoritas* with the praetor to emerge as *mulierculae publicanae,* tax-farming rivals to Apronius.[68] And it is not just that both types of *deliciae* acquire too much control over Verres. The sexual innuendo implicit in *in omnibus stupris* (3.23) becomes explicit in the references to the bedroom. Apronius has a tête-à-tête with Verres *in cubiculo* (3.23), the door of Verres' bedroom opens only for a woman and a tithe collector (*decumanus,* 3.56), and so on.[69] Apronius' bad breath, too, may be an indicator of sexual practices of which Cicero expected his audience to disapprove.[70]

What does Cicero hope to accomplish by this concatenation of caricatures? Was Apronius not objectionable enough as a parasite? Well, *he* was objectionable, but he was not the man on trial. Hosting a parasite did not necessarily reflect poorly on a rich man. The wealthy father of Plautus' *Captivi,* Hegio, was, as we saw, treated with remarkable sympathy. But being so infatuated with a dependent as to make him *dominus* in his dining room and give him *arbitrium* over the praetorian edict did most certainly reflect poorly on Verres. In presenting Apronius as a parasite, Cicero suggests that he was at Verres' service in affairs no matter how disreputable; in presenting him as a *meretrix,* he suggests that Verres had relinquished the responsibilities of the dominant member of the relationship and allowed himself to be governed by his subordinate.

Cicero repeats the tactic of endowing agents with personal intimacy with their principal in his description of Verres' lesser *ministri,* too. We

---

67. illa cuius modi sunt quae ex tempore ab Apronio admonitus edixit? (*Ver.* 3.36); ne totum edictum ad Chelidonis arbitrium scriptum videretur (1.106). Cf. 1.136: [Chelido] isto praetore non modo in iure civili privatorumque omnium controversiis populo Romano praefuit, verum etiam in his sartis tectisque dominata est. Apropos of Verres' Sicilian mistresses, Cicero says, *iste quarum arbitrio praeturam per triennio gesserat* (4.136).

68. *Ver.* 3.78; cf. *decumana mulier,* 3.77.

69. For the imputation of effeminacy see *Ver.* 2.92, where Verres is called a *vir inter mulieres, impura inter viros muliercula,* and 4.39, where Verres' passion for precious objects is likened to that of Amphiaraus' wife Eriphyle.

70. *Ver.* 3.23, 134. Cf. Martial 11.30, and see Kay's note (1985, ad loc.) for further passages. Cicero has anticipated Juvenal's portrait of Naevolus.

have already examined the case of Volcatius. C. Claudius was another instigator of false (but profitable) prosecutions.

> You see the man with the rather curly hair and the dark complexion? The one who looks as though he thinks himself ever so clever? Who holds a notebook, who writes, advises, sits close? That is Claudius. In Sicily he was this fellow's agent, interpreter, and cooker-up of schemes. He was practically counted as a colleague of Timarchides then, but now he is positioned so close as scarcely to yield precedence to Apronius, to the man who used to say that he was the colleague and partner not of Timarchides but of Verres himself. Can you help but think that Verres decided that this man, most hostile to [sc. the victim of the plot] and most friendly to himself, was the one to whom he would assign the shameful role of false prosecutor?[71]

Claudius' long-standing enmity with a wealthy Sicilian was eventually turned to his own profit and to that of the praetor himself. Two tithe collectors of Herbita, Apronii writ small, had other qualities that recommended them to Verres.

> Aeschrio and Docimus, men who made no difficulty about sharing their women with the praetor, shifty agents of these awful women, came to Herbita. They start making requests, demands, threats. They want to imitate Apronius, but can't quite do it; Sicilians just aren't intimidated by other Sicilians. Nevertheless, they make up all sorts of false charges, so that the Herbitans give security for an appearance in court at Syracuse. [The terms of the wheat tithe settlement are described here.] They think everything settled, when Verres says, "What about the barley and my friend

---

71. Videtis illum subcrispo capillo, nigrum, qui eo vultu nos intuetur ut sibi ipse peracutus esse videatur, qui tabulas tenet, qui scribit, qui monet, qui proximus est. Is est Claudius, qui in Sicilia sequester istius, interpres, confector negotiorum, prope conlega Timarchidi numerabatur, nunc obtinet eum locum ut vix Apronio illi de familiaritate concedere videatur, ei qui se non Timarchidi se ipsius Verris conlegam et socium esse dicebat. Dubitate etiam, si potestis, quin eum iste potissimum ex omni numero delegerit cui hanc cognitoris falsi improbam personam imponeret, quem et huic inimicissimum et sibi amicissimum esse arbitraretur! (*Ver.* 2.108–9).

[*amiculo*] Docimus here? What do you think?" (The whole business was transacted in his bedroom, with the praetor still in bed.) They said that they had nothing for him. Says Verres, "Didn't hear what you said. Pay him twelve thousand sesterces."[72]

If the Sicilians Aeschrio and Docimus are like the parasites we saw in the satires of Horace and Lucian who accommodated their patron with their own women, Rubrius (whom Cicero calls Verres' "companion" [*comes*] and "darling" [*deliciae*] in Asia [1.64]) was performing services equally parasitical in finding other men's women for him.[73] Cicero describes Rubrius as "a man made to serve that fellow's lusts." "Wherever they went," he says, "he showed amazing skill at tracking down delights of all sorts for Verres" (*homo factus ad istius libidines, qui miro artificio, quocumque venerat, haec investigare omnia solebat*, 1.64). The evidence for this was an incident at Lampsacus, where Rubrius made elaborate arrangements for the abduction of the daughter of a prominent citizen (his own host) and was injured in the resulting brawls.[74] Like Volcatius and C. Claudius, he would seem to have been willing to sacrifice his own reputation (and skin) to satisfy his patron's wants.

Volcatius the stooge, the easygoing "rivals" Aeschrio and Docimus, the *canes Cibyratae*, Rubrius the procuror, Claudius the false prosecutor, and the gluttonous Apronius, who danced naked in the dining room (not to mention what he did in the bedroom)—these are all suitable friends for a man who (Cicero would have us believe) gave too much thought to his pleasures and too little to his responsibilities. But they provided two distinct types of service. Rubrius and the *canes*, along

---

72. Veniunt Herbitam duo praetoris aemuli non molesti, muliercularum deterrimarum improbissimi cognitores; incipiunt postulare, poscere, minari; non poterant tamen, cum cuperent, Apronium imitari; Siculi Siculos non tam pertimescebant. Cum omni ratione tamen illi calumniarentur, promittunt Herbitenses vadimonium Syracusas . . . Transactum putabant Herbitenses, cum iste, 'Quid? de hordeo,' inquit, 'et de Docimo, amiculo meo, quid cogitatis?' Atque hoc agebat in cubiculo, iudices, atque in lecto suo. Negabant illi quicquam sibi esse mandatum. 'Non audio: numerate HS. XII.' (*Ver.* 3.78–79).

73. Hor. *Sat.* 2.3.237–38, Lucian *Symp.* 32. For a discussion of the incident involving Rubrius see Fuhrmann 1980.

74. *Ver.* 1.65–67; see 80 for the "proof" that he was acting on Verres' behalf. Cicero does not mention Rubrius' social standing, but Münzer (1914) tentatively connects him with the likes of the Capuan *praeco* A. Rubrius A.f. at *CIL* 1.573 (= *CIL* 10.3783 = *ILS* 6303).

with the doctor Cornelius, belong to the category that Cicero would later label "live-in companions or . . . personal staff" (*Qfr.* 1.1.12). Their services were essentially personal. But the services of Verres' tithe-collecting and prosecuting friends went well beyond the private arena. Volcatius, Claudius, and Apronius—to name only three—helped Verres turn the prerogatives of a provincial governor into a source of private profit.

The latter group of useful friends proves useful to us, too: they help us identify practices that a Roman might feel were beyond the legitimate uses of the governor's prerogatives. That a governor might exercise his powers selectively or partially was an accepted fact of provincial administration: Cicero wrote numerous letters of recommendation urging the governors of Asia, Africa, Achaia, Bithynia, and Sicily to get to know his friends, to preserve their privileges, to expedite their affairs, to help them collect from their debtors, to look favorably on their claims to inheritances, and so on. All of these requests were, it seems, perfectly legitimate expressions of a patron's interest in his friends' well-being.[75] And the governor who used his resources of power on behalf of his own friends or his friends' friends might expect to profit thereby. But the "profit" specified in Cicero's letters, at least, takes the form of gratitude; a helpful governor lays up a credit balance in his friends' goodwill, not in the bank. And he is not expected to go to any and all lengths to help his friends. Again and again we find variations on a formula: "I ask you to do X, insofar as seems proper to you or just," "insofar as is consonant with your honor or your position or your convenience," or "unless you think that your reputation will be damaged thereby."[76] No doubt the letters show us the presentable face of the system, the ideal parameters. But Verres, as Cicero draws him, went well beyond the limits prescribed by propriety, justice, and honorable behavior. He converted the patronal resources inherent in a governor's position into cash. And he did it not *pro amicis* (on behalf of his friends) but *per amicos* (by means of his friends). Verres' prosecutor must have felt that this form of profit taking would be seen as an intolerable perversion of a system that in other hands—even less-than-ideal

---

75. The range of services attested in the imperial period are discussed by Saller (1982, 145–94).

76. The recommendations are collected in book 13 of the *Letters to His Friends*. The provisos translated in the text can be found in letters 14, 22, 23, 25, 27, 28b, 31, 37, 54, 58, 61, 63, 69, 72, 73.

hands—worked reasonably well. He would feel the same a decade later, when advising his brother (who was threatened with prosecution for extortion when his term was up) about the limits he should impose on the activities of his subordinates: "If any of them is a scoundrel, you may turn a blind eye as long as *he* will be held accountable for neglecting the limits imposed on him by the law, but not so far as to let him use the resources of power with which you have reinforced his authority for his own personal profit."[77] In this same letter he warned his brother about the dangers of associating too closely with provincials and local businessmen, men who "have all kinds of moneymaking schemes and do everything for the sake of money"—men, in fact, who sound remarkably similar to Verres' helpers. Cicero's letter suggests that many of the projects devised for the plundering of Sicily may have originated in the clever and crooked brains of men like Apronius.[78] Verres may have been the beneficiary of many men's endeavors, but Verres' prosecutor needed to reverse the charges, so to speak—to make Verres accountable for the illegal exactions that other men engineered. The image of the parasite helped Cicero do just this.

Irresponsible heirs and voluptuaries are the sorts of men that comedy shows preyed on by parasites. Their weaknesses give the parasites the hold they need. The speech that Cicero wrote on behalf of Aulus Caecina shows that propertied women found themselves exposed to the same hazard of Roman social life. Cicero plainly felt that a combination of legal freedom and womanly weakness made a woman named Caesennia a plausible victim for a parasite.[79]

The *pro Caecina* centers around a property dispute generated by Caesennia's death. Her second husband and principal heir, A. Caecina (Cicero's client), and her friend and former legal representative, Sex.

77. quorum si quis forte esset sordidior, ferres eatenus, quoad per se neglegeret eas leges, quibus esset astrictus, non ut ea potestate, quam tu ad dignitatem permisisses, ad quaestum uteretur (*Qfr.* 1.1.11). For the threatened prosecution see *Att.* 3.9.1, 3.17.1.

78. On Apronius cf. *Ver.* 3.36: illa cuius modi sunt quae ex tempore ab Apronio admonitus edixit? For other helpers see 2.89, where Verres is spurred to a profitable seizure by the victim's enemies.

79. Frier 1985 is the most recent extended treatment of the *pro Caecina*. References to earlier work can be found in Stroh 1975, 309–10. Particular facets of the law involved in the case are discussed in Tellegen and Tellegen-Couperus 1989 and Corbino 1982.

Aebutius, were rival claimants for a farm. The property in question had been auctioned off to settle the estate of Caesennia's son, who predeceased her. It was adjacent to a farm that was part of Caesennia's dowry. The highest bidder at the auction was Aebutius. Caecina asserted that the farm was purchased for Caesennia and with her money, Aebutius that he bought it for himself. Cicero's job was to get Caecina reinstated in possession. As was observed long ago, if Cicero won this case for his client (we do not know), he won it by means of characterizations.[80]

Sextus Aebutius is introduced first, near the beginning of the *narratio*. The events described in this portion of the *narratio*, as Cicero himself confesses (10), are not strictly relevant to the issue before the *recuperatores* (adjustors), but they are essential for the blackening of Aebutius.

Aebutius had long since been feeding on [*aleretur*] Caesennia's widowhood and lonely state. He had insinuated himself into her good graces, thinking that he would take charge of whatever business and legal affairs the woman had and make a profit of a sort for himself, too. When the property [sc. of Caesennia's son] was being auctioned off, friend Aebutius was involved in the accounting and in the division of proceeds. In fact, he quite applied himself to and got inside of the matter, and he succeeded in persuading Caesennia—she knew nothing of such things—that no clever bit of business could be done without Aebutius. You see the type [*personam*] every day, judges: a fellow who says just what a woman wants to hear [*mulierum adsentatoris*], a "legal representative" who specializes in widows' business [*cognitoris viduarum*], an advocate overeager for trade, a fellow used to hanging about the forum. Men think that sort an inept clod, women an attorney both knowledgeable and clever. See if the picture doesn't fit.

---

80. Keller 1842, 390. He saw, rightly, that *quae de emptione fundi Cicero narrat, opinione hominum plus quam legitimis probationibus ad capiendos recuperatorum animos valerent*. The characterizations in the speech as we have it are probably more elaborate than those contained in the courtroom speech on which it is based (his third in this case before these same *recuperatores, Caec.* 6), but Cicero will have taken care to paint these portraits at least piecemeal over the course of the trial. Note his complaint that the defense has (understandably enough) diverted the point at issue from the *improbitas Sex. Aebuti* to a point of *ius civile* (4). On the question of postdelivery revisions see Stroh 1975, 31–54, and Frier 1985, 117 and n. 67.

What was Aebutius to Caesennia? Don't ask whether he was a relative. There's not a shred of connection. A friend of her father or husband, then? Nothing of the sort. Who, then? Why, the fellow I've just sketched for you, a self-selected "friend" [*voluntarius amicus*] for the woman, no connection of hers. All that tied him to her was a pretended sense of duty [*ficto officio*] and a contrived display of concern [*simulata sedulitate*]. His efforts were occasionally well timed but never well motivated.[81]

Aebutius is reduced to preying on women, to being an *adsentator mulierum*, because men are not deceived by his apparent cleverness. He insinuated himself into a position of dependence on Caesennia—a situation summed up in the verb *aleretur*—by making himself useful, primarily in legal affairs. But his position of intimacy and trust is one to which he has no legitimate claim, and self-interest underlies all of his services to her (*voluntarius amicus*).

The formal portrait concludes here, but more information is provided indirectly. Cicero does not say, for instance, that Aebutius is a poor man (he will later need to suggest that Aebutius bribed his ten witnesses, 28), but he implies as much by claiming that the rival bidders at the auction assumed that Aebutius was buying property for Caesennia, because they knew he could not have afforded it for himself.

When, as I was saying, the property was being auctioned off in Rome, . . . [Caesennia] gets someone to buy the farm for her. Who?

---

81. Cum esset haec auctio hereditaria constituta, Aebutius iste, qui iam diu Caesenniae viduitate ac solitudine aleretur ac se in eius familiaritatem insinuasset, hac ratione ut cum aliquo suo compendio negotia mulieris, si qua acciderent, controversiasque susciperet, versabatur eo quoque tempore in his rationibus auctionis et partitionis atque etiam se ipse inferebat et intro dabat et in eam opinionem Caesenniam adducebat ut mulier imperita nihil putaret agi callide posse, ubi non adesset Aebutius. (14) Quam personam iam ex cotidiana vita cognostis, recuperatores, mulierum adsentatoris, cognitoris viduarum, defensoris nimium litigiosi, contriti ad Regiam, inepti ac stulti inter viros, inter mulieres periti iuris et callidi, hanc personam imponite Aebutio. Is enim Caesenniae fuit Aebutius—ne forte quaeratis, num propinquus?—nihil alienius—amicus a patre aut a viro traditus?—nihil minus—quis igitur? ille, ille quem supra deformavi, voluntarius amicus mulieris non necessitudine aliqua, sed ficto officio simulataque sedulitate coniunctus magis opportuna opera non numquam quam aliquando fideli (*Caec.* 13–14; the text is from Clark 1909).

Who do you think? Surely you can see that this was a job for that
fellow who was so ready to handle this woman's business, without whom no transaction could be done carefully or cleverly
enough? You've been paying attention, I see. The task was given
to Aebutius. He shows up at the sale and places a bid. Many
potential buyers back off, as a favor to Caesennia. Others can't
meet the price. The farm is knocked down to Aebutius. Aebutius
promises to pay the banker. He's the man whose testimony
proves, according to our fine friend here, that he bought the farm
for himself, as if we were denying that the property was knocked
down to him—or that there was anyone there who didn't think he
was buying it for Caesennia. In fact, many people knew he was
doing this; almost everyone had heard it, and anyone who hadn't
heard it would have been able to figure out that this was the case,
since Caesennia was owed money from her son's estate, since real
estate was the best investment, since the real estate in question
was the real estate most suitable for the woman, and since the bidder was someone whom no one was surprised to see helping Caesennia out. That he would be buying it for himself couldn't have
occurred to anyone.[82]

In a similar fashion, Cicero avoids saying that Aebutius is a hired agent
(though *conductus* and its cousins *mercennarius* and *egens* are among his
favorite terms of abuse in other speeches, he will later want to contrast
Aebutius' *audacia, impudentia,* and *violentia* with Caecina's *modestia,* so
he cannot draw him too abject here), but he suggests that Caesennia

---

82. Cum esset, ut dicere institueram, constituta auctio Romae, . . . mandat ut
fundum sibi emat—cui tandem?—cui putatis? an non in mentem vobis venit
omnibus illius hoc munus esse ad omnia mulieris negotia parati, sine quo nihil
satis caute, nihil satis callide posset agi? (16) Recte attenditis. Aebutio negotium
datur. Adest ad tabulam, licetur Aebutius; deterrentur emptores multi partim
gratia Caesenniae, partim etiam pretio. Fundus addicitur Aebutio; pecuniam
argentario promittit Aebutius; quo testimonio nunc vir optimus utitur sibi
emptum esse. Quasi vero aut nos ei negemus addictum aut tum quisquam
fuerit qui dubitaret quin emeretur Caesenniae, cum id plerique scirent, omnes
fere audissent, qui non audisset, is coniectura adsequi posset, cum pecunia
Caesenniae ex illa hereditate deberetur, eam porro in praediis conlocari
maxime expediret, essent autem praedia quae mulieri maxime convenirent, ea
venirent, liceretur is quem Caesenniae dare operam nemo miraretur, sibi emere
nemo posset suspicari (*Caec.* 15–16).

thinks of him as such by saying that the trifling inheritance that she left him (half that left to a freedman of her former husband) was intended as *merces* (payment) and was casually given (*aspergit*, 17), not rendered with gratitude.

> After the sale the money was paid by Caesennia. The fellow thinks that this payment can't be proved because he stole her account books, whereas he has the banker's account books with their records of money paid in [by Aebutius] and then disbursed [by the banker to the seller]. As if the transaction was supposed to have been done in any other way. When all this was done the way I've been telling it, Caesennia took possession of the farm and found a tenant for it. It wasn't long afterward that she married A. Caecina. I'll finish the story briefly. She makes a will and dies. Caecina inherits 23/24. M. Fulcinius, a freedman of her first husband, gets 1/36, and she throws 1/72 the way of Aebutius. This seventy-second portion she meant as payment for his attentions, in case they caused him any inconvenience. But he thinks that with this 72nd portion he's got a hold of all sorts of litigatory opportunities.[83]

The characterization of Aebutius that Cicero has assembled so far has a precise aim. Cicero is trying to get around the awkward fact (based on the testimony of the seller of the property and the banker who handled the money, 27) that Aebutius acquired the farm in his own name (*fundus addicitur Aebutio*, 16). Cicero's claim, that Aebutius was acting at Caesennia's behest (*mandatu Caesenniae*, 19) rests entirely on probability. To establish this, he emphasized the suitability, or rather the inevitability, of Caesennia's acquiring this piece of land

---

83. Hac emptione facta pecunia solvitur a Caesennia; cuius rei putat iste rationem reddi non posse quod ipse tabulas averterit; se autem habere argentarii tabulas in quibus sibi expensa pecunia lata sit acceptaque relata. Quasi id aliter fieri oportuerit. Cum omnia ita facta essent, quem ad modum nos defendimus, Caesennia fundum possedit locavitque; neque ita multo post A. Caecinae nupsit. Ut in pauca conferam, testamento facto mulier moritur; facit heredem ex deunce et semuncia Caecinam, ex duabus sextulis M. Fulcinium, libertum superioris viri, Aebutio sextulam aspergit. Hanc sextulam illa mercedem isti esse voluit adsiduitatis et molestiae si quam ceperat. Iste autem hac sextula se ansam retinere omnium controversiarum putat (*Caec.* 17).

(15–16). Then, drawing on the description provided in sections 13–14, he reminded the judges that Aebutius had frequently acted as Caesennia's agent, and he suggested that Aebutius must have been doing so at the auction as well.

The characterization of Aebutius is detailed, but it is not personal. Cicero asserts, in fact, that what he has described is a familiar type (*persona*), one that the judges might see any day in the forum.[84] Cicero even urges the judges to fill in the details of Aebutius' portrait from their own experience (*hanc personam inponite Aebutio*, 14). To facilitate the application of the stereotype to Aebutius, Cicero omits any description of Aebutius' background. Caesennia and her husbands, by contrast, are placed in their respectable, even eminent, municipal context.[85] What *persona* did Cicero want the *recuperatores* to use in masking the real Aebutius?[86]

In his second book of *Satires*, Horace created a character very like Aebutius. A thoroughly modern "Tiresias" gives the following advice to an impoverished "Ulysses."

> Suppose a case, any case, comes up in the forum; whichever of the two litigants is rich and childless, no matter if he's a scoundrel so bold as to bring a better man to court, he's the one whose side you should take. Avoid the citizen with the better character and the better case, if he's got a child or a child-bearing wife. "Quintus," suppose you say, or "Publius" (tender little ears love those first names), "a fine man like yourself finds a friend in me. I know where the law leaves one room to maneuver, and I can handle

---

84. If "hanging about in the forum" is what the expression *contriti ad Regiam* implies. Keller (1842, 445–46) objected to the use of *ad Regiam* as a rough equivalent for "in the forum" and printed Beroaldus' *conciti ad rixam* instead. H.G. Hodge, the Loeb editor, emends to *cogniti ad Regiam*, with a note to the effect that *ad Regiam* = βασιλική = "a colonnade in the forum, apparently a common resort of disreputable characters." But *cogniti* is surely unlikely so soon after *cognitoris viduarum*. Frier (1985, 57–63) retains the transmitted text and explains *ad Regiam* as a reference to the area of the urban praetor's tribunal and *contriti* as a sneer at Aebutius' legal "expertise." Cf. Cic. *de Or.* 1.249 for *conterere* of legal business, Martial 4.8.1 for the tone.

85. Fulcinius and Caesennia, *Caec.* 10; Caecina, 103. On their background and status see Frier 1985, 18–20, 35, and Hohti 1975.

86. According to Frier (1985, 275–76), Aebutius was "plainly better connected than Cicero cared to admit."

cases. No one will think you easy prey or get so much as a nut-
shell away from you as long as I am here to watch out for you. My
one thought is to make sure that no one takes anything from you
or laughs at you." Tell him to go home and relax; you be his representative in court.[87]

This *voluntarius cognitor* is an inheritance-hunter, of course, but we
have seen that he learned his ingratiating ways from the parasites of
comedy. And Aebutius has his own parasitical stigmata: a metaphor
derived from the dining room (*aleretur*, 13), for example, as well as
ingratiating behavior (*insinuasset*, 13; *adsentator*, 14), self-interest
behind a false front of friendship (*voluntarius amicus*, 14), poverty (16),
and petty services (*molestia si quam ceperat*, 17).

But a parasite preying on a woman is unheard of, at least in extant
comedy. Peniculus' attempt to transfer his attachment from Menaechmus to Menaechmus' wife was a complete failure, as we saw (Plaut.
Men. 664–65). However, there is a comedy in which a shady character
acts as a woman's representative in court, and in the speech under consideration Cicero likens that comedy's title character, Phormio, to one
of his opponent's witnesses: ". . . and then there is the banker Sex.
Clodius, whose other name is Phormio, whose character is no less dubious and brash than is that of Terence's Phormio."[88] Cicero does not
dwell on this likeness, however, for he is far more interested in establishing the points of contact between Aebutius and *ille Terentianus
Phormio.*

---

87.   magna minorve Foro si res certabitur olim,
         vivet uter locuples sine gnatis, improbus, ultro
         qui meliorem audax vocet in ius, illius esto
         defensor; fama civem causaque priorem
         sperne, domi si gnatus erit fecundave coniunx.
         'Quinte,' puta, aut 'Publi' (gaudent praenomine molles
         auriculae), 'tibi me virtus tua fecit amicum.
         ius anceps novi, causas defendere possum;
         eripiet quivis oculos citius mihi quam te
         contemptum cassa nuce pauperet. haec mea cura est,
         ne quid tu perdas neu sis iocus.' ire domum atque
         pelliculam curare iube. fi cognitor ipse.
                                        (Hor. *Sat.* 2.5.27–38)
88. . . . . et argentarius Sex. Clodius cui cognomen est Phormio, nec minus
niger nec minus confidens quam ille Terentianus est Phormio (*Caec.* 27).

We have seen that Phormio combines the attributes of *sycophanta* and *parasitus*. Cicero's Aebutius does the same: he rejoices in getting "a hold of all sorts of litigatory opportunities" (*Caec.* 17). Malicious prosecution is the hallmark of the *sycophanta,* and Cicero reproaches Aebutius with *calumnia* (bringing false accusations) and its equivalents seven times in the course of the speech.[89] He compounds the insult by saying that Aebutius works for women (no man being fool enough to trust him). Phormio has the same specialization. He says, "Perhaps you think that I only defend women without dowries? On the contrary, I take cases for dowered ones as well."[90] The principal object of Phormio's *patrocinium,* however, was not to benefit either of the women he serves but to win (and bank) the gratitude of their menfolk. Aebutius, too, is out for his own profit.

The *Phormio* ends with an unusual twist when Nausistrata, the "dowered woman" whose interests Phormio professed to be watching out for, takes it on herself to invite Phormio to dinner.

NAUSISTRATA: Your name—what is it, please?

PHORMIO: Mine? Phormio. Friend of your family, ma'am, and best of friends to your son Phaedria.

NA: Well, Phormio, you can be sure that hereafter, insofar as I am able, I will be doing and saying whatever pleases you.

PH: Your words are too kind.

NA: But you deserve it.

PH: Nausistrata, would you like to start right off today with something that will give me pleasure and make your husband see red?

NA: Indeed!

PH: Then invite me to dinner.

NA: Consider yourself invited.[91]

Cicero's Aebutius, by contrast, never appears in Caesennia's dining room. But then Cicero's client may not have wanted his deceased wife to be made to look like a proto-Clodia.

---

89. *Caec.* 2 (*malitia*), 18 (*calumnia;* cf. 102), 19 (*nihil se ab A. Caecina posse litium terrore abradere*), 20 (*malitiose*), 61 (*calumnia*), 65 (*scriptum sequi calumniatoris esse*).

90. vos me indotatis modo / patrocinari fortasse arbitramini: / etiam dotatis soleo (Ter. *Phorm.* 938–40; cf. Demipho's sneer at *istum patronum mulieris,* 307).

91. Ter. *Phorm.* 1048–54.

Clodia is painstakingly painted in the *pro Caelio,* where part of her characterization is that of a *miles gloriosa,* a female boastful soldier.[92] As such, she marshals troops, plans campaigns (in a bathhouse), and has helpful gentlemen in to dinner. Cicero maintains that the witnesses whom (he says) Clodia hopes to use against his client Caelius ought to keep to their accustomed places in her dining room.

> Suppose they are amusing at parties, witty, even eloquent when the wine is flowing. Still, what works in the dining room won't necessarily work in the forum. You have to deal differently with couches and courtroom benches. Judges and partygoers are not at all the same sort of audience. And how can you compare lamps to the broad light of day? Therefore we will throw out all of their trifling jokes and absurdities—if they come forward, that is. But they should take my advice instead: let them take up some other task, do some other favor, make a show of themselves in some other matter. It is fine with me if charm gives prosperity and extravagance mastery—at Clodia's house. Let them cling to her, let them lie at her feet and grovel. But let them spare the life and fortunes of an innocent man.[93]

Cicero maintains that these men were false witnesses ready to swear to having observed an event that never occurred. Their testimony, according to Cicero, was the sole support for the trumped-up charge of poisoning (*haec causa . . . ad testes tota traducta est,* 66).[94] He clearly expects his audience to (a) enjoy the lively dining-room scene with which he

---

92. Geffcken 1973, 37–40.

93. Quam volent in conviviis faceti, dicaces, non numquam etiam ad vinum diserti sint, alia fori vis est, alia triclinii, alia subselliorum ratio, alia lectorum; non idem iudicum comissatorumque conspectus; lux denique longe alia est solis, alia lychnorum. Quam ob rem excutiemus omnes istorum delicias, omnes ineptias, si prodierint. Sed me audiant, navent aliam operam, aliam ineant gratiam, in aliis se rebus ostentent, vigeant apud istam mulierem venustate, dominentur sumptibus, haereant, iaceant, deserviant; capiti vero innocentis fortunisque parcant (Cic. *Cael.* 67).

94. Wiseman (1985, 30) argues that these are portrayed like the *cultus adulter* character in mime (rather than as parasites), but the parallels he cites (Ovid *Tr.* 2.499, 505, and Apul. *Met.* 9.22 ff.) do not explain a number of important features of the description, namely, the wit, the dependency, the convivial setting, and the plural number.

regales them and (b) believe that Clodia would be offered such a disreputable service by men dependent on her goodwill. The picture of Aebutius and Caesennia is drawn in much less garish colors, of course, but the dependents of both women display the same incompetence in the company of men and the same ingratiating behavior.

The figure of the parasite, then, is what Cicero uses to describe Aebutius' position vis-à-vis Caesennia. But that role belonged to the past. Caesennia was now dead, and Aebutius faced Caecina in court. When Cicero tells the story of the conflict between his client, Caecina, and Aebutius, a rather different picture of the man emerges.[95]

The presentation of the two men is largely a study in contrast. Caecina was, according to Cicero, an upstanding man. His character is presented much more subtly than was that of Aebutius; he is not a type at all and has no formal portrait. His virtues emerge "naturally" from the events narrated; they "just happen to be" the precise opposites of Aebutius' defects. Aebutius is a nobody with no connections; Caecina is a member of "the most important family in Etruria" (*amplissimo totius Etruriae nomine*, 103). Aebutius is litigious, *audax,* and *impudens;* Caecina is anxious that there be no unnecessary legal fuss (10, 23, 25). Aebutius' associates are a woman and a crew of disreputables (27); Caecina takes counsel and acts with his *amici* as any good Roman should do (2, 20). Aebutius employs violence; Caecina, ever the good citizen, defends himself with a lawsuit. Aebutius can only convince an ignorant woman that he has legal expertise, and his violence is all bluster: nobody thought he would dare fight, and in fact it was not he who issued the command to attack when things did get violent (25). Caecina, in contrast, is neither cowardly nor ignorant of the law: like the *vir fortis et sapiens* that Cicero dubs him (18), he refuses to yield his rights to such a scoundrel.[96] And so on. After all this, it is hardly a surprise to find Cicero suggesting in the peroration that character (that is to say, Caecina's good character and Aebutius' bad one) ought to count heavily in the judges' decision (104).

Yet one may suspect that Aebutius was not quite the insignificant creature Cicero tried to sketch in the *narratio.* Certain facts were refrac-

---

95. Cf. Frier 1985, 120: "Aebutius, who is introduced in the *narratio* simply as an unscrupulous parasite, emerges in the argument as a sinister figure whose actions are opposed to *ius* and *aequitas.*"

96. *Obtrivit et contudit* (*Caec.* 18) puts his scorn for Aebutius on display; see also 10, 103.

tory. It comes as a surprise, for instance, that the neighbors of the farm were willing to join him in armed resistance to Caecina and to appear in court, ten strong, on his behalf.[97] Would they be willing to do so if Aebutius was a nobody? Caecina was the undisputed owner of at least one property in the neighborhood (the one that came to him from Caesennia's dowry) and, as Cicero claims, had already taken possession of the disputed farm (19, 94–95). Either Aebutius had the wherewithal for massive bribes, or he had some clout in the neighborhood. Also, he managed, somehow, to survive without Caesennia's support during the four years of her marriage to Caecina (17), yet Cicero has no other victim to reproach him with.[98] One feels, too, a certain discrepancy between the personae created, between the tool of Caesennia and the foe of Caecina. Each caricature serves its own end—that of the parasite casts doubt on Aebutius' case for ownership, and that of the violent aggressor allows Cicero to parade Caecina's manly virtues.

In the years between the death of her first husband Fulcinius and her marriage to Caecina, Caesennia was in a position to make the most of her legal freedoms. She was not subject to her father's control (the farm that she bought with money from her dowry returned to her, not to her father, after Fulcinius' death), and she had no husband.[99] Caesennia needed the authorization of a *tutor* for transactions involving assets of land and personnel and for the making of her will, but this need not have been a great impediment. Cicero would remark just a few years later that *tutores* had been effectively stripped of their powers of control.

Many excellent practices were founded on our laws, but most of these have been vitiated or perverted by the cleverness of our "legal experts." Because women are not good managers, our forebears wanted them all to be under the control of guardians. But

97. We are not informed about the social status of these neighbors, which may indicate that Cicero could not plausibly discredit them by claiming that they were negligible types available for hire.

98. Frier (1985, 275–76; cf. 35–36) suggests that Aebutius is described as a "social parasite living off his legal representation of Roman women," but Cicero provides no evidence for the generalization.

99. Even independent-minded women like Cicero's wife Terentia and the woman commemorated in the inscription called the *laudatio Turiae* will have noticed that husbands took a strong interest in the management of their wives' property.

our legal experts have given us guardians who are under the control of women![100]

Being entitled to manage property did not, however, necessarily mean that Caesennia would want to play an active role in doing so. Men who wished to free themselves of the legal side of asset management would find themselves a *cognitor*, a legal representative. The author of the *Rhetorica ad Herennium* heartily approved of a legal development that allowed someone who was elderly or unwell to appoint a *cognitor* to represent him in court.[101] Other *cognitores* seem to have been appointed purely as a matter of convenience.[102] Certainly that is the case with the *voluntarius cognitor* in Horace's *Satire* 2.5. Horace's picture was quite negative, of course, since his *cognitor* was really an inheritance-hunter in disguise, but the services that the *cognitor* offered his prey were not so very different from those performed for Antony's wife Fulvia by Cicero's friend Atticus in 42 B.C.: "When Fulvia was harried by lawsuits and beset by bigger worries, too, Atticus was so active in helping her that he was at her side whenever she made a promise to appear in court. He backed her in all her affairs."[103] Fulvia's husband was still very much alive at this time, of course, but he was not in any position to stand between his wife and the opportunists who were advancing claims against her. We do not know whether Fulvia

---

100. Nam, cum permulta praeclare legibus essent constituta, ea iure consultorum ingeniis pleraque corrupta ac depravata sunt. Mulieres omnis propter infirmitatem consili maiores in tutorum potestate esse voluerunt; hi invenerunt genera tutorum quae potestate mulierum continerentur (Cic. *Mur.* 27).

101. Ex aequo et bono ius constat quod ad veritatem et utilitatem communem videtur pertinere; quod genus, ut maior annis LX et cui morbus causa est cognitorem det (*Rhet. Her.* 2.20). On the legal procedures and constraints see Kaser 1966, 153–56.

102. Cicero does not trouble to explain why Q. Roscius made Fannius his *cognitor* (Cic. *pro Q. Rosc.* 32, 38, 53–56).

103. ipsi autem Fuluiae, cum litibus distineretur magnisque terroribus uexaretur, tanta diligentia officium suum praestitit, ut nullum illa stiterit uadimonium sine Attico, <Atticus> sponsor omnium rerum fuerit (Nep. *Att.* 9.4). In a letter to Crassus, Cicero mentions his own services to Crassus' wife and daughter-in-law: praestantissima omnium feminarum, uxor tua, et eximia pietate, virtute, gratia tui Crassi *meis consiliis, monitis, studiis, actionbusque* nituntur (Cic. *Fam.* 5.8.2).

expressed her gratitude to Atticus in her will, but Antony was later able to even up the balance of services between them.[104]

What are we to make of the inheritance of 1/72 that Caesennia willed to Aebutius? Was it, as Cicero would have us believe, an insult, a reflection of the triviality of the man's services? Or is any inheritance a public declaration of the testator's gratitude and respect? The latter explanation is more likely, but it is difficult to be sure that one is correcting accurately for the bias with which Cicero interprets the situation.[105] It is not at all difficult, however, to see that when Cicero wanted to show that Aebutius was to be regarded not as a true friend, not as an Atticus vis-à-vis Fulvia, but as a predatory scoundrel like the *cognitor* in *Sat.* 2.5, it was the figure of the parasite that helped him to do so.

We do not have to look far in Cicero's corpus to see that the negative picture created by the parasite/patron(ess) model is a function not of the relationship itself but of Cicero's purpose in describing it. A decade earlier he had placed another propertied woman in a very much more flattering light.

> As soon as Sex. Roscius became aware of his enemies' plot, he followed the advice of his friends and relatives and fled to Rome. He took refuge with Caecilia (sister of Metellus Nepos, daughter of Metellus Baliaricus), since she had done a great deal for his father. I mention her name to do her honor. One can find still today a model for behavior in her old-fashioned sense of duty. When Roscius was helpless, when he had been driven out of his home and possessions and was being pursued by the weapons and threats of these thieves, she took him into her home. She gave help to a friend in need when everyone else had despaired of his cause.[106]

---

104. Nep. *Att.* 10.4; cf. 21.1 for the inheritances left to Atticus: multas enim hereditates nulla alia re quam bonitate consecutus est.

105. The lowest partial inheritance mentioned in a recent discussion of Roman wills is 1/40 (Champlin 1991, 142–54). However, Champlin also lists numerous bequests to friends of trifling amounts. These were manifestly *honoris causa*.

106. Quod hic simul atque sensit, de amicorum cognatorumque sententia Romam confugit et sese ad Caeciliam, Nepotis sororem, Baliarici filiam, quam honoris causa nomino, contulit, qua pater usus erat plurimum; in qua muliere, iudices, etiam nunc, id quod omnes semper existimaverunt, quasi exempli causa vestigia antiqui offici remanent. Ea Sex. Roscium inopem, eiectum domo

Cicero praises Caecilia for having taken Sex. Roscius under her patronal wing (and into her house). And Sextus' father, too, had apparently benefited from his connection with her. One may suspect that both Sextus and his father would have been "at her service" should Caecilia have needed anything they could offer. In short, if women had enough resources to attract *clientes*, they could be caricatured as hosts to parasites as well.

In creating a parasite dependent on a woman, Cicero put an old caricature to use in grappling with a relatively new problem. In characterizing the contemporary philosopher Philodemus as a parasite, by contrast, he had a long tradition behind him, for philosopher-parasites were favorite targets of comedy.

The term φιλόσοφος and its Latin transliteration *philosophus* had a wide range of applicability—being used of many others besides those who passed along and modified the doctrines of the various "schools"—but one can identify as the lowest common denominator of its meaning a privileging of intellectual over material goods. Philosophers in pursuit of material gain (however modest) were thus easy prey for critics. The emperor Antoninus Pius gave a particularly clear statement of the charge: "It seems to me that [sc. philosophers] who have plenty of money ought to be willing to pay their municipal dues like anyone else. If they are going to niggle about money, it will be clear that they do not really live a life in accordance with the dictates of philosophy."[107]

The philosopher-parasite can be traced as far back as Middle Comedy. A fragment from a play of Eubulus contains an abusive comment directed at a group of men defined by the phrase "dirty-footed men who make their beds in the dirt and their homes in the open." They are, says an unspecified speaker, "impious tongues, 'women' who feed at the expense of another and clutch at plates full of white fish-

---

atque expulsum ex suis bonis, fugientem latronum tela et minas recepit domum hospitique oppresso iam desperatoque ab omnibus opitulata est (Cic. *pro Sex. Rosc.* 27).

107. οἶμαι δὲ ὅτι οἱ πλούτῳ ὑπερβάλλοντες ἐθελονταὶ παρέξουσιν τὰς ἀπὸ τῶν χρημάτων ὠφελείας ταῖς πατρίσιν· εἰ δὲ ἀκριβολογοῖντο περὶ τὰς οὐσίας, αὐτόθεν ἤδη φανεροὶ γενήσονται μὴ φιλοσοφοῦντες (*Dig.* 27.1.6.7 [Modestinus, quoting a rescript of Antoninus Pius]).

paunches."[108] The term παραδειπνίδες (meaning "women who feed beside [and at the expense of] others") is obviously a by-form of παράσιτοι;[109] a character in Athenaeus' *Scholars' Dinner Party* quotes these lines in attacking a philosopher of the Cynic persuasion. Cynics and parasites are also connected in Plautus' *Persa*.

> "Moneybags" won't make it as a parasite. Anyone who has the wherewithal will want to start the party right away and stuff himself at his own expense. A parasite really ought to be like the Cynic, penniless. He needs an oil flask, a strigil, a cup, shoes, a cloak, and a pouch with not enough in it to provide him and his with sufficient cheer.[110]

The authors of *Lives* of the various philosophers, writing often centuries after the men they were writing about, even seem to have drawn on comic sources for "historical" anecdotes about their subjects. Apropos of Diogenes (the original Cynic), for example, we read that "when someone showed Diogenes a sundial, he remarked that it was a useful

---

108.   οὗτοι ἀνιπτόποδες χαμαιευνάδες ἀερίοικοι,
       ἀνόσιοι λάρυγγες,
       ἀλλοτρίων κτεάνων παραδειπνίδες, ὦ λοπαδάγχαι
       λευκῶν ὑπογαστριδίων.

(Eubulus, 137 K-A)

See Hunter 1983, ad loc., for discussion.

109.   Eustathius 1058.12 ff. Valk: φέρεται γοῦν Εὐβούλου περὶ φιλοσόφων τὸ "ἀνιπτόποδες ... παραδειπνίδες," ὃ παραπεποίηκεν ἐκεῖνος ἐκ τοῦ παρασίτου. The contemptuous feminine synonym is unusual, since the inferior *comparandi* used for parasites are generally slaves or beasts, not women.

110.   nihili parasitus est qui Argentumdonidest:
       lubido extemplo coeperest convivium,
       tuburcinari de suo, si quid domist.
       cynicum esse egentem oportet parasitum probe:
       ampullam, strigilem, scaphium, soccos, pallium,
       marsuppium habeat, inibi paullum praesidi
       qui familiarem suam vitam oblectet modo.

(Plaut. *Persa* 123–26)

Leo (1906) felt that the Cynic described in the Greek original of this passage was Diogenes himself, but chronological difficulties arise on that interpretation. See Woytek 1982, 65–79 and *ad* 123.

device: it would keep one from arriving too late for dinner."[111] A similarly comic trait is credited to the Academic philosopher Ctesibius of
Chalcis: "When someone asked Ctesibius what he had gained from
philosophy, he replied, 'Being able to dine at someone else's
expense.'"[112] In the second century A.D. Lucian was still drawing an
analogy between the two professions. In the dialogue *On the Philosophy
of Nigrinus*, for example, he has the title character profess himself irritated by the behavior of "self-styled philosophers" (τῶν φιλοσοφεῖν
προσποιουμένων) who, despite their intellectual pretenses, are less
restrained even than ordinary folk (ἰδιῶται) in making themselves
amusing.

Take their behavior at parties—how can we describe this as a
form of virtue? They stuff themselves with abandon, there's no
hiding their drunkenness, they are the last to take their leave, and
when they do go they've stuffed their pockets fuller than anyone
else. Some of the more amusing ones can even be induced to sing.

"They don't use props," he says, "but in every other respect they are
just like characters in a play."[113] Let us see what use Cicero makes of

---

111. ὁ γοῦν Διογένης πρὸς τὸν ἐπιδεκνύοντα αὐτῷ ὡροσκοπεῖον χρήσιμον
ἔφη τὸ ἔργον πρὸς τὸ μὴ ὑστερῆσαι δείπνου (Diog. Laert. 6.104). For a discussion of comic elements in ancient biographies of philosophers see Fairweather
1974, 238, 247–49, 267–68 (on the migration of anecdotes from one *Life* into others), and Gaiser 1981.

112. The tale is told by the biographer Antigonus of Carystus (fl. 240 B.C.):
Κτησίβιος δ' ὁ Χαλκιδεὺς ὁ Μενεδήμου γνώριμος, ὥς φησιν Ἀντίγονος ὁ
Καρύστιος ἐν τοῖς βίοις, ἐρωτηθεὶς ὑπό τινος τί περιγέγονεν ἐκ φιλοσοφίας
αὐτῷ ἔφη "ἀσυμβόλως δειπνεῖν" (p. 102 Wilamowitz). Ctesibius was reviled
by the third-century B.C. Skeptic Timon: δειπνομανές, νεβροῦ ὄμματ' ἔχων,
κραδίην δ' ἀκύλιστον (Timon fr. 188 Diels). According to Athenaeus' character Magnus, he was εὔστοχος . . . καὶ χαρίεις περὶ τὸ γελοῖον. διὸ καὶ
πάντες αὐτὸν ἐπὶ τὰ συμπόσια παρεκάλουν (Ath. 4.163a).

113. καὶ ὃ μάλιστα ἀγανακτῶ, ὅτι μὴ καὶ τὴν σκευὴν μεταλαμβάνουσι,
τὰ ἄλλα γε ὁμοίως ὑποκρινόμενοι τοῦ δράματος· ἃ μὲν γὰρ ἐν τοῖς συμπο-
σίοις ἐργάζονται, τίνι τῶν καλῶν εἰκάσομεν; οὐκ ἐμφοροῦνται μὲν
ἀπειροκαλώτερον, μεθύσκονται δὲ φανερώτερον, ἐξανίστονται δὲ πάντων
ὕστατοι, πλείω δὲ ἀποφέρειν τῶν ἄλλων ἀξιοῦσιν; οἱ δὲ ἀστειότεροι
πολλάκις αὐτῶν καὶ ᾆσαι προήχθησαν (Lucian *Nigr.* 24–25). This passage is
one of many in which Lucian uses the figure of the parasite to

these characters in the speech he composed attacking L. Calpurnius
Piso in 55 B.C.

The *in Pisonem* is not a courtroom speech but a harangue on the political, military, personal, social, and ethical inadequacies of the ex-consul
of 58. Much of the evidence that Cicero cites concerning the latter two
categories was, he claims, already in the public domain in the form of
occasional poems that reflected Piso's lifestyle "as if in a mirror" (*Pis.*
71). Cicero reinforces his argument by describing the character and
position of the author of those poems, Philodemus.

> There is a certain Greek who spends a lot of time with Piso. He's
> an agreeable chap, really (I know the man), but only so long as he
> is in the company of other men than Piso or is by himself. This
> Greek fellow, although he saw that our friend here was showing
> already as a youth his hideous grimace, nevertheless did not
> scorn his friendship, since he had been specially sought out. In
> fact, he devoted himself to keeping the man company and from
> then on spent all his time with Piso and practically never left his
> side. . . . And as soon as our fine stallion here heard this philoso-
> pher give high praise to pleasure, he sought no further. His pas-
> sions were roused and he positively whinnied his appreciation of
> the lecture, as if he thought he had found not a morals teacher but
> a pleasure preacher. At first, the Greek tried to draw some dis-
> tinctions and define the terms he was using, but Piso, in the man-
> ner of the lame man in the story, catches the ball and holds onto it.
> He gives evidence in support of the proposition, is ready to write
> an affidavit, decrees that Epicurus is a clever one. What Epicurus
> says (I think) is that he can perceive no good but bodily pleasure.
> You can guess the outcome. An easygoing [*facilis*] and agreeable
> [*valde venustus*] Greek was unwilling to oppose a senator of the
> Roman people.[114]

make a point about contemporary philosophers. For a discussion of Lucian on
philosophers see Jones 1986, 24–32.

114. Est quidam Graecus qui cum isto vivit, homo, vere ut dicam—sic enim
cognovi—humanus, sed tam diu quam diu aut cum aliis est aut ipse secum. Is
cum istum adulescentem iam tum hac distracta fronte vidisset, non fastidivit
eius amicitiam, cum esset praesertim appetitus; dedit se in consuetudinem sic
ut prorsus una viveret nec fere ab isto umquam discederet. . . . (69) Itaque
admissarius iste, simul atque audivit voluptatem a philosopho tanto opere laudari, nihil expiscatus est, sic suos sensus voluptarios omnis incitavit, sic ad

In this sketch Cicero avoids impugning Philodemus qua philosopher: the good intentions of the *magister virtutis* (morals teacher) are overthrown by a *discipulus* who was not particularly bright (*non acriter intellegenti*, 68) and who insisted on a willfully superficial interpretation of the key term *voluptas* (68–69).[115] Philodemus does not emerge unscathed, however, for "easygoing" and "agreeable" suggest a man whose position in society is such that he must follow, not lead. And Cicero does not scruple to say that Philodemus made a habit of taking his cues from Piso. For the philosopher also produced poetry, a form of discourse that, Cicero reminds his audience, was not approved by Epicureans: "Now the Greek of whom I am speaking had at his fingertips not only philosophy but also other accomplishments that Epicureans are said commonly to neglect. He proceeded to compose a poem so witty, neat, and elegant that nothing could be cleverer."[116] A philosopher writing frivolous verse? Cicero explains that Philodemus was a reluctant versifier: rather than risk being thought insufficiently attentive to duty, he silenced his doctrinal scruples and wrote the occasional verses his patron wanted.

> He came to (or rather, fell in with) Piso. It is no wonder if a Greek newly arrived in Italy was fooled by the austere grimace that had already fooled so many wise men and so great a state as ours.

illius hanc orationem adhinnivit, ut non magistrum virtutis sed auctorem libidinis a se illum inventum arbitraretur. Graecus primo distinguere et dividere, illa quem ad modum dicerentur; iste, 'claudus' quem ad modum aiunt 'pilam', retinere quod acceperat, testificari, tabellas obsignare velle, Epicurum disertum decernere. Et tamen dicit, ut opinor, se nullum bonum intellegere posse demptis corporis voluptatibus. (70) Quid multa? Graecus facilis et valde venustus nimis pugnax contra senatorem populi Romani esse noluit (*Pis*. 68–70; the text is from Nisbet 1961).

115. Cf. *Pis*. 74: Quaere ex familiari tuo Graeco illo *poeta*. It is rather Piso's conspicuous and, according to Cicero, hypocritical Epicureanism that bears the brunt of the attack (*Pis*. 19–22, 37, 58–60, 62, 92, *Sest*. 212–24, *Red. Sen*. 13). The portrait of Philodemus is discussed in some detail in Gigante 1983b, 35–53. He explains the ambivalence of the description as a reflection of the two areas—political and scholarly—of Cicero's own interests.

116. Est autem hic de quo loquor non philosophia solum sed etiam ceteris studiis quae fere Epicureos neglegere dicunt perpolitus; poema porro facit ita festivum, ita concinnum, ita elegans, nihil ut fieri possit argutius (*Pis*. 70). The Epicurean position on poetry was of course a good deal more complex than Cicero lets on. For recent discussion and bibliography see Asmis 1992.

Once caught, he was unable to extricate himself from the relation-ship—he was afraid he might get a reputation for being unreli-able. When Piso asked him, urged him, pressed him to write, he wrote for him and also about him. The man's diversions, dinner and drinking parties of all sorts (not to mention affairs with mar-ried ladies)—all these he described in the most delicious verses. Piso's lifestyle is on show for anyone who cares to read them. Many people have read or heard them, and I'd give you a sample here if I didn't feel that even in mentioning this sort of thing I've gone beyond the custom of this court. And anyway, I don't want to harm the fellow who wrote the verses. If he had had better luck in finding a disciple, it would probably have been better for his gravity and his dignity. But Philodemus' bad luck reduced him to writing stuff utterly unworthy of a philosopher, if it really is the case that philosophy teaches virtue and duty and how to live a good life. Anyone who teaches philosophy ought to act the part, however difficult it is to do so. Philodemus didn't really realize what task he set himself when he claimed to be a philosopher, and that bad luck of his spattered him with the mud and filth of this disgusting and ungovernable brute.[117]

Cicero's target in this speech is not Philodemus, of course, but Philode-mus' patron, Piso, so he can afford to dismiss the philosopher's moral collapse with a tolerant wave: "Go ahead and criticize him for writing

---

117. Devenit autem seu potius incidit in istum eodem deceptus supercilio Graecus atque advena quo tot sapientes et tanta civitas; revocare se non poterat familiaritate implicatus, et simul inconstantiae famam verebatur. Rogatus invi-tatus coactus ita multa ad istum de isto quoque scripsit ut omnis hominis libidines, omnia stupra, omnia cenarum genera conviviorumque, adulteria denique eius delicatissimis versibus expresserit, (71) in quibus si qui velit pos-sit istius tamquam in speculo vitam intueri; ex quibus multa a multis et lecta et audita recitarem, ni vererer ne hoc ipsum genus orationis quo nunc utor ab huius loci more abhorreret; et simul de ipso qui scripsit detrahi nil volo. Qui si fuisset in discipulo comparando meliore fortuna, fortasse austerior et gravior esse potuisset; sed eum casus in hanc consuetudinem scribendi induxit philosopho valde indignam, si quidem philosphia, ut fertur, virtutis continet et offici et bene vivendi disciplinam; quam qui profitetur gravissimam mihi sustinere personam videtur. Sed idem casus illum ignarum quid profiteretur, cum se philosophum esse diceret, istius impurissimae atque intemperantissi-mae pecudis caeno et sordibus inquinavit (Pis. 70–71).

these verses, but do it gently. He's not a low, barefaced rogue but a foreigner, a flatterer, a poet" (*non ut improbum, non ut audacem, non ut impurum, sed ut Graeculum, ut adsentatorem, ut poetam, Pis.* 70).[118] Philodemus the Epicurean ought to have had nothing to do with poetry or with the kind of *voluptates* that Piso reveled in, but Philodemus the *Graeculus* and *adsentator* yields to his patron's taste on both counts.

Why does Cicero tell this painful tale? Cicero does give a reason (not necessarily the right reason): he needs details of Piso's personal life to fuel this portion of his invective, but as a long-standing enemy to Piso Cicero cannot produce such details on his own authority.[119] Philodemus, who "spent all his time with Piso and practically never left his side," had produced verses that served Cicero's needs admirably. So Cicero exploits the stereotype of the hypocritical philosopher-parasite, who obeys the dictates of his belly more readily than the philosophical doctrines he professes, to show that his allegations about Piso's private life are based on inside information.[120]

The *in Pisonem* is not the only source of information about Philodemus' place in the world. Philodemus himself had produced writings that contributed to his public image, and these writings help us see what Cicero had to work with in creating the picture of Philodemus that he uses in his attack on Piso.

By origin from Syrian Gadara, Philodemus spent a number of years

---

118. In quo [sc. poemate] reprehendat eum licet si qui volet, modo leviter, non ut improbum, non ut audacem, non ut impurum, sed ut Graeculum, ut adsentatorem, ut poetam (*Pis.* 70).

119. *Pis.* 68: Dicet aliquis 'unde haec tibi nota sunt?' Cf. *Sest.* 23–24, *Prov.* 14, and *Red. Sen.* 14 for the privacy of Piso's *libidines.* The phrase *nec fere ab isto umquam discederet* (*Pis.* 68) has been taken to imply that Philodemus was with Piso in Macedonia, but if that fact is true, Cicero fails to exploit it in his other references to the *Graecus comitatus* (see n. 120 in this chapter). The identification of Catullus' Socration with Philodemus will not be convincing until an appropriate identity for Porcius can be found (*Carm.* 47). Perhaps *Porcius* is not a *gentilicium* but a nickname drawing its meaning from the frequent association of Epicureans and pigs (e.g., *Pis.* 19–20, 37, 42, 71; also *Amic.* 32 and Hor. *Epist.* 1.4.16). See Fordyce 1961 for discussion and bibliography.

120. Cicero is not always punctilious about supporting his allegations, but he is so here, probably because the description of the relationship between Philodemus and his patron contributes to two other forms of insult as well: first, it serves to particularize the *Graecus comitatus* with which he reproaches Piso on numerous occasions (*Pis.* 22, 42, 67, 89, *Prov.* 14); second, it provides a response to Piso's critique of his poetry (*Pis.* 72–75).

in Athens studying under the Epicurean Zeno of Sidon, a master of whom he speaks fondly and whose teachings he cites frequently.[121] This will have been in the eighties and perhaps early seventies B.C., when Zeno is known to have been active there.[122] But at some point Philodemus transferred his activities to Italy, where he was well established in the early fifties.[123]

We find him dedicating works to well-placed Romans, for example. The treatise *On the Good King according to Homer* goes to Piso's address, as does an invitation poem (not to mention the frivolous verses held up to scorn in the *in Pisonem*).[124] He seems to have favored a connection of Piso's with another work, the *Rhetorica*, which is addressed to a Γάιε παῖ who is generally taken to be C. Calpurnius Piso Frugi, Cicero's sometime son-in-law who died young in 57.[125]

Apart from the fact of the dedication, however, and the choice of subject matter of interest to Roman *principes,* these two treatises are at present in too fragmentary a state to reveal much about the relationship between author and dedicatee. The invitation poem, however, was preserved in its entirety in the *Garland of Philip.*[126] Let us see what it reveals about Philodemus' view of his relationship with Piso.

> My dear Piso, your muse-loved mate wants to drag you to his
> humble abode tomorrow at three for dinner, for the annual cele-

---

121. Origin: Strabo 16.759. Zeno: *P. Herc.* 1003, 1389, and 1471 are labeled ἐκ τῶν Ζήνωνος σχολῶν. There are also references to him in περὶ σημείων, περὶ τῆς τῶν θεῶν περὶ τῆς τῶν θεῶν ἀγώγης, περὶ θεῶν, and περὶ εὐσεβείας. Philodemus' fondness: *P. Herc.* 1005, col. 9.5.

122. Cic. *N.D.* 1.59, *Fin.* 1.16, *Tusc.* 3.38.

123. For a brief discussion see Allen and Delacy 1939.

124. The date of the treatise is uncertain, but recent opinion puts it early, in the seventies (when Piso was in his thirties), rather than later. Views on the precise relevance of the topic to a Roman magistrate vary as well. See, e.g., Murray 1965 and 1984, 157–60; Dorandi 1982, 39–47; Fowler 1986, 82; Asmis 1991. On the dating of Philodemus' epigrams see Griffiths 1970, 37–38.

125. 1.223 Sudhaus (1892). At least one of the interlocutors in the dialogue contained in *P. Herc.* 312 was Roman, too: at fragment III 2.1 we read "καθόλου," ἔφη πρὸς τὸν Σκατίνιον. For discussion see Gigante 1983a, 35, and Dorandi 1982, 28 and 43.

126. These works are most easily available in the edition of Gow and Page (1968). For discussion of a papyrus roll that contains a larger set of Philodemus' epigrams see Gigante 1989a.

bration of Epicurus' birthday. You'll have to pass up sow's udders and toasts of Chian wine, but the company will be utterly honest, and the conversation will be even sweeter than the tales told in the land of the Phaeacians. And if you favor me, too, with your glance, Piso, my feast will be sumptuous, not simple, after all.[127]

The first two couplets are pleasantly familiar in tone. Philodemus affects to read the invitation with Piso's eyes—it is as much an importunity as an opportunity to dine out, and the fare will not be as lavish as he could get elsewhere. In the third couplet, however, Philodemus mentions the compensations: unpretentious company, amusing conversation, a host who will be truly grateful if Piso makes an appearance (and whose gratitude will perhaps manifest itself in further elegant occasional poems attesting Piso's cultured *clientela*). Philodemus is still very cordial, but he betrays an awareness of the necessity of offering compensations. The tone is more like that of Horace's invitations to Maecenas (e.g., *Odes* 1.20, 3.29) than like that of Catullus' unabashedly jocular invitation to Fabullus (*C.* 13).[128] And in the final couplet, with its reference to Piso's favor, deference comes to the surface. These lines have even been criticized as begging flattery.[129] They do place Piso firmly on a plane above that of the passive objects of his godlike glance, but it does not necessarily follow from this that "sumptuous" is to be taken as a bid for material support.[130] In fact, the humbleness of Philodemus' abode and the simplicity of the fare are matters of doctri-

---

127. αὔριον εἰς λιτήν σε καλιάδα, φίλτατε Πείσων,
    ἐξ ἐνάτης ἕλκει μουσοφιλὴς ἕταρος
    εἰκάδα δειπνίζων ἐνιαύσιον· εἰ δ' ἀπολείψεις
    οὔθατα καὶ Βρομίου Χιογενῆ πρόποσιν,
    ἀλλ' ἑτάρους ὄψει παναληθέας, ἀλλ' ἐπακούσηι
    Φαιήκων γαίης πουλὺ μελιχρότερα.
    ἢν δέ ποτε στρέψηις καὶ ἐς ἡμέας ὄμματα, Πείσων,
    ἄξομεν ἐκ λιτῆς εἰκάδα πιοτέρην.

                                        (*A.P.* 11.44)

128. Gigante (1985) suggests that Horace and perhaps even Catullus drew on Philodemus' poem when writing their own.

129. Previous interpretations are summarized in Gigante 1985, 861–62. He himself thinks it a compliment modeled on Callimachus' *Hymn to Apollo* 9–11, where those privileged to see Apollo are οὔποτε λιτοί.

130. Kaibel 1885, 24.

nal choice, and the "richness" to be provided by Piso would result from his welcome presence, not from presents.[131] For Piso's presence (both at the party and in the poem) renders visible Philodemus' connections with the powerful. The Greek was not the only one to benefit from the connection: poems like this invitation were both personal and public documents—"many people" had "read and heard" the occasional verse that Cicero makes so much of in the *in Pisonem*, for example (*Pis.* 71)—and Philodemus clearly writes with the assumption that Piso will be pleased to have his association with cultured men like Philodemus and his ἐτάροι broadcast.[132]

The fundamental elements of the relationship between Philodemus and Piso are much the same in Cicero's description and Philodemus' own. In both, Philodemus is seen to suit his behavior to the taste and social position of his patron. But the situation gives rise to what in Philodemus' hands looks like graceful and appropriate deference to a superior he wants and expects to please, while in Cicero's hands it looks like a rather spineless capitulation to the Roman's overwhelming boorishness. Shall we discard Cicero's version as irresponsible invective or Philodemus' as special pleading? In fact, both versions shed light on important aspects of the relationship between Roman patron and literary Greek, and in recognizing their simultaneous validity, we achieve, I hope, a more sophisticated understanding of the way patronage worked in Roman society.

A much-quoted modern definition of patronage reads, "Patronage is a social relationship that is essentially (i) reciprocal, involving exchanges of services over time between two parties, (ii) personal as opposed to, e.g., commercial, and (iii) asymmetrical, i.e., between par-

---

131. The fare in *A.P.* 9.412 and 11.35 is no more opulent. The occasion mentioned in 11.44 was one of special relevance to the followers of Epicurus. On the Epicurean tenor of the poem see Hiltbrunner 1972, 168–72.

132. Despite the abuse he received in the *in Pisonem*, Philodemus continued to be successful in making useful Roman connections in the last decades of the Republic. Cicero himself is mentioned in and may be the dedicatee of a dialogue written sometime in or after 51 (Capasso 1992). He speaks in flattering terms of the philosopher in a treatise of 45 B.C. (*familiares nostros Sironem et Philodemum, cum optimos viros tum homines doctissimos, Fin.* 2.119). Vergil and three other literary Augustans (L. Varius, Quintilius Varus, and Plotius Tucca) are the dedicatees of a treatise *on Greed* and of at least one volume of *on Flattery* (see Körte 1890, 172–77; Gigante 1983b, 31–50, and 1989b, 3–6). One of the more technical treatises (*P. Herc.* 1005) seems to be addressed to a Greek]χαιε.

ties of different status."[133] Reciprocity would seem to entail at least a rough balance between services rendered and benefits received, and we can see Cicero worrying about the balance point in a letter to his younger friend Curio.

> If my services to you were as great as you are in the habit of saying they are (they don't seem to me so substantial), I would have greater scruples about asking a big favor of you. For no modest man enjoys seeking a large favor from someone he knows to be in his debt, lest he seem not to seek but to demand and to count the service as a payment, not a favor. But since you have done so many wonderful things for me already (everyone knows about them since my situation is so very unusual), and since a gentleman is always ready to increase his indebtedness, I haven't hesitated to write to ask for something that is of the very greatest importance to me. I am not worried that I'll be crushed by the weight of your countless services to me, for my spirit sets no limits on what it can owe to you or what it can multiply and magnify in repayment.[134]

This passage does something that the definition does not: it makes it clear that there has to be someone to do the balancing.[135] This stipulation is crucial. The relationships that we have examined in this chapter help show that the services/benefits equation looks very different from different points of view. Philodemus and Piso may have been perfectly

---

133. Wallace-Hadrill 1989, 3.

134. Ego, si mea in te essent officia solum, Curio, tanta quanta magis a te ipso praedicari quam a me ponderari solent, verecundius a te, si quae magna res mihi petenda esset, contenderem. grave est enim homini pudenti petere aliquid magnum ab eo de quo se bene meritum putet, ne id quod petat exigere magis quam rogare et in mercedis potius quam benefici loco numerare videatur. sed quia tua in me [vel] nota omnibus vel ipsa novitate meorum temporum clarissima et maxima beneficia exstiterunt estque animi ingenui, cui multum debeas, eidem plurimum velle debere, non dubitavi id a te per litteras petere quod mihi omnium esset maximum maximeque necessarium. neque enim sum veritus ne sustinere tua in me vel innumerabilia <officia> non possem, cum praesertim confiderem nullam esse gratiam tuam quam non vel capere animus meus in accipiendo vel in remunerando cumulare atque illustrare posset (*Fam.* 2.6.1–2).

135. See Saller 1982, 16–17, for the difficulties of finding exact equivalences between services of different types.

content with the "balance of trade" between them—we have no indication that they were not. But that does not mean that Cicero could not
feel that he was on rhetorically strong ground in criticizing the relationship, in pointing out that Philodemus' half of the exchange
involved not just philosophical instruction and the production of occasional verse and diligent attendance on his patron but also a kind of
moral capitulation. Cicero expects to be persuasive when he asserts
that, for Philodemus, obliging his patron involved a retreat from his
Epicurean principles. From this point of view (that of an observer external to the relationship), it is difficult to believe that the accounts
between Philodemus and his patron can ever balance. How can one
assess what Philodemus' "services" cost him, and what could Piso do
that would cost him as much? In fact, the relationship between philosopher and patron seems often to have looked (to external observers) like
an exchange that required, on the one side, a moral sacrifice and, on the
other, the expenditure of some superfluous cash. From this point of
view the mask of the parasite fit snugly onto the philosopher. And it is
no less important to consider this point of view in evaluating the
ancient experience of patronage than it is to consider the views of the
patron and client themselves.

Yet descriptions of the service provided by philosophers frequenting
Roman households often content themselves with the view from one of
the various vantage points. Philodemus gives us (not surprisingly) the
philosopher's point of view when he maintains that the migration of
philosophers in pursuit of patronage was a perfectly justifiable phenomenon: "Some philosophers take up residence in powerful cities like
Alexandria and Rome, motivated either by necessity or by the possibility of serving their own hometown's interests greatly thereby."[136] Not
all philosophers shared Philodemus' point of view, however, for

---

136. ἐνίους δὲ καὶ δυναστευτικαὶ πόλεις καὶ χῶραι κατέσχον ὥσπερ
Ἀλεξάνδρεια καὶ Ῥώμη τοῦτο μὲν ἀνάγκαις τοῦτο δὲ μεγάλαις ἑαυτῶν τε
καὶ πατρίδων χρείαις (Rhet. 2.145 Sudhaus). For "necessity" cf. P. Herc. 222,
col. IV.4–6. χρεῖαι πατρίδων are not, in fact, particularly well attested: "Most
of the cultivated Greeks who appeared regularly in the retinues of Roman
luminaries did not use their good offices in the interests of particular Greek
communities" (Bowersock 1965, 4). Philodemus' is an apologist's view: καὶ
ταῦτα μὲν ἐγὼ λέγω περὶ τῶν φιλοσόφων αὐτῶν ἀπολογούμενος (Rhet. 2.145
Sudhaus).

Epictetus looks at the spectacle of philosophers in pursuit of security and influence from outside the rat race, so to speak.

> Does it seem right to us that the philosopher should leave his home hoping and expecting that others will provide for him? Should he not attend to his own needs himself? Or is he to be weaker and more abject than the unreasoning beasts, who are able to provide for themselves? They do not lack the food they need, and they manage their lives in accordance with their own natures.

He puts the matter with characteristic bluntness: for philosophers of his day and age, going abroad was an inappropriate solution to the question "how am I to feed myself?"[137] The dependence of one man on another creates an "incentive for flattery" (κολακείας ἀφορμή, 1.9.20): "We think of ourselves as bellies, as bowels, as genitals, and because we have fears and desires, we fawn on those who can help us allay fear and desire. But we end up fearing them, too."[138] Epictetus, when he adopts the point of view of an external observer, finds what he observes troubling because of the effects of dependency on the character of the philosopher—he becomes a craven flatterer whose reason and training are of less use to him than instinct is to animals. The relationship can also worry those who see a potential danger to the patron, as one can see from the arguments against philosophers that Dio puts in the speech that "Maecenas" makes to the new *princeps* Augustus (dramatic date 29 B.C.):

> This is the very thing [sc. speaking the truth occasionally, but more often falsehoods] that no small number of those self-styled philosophers do. Which is why I urge you to be wary of them, too.

---

137. τὸν δὲ φιλόσοφον ἡμῖν δεήσει ἄλλοις θαρροῦντα καὶ ἐπαναπαυόμενον ἀποδημεῖν καὶ μὴ ἐπιμελεῖσθαι αὐτὸν αὑτοῦ καὶ τῶν θηρίων τῶν ἀλόγων εἶναι χείρονα καὶ δειλότερον, ὧν ἕκαστον αὐτὸ αὑτῷ ἀρκούμενον οὔτε τροφῆς ἀπορεῖ τῆς οἰκείας οὔτε διεξαγωγῆς τῆς καταλλήλου καὶ κατὰ φύσιν· (Epict. *Diss.* 1.9.9); πόθεν φάγω; (1.9.8).

138. ἡμεῖς οὖν ὡς κολίαι, ὡς ἔντερα, ὡς αἰδοῖα, οὕτω περὶ αὐτῶν διανοούμεθα, ὅτι φοβούμεθα, ὅτι ἐπιθυμοῦμεν· τοὺς εἰς ταῦτα συνεργεῖν δυναμένους κολακεύομεν, τοὺς αὐτοὺς τούτους δεδοίκαμεν (Epict. *Diss.* 1.9.26).

I know you have found Areius and Athenodorus to be honorable and good men, but don't for that reason believe that all the others who claim to be philosophers are like them. For those who make this pretense do immeasurable harm to states and to individuals, too.[139]

Cicero is able to view the relationship of patron and philosopher from different vantage points at different times, as we have seen. In the *in Pisonem* he speaks as the external observer of a troubling social phenomenon, much the way Epictetus does, though more pointedly, of course, to suit the invective context of that speech. In the treatise *on Duties*, however, Cicero speaks of the presence of an intellectual companion as a (self-evident) desideratum.

Some argue (wrongly) from the fact that we are unable to obtain or produce the things we need without others that the human tendency to community and society is inborn. It follows that if everything that was necessary for human feeding and care were supplied by a magic wand, so to speak, then people with intellectual powers—relieved of all human tasks—would give themselves up to the pursuit of knowledge. But this is not the case: such people would flee solitude and seek a companion for their studies; they would want both to teach and to be taught, to listen and to speak.[140]

---

139. τὸ δ᾽ αὐτὸ τοῦτο καὶ τῶν φιλοσοφεῖν προσποιουμένων οὐκ ὀλίγοι δρῶσι. διὸ καὶ ἐκείνους φυλάσσεσθαί σοι παραινῶ. μὴ γὰρ, ὅτι καὶ Ἀρείου καὶ Ἀθηνοδώρου καλῶν καὶ ἀγαθῶν ἀνδρῶν πεπείρασαι, πίστευε καὶ τοὺς ἄλλους πάντας τοὺς φιλοσοφεῖν λέγοντας ὁμοίους αὐτοῖς εἶναι. μυρία γὰρ κακὰ καὶ δήμους καὶ ἰδιώτας τὸ πρόσχημά τινες τοῦτο προβαλλόμενοι δρῶσι (Dio 52.36.4).

Crawford (1978, 203) is an even more detached observer: Greek intellectuals provided not civilized entertainment but "flattery of Roman cultural pretensions." Cf. the "cultural ego-trip" provided Pompey by Theophanes (204) and Archias' "aiding and abetting Lucullus' cultural pretensions" (205). The Romans involved, it seems, were the willing victims of intentional flattery, and the whole crew, patrons and philosophers alike, looks rather silly.

140. Nec uerum est quod dicitur a quibusdam, propter necessitatem uitae, quod ea quae natura desideraret, consequi sine aliis atque efficere non possemus, idcirco insitam esse cum hominibus communitatem et societatem; quodsi omnia nobis quae ad uictum cultumque pertinent, quasi uirgula diuina, ut aiunt, suppeditarentur, tum optimo quisque ingenio negotiis omnibus omissis

Here Cicero stresses the desirability of the patron/philosopher relationship for the man who would seek out a companion for his studies. Another way of looking at the advantage of the connection for the Roman involved can be seen in Cicero's proud reference to "the learned men who were always present as ornaments to my household."[141] One of these ornaments was the Stoic Diodotus, who lived in Cicero's house and favored him with lessons in dialectic (*Brut.* 309). He remained with Cicero (though Cicero was never a Stoic) until his death in 59. It would seem that he was well known to Atticus (*Att.* 2.20.6) and Varro (*Fam.* 9.4.1), but he had to be described to Cicero's more distant connections, including Caesar (*Fam.* 13.16.4) and the "Lucullus" of the dialogue entitled *Lucullus* (*Luc.* 115). Cicero speaks of Diodotus with respect and affection, never alluding directly to his dependence, but the terms in which he couches his praise give a sufficient indication of dependence nevertheless. After describing Diodotus' admirable refusal to be handicapped by his blindness, he generalizes: "Just as a man can make do without financial resources, if he can rely on the kind of support that certain Greeks have nowadays, so blindness is bearable, as long as there are aids for one's infirmity."[142] The patron is pleased to have a status symbol and an interesting person about the house, as well as the

---

totum se in cognitione et scientia collocaret. Non est ita; nam et solitudinem fugeret et socium studii quaereret, tum docere, tum discere uellet, tum audire, tum dicere (*Off.* 1.158).

141. doctissimorum hominum familiaritates quibus semper domus nostra floruit (*N.D.* 1.6). The value of this ornament was rather variable, however. Cicero worries that the philosophical expertise with which he credits Lucullus in the *Academica* will not enhance Lucullus' reputation: ac vereor interdum ne talium personarum [sc. Luculli] cum amplificare velim minuam etiam gloriam. sunt enim multi qui omnino Graecas non ament litteras, plures qui philosophiam; reliqui etiam si haec non improbant, tamen earum rerum disputationem principibus non ita decoram putant (*Luc.* 5). One gathers that Lucullus had not troubled to advertise his long-standing connection with the Academic philosopher Antiochus, for Cicero calls his taste for philosophy *laudes minus notae minusve pervolgatae* (*Luc.* 7). Public hostility toward philosophy and philosophers is well attested. See, e.g., *N.D.* 1.8, *Fin.* 1.1, *Off.* 2.2, and Jocelyn 1977, 358.

142. ut enim vel summa paupertas tolerabilis sit, si liceat quod quibusdam Graecis cotidie, sic caecitas ferri facile possit, si non desunt subsidia valetudinum (*Tusc.* 5.113).

gratifying sensation of providing support for someone who could not (he thinks) get along without it.[143]

None of these evaluations of the relationship between Romans and dependent philosophers is wrong, but none is complete either. Plutarch has a wider optic than most ancient observers.[144] In an essay entitled "That a Philosopher Ought to Converse Especially with Men in Power," he discusses the relationship appropriate for such a conversation.

> Therefore a philosopher should not avoid befriending and cherishing a man in a position of leadership and power (provided the man behaves with moderation and civility, of course). Nor should he worry if people label him a hanger-on or call him servile. "Shunning the goddess of love is as unhealthy as pursuing her too avidly." The same applies to philosophers who seek to make a name for themselves by befriending the powerful. The unworldly philosopher will not avoid such men, while the philosopher interested in politics will positively seek them out. He won't make himself a nuisance with his talk, of course, or fill up his friend's ears with unseasonable or trivial discussion, but when the man wants it, he'll oblige with conversation, happy to share his hours of leisure with him.[145]

Plutarch sees that some philosophers (the ambitious ones) may want to initiate a connection with a man of power and influence and that men of power and influence may want to hear what a philosopher has to say. What is more, he sees that interaction between the two may be ben-

---

143. Rawson (1985, 59) uses the phrase *status symbol* apropos of Philodemus and Piso.

144. Personal experience may have broadened his perspective. For his Roman friends see Jones 1971, 20–38, 48–64.

145. οὕτως οὖν ἀξίας ἡγεμονικῆς καὶ δυνάμεως ἀνδρὶ μετρίῳ καὶ ἀστείῳ προσούσης. οὐκ ἀφέξεται [sc. ὁ φιλόσοφος] τοῦ φιλεῖν καὶ ἀγαπᾶν οὐδὲ φοβήσεται τὸ αὐλικὸς ἀκοῦσαι καὶ θεραπευτικός·

οἱ γὰρ Κύπριν φεύγοντες ἀνθρώπων ἄγαν

νοσοῦσ᾽ ὁμοίως τοῖς ἄγαν θηρωμένοις.

καὶ οἱ πρὸς ἔνδοξον οὕτως καὶ ἡγεμονικὴν φιλίαν ἔχοντες. ὁ μὲν οὖν ἀπράγμων φιλόσοφος οὐ φεύξεται τοὺς τοιούτους, ὁ δὲ πολιτικὸς καὶ περιέξεται αὐτῶν ἄκουσιν οὐκ ἐνοχλῶν οὐδὲ ἐπισταθμεύων τὰ ὦτα διαλέξεσιν ἀκαίροις καὶ σοφιστικαῖς, βουλομένοις δὲ χαίρων καὶ διαλεγόμενος καὶ σχολάζων καὶ συνὼν προθύμως (Plut. *Mor.* 778a–b).

eficial to society at large (776b and passim).[146] But he also sees that there will be people to whom the philosopher who tries to avoid untimely intrusions, who is called on to provide entertaining discussions in moments of leisure, and who is eager to serve merits the labels "courtier-like" (αὐλικός), "servile" (θεραπευτικός), or, I might add, "parasitical" (παρασιτικός).

---

146. This is in fact the "theme song" of the essay. See Pelling 1989 for this theme elsewhere in Plutarch.

Conclusion

We have now seen some fifty passages of a widely assorted variety in which a Roman evokes the parasite by name or by type to serve as an unflattering description of a dependent. Doubtless more could be found, especially if one looked to Greek literature of the Roman period; Lucian in particular found the type serviceable in his satirical representations of the world around him. The evidence that the passages we have looked at provide for friction in the operation of patronage in Roman society can be divided into two broad categories. The satirists were primarily concerned with the (bad) effects of dependence on the moral character of the people involved, while Cicero revealed more about its effects in the structure of Roman society at large.

In focusing on the moral consequences of dependence, the satirists remained close to the thematic territory of the parasite of comedy. The parasite, subservient to the needs and desires of his belly, had long served as an emblem of a pleasure-oriented way of life, one unworthy of a virtuous man. Horace's Mulvius (the lightweight of *Sat.* 2.7, who did what his belly ordered) and Maenius (the bottomless pit into which one could upend the marketplace, *Epist.* 1.15) are blood brothers to the pleasure-seeking parasites of comedy, though what these and other parasites experience is a far cry from pleasure, of course. Moral capitulation, such as that shown by Juvenal's Trebius, does not meet with significant material rewards in the world of satire—"if you can put up with anything, you deserve to put up with anything" (*omnia ferre / si potes, et debes, Sat.* 5.170–71). Parasitical behavior is always the wrong answer to the question "how am I to feed myself?" (πόθεν φάγω; Epict. *Diss.* 1.9.8). What makes some of the parasites of Roman satire more contemporary than comic is the object of their hunger—the pest of Horace's *Satire* 1.9 is hungry for connections, while the captatorial Ulysses of *Satire* 2.5 has his eye on potential inheritances; Juvenal's *Graeculus esuriens* and Naevolus both want to be set up in a life of relative luxury (*viscera magnarum domuum dominique futuri*, 3.72; *aliquid quo sit mihi tuta senectus,* 9.139). The means, too, by which these latter-day parasites pursue their ends differ somewhat from those of the comic parasite, but the formula remains in general terms the same: the dependent uses unworthy means (flattery, entertainment, services of dubious propriety or legality) for unworthy ends (food, clothing, connections, property). Both Horace and Juvenal in their very different ways explore the obstacles to virtue inherent in dependence: "Virtue is praised and shivers" (*probitas laudatur et alget,* Juv. *Sat.* 1.75).

Satire also extrapolates on what was already present in comedy in depicting the deleterious effect on a patron of associating with a dependent who has only his own interests in view. Lucilius gave the rich man a touchstone by which to distinguish real friends from parasites (Lucil. 716–17 Marx). Persius provides a brutally logical argument instead: "You serve a nice warm sow's udder and do it well, you give a shivering friend a cast-off cloak, and then you say, 'Please, tell me the truth about myself, the truth, mind you.' How can he?" (*Sat.* 1.53–56). Such passages might make one think it was easy for the patron to protect himself from the effects of a dependent's self-serving behavior, as do the epigrams of Martial in which the services peddled by the dependent are tiresome to the recipient (e.g., 2.27, 12.82). But both Horace and Juvenal show patrons whose weaknesses have been at least encouraged, if not caused, by their association with parasites. Surrounded as he is by parasites who defer to his wishes (Porcius), ape his behavior (Nomentanus), and encourage his pretensions (Balatro), Nasidienus is not likely to be any less ambitiously hospitable after the dinner party described in *Satire* 2.8. And the arrogant hosts of Juvenal are, as we have seen, as much the object of satire as are their parasitical dependents. Martial makes much the same point with his epigrams illustrating the impoverishment of the patron/client relationship (2.19, 6.51, 9.14). The material components of the exchange persist—meals on the one hand, cliental *munera* on the other—but the relationship that gave these "goods" an acceptable context has withered away to nothing. Patrons expect gratitude for a meal given grudgingly, and clients expect generosity in return for services they resent. Both sides are diminished when a dinner guest views his presence at the table as a form of revenge on his host (*Ep.* 6.51).

The satirists, then, concentrate their attention on the ways in which the behaviors that dependency makes profitable are damaging to the characters of both parties to the relationship. Cicero makes use of this theme in his speech against Piso, in his depiction of Philodemus, but his other parasites are social types rather than moral exempla. (His Philodemus is both.) In Naevius (that is, of course, in Cicero's picture of Naevius) we see the nouveau riche who outstrips those who have helped him along the way. C. Quinctius, the man who elevated him from the auction halls into polite society, is dead, and Naevius shows how superficial his sense of gratitude is by harassing his benefactor's brother in court. Though successful, he retains the objectionable habits and values that got him his start in life: "it's an old saying that 'a *scurra* will sooner become rich than responsible'" (Cic. *Quinct.* 57). Cicero's portrait is calculated to arouse the scorn of his social peers (members of the board of adjustors) for those they see climbing up the social ladder toward them, often at their own expense. (Naevius' opportunistic betrayal of his "friends" during the civil-war years was a particularly vivid indication of the expense.) This social process was not per se objectionable, as one can see from Seneca's complacent catalog of the factors that accounted for his friend Lucilius' success—"the force of your talent, the elegance of your writings, and the friendships you have made among the eminent and well born"—but particular instances of it could be made objectionable by the attitudes and actions of the individuals involved. To exploit these objections (scorn, resentment, even fear) in his attack on Naevius, Cicero characterizes Naevius' attitudes and actions as those of a parasite.

The same objectionable character is used to interpret Q. Apronius, though in the *Verrines* Cicero's rhetorical task was very different. Problematic for Cicero was not Apronius' manifest success but his degree of responsibility for the various crimes committed in Sicily. To emphasize Verres' guilt over Apronius', Cicero draws the latter as someone who courts and wins a powerful man's favor by defying social norms and legal boundaries, a willing agent for a provincial governor's dirty work. "Dear to Verres is the man who can accuse him whenever he pleases" (*carus erit Verri qui Verrem tempore quo vult / accusare potest*, Juv. *Sat.* 3.53–54). Defining (and policing) the acceptable limits on patronal clout was a task that the Romans were struggling with ever more desperately in these final decades of the Republic, and it was one at which Cicero and his fellow senators ultimately failed. They won the battle against Verres but lost the war to Caesar and his heir. The parasite could be evoked in connection with less egregiously criminal agents as well: the well-fed fellows who were willing to give false testimony to please

Mithridates (Cic. *Flac.* 17) and the wits who would do the same for Clodia (*Cael.* 67).

The parasite of Cicero's *pro Caecina* appears on a more humble social plane and in connection with a domestic problem rather than a political one. Men like Aebutius made it possible for a woman in Caesennia's position to be worrisomely free of familial control: "What was Aebutius to Caesennia? Don't ask whether he was a relative. There's not a shred of connection. A friend of her father or husband, then? Nothing of the sort. Who, then? Why, the fellow I've just sketched for you, a self-selected 'friend' for the woman, no connection of hers" (*Caec.* 14). Cicero is confident that his audience would have preferred Caesennia to have entrusted her affairs to someone chosen for her by a male relative. The figure of the parasite offers a negative interpretation of the friend and helper she chose for herself. Again, Caesennia's freedom was not in itself a problem—Cicero's contemporaries gave women the right to change their *tutores* at will (Cic. *Mur.* 27)—but people had experienced (or feared) unhealthy uses of that freedom. Caecilia's protection of Sex. Roscius could be mentioned in court to do her honor, but Caesennia, so Cicero argues, had been taken advantage of by an ingratiating shyster. If the one relationship is possible, so is the other.

In following the tracks of the parasite, we have discovered some sites of discomfort in this social system dominated by the patron/client relationship. He has not led us to all of the sites that one might expect to find, given what we know about Roman history and what we can predict on the basis of comparisons with better-documented societies—there is little here about the late republican competition among patrons for ever larger client groups, and there is nothing at all about economic exploitation or political coercion of *clientes.* Perhaps the problems outgrew the capacity of the parasite to represent them. We are also ill informed as to differences between the republican and imperial periods. This, however, is a fault not of the parasite but of the haphazard preservation of ancient literature. Satirists, as we saw, were more intent on the timeless problems of character, and there is nothing from the imperial period even remotely comparable to Cicero's more historically located speeches. Still, the parasite has shown us, I think, that although the patron/client relationship was part of the *mos maiorum,* the ancestral constitution, it was not a problem-free inheritance. With all his faults, the parasite has improved our understanding of the Roman experience.

Appendices

Appendix 1

Parasitus in Latin from Plautus to Apuleius (Outside of Comedy and References to Comedy)

1. In convivial contexts (Schol. Ter. p. 98.18–21 Schlee: parasitus sonat mecum cibatus vel apud me, quia παρά apud σῖτος cibus dictus est . . .)

   a. Cato *Agr.* 5.4 (in the list of *vilici officia*): nequem **parasitum** habeat. (Cf. *vicinas aliasque mulieres quam minimum utatur neve domum neve ad sese recipiat* in the list of the *vilicae officia*, 143.1.)

   b. Suetonius (quoting a letter of Augustus to Maecenas about the poet Horace): veniet ergo ab ista **parasitica** mensa ad hanc regiam et nos in epistulis scribendis adiuvabit.

   c. Juv. 1.139:
   vestibulos abeunt veteres lassique clientes
   votaque deponunt, quamquam longissima cenae
   spes homini; caulis miseris atque ignis emendus.
   optima silvarum interea pelagique vorabit
   rex horum vacuisque toris tantum ipse iacebit.
   nam de tot pulchris et latis orbibus et tam
   antiquis una comedunt patrimonia mensa.
   nullus iam **parasitus** erit.

   d. Juv. 5.145 (with reference to the [hypothetical] child of the parasite-like Trebius; *ipse* is Trebius' patron Virro):
   sed tua nunc Mycale pariat licet et pueros tres
   in gremium patris fundat semel, ipse loquaci
   gaudebit nido, viridem thoraca iubebit
   adferri minimasque nuces assemque rogatum,
   ad mensam quotiens **parasitus** venerit infans.

   e. Apul. *Met.* 10.16.8 (the ass as *conviva*): et 'heus,' ait , 'puer, lautum diligenter ecce illum aureum cantharum mulso contempera et offer **parasito** meo.'

f.   Apul. *Apol.* 100.4 (Apuleius characterizes his accuser's associ-
     ates): cape istud matris tuae testamentum, vere hoc quidem
     inofficiosum; quidni?   in quo obsequentissimum maritum
     exheredavit, inimicissimum filium scripsit heredem, immo
     enimvero non filium, sed Aemiliani spes et Rufini nuptias, set
     temulentum illud collegium, **parasitos** tuos.

2.   Outside the convivial context (. . . vel parasiti dicuntur a parendo et
     assistendo eo quod assidentes ipsi maioribus personis illorum
     voluptati per adulationem obsequuntur.)

a.   Lucilius 716–17 Marx (from book 27, trochaic septenarii): cocus
     non curat caudam insignem esse illam, dum pinguis siet. / sic
     amici quaerunt animum, rem **parasiti** ac ditias.

b.   Hor. *Sat.* 1.2.98–99 (a list of things that make the *matrona* hard
     to get at): custodes, lectica, ciniflones, **parasitae,** / ad talos stola
     demissa et circum addita palla.

c.   Pliny *HN* 10.68 (on a small owl, the *otus*): imitatrix alias avis ac
     parasita et quodam genere saltatrix.

d.   Juv. 14.44–46 (on the father's duty of providing a good exem-
     plum):

     nil dictu foedum visuque haec limina tangat
     intra quae pater est. procul, a procul inde puellae
     lenonum et cantus pernoctantis **parasiti.**

3.   In declamations

a.   Seneca (rhetor) *Contr.* 2.6.9 (a son bringing an accusation of
     madness against a spendthrift father): (Arellius Fuscus) subito
     furore conlapsam patri mentem. meretricem vidi pendentem
     collo senis et **parasitorum** circumfusum patri gregem, turpes
     cum rivalibus rixas et ebrietati nocturnae additum diem.

b.   Seneca (rhetor) *Contr. Exc.* 3.4 (a father justifying disowning his
     son): redivivum me senem meretrix vocat, **parasitorum** iocan-
     tium materia sum; omnibus istis tamquam servatoribus tacere
     iubeor.

c.   Seneca (rhetor) *Contr.* 10.1.7 (a poor man explains why he was
     reluctant to take a rich man to court): venit iste cum turba cli-
     entium ac **parasitorum** et adversus paupertatem totam regiam
     suam effundit.

d.   Quint. *I.O.* 2.4.23 (how to use labels [e.g., *adulter, aleator, petu-
     lans*] in attacking your opponent's character): quamquam hi

quoque ab illo generali tractatu ad quasdam deduci species
solent, ut si ponatur adulter caecus, aleator pauper, petulans
senex. habent autem nonnumquam etiam defensionem; nam
et pro luxuria et pro amore dicimus, et leno interim **parasitus**que defenditur sic ut non homini patrocinemur sed crimini.

e. Quint. *I.O.* 4.2.94–95 (a declamation scenario): ut ille **parasitus**
qui ter abdicatum a divite iuvenem et absolutum tamquam
suum filium adserit, habebit quidem colorem quo dicat et paupertatem sibi causam exponendi fuisse, et ideo a se **parasiti**
personam esse susceptam quia in illa domo filium haberet, et
ideo illum innocentem ter abdicatum quia filius abdicantis non
esset.

f. [Quint.] *Decl. min.* 252 (a *virgo* who hopes to be made a priestess is raped and claims that her rival's rich father engineered
the crime): rapuit eam **parasitus** divitis. (Cf. 370 on the same
theme: *eam parasitus sub diem comitiorum rapuit.*) The term *parasitus* is used repeatedly in this declamation as a matter-of-fact
label for the agent of the crime.

g. [Quint.] *Decl. min.* 260.8 (a young man who entertained people
who had been disinherited by their fathers is accused of *res
publica laesa;* this text is from the defense): et tamen si faciendae
sunt inpensae, si perdendum aliquid, non potest honestiore via
inpendere. non meretricibus donat, non in **parasitos** profundit, non illi magno cupiditates suae constant: sumptuosus est
misericordiae.

h. [Quint.] *Decl. min.* 296.1, 6 (a young man is accused of having
engineered the murder of his brother): obicimus adulescenti
ante omnia quod **parasitum** habuerit. . . . quid enim est **parasitus** nisi comes vitiorum, turpissimi cuiusque facti laudator?
. . . persona crimini idonea est: habes **parasitum,** et causa occidendi manifesta est: coheres es fratris. occasio adiuvit consilium: intra fines occidi potest. minister non defuit: **parasitus** in
tua potestate est. cetera vero cui non etiam manifesta sint?
parasitus sine tua voluntate conviciari fratri tuo auderet?
homo in adulationem natus, homo cuius famem tantum tu propitius differebas, non fecisset utique quo te putaret offendi
(etc.).

　　i.　[Quint.] *Decl. min.* 298: rusticus **parasitum** filium abdicat (etc.).
　　j.　[Quint.] *Decl. min.* 379: dives a **parasito** sacrilego reus caedis (etc.)
4.　*Parasiti Apollinis*
　　a.　Martial 9.28.9–10 (epitaph for the mime actor Latinus): vos me laurigeri / parasitum dicite Phoebi, / Roma sui famulum dum sciat esse Iovis.
　　b.　Inscriptions for mime actors et al. (a selection): *ILS* 5186, 5189, 5193, 5194, 5196, 5200, 5201, 5209, 5275; *CIL* 6.37816, 9.1578, 11.7767; possibly also *CIL* 6.37418, 8.25574.

Appendix 2

Possible Traces of Parasites in the *Satires* of Lucilius

Finding parasites in what survives of Lucilius is a difficult business. The difficulties, both textual and contextual, are well illustrated by fragment 882–83 Marx. The fragment is a bit of character description: "When he sees me he acts oh-so-nicely to me, gives me a rub, scratches my head for me, and starts picking off my lice."[1] The activities mentioned here are very like the personal services performed by the parasites of comedy for their patrons—brushing off dandruff, plucking gray hairs, removing fuzz—especially if one accepts, as I have done in the translation, Krenkel's text <sub>*palpatur*, "he gives me a rub," and takes *caput* to mean *caput meum*, "my head." The context probably is comic, for in this *Satire* Lucilius seems to be parading objectionable features of Roman drama.[2] One specific target is thought to be a play in which a *meretrix* named Hymnis appeared, possibly the play by Caecilius in which she has the title role. Yet the only identifiable figures in the satire here or in the scant remains of Caecilius' play are, besides Hymnis herself, an *adulescens*, a *senex*, and a *servus callidus;* there is no parasite. Moreover, the various parallels adducible for the language of this fragment led both Marx and Krenkel to apply the description to a character with a bad conscience. They take *caput* to mean *caput suum*, "his head," and the person who scratches his head and tries to catch (his own) vermin is presumably a clever slave who is planning a trick.[3] By itself this passage clearly does not constitute evidence for the presence of parasites in the *Satires* of Lucilius.

---

1. hic me ubi videt / subblanditur, <sub>palpatur, caput scabit, pedes legit (Lucil. 882–83 Marx = Krenkel 859–60, with Krenkel's emendation. The first part of the fragment in Marx' edition is *hic me ubi videt / subblanditur <fur>, palpatur . . .*).

2. Krenkel 1970, 1:93–95.

3. According to Marx' text he is a "thief," but *fur* is an accusation leveled at a number of *servi callidi* (e.g., Plaut. *Asin* 421, 681, *Trin.* 1024).

Another fragment that has deceptive parasite features is a bit of direct address from book 2: "Long live gluttons and gobblers-down, long life to bellies."[4] The connection between Lucilius' "bellies" and comic parasites is made by Donatus, who preserves this passage for us. He cites the line in support of his interpretation of the phrase *pugnos in ventrem ingere*, "apply your fists to the belly," at Terence *Phormio* 988. This phrase occurs in a scene in which the parasite Phormio is being subjected to force, and Donatus takes *ventrem* to mean not "the belly" but "The Belly" (i.e., the parasite himself). This interpretation works well enough for the *Phormio* passage, but it does not tell us anything about the Lucilius fragment other than that *venter*, "The Belly," could be used as a label for people whose behavior one wanted to criticize. And the appropriate implication of *venter* in the Lucilius fragment would seem to be gluttony, not parasitism, since the satire contains an accusation of the luxury-loving propraetor Scaevola by one Albucius.

Possibly parasitical is fragment 658 M.: "People find it easy to make fun of us, for we know that it will cost us our living if we get angry."[5] This sentence would work well if spoken by a parasite: it correctly connects the abuse that parasites were willing to tolerate and the amusement value they had for their hosts, and it has the plural form of self-reference that comic parasites used to evoke their membership in a "professional group." However, the fragment has no specifically parasitical marks, and I have rather overtranslated in using "cost us our living" to render *capital*, which properly refers to a loss of citizen rights. This is not the sort of food-related punishment that would really hit the parasite where it hurts.

About fragment 1181–82 M. we can feel a bit more confident, since it contains a term very closely associated with comic parasites, namely, *reges*. The fragment is a bon mot attributed to a witty civil servant (a public crier) named Granius: "Granius said that he wasn't at all ashamed of himself and that he hated haughty *reges*."[6] The term *reges* in this famous dictum may originally have referred not to men with political clout (which is how Cicero uses it when he adopts the phrase at *Att.* 6.3.7; cf. 2.8.1) but to the alter ego of the comic parasite, his *rex*, for the setting of this *Satire* is a dinner party. Even if one reckons with a con-

---

4. vivite lurcones, comedones, vivite ventris (Lucil. 75 M.).

5. facile deridemur. scimus capital esse irascier (Lucil. 658 M.).

6. Granius autem / non contemnere se et reges odisse superbos (Lucil. 1181–82 M.).

vivial context, however, it is difficult to know how Granius means his statement about haughty *reges*. Granius was a *praeco* who had risen in the world by means (at least partly) of his wit; does he speak as an ex-parasite whose experience with arrogant hosts was a bitter memory? Or is the statement a promise about his own hospitable behavior? Does he mean that he will be not your average haughty *rex* but the soul of convivial equality? Given that the first part of his dictum—"I am not at all ashamed of myself"—would seem to be part of a justification of current behavior, the latter of the two explanations offered above may be marginally more probable (though in neither case do I feel the ground very firmly beneath my feet). But even if one ventures this far, one only arrives at more questions. To whom was Granius addressing himself? He is serving as host to his betters at this party (a good sign of his good opinion of himself)—is his dictum a tacit reproach to those of his guests who are in a position to be *reges* themselves? Or is it meant to reassure parasites among the company, a promise that they will be treated decently? We simply do not know enough to make good use of this fragment.

Another fragment with a convivial context is fragment 1307 M., where some well-fed guests (? the text is problematical here) are laughing at the *lex Tappula*.[7] This *lex* was in fact a legal travesty, a set of "dinner-party regulations." Among the backers of this formally cast law were M. Multivorus ("Marcus the Big Eater") and P. Properoc[ibus] ("Publius Hurry-up-with-the-food"); its ratification was begun by the *tribus Satureia*, "the Well-fed tribe."[8] This sounds like good territory for a parasite to operate in; it also happens to be paralleled by a dinner-party *lex* proposed by the parasite in a late antique comedy called the *Querolus*. This latter parasite law specified that the parasite was to receive food as recompense for the injuries he suffered.[9] But the text of the *lex Tappula* was composed by one Valerius Valentinus, not by Lucilius, so we do not know who was laughing or why in fragment 1307 M. (or even where in Lucilius' corpus this fragment fits).

Another fragment in which the terminology evokes the parasite is

---

7. Tappulam rident legem †conter⁻ opimi (Lucil. 1307 M.). For *conter⁻* Marx records the emendations *congerrae* ("potluck partners," Scaliger), *concenae* ("dinner companions," I. Dousa), and *canterii* ("impotent old guys," Marx).

8. These details are preserved on an inscription containing parts of the *lex*, *ILS* 8761 (cf. Festus 363.21 Müller).

9. mercedem vulnerum victus accipiat [sc. parasitus] (*Querolus* p. 59 Peiper).

fragment 718 M.: "At your house you feed twenty or thirty or a hundred alimentary assassins."[10] The verb *alo*, "feed," is the *vox propria* for supporting a parasite—it is the Latin equivalent for the verb τρέφειν, which Crito used of his support for Archedemus—and the term *cibicida* is an abusive compound (modeled on *parricida*) for which there are parasite parallels in Greek. According to a second-century A.D. collector of convivial trivia, a compound word of similar etymology, σιτόκουρος (slayer of food), is a synonym for παράσιτος.[11] *Cibicida* is not attested elsewhere, but both of the plays of Menander in which its Greek equivalent σιτόκουρος is attested received Latin adaptations that predate (or are contemporary with) the *Satires* of Lucilius.[12] W. Krenkel suggests that the *cibicidae* of fragment 718 M. are clients, parasites, and/or slaves, and while the numbers mentioned in the fragment seem rather high for specifically comic parasites, who tended to work alone, the abusive compound may well add a taint of parasitism to a reference to *clientes*, if this is one.[13] This possibility is strengthened by the presence in the same book (27) of the one certain reference to parasites (in the plural, no less), the moralizing fragment 716–17 M.: *cocus non curat caudam insignem esse illam, dum pinguis siet; / sic amici quaerunt animum, rem parasiti ac ditias* (discussed in chap. 4).

The extant fragments contain one final possible parasite, identifiable as such by the company he keeps. Coelius, who is the "games partner of Gallonius" may well have been drawn as the parasite of Gallonius, an extravagant upstart *praeco* like Granius who dined sumptuously rather than well (1238–40 M.; cf. Cic. *Fin.* 2.8.24–25). All of the context that remains to us, however, is the predinner game of ball (*trigonum*): "When the *scurra* Coelius, games partner of Gallonius, plays, he plays a clever game and wins it."[14] The expenditure for which Gallonius is crit-

---

10. viginti domi an triginta an centum cibicidas alas (Lucil. 718 M.).

11. Ath. 6.247e. The term σιτόκουρος may have arisen out of an unusual metaphor applied repeatedly to the suitors' consumption of Odysseus' wealth: ἐκείρετε πολλὰ καὶ ἐσθλὰ κτήματα (2.312, which Eustathius explains as τὸ εἰς κόρον δαπανᾶν [1447.1]; cf. 1.378, 2.143, 22.369, 24.459).

12. Menander's Πωλούμενοι was the source of the *Polumeni* of Caecilius Statius, his Θρασυλέων the source of the *Thrasyleon* of Sextus Turpilius.

13. Krenkel 1970, ad loc.

14. Coelius conlusor Galloni scurra, trigonum / cum ludet, scius ludet et eludet (Lucil. 1150–51 Krenkel, an emendation of 1134–36 M.). Cf. Petron. *Sat.* 27, where a game with balls is the prelude to Trimalchio's fancy dinner.

icized in the texts we have is on food, not parasites, but the two forms of extravagance are perfectly compatible.

In sum, Lucilius provides us a handful of fragments with some claim to containing parasite material. It is a tantalizing collection, enough to suggest that Lucilius did take up various facets of the parasite persona for use in his critique of contemporaries, but not enough to show how he used it.

Appendix 3

Patronage and the *pro Archia*

Archias has figured largely in a number of recent studies of literary patronage.[1] The picture of Archias that emerges from these works may be summarized as follows: Archias is a poet who goes with his patrons to where he is bid (to Sicily, to the East) and writes, if not what he is told, at least what he guesses will be acceptable (the epic poem on Lucullus' fight against Mithridates, for example, or the verses that pleased Marius on the war against the Cimbri [Cic. *Arch.* 19]). He sets himself to be companionable and amusing; his facility at metrical impromptu will have recommended him as an entertainer, as will the subjects that he treated so spontaneously: he spoke on "matters pertaining to the occasion on which he was speaking" (*res quae tum agerentur, Arch.* 18), and the occasions were probably convivial (birthdays, betrothals, gatherings of friends, and so on). The picture is familiar, and most aspects of it can be supported by parallels from the lives of other dependent intellectuals. If anyone ought to be liable to caricature as a parasite, it is Archias.

But this picture is far from the one Cicero paints of him in the *pro Archia*. Cicero attaches Archias as a kind of caboose to the train of poetic glory pulled by the Homeric engine: Archias is, Cicero insists, a poet who has devoted the whole of his considerable talent to "celebrating the glory and merits of the Roman people" (*ad populi Romani gloriam laudemque celebrandam,* 19). Cicero's Archias takes up Homer's mantle as "best of poets" (*summus poeta,* 3), with Ennian *sanctitas* as trimming (*Arch.* 18–19, 31), and his presence seems to be positively essential to the well-being of the res publica (*Arch.* 14, 23, 28–30).

Throughout the speech, Cicero lays great stress on Archias' services to the *populus Romanus.* According to Cicero, Archias' epic on Lucullus' Mithridatic campaigns, for example, celebrates not only, not even primarily, the glory of the commander but the achievements of the Roman

---

1. For a lively description see Wiseman 1982, 31–34. For a more general picture see Treggiari 1977 and Hardie 1983, 15–36.

people (*Arch.* 21). This assertion is followed by a carefully filtered report of the highlights of that poem. First comes the acquisition of new territory: "the Roman people opened up the area of Pontus—Lucullus was the commander at the time" (*populus enim Romanus aperuit Lucullo imperante Pontum*). Next comes the victory over the vastly superior forces of Tigranes: "the army of the Roman people crush the uncountable forces of the Armenians—the same man was commanding, and he had only a small force at his disposal" (*populi Romani exercitus eodem duce non maxima manu innumerabilis Armeniorum copias fudit*). Then comes the lifting of the siege of Cyzicus: "it is to the credit of the Roman people that the city of our friends the Cyzicenes was saved—the plan was Lucullus'" (*populi Romani laus est urbem amicissimam Cyzicenorum eiusdem consilio . . . servatam*). Then Cicero mentions "that incredible naval battle of ours off Tenedos—Lucullus led the struggle" (*nostra semper feretur et praedicabitur L. Lucullo dimicante, cum interfectis ducibus depressa hostium classis est, incredibilis apud Tenedum pugna illa navalis*). The report goes on. In brief, says Cicero, "these are our trophies, our monuments, our triumphs" (*nostra sunt tropaea, nostra monumenta, nostri triumphi,* 21). The *populus Romanus*, Cicero implies, if it is sensible and retains Archias as a citizen, will be as well served by its poet as Achilles was by his Homer.

This equation between the *populus Romanus* and Achilles is peculiar; Lucullus would have been a more natural equivalent for Achilles. The tokens of victory that Cicero mentions, for example—trophies, monuments, triumphs—are properly celebrations of the commander's merit, not of that of the state. The peculiar emphasis of this passage is best revealed by a comparison with another speech of Cicero's, the speech on Pompey's command, in which Cicero puts the same achievements in a very different light. He identifies Cyzicus as "a city that L. Lucullus freed from the extreme danger of a siege by means of his courage, his determination, and his strategy" (*quam* [sc. *urbem Cyzicenorum*] *L. Lucullus virtute, adsiduitate, consilio summis obsidionis periculis liberavit,* 20). In regard to the naval battle he writes, "by this very same commander a large and well-equipped fleet . . . was defeated and sunk (***ab eodem imperatore*** *classem magnam et ornatam . . . superatam esse et depressam,* 21). In regard to the opening of Pontus he writes, "Sinope and Amisus . . . and many other cities of Pontus and Cappadocia were retaken at his very approach and arrival" (*Sinopen atque Amisum . . . ceterasque urbis Ponti et Cappadociae permultas **uno aditu adventuque** esse* *captas,* 21). Lucullus' *res gestae* are listed yet again in Cicero's speech on behalf of Lucullus' lieutenant, Murena, after the following introduction: "Lucullus' achievements are so very distinguished that I can cite neither a greater war nor any war conducted with greater strategy or fortitude" (*L. Luculli vero res tantae exstiterunt ut neque maius bellum commemorari possit neque maiore consilio et virtute gestum,* 33). In neither of these latter speeches does the *populus Romanus* come in for any special praise. And as Cicero's defense of Archias continues, so too does his avoidance of Lucullus.

Cicero can (and does) cite a precedent for what he wants (recognition of Archias as a citizen), namely, the gift of citizenship to the poet Ennius, who praised so many Roman notables, "not without praise that pertains to all of us" (*non sine communi omnium nostrum laude,* 22). But note how he describes his precedent: "our ancestors received Ennius into the state" (*maiores nostri* [sc. *Ennium*] *in civitatem receperunt,* 22).[2] The grant of citizen status in this case was a *beneficium* from patron to poet[3]—the *maiores* had nothing to do with it, really. That Cicero asks his jury to view the precedent from such a peculiar angle is due to the avoidance of Lucullus here.

Cicero has another speech defending a dependent ex-foreigner in a case brought under the same *lex Papia* that was invoked against Archias, the speech on behalf of Caesar's aide and friend Cornelius Balbus. In that speech Cicero uses a very different strategy from the one he used to defend Archias, and the differences between the two speeches shed further light on the avoidance of Lucullus in the *pro Archia.* Balbus' claim to Roman citizenship, like that of Archias, was contested, and as a result he too was threatened with expulsion under the *lex*

---

2. A more ordinary expression occurs apropos of a different writer later in the speech: noster hic Magnus . . . nonne Theophanem Mytilenaeum, scriptorem rerum suarum, in contione militum civitate donavit (*Arch.* 24). Cf. the expressions used in another speech about citizenship, the *pro Balbo: donatus igitur est* [sc. *Balbus*] *ob eas causas a Cn. Pompeio civitate* (6), *eum Pompeius civitate donavit* (7), and *is* [sc. *C. Marius*] *Iguvinatem M. Annium Appium, fortissimum virum summa virtute praeditum, civitate donavit* (52).

3. Which patron is less clear. Q. Fulvius Nobilior, the ostensible grantor (Cic. *Brut.* 80), was twelve years old at the time of the *colonia* foundation by means of which Ennius was enrolled. Badian (1972, 183–85) concludes his examination of the matter as follows: "If, as seems quite certain, the man who gave Ennius his citizenship in 184 was not Quintus, the son of the consul of 189, it becomes quite uncertain who he in fact was."

Papia. Once again the legal issue seems to have generated very little steam.[4] Already in section 15 (of 65) Cicero is summing up (*atque, ut ego sentio, iudices, causa dicta est,* 15).[5] Much of the rest of the speech is devoted to undoing the work of what Cicero calls "the spot and stain of our time, begrudging merit its due" (*haec saeculi quaedam macula atque labes, virtuti invidere,* 15). Cicero is repeatedly moved to deprecate the ill will aroused by the conspicuous success of Caesar's adjutant (*Balb.* 18–19, 56–57, 59–60, 65). The *invidia* he tries to argue away operates by measuring the distance between point A, where Balbus started out, and point B, where he is now, and comparing that distance with some vaguely defined social norm that would claim Balbus has gone farther than he ought. To counter this argument, Cicero does not try to relocate either point A or point B (that would be cutting off his nose to spite his face); rather, he concentrates on the means Balbus used to get from A to B. For the fact that Balbus' rise was due to Caesar's influence, Cicero argues, ought to help mitigate its offensiveness.

> At different times Balbus has shared in many of his toils; today, possibly, he shares in some of his advantages. And if these matters should harm him in your eyes, I fail to see what advantage any man will gain from virtue with such men as you.[6]

Cicero further emphasizes Balbus' dependent position by insisting that the enemies of Balbus' powerful friends are behind the attack on him (*Balb.* 59, 64–65) and by describing the unassuming behavior with which Balbus tried to make his success palatable.

> Who of the worthy did he not cultivate? Was there anyone with fortune or reputation to whom he did not yield place? He was an intimate companion of the most powerful of men, but even in our darkest and most troubled days he never offended any of Cae-

---

4. Gruen 1974, 313.

5. Cicero does not actually conclude his argument here (though presuming to do so was an extremely effective way of registering scorn for the opponent's plaint); he returns to the legal details of citizenship grants in sections 20–24.

6. fuit hic multorum illi [sc. Caesari] laborum socius aliquando; est fortasse nunc non nullorum particeps commodorum. quae quidem si huic obfuerint apud vos, non intellego, quod bonum cuiquam sit apud tales viros profuturum (*Balb.* 63).

sar's opponents in word or deed and not even by the expression on his face.[7]

To complete his case for Balbus' deserts, Cicero points out that if Balbus owed his success to Caesar, he owed his citizenship to Pompey. With such backing, the argument goes, he ought to be a welcome addition to the citizen list: "Remember, judges, that in this case today you are pronouncing judgment not on any misdeed of Cornelius Balbus but on the service that Pompey rendered him" (*postremo illud, iudices, fixum in animis vestris tenetote, vos in hac causa non de maleficio L. Corneli, sed de beneficio Cn. Pompeio iudicaturos,* 65). It is interesting, then, that in the case for Archias, who had achieved so much less than Balbus, Cicero insists that Archias' services to the *populus Romanus* (not his services to Lucullus) ought to have earned him Roman citizenship.

By examining the *pro Archia* in light of the *pro Balbo,* we can see that Cicero is trying to minimize the extent of Archias' debt to Lucullus. One naturally wonders whether the prosecution played up the relationship. It is a very real possibility, for in chapter 7 we saw that Cicero adopted this tactic in 57 when speaking for the "prosecution" in a case that involved another poet/patron relationship, that of Philodemus and Piso. It is naturally impossible to know whether Archias' prosecutor (who will if anything have been more severe) used a similar line of argument. All that we can say is that a negative stereotype was available to him and that his application of it would parallel not only what Cicero says about Philodemus but also what so many Romans had said about dependents of whom they disapproved.

We have seen that the *parasitus/rex* relationship was an efficient caricature of a patron/client pair, and the conspicuously luxurious Lucullus would have been peculiarly liable to the charge of consorting with a creature of this sort. The patrons of Philodemus, Horace, and Archias, though vastly different in character and achievements, have one thing in common, namely, a biographical tradition stressing a pleasure-oriented way of life. In the mid-fifties Cicero was always harping on Piso's dedication to pleasure, while Maecenas' luxurious softness was teased

---

7. quem bonum non coluit? cuius fortunae dignitatique non concessit? versatus in intima familiaritate hominis potentissimi, in maximis nostris malis atque discordiis neminem umquam alterius rationis ac partis non re non verbo non vultu denique offendit (*Balb.* 58).

by Augustus and derided by Seneca.[8] And everyone has heard of Lucullus' fishponds.[9] The extant references to the costly ponds date from 60 and 59, when Cicero was rather annoyed by Lucullus' disengagement from public affairs, but Lucullus' taste for sumptuous living had come under attack as early as 67.[10] If you need to persuade a jury that a man deserves to be a Roman citizen, you will be very careful to avoid the nexus of *parasitus/rex* images.

One of the all-too-infrequent bits of information about the context in which Cicero delivered his speeches may help us understand the significance of Cicero's strategy in the *pro Archia*. Lucullus apparently absented himself from Archias' trial.[11] In the discussion of Plautus' *Menaechmi* in chapter 2, we saw that a key way of showing oneself a patron was to appear in court on behalf of a dependent. However much this aspect of patronage may have been abused by selfish or overbusy patrons, it was never relegated to an attic of outdated morals. So it is surely a remarkable thing if the man in whose provincial entourage Archias had spent some ten years of his life and to the greater glory of whom he had recently produced an epic poem in more than one volume did nothing to keep Archias from being expelled from Rome (his home base for nearly forty years) and losing all of the entitlements

---

8. For Piso see Cic. *Sest.* 23, *Pis.* 68, *Red. Sen.* 14; for Maecenas see Macrobius *Sat.* 2.4.12, Sen. *Ep. Mor.* 114.4–5.

9. Cic. *Att.* 1.18.6 (from this letter it sounds as though the *piscinarii* have been notorious for some time: . . . *qui ita sunt stulti ut amissa re publica piscinas suas fore salvas videantur*), 1.19.6, 1.20.3, 2.9.1; cf. Ath. 6.274f: ὤκειλεν εἰς πολυτελῆ δίαιταν ἐκ τῆς παλαιᾶς σωφροσύνης, from book 112 of the Augustan-period *Histories* of Nicolaus of Damascus.

10. *Sest.* 93; cf. Plut. *Pomp.* 46.3 (a passage that suggests that Lucullus' *luxuries* began before 63). It is unfortunately impossible to pin down the date at which Pompey was referring to Lucullus as an oriental despot (*Xerxes togatus,* Vell. 2.33.4), but there was apparently a vigorous exchange of insults between the two in 66 (Vell. 2.33.2).

11. Lucullus' most recent biographer, Keaveney (1992, 138), asserts that Lucullus was present at the trial ("Now he came once more to lend support to a friend in peril") but provides no discussion of the textual and chronological problems arising from such a claim. Gold's view is less clear. In 1987, 73, 74, 77, and 84 she seems to think that L. Lucullus *cos.* 74 is the man to whom Archias owes his citizenship and who spoke at his trial, but elsewhere (75) she asserts that his brother, M. Lucullus, spoke and that his father, L. Lucullus *pr.* 104, moved the citizens of Heraclea to enroll Archias as a citizen.

inherent in Roman citizenship.¹² One of Lucullus' biographers, Jules
van Ooteghem, does remark on Lucullus' absence but contents himself
with repeating the not very satisfactory explanation of Laurand, that
Cicero was the better advocate.¹³ Rhetorical skill was by no means the
only desideratum in a *patronus,* and in any case it was entirely possible
and indeed increasingly customary for a defendant to have more than
one *patronus.*¹⁴ We know of no technical barrier that would have kept
Lucullus away—he had celebrated his triumph in 63 and returned to
privatus status thereafter. He was intermittently active in politics at this
period, not active enough to suit the most vocal of the optimates, of
course, but not yet given up entirely to the cultivation of fishponds.
Among other things, he appeared at the trial of his legate Murena in
November of 63.¹⁵ To be sure, Archias had Cicero to speak for him, and
Cicero's original audience may have believed him when he expatiated
on his long-standing familiarity with Archias and his intellectual debt
to the man (*Arch.* 1–4, 12–14, 28–30), but his modern audience, finding
nothing much about Archias in the letters and no mention at all of

---

12. Archias was with Lucullus on his two long tours of duty in the East; the
years were 88–84 and 74–68. Cicero mentions the trips to explain why Archias'
citizenship was not registered for so long (he missed two censuses while he was
away, *Arch.* 11). Between his two campaigns in the East, Lucullus was governor
of Africa (in 76). If Archias accompanied him, Cicero did not bother to mention
it in his speech (76 was not a census year).

13. Ooteghem 1959, 170–72.

14. Cicero felt that his single-handed defense of Cluentius in 66 was something remarkable (*Clu.* 199). Just twelve years later there were six *patroni* speaking for M. Aemilius Scaurus, and these were supported by ten *laudatores* and
nine other men *qui pro eo rogabant* (Asc. *Scaur.* 20.13, 28.17 Clark). In his commentary on Cicero's speech for Scaurus, Asconius remarks that at that period it
was rare for there to be more than four *patroni* (20.13 Clark).

15. Lucullus himself did not speak—Murena had assembled an exceptionally able group of advocates, Cicero, M. Crassus, and Q. Hortensius—but in
case anyone failed to notice the *triumphator,* Cicero obligingly pointed him out:
haec quamquam praesente L. Lucullo loquor (*Mur.* 20). Earlier Lucullus had
used his troops to support Murena's candidacy (Cic. *Mur.* 37, 69). Later in 63 he
was present at the debate on the handling of the captured Catilinarians (Cic.
Att. 12.21.1). In 61 he gave evidence against Clodius in the Bona Dea trial (Cic.
Mil. 73, Plut. *Cic.* 29.4, Dio 37.46.2), and in 60 he joined Cato and Q. Caecilius
Metellus in trying to stymie Pompey (Plut. *Luc.* 42.6, *Pomp.* 46.6, Vell. 2.40.5).
According to Plutarch, the two things that would still bring Lucullus to the
forum after his triumph were "helping his friends and harming Pompey" (*Luc.*
52.5). See further discussion in Hillman 1993.

Archias in the detailed description that Cicero gives of his own forma-
tive years in the *Brutus* (304–29), will not.[16] Archias did have support
from Lucullus' family, in the form, it appears, of eyewitness testimony
from Lucullus' younger brother, M. Terentius Varro Lucullus, but this
Lucullus was not the one to whose campaign for glory Archias had contributed so much.

The possibility that L. Lucullus' absence was due to some unforsee-
able (and unmentioned) obstacle can be discounted, I think, given the
lengths to which Cicero goes to avoid references to Archias' debt to his
patron. Whatever Grattius may have said about Archias, it is abun-
dantly clear that Cicero did not try to counter it by aligning Archias'
position vis-à-vis Lucullus with the often-described ideal of
patrocinium. Instead, he presented Archias' merit in terms of a com
pletely different value system. The *auctoritas* and *gratia* of the Luculli
might suffice to win Archias citizenship in Heraclea, but Cicero does
not assume that they will do so in Rome. He argues not that Archias is
worthy because Lucullus (or Metellus or I) say he is but that he
deserves Roman citizenship because he has served and will continue to
serve the *populus Romanus*.[17] If Lucullus' absence from the trial was
deliberate, the strategy that Cicero uses for Archias' defense becomes of
interest to the student of the workings of patronage in Rome.

It is useful to think of patronage in terms of two conceptual continuums, one practical, the other ideological. At the left end point of the
practical continuum is a (hypothetical) society in which patronage is
the normal mode for distributing resources of power and material
goods, while at the right end point is one in which resources are at the
disposal of officials who use essentially impersonal criteria in their distribution.[18] Parallel with this practical continuum is an ideological one,
of which the end points are societies in which on the left patronage is
openly avowed and associated with ideals such as duty, friendship,

---

16. The only mention in the letters is the notice that Archias would not be
requiting his lawyer with an epic on the great consulship of 63 (*Archias nihil de
me scripserit, Att.* 1.16.15 [July 61]).

17. Pace Fowler 1990.

18. Examples of impersonal criteria are age (all children will receive an education), income (all citizens with incomes under X get Y), examination results
(all examinees with a score of X receive Y), seniority (all candidates who have
served X years get Y), and so on. For a stimulating discussion of such criteria
see Saller 1982, 79–117.

and so on, while on the right patronage operates covertly and is equated with favoritism, bribery, special interests, graft, and other bad things. One needs these two continuums rather than just one because a society is not necessarily at the same point on both. In fourth-century Athens, for example, patronage was operational but not approved of by a demos-oriented society. That is to say, it is left of center on the practical continuum and right of center on the ideological one. The investigation of the workings of patronage in such societies is hindered by a dearth of sources, since patronal influence tends to be masked by euphemism when it is not left altogether unattested.[19] Republican Rome is often thought to be rather far to the left of center on both continuums. But Roman historians have begun challenging this view, demonstrating the necessity of admitting other influences than patronage in practical politics, for example.[20] In an essay entitled *"Libertas* in the Republic,"* P.A. Brunt looks at what I have called the ideological continuum, assembling the evidence for the nature and power of the concept of democratic freedom in republican Rome.[21] One can see a conflict between one of the components of this ideal, civil behavior (that is, behavior appropriate between fellow citizens), and the reality of dependence in Juvenal's fifth *Satire,* where the satirist says to Virro (a *rex* who begrudges even the meager support he provides to his parasite) that what is desired of him is not greater generosity but civility, *ut cenes civiliter* (5.112). We are now beginning to see that there were perhaps several ideals, some even mutually incompatible, that might be used to move the *populus Romanus.*

Because, instead of bringing Lucullus' influence to bear on Archias' behalf, Cicero appealed to the poet's services to the *populus Romanus,* we may conclude that the ideal of the patron/client relationship—the sort of thing that he used to defend Balbus—was not the most effective argument in Archias' case. Patron/client ties, while important to the structure of Roman society and the function of the Roman polity, were not the only structural members on which Rome rested. By studying the figure of the parasite, we have, I hope, improved our ability to see that the Romans perceived both the problems in and the limitations of a system based on patronage.

---

19. There is a good discussion in Millett 1989.
20. Rouland 1979; Millar 1984, 1986.
21. Brunt 1988, 334–50.

Works Cited

Allen, W., Jr., and P.H. Delacy. "The Patrons of Philodemus." *CP* 34 (1939): 59–65.

Aloni, A. "Due note Menandree." *Acme* 25 (1972): 217–19.

Anderson, W.S. "Anger in Juvenal and Seneca." *California Studies in Classical Philology* 19 (1964): 127–96. Reprinted in *Essays on Roman Satire*, 293–361, Princeton, 1982.

Antidosis. Festschrift für W. Kraus. Edited by R. Hanslik et al. Vienna, 1972.

Arnott, W.G. *Menander.* 3 vols. Loeb Classical Library. Cambridge, Mass., 1979–.

———. "*Phormio Parasitus:* A Study in Dramatic Methods of Characterization." *G&R* 17 (1970): 32–57.

———. "Studies in Comedy." Part 1, "Alexis and the Parasite's Name." *GRBS* 9 (1968): 161–68.

———. "Targets, Techniques, and Tradition in Plautus' *Stichus.*" *BICS* 19 (1972): 54–79.

Asmis, E. "An Epicurean Survey of Poetic Theories." *CQ* 42 (1992): 395–415.

———. "Philodemus' Poetic Theory and *On the Good King according to Homer.*" *CA* 10 (1991): 1–45.

Athlon, satura grammatica in honorem F.R. Adrados. Edited by P. Bádenas de la Peña et al. 2 vols. Madrid, 1987.

Austin, J.C. *The Significant Name in Terence.* University of Illinois Studies in Language and Literature 7, no. 4. Urbana, 1922.

Badian, E. "Ennius and His Friends." In *Ennius,* edited by O. Skutsch, Fondation Hardt, Entretiens sur l'Antiquité Classique, no. 17, 151–208. Geneva, 1972.

———. "*Nobiles amici:* Art and Literature in an Aristocratic Society." *CP* 80 (1985): 341–57.

———. *Publicans and Sinners.* Ithaca, 1983.

Baldwin, B. "Gregory Nazianzenus, Ammianus, *scurrae,* and the *Historia Augusta.*" *Gymnasium* 93 (1986): 178–80.

Bardon, H. "Réflexions sur réalité et imaginaire chez Juvénal." *Latomus* 36 (1977): 996–1002.

Barsby, J. Bacchides/ *Plautus.* Warminster, 1986.

———. *Terence,* The Eunuch, Phormio, The Brothers. Bristol, 1991.

Beaufils, C. "De parasitis apud veteres." Konstanz, 1861.

Bell, A. "A New Approach to the *Laus Pisonis.*" *Latomus* 44 (1985): 871–78.

Bellandi, F. "*Naevolus cliens.*" *Maia* 26 (1974): 279–99.

Bentley, R. *Horace.* 3d ed. 2 vols. Berlin, 1869.

Bettini, M. "Il parasito Saturio, una riforma legislativa e un testo variamente tormentato (*Persa* vv. 65–74)." *SCO* 26 (1977): 83–104.

Bieber, M. *The History of the Greek and Roman Theatre.* Princeton, 1961.

Boissevain, J. *Friends of Friends: Networks, Manipulators, and Coalitions.* New York, 1974.

Bolkestein, H. *Wohltätigkeit und Armenpflege im vorchristlichen Altertum.* Utrecht, 1939.

Bowersock, G. *Augustus and the Greek World.* Oxford, 1965.

Braund, D. "Function and Dysfunction: Personal Patronage in Roman Imperialism." In *Patronage in Ancient Society,* edited by A. Wallace-Hadrill, 137–52. London, 1989.

Braund, S.H. *Beyond Anger: A Study of Juvenal's Third Book of Satires.* Cambridge, 1988.

Brinkhoff, J. "De parasiet in Plautus' *Menaechmi.*" *Hermeneus* 38 (1965): 38–45.

———. "De parasiet op het romeinsche tooneel." *Neophilologus* 32 (1948): 127–41.

Brown, P.G. McC. "Menander, Fragments 745 and 746 K–T, Menander's *Kolax,* and Parasites and Flatterers in Greek Comedy." *ZPE* 92 (1992): 91–107.

Bruns, C. G. *Fontes iuris romani antiqui.* 7th ed. Edited by O. Gradenwitz. 2 vols. Tübingen, 1909.

Brunt, P.A. *The Fall of the Roman Republic and Related Essays.* Oxford, 1988.

Capasso, M. "Una pretesa allusione di Filodemo a Cicerone [P. Herc. 986, fr. 19]." *CrE* 22 (1992): 169–71.

Cary, E. trans. *Dionysius of Halicarnassus, Roman Antiquities.* 7 vols. Loeb Classical Library. Cambridge, Mass., 1937–50.

Castillo, C. "El tipo del parásito en la comedia Romana." In *Athlon, satura grammatica in honorem F.R. Adrados.* Edited by P. Bádenas de la Peña et al., 2:173–82. Madrid, 1987.

Champlin, E. *Final Judgments: Duty and Emotion in Roman Wills, 200 B.C.–A.D. 250.* Berkeley, 1991.

Charpin, F. *Lucilius, Satires.* 3 vols. Paris, 1978–.

Chiarini, G. *La recita: Plauto, la farsa, la festa.* Bologna, 1979.

Christ, M. "Ostracism, Sycophancy, and Deception of the Demos: [Arist.] *Ath. Pol.* 43.5." *CQ* 42 (1992): 336–46.

Citroni, M. *M. Valerii Martialis* Epigrammaton *liber primus.* Florence, 1975.

Clark, A.C. *M. Tulli Ciceronis orationes* pro P. Quinctio, *etc.* Oxford, 1909.

Classen, C.J. "Verres Gehilfen in Sizilien nach Ciceros Darstellung." *Ciceroniana,* n.s., 4 (1980): 93–114.

Clausen, W.V. *A. Persi Flacci et D. Iuni Iuuenalis* Saturae. Rev. ed. Oxford, 1992.

Coleman, K.M. *Statius, Siluae IV.* Oxford, 1988.

Concentus hexachordus: Beiträge zum 10. Symposion der bayerischen Hochschullehrer für kl. Ph. in Eichstätt (24–5 Feb. 1984). Edited by P. Krafft and H.J. Tscheidel. Regensburg, 1986.

Conrad, C.C. "The Rôle of the Cook in Plautus' *Curculio.*" *CP* 13 (1918): 389–400.

Corbett, P. *The Scurra.* Edinburgh, 1986.

Corbino, A. "La *pro Caecina* di Cicerone e l'acquisto della proprietà mediante intermediario estraneo." In *Studi in onore di Arnaldo Biscardi*, 3:277–87. Milan, 1982.

Courtney, E. *A Commentary on the* Satires *of Juvenal.* London, 1980.

———. *The Fragmentary Latin Poets.* Oxford, 1993.

———. *P. Papini Stati* Siluae. Oxford, 1990.

Crawford, M.H. "Greek Intellectuals and the Roman Aristocracy in the First Century B.C." In *Imperialism in the Ancient World*, edited by P.D.A. Garnsey and C.D. Whittaker, 193–207. Cambridge, 1978.

Csapo, E. "Plautine Elements in the Running-Slave Entrance Monologues?" *CQ* 39 (1989): 148–63.

Cupaiuolo, F. "Una pagina della vita di Cicerone: Tra pubblico e privato." *BSL* 19 (1989): 17–32.

D'Agostino, V. "La figura del parassito in Plauto." *Mondo Classico* 7, supplement (1937): 90–110.

Damon, C. "Statius *Silvae* 4.9: *Libertas Decembris*?" *ICS* 17 (1992): 301–8.

D'Arms, J.H. "Control, Companionship, and *Clientela:* Some Social Functions of the Roman Communal Meal." *EMC* 3 (1984): 327–48.

———. "The Roman *Convivium* and the Idea of Equality." In *Sympotica: A Symposium on the Symposion*, edited by O. Murray, 308–19. Oxford, 1990.

———. "Slaves at Roman *Convivia.*" In *Dining in a Classical Context*, edited by W. J. Slater, 171–83. Ann Arbor, 1991.

Danek, G. "Parasit, Sykophant, Quadruplator; zu Plautus, *Persa* 62–76." *WS* 101 (1988): 223–41

Davies, J.K. *Athenian Propertied Families 600–300 B.C.* Oxford, 1971.

Democracy, Clientelism, and Civil Society. Edited by L. Roniger and A. Günes-Ayata. Boulder, 1994.

Diehl, E. *Anthologia lyrica graeca.* 2 vols. Leipzig, 1925.

Diels, H. *Poetarum philosophorum fragmenta.* Poetarum graecorum fragmenta, vol. 3, pt. 1. Berlin, 1901.

Dittenberger, W. *Orientis graeci inscriptiones selectae: Supplementum sylloges inscriptionum graecarum.* 2 vols. Leipzig, 1903–5.

Dorandi, T. *Filodemo, Il buon re secondo Omero.* Naples, 1982.

———. *Filodemo*, Storia dei filosofi: *La Stoa da Zenone a Panezio*, PHerc. *1018.* Leiden, 1994.

———. *Filodemo*, Storia dei filosofi: *Platone e l'Academia*, PHerc. *1021 e 164. La Scuola di Epicuro*, vol. 12. Naples, 1991.

———. "Filodemo storico del pensiero antico." *ANRW* II.66.4 (1990): 2407–23.

Dover, K.J. *Greek Popular Morality in the Time of Plato and Aristotle.* Berkeley, 1974.

Dziatzko, K.F.O. *Phormio.* 3d ed. Edited by E. Hauler. Leipzig, 1898.

Eppers, M., and H. Heinen. "Zu den *servi venerii* in Ciceros *Verrinen.*" In *Soda-*

litas: Scritti in onore di Antonio Guarino, edited by V. Giuffrè, 1:219–32. Naples, 1984–85.

Fabia, P. *P. Terenti Afri* Eunuchus. Paris, 1895.

Fairweather, J.A. "Fiction in the Biographies of Ancient Writers." *Ancient Society* 5 (1974): 231–75.

Fordyce, C.J. *Catullus, a Commentary.* Oxford, 1961.

Fowler, D.P. Review of *Filodemo, Il buon re secondo Omero,* by T. Dorandi. *CR* 36 (1986): 81–85.

———. Review of *The Scurra,* by P. Corbett. *G&R* 34 (1987): 90.

Fowler, W. M. "Cicero's *pro Archia* and the Responsibility of Reading." *Rhetorica* 8 (1990): 137–52.

Fraenkel, E. *Elementi Plautini in Plauto.* Translated by F. Munari. Florence, 1960.

———. *Horace.* Oxford, 1957.

Frank, T. *Life and Literature in the Roman Republic.* Berkeley, 1957.

Freudenberg, K. *The Walking Muse: Horace on the Theory of Satire.* Princeton, 1993.

Frier, B. *The Rise of the Roman Jurists.* Princeton, 1985.

Frisk, H. *Griechisches Etymologisches Wörterbuch.* Heidelberg, 1960.

Fuhrmann, M. "Tecniche narrative nella seconda orazione contro Verre." *Ciceroniana,* n.s., 4 (1980): 27–42.

Gaiser, K. "Platone come 'kolax' in una letter apocrifa (13a Epist.)." *Sandalion* 4 (1981): 71–94.

García Hernández, B. "*Summanus.*" Part 1. "El enigmático dios del fulgor nocturno." *EM* 60 (1992): 57–69.

Geffcken, K.A. *Comedy in the* pro Caelio. *Mnemosyne Supplementum* 30. Leiden, 1973.

Gérard, J. *Juvénal et la réalité contemporaine.* Paris, 1976.

Giese, A. "De parasiti persona capita selecta." Berlin, 1908.

Gigante, M. "Filodemo e Pisone: Da Ercolano a Roma." *ASNP* 15 (1985): 855–66.

———. "Filodemo tra poesia e prosa (a proposito do POxy. 3724)." *SIFC,* 3d ser., 7 (1989a): 129–51.

———. "Il ritorno di Virgilio a Ercolano." *SIFC,* 3d ser., 7 (1989b): 3–6.

———. *Ricerche Filodemee.* 2d ed. Naples, 1983a.

———. "Virgilio fra Ercolano e Pompei." *A&R* 28 (1983b): 31–50.

Gil, L. "El 'alazon' y sus variantes." *Estudios Classicos* 86 (1981–83): 39–57.

Gilmartin, K. "The Thraso-Gnatho Subplot in Terence's *Eunuchus.*" *CW* 69 (1976): 263–67.

Gold, B. *Literary Patronage in Greece and Rome.* Chapel Hill, 1987.

Goldberg, S.M. *Understanding Terence.* Princeton, 1986.

Gomme, A.W., and F.H. Sandbach. *Menander, a Commentary.* Oxford, 1973.

Gotoff, H. "Oratory: The Art of Illusion." *HSCP* 95 (1993): 289–313.

Gow, A.S.F., and D.L. Page. The Greek Anthology: The Garland of Philip *and Some Contemporary Epigrams.* Cambridge, 1968.

Gratwick, A.S. "Curculio's Last Bow: Plautus, *Trinummus* IV.3." *Mnemosyne* 34 (1981): 331–50.

———. *Plautus, Menaechmi.* Cambridge, 1993.

———. "Sundials, Parasites, and Girls from Boeotia." *CQ* 29 (1979): 308–23.

Griffiths, A.H. "Six Passages in Callimachus and the *Anthology." BICS* 17 (1970): 37–38.

Gruen, E.S. *The Last Generation of the Roman Republic.* Berkeley, 1974.

Handley, E. *The* Dyskolos *of Menander.* London, 1965.

Hardie, A. *Statius and the* Silvae: *Poets, Patrons, and Epideixis in the Graeco-Roman World.* Liverpool, 1983.

Harsh, P.W. "Possible Greek Background for the Word *Rex* as used in Plautus." *CP* 31 (1936): 62–68.

Harvey, D. "The Sykophant and Sykophancy: Vexatious Redefinition?" In *Nomos: Essays in Athenian Law, Politics, and Society,* edited by P. Cartledge et al., 103–21. Cambridge, 1990.

Highet, G. *The Classical Tradition.* Oxford, 1949.

———. "Masks and Faces in Satire." *Hermes* 102 (1974): 321–37.

Hillman, T.P. "When Did Lucullus Retire?" *Historia* 42 (1993): 211–28.

Hiltbrunner, O. "Einladung zum epikureischen Freundesmahl (Thema mit Variationen)." In *Antidosis, Festschrift für W. Kraus,* edited by R. Hanslik et al., 168–72. Vienna, 1972.

Hinard, F. "Le *pro Quinctio,* un discours politique?" *REA* 77 (1975): 88–107.

———. "Remarques sur les *praecones* et le *praeconium* dans la Rome de la fin de la République." *Latomus* 35 (1976): 730–46.

Hodge, H.G. *Cicero, the Speeches:* Pro lege Manilia, pro Caecina, pro Cluentio, pro Rabirio perduellionis. Loeb Classical Library. Cambridge, Mass., 1966.

Hohti, P. "Aulus Caecina the Volaterran: The Romanization of an Etruscan." In *Studies in the Romanization of Etruria,* edited by P. Bruun and P. Hohti, 405–33. Acta Instituti Romani Finlandiae 5. Rome, 1975.

Hough, J. "The Structure of the *Captivi." AJP* 63 (1942): 26–37.

Howell, P. *A Commentary on Book One of the* Epigrams *of Martial.* London, 1980.

Hunter, R.L. *Eubulus, the Fragments.* Cambridge, 1983.

Imperialism in the Ancient World. Edited by P.D.A. Garnsey and C.D. Whittaker. Cambridge, 1978.

Jocelyn, H.D. "The Ruling Class of the Roman Republic and Greek Philosophers." *BRL* 59 (1977): 323–66.

Jones, C.P. *Culture and Society in Lucian.* Cambridge, Mass., 1986.

———. *Plutarch and Rome.* Oxford, 1971.

Jory, E.J. "Associations of Actors in Rome." *Hermes* 98 (1970): 237–53.

Kaibel, G. *Comicorum graecorum fragmenta.* Berlin, 1899.

———. *Index scholarum in universitate litteraria Gryphiswaldensi per semestre aestivum anni 1885 a die 15 mens April. habitarum.* Greifswald, 1885.

Kaser, M. *Das Römische Zivilprozessrecht.* Munich, 1966.

Kassel, R., and C. Austin. *Poetae Comici Graeci.* 7 vols. Berlin, 1983–.

Kauer, R., and W.M. Lindsay. *P. Terenti Afri Comoediae.* Oxford, 1926.

Kay, N.M. *Martial, Book XI, A Commentary.* New York, 1985.

Keaveney, A. *Lucullus, a Life.* London, 1992.

Keil, H. *Grammatici latini.* 7 vols. Leipzig, 1857–80.
Keller, F.L. *Semestrium ad M. Tullium Ciceronem libri sex.* Turicum, 1842.
Kilpatrick, R.S. *The Poetry of Friendship: Horace,* Epistles *I.* Edmonton, 1986.
Kinsey, T.E. *M. Tulli Ciceronis* pro P. Quinctio *oratio.* Sydney, 1971.
Knoche, U. *D. Iunius Iuuenalis, Saturae.* Munich, 1950.
Konstan, D. *Roman Comedy.* Ithaca, 1983.
Körte, A. "Augusteer bei Philodem." *RhM* 45 (1890): 172–77.
———. *Menandri quae supersunt.* Addenda added by A. Thierfelder. 3d ed. 2 vols. Leipzig, 1957–59.
Krenkel,W. *Lucilius,* Satiren. 2 vols. Leiden, 1970.
Labate, M. *L'arte di farsi amare: Modelli culturali e progetto didascalico nell' elegia ovidiana.* Pisa, 1984.
Leach, E.W. "Ergasilus and the Ironies of the *Captivi.*" *Classica et Medievalia* 30 (1969): 262–96.
———. "Horace's *'pater optimus'* and Terence's Demea: Autobiographical Fiction and Comedy in *Sermo* 1.4." *AJP* 92 (1971): 616–32.
Lefèvre, E. *Der* Phormio *des Terenz und der* Epidikazomenos *des Apollodor von Karystos.* Zetemata 74. Munich, 1978.
Lejay, P. *Oeuvres d'Horace:* Satires. Paris, 1911.
Leo, F. "Diogenes bei Plautus." *Hermes* 41 (1906): 441–46.
———. *Plautinische Forschungen.* 2d ed. Berlin, 1912.
Levi, M.A. "Aspetti sociali della poesia di Giovenale." In *Studi in onore di Gino Funaioli,* edited by E. Paratore, 170–80. Rome, 1955.
Lindsay, W.M. *Early Latin Verse.* Oxford, 1922.
———. *Plautus,* Comoediae. 2 vols. Oxford, 1904–5.
Literary and Artistic Patronage in Ancient Rome. Edited by B. Gold. Austin, 1982.
Lofberg, J.O. "Phormio and 'Art for Art's Sake.'" *CW* 22 (1929): 183–84.
———. *Sycophancy in Athens.* Chicago, 1917.
———. "The Sycophant-Parasite." *CP* 15 (1920): 61–72.
Long, G. *M. Tullii Ciceronis orationes.* 4 vols. London, 1851–58.
Lowe, J.C.B. "Aspects of Plautus' Originality in the *Asinaria.*" *CQ* 42 (1992): 152–75.
———. "Cooks in Plautus." *Cl. Ant.* 4 (1985): 72–102.
———. "The *Eunuchus:* Terence and Menander." *CQ* 33 (1983): 428–44.
———. "Plautus' Choruses." *RhM* 133 (1990): 274–97.
———. "Plautus' Parasites and the *Atellana.*" In *Studien zur vorliterarischen Periode im frühen Rom,* edited by G. Vogt-Spira, 161–69. ScriptOralia 12. Tübingen, 1989a.
———. "The *Virgo Callida* of Plautus, *Persa.*" *CQ* 39 (1989b): 390–99.
Luck, G. *Der Akademiker Antiochos.* Noctes Romanae 7. Bern, 1953.
Ludwig, W. "Von Terenz zu Menander." *Philologus* 103 (1959): 1–38. Reprinted in *Der römische Komödie: Plautus und Terenz,* edited by E. Lefèvre, 354–408. Wege der Forschung 236. Darmstadt, 1973.
Lyne, R.O.A.M. *Horace: Behind the Public Poetry.* New Haven, 1995.
Macleod, C.W. "The Poetry of Ethics: Horace, *Epistles* I." *JRS* 69 (1979): 16–27.
MacMullen, R. "Personal Power in the Roman Empire." *AJP* 107 (1986): 512–24.

Marache, R. "Juvénal, peintre de la société de son temps." *ANRW* 2.33.1 (1989): 593–639.

———. "La revendication sociale chez Martial et Juvenal." *RCCM* 3 (1961): 30–67.

Marti, H. Review of *T. Maccius Plautus,* Persa: *Einleitung, Text, und Kommentar,* by E. Woytek. *Gnomon* 56 (1984): 391–99.

Martina, M. "*Grassatores e Carmentarii.*" *Labeo* 26 (1980): 155–75.

Marx, F. *C. Lucilii* Carminum *reliquiae.* 2 vols. in 1. Leipzig, 1904–5.

Maurach, G. "Der Grundriss von Horazens erstem Epistelbuch." *Act. Class.* 17 (1968): 73–124.

May, J.M. *Trials of Character: The Eloquence of Ciceronian Ethos.* Chapel Hill, 1988.

McGann, M.J. *Studies in Horace's First Book of* Epistles. Collection Latomus, no. 100. Brussels, 1969.

Millar, F. "The Political Character of the Classical Roman Republic, 200–151 B.C." *JRS* 74 (1984): 1–19.

———. "Politics, Persuasion, and the People before the Social War (180–90 B.C.)." *JRS* 76 (1986): 1–11.

Millett, P. "Patronage and Its Avoidance in Classical Athens." In *Patronage in Ancient Society,* edited by A. Wallace-Hadrill, 15–47. London, 1989.

Momigliano, A. "*Panegyricus Messallae* and 'Panegyricus Vespasiani': Two References to Britain." *JRS* 40 (1950): 39–42.

Müller, A. "Die Parasiti Apollinis." *Philologus* 63 (1904): 342–61.

Müller, C.O. Sex. Pompei Festi De verborum significatu *quae supersunt, cum Pauli* Epitome. Leipzig, 1839.

Münzer, F. "Rubrius." *RE,* 2d ser., 1 (1914): 1169.

Murray, O. "Philodemus *On the Good King according to Homer.*" *JRS* 55 (1965): 161–82.

———. "Rillegendo *Il buon re secondo Omero.*" *CrE* 14 (1984): 157–60.

Nencini, F. *De Terentio eiusque fontibus.* Liburnum, 1891.

Nesselrath, H.-G. *Die Attische Mittlere Komödie: Ihre Stellung in der antiken Literaturkritik und Literaturgeschichte.* Berlin, 1990.

———. *Lukians Parasitendialog: Untersuchungen und Kommentar.* Berlin, 1985.

New Perspectives in the Roman Law of Property. Edited by P. Birks. Oxford, 1989.

Nicolet, C. *L'ordre équestre à l'époque républicaine.* 2 vols. Paris, 1974.

Nisbet, R.G.M. "How Textual Conjectures Are Made." *MD* 26 (1991): 65–91.

———. *M. Tulli Ciceronis* in L. Calpurnium Pisonem *oratio.* Oxford, 1961.

Noirfalise, A. "L'art de réussir auprès des grands d'après les *Épîtres* d'Horace." *LEC* 20 (1952): 358–63.

Nomos: Essays in Athenian Law, Politics, and Society. Edited by P. Cartledge et al. Cambridge, 1990.

Nuchelmans, J. "De tafelschuimer in de Griekse komedie." *Lampas* 10 (1977): 362–75.

Ooteghem, J. van. *Lucius Licinius Lucullus.* Académie Royale de Belgique, Classes des Lettres des Science Morales et Politiques, Mémoires, vol. 53. Brussels, 1959.

Osborne, R. "Vexatious Litigation in Classical Athens: Sykophancy and the

Sykophant." In *Nomos: Essays in Athenian Law, Politics, and Society,* edited by P. Cartledge et al., 83–102. Cambridge, 1990.

Paoli, U.E. "Nota giuridica su Plauto (Plauto, *Persa,* vv. 67–71)." *Iura* 4 (1954): 174–81.

Papke, R. "*Panegyricus Messallae* und *Catalepton* 9: Form und gegensitiger Bezug." In *Concentus hexachordus: Beiträge zum 10. Symposion der bayerischen Hochschullehrer für kl. Ph. in Eichstätt (24–5 Feb. 1984),* edited by P. Krafft and H.J. Tscheidel, 123–68. Regensburg, 1986.

Patronage in Ancient Society. Edited by A. Wallace-Hadrill. London, 1989.

Peiper, R. Aulularia, *sive* Querolus: *Theodosiani aevi comoedia Rutilio dedicata.* Leipzig, 1875.

Pelling, C. "Plutarch: Roman Heroes and Greek Culture." In *Philosophia Togata,* edited by M. Griffin and J. Barnes, 199–232. Oxford, 1989.

Perret, J. *Horace.* Paris, 1959.

Petersmann, H. *T. Maccius Plautus:* Stichus. Heidelberg, 1973.

Peterson, W. *M. Tulli Ciceronis orationes,* divinatio in Q. Caecilium, in C. Verrem. Rev. ed. Oxford, 1917.

Petrone, G. "*Campi Curculionii,* ovvero il bestiario del parassita (Plauto, *Mi.* 13 ss.)." *SIFC,* 3d ser., 7 (1989): 34–55.

Philosophia Togata. Edited by M. Griffin and J. Barnes. Oxford, 1989.

Powell, J.G.F. *Cicero,* Cato maior de senectute. Cambridge Classical Texts and Commentaries, no. 28. Cambridge, 1988.

Prescott, H.W. "Inorganic Roles in Roman Comedy." *CP* 15 (1920): 245–81.

Ramin, J., and P. Veyne. "Droit romain et société: Les hommes libres qui passent pour esclaves et l'esclavage volontaire." *Historia* 30 (1981): 472–97.

Rauh, N.K. "Auctioneers and the Roman Economy." *Historia* 38 (1989): 451–71.

Rawson, E. "Freedmen in Roman Comedy." In *Theater and Society in the Classical World,* ed. R. Scodel, 215–33. Ann Arbor, 1993.

———. *Intellectual Life in the Late Roman Republic.* London, 1985.

Reeve, M.D. "The Addressee of *Laus Pisonis.*" *ICS* 9 (1984): 42–48.

———. *M. Tulli Ciceronis oratio* pro P. Quinctio. Stuttgart, 1992.

———. "The Textual Tradition of Donatus' Commentary on Terence." *CP* 74 (1979): 310–26.

Ribbeck, O. *Kolax, eine ethologische Studie.* Abhandlungen der philologisch-historischen Klasse der königlichen sächsischen Gesellschaft der Wissenschaften, vol. 9, no. 1. Leipzig, 1883.

———. *Scaenicae Romanorum Poesis Fragmenta.* 3d ed. 2 vols. Leipzig, 1897–98.

Rohdich, H. "Die 18. Epistel des Horaz." *RhM* 105 (1972): 261–88.

Roniger, L. "Modern Patron-Client Relations and Historical Clientelism: Some Clues from Ancient Republican Rome." *Arch. Europ. Sociol.* 29 (1988): 63–95.

Roniger, L., and A. Günes-Ayata. *Democracy, Clientelism, and Civil Society.* Boulder, 1994.

Rosand, E. "Iro and the Interpretation of *Il ritorno d'Ulisse in patria.*" *Journal of Musicology* 7 (1989): 141–64.

Rose, V. *Aristotelis qui ferebantur librorum fragmenta.* Leipzig, 1886.

Rosivach, V.J. "The *Aduocati* in the *Poenulus* and the *Piscatores* in the *Rudens.*" *Maia* 35 (1983): 83–93.

Rostagni, A. *Suetonio* de Poetis *e biografi minori.* Turin, 1956.

Rouland, N. *Pouvoir politique de dépendance personnelle dans l'antiquité romaine: Genèse et rôle des rapports de clientèle.* Collection Latomus, no. 166. Brussels, 1979.

Rudd, N. Review of *The Scurra*, by P. Corbett. *CR* 37 (1987): 319–20.

———. *The* Satires *of Horace.* Cambridge, 1966.

Saggese, P. "Lo *scurra* in Marziale." *Maia* 46 (1994): 53–59.

Saller, R. "Martial on Patronage and Literature." *CQ* 33 (1983): 246–57.

———. "Patronage and Friendship in Early Imperial Rome: Drawing the Distinction." In *Patronage in Ancient Society*, edited by A. Wallace-Hadrill, 49–62. London, 1989.

———. *Personal Patronage under the Early Empire.* Cambridge, 1982.

Sandbach, F.H. *Menandri reliquiae selectae.* Oxford, 1972.

Schaaf, L. *Der* Miles gloriosus *des Plautus und sein griechisches Original: Ein Beitrag zur Kontaminationsfrage.* Munich, 1977.

Schlee, F. *Scholia Terentiana.* Leipzig, 1893.

Schneider, K. "Praeco." *RE* 22 (1953): 1193–99.

Schoonhoven, H. "The *Panegyricus Messallae*: Date and Relation with *Catalepton* 9." In *ANRW* 2.30.3 (1983): 1681–1707.

Seel, A. Laus Pisonis: *Text, Übersetzung, Kommentar.* Hogl, 1969.

Segal, E., and C. Moulton. "*Contortor legum*: The Hero of the *Phormio.*" *RhM* 121 (1978): 276–88.

Serres, M. *Le Parasite.* Paris, 1980.

Shackleton Bailey, D.R. *Cicero's* Letters to Atticus. 7 vols. Cambridge, 1965–70.

———. *Epistulae ad Familiares.* 2 vols. Cambridge Classical Texts and Commentaries, nos. 16–17. Cambridge, 1977.

———. *Q. Horati Flacci Opera.* Stuttgart, 1985.

———. *M. Valerii Martialis* Epigrammata. Stuttgart, 1990.

———. *Onomasticon to Cicero's Speeches.* Norman, Okla., 1988.

———. *Profile of Horace.* London, 1982.

Shipp, G.P. "Linguistic Notes." *Antichthon* 11 (1977): 1–9.

Skinner, M. "Parasites and Strange Bedfellows: A Study in Catullus' Political Imagery." *Ramus* 8 (1979): 137–52.

Skutsch, O. *The* Annals *of Q. Ennius.* Oxford, 1985.

Sodalitas: Scritti in onore di Antonio Guarino. Edited by V. Giuffrè. 9 vols. Naples, 1984–85.

Spranger, P. *Historische Untersuchungen zu den Sklavenfiguren des Plautus und Terenz*, 2d ed. Stuttgart, 1984.

Stangl, T. *Ciceronis orationum scholiastae.* Vienna, 1912.

Stroh, W. *Taxis und Taktik: Die advokatische Dispositionskunst in Ciceros Gerichtsreden.* Stuttgart, 1975.

Studi in onore di Arnaldo Biscardi. 6 vols. Milan, 1982.

Studi in onore di Gino Funaioli. Edited by E. Paratore. Rome, 1955.

Studien zur vorliterarischen Periode im frühen Rom. Edited by G. Vogt-Spira. ScriptOralia 12. Tübingen, 1989.

Studies in the Romanization of Etruria. Edited by P. Bruun and P. Hohti. Acta Instituti Romani Finlandiae 5. Rome, 1975.

Sudhaus, S. *Philodemi volumina rhetorica.* 2 vols. Leipzig, 1892–96.

Sullivan, J.P. *Martial, the Unexpected Classic: A Literary and Historical Study.* Cambridge, 1991.

Sympotica: A Symposium on the Symposion. Edited by O. Murray. Oxford, 1990.

Tellegen, J.W., and O. Tellegen-Couperus. "Joint Usufruct in Cicero's *pro Caecina.*" In *New Perspectives in the Roman Law of Property,* edited by P. Birks, 195–205. Oxford, 1989.

Texte, politique, ideologie: Cicéron. Paris, 1976.

Theater and Society in the Classical World. Edited by R. Scodel. Ann Arbor, 1993.

Treggiari, S.M. "Intellectuals, Poets, and Their Patrons in the First Century B.C." *EMC* 21 (1977): 24–29.

———. *Roman Freedmen during the Late Republic.* Oxford, 1969.

Ussher, R.G. *The* Characters *of Theophrastus.* London, 1960.

Vahlen, J. *Ennianae poesis reliquiae.* 2d ed. Leipzig, 1903.

Valk, M. van der. *Eustathii episcopi Thessalonicensis commentari ad Homeri* Iliadem *pertinentes.* 4 vols. Leiden, 1971–87.

Vasaly, A. *Representations: Images of the World in Ciceronian Oratory.* Berkeley, 1993.

Viljoen, G. "The Plot of the *Captivi* of Plautus." *Acta Classica* 6 (1963): 38–63.

Walbank, F.W. "Political Morality and the Friends of Scipio." *JRS* 55 (1965): 1–16.

Wallace-Hadrill, A. "Patronage in Roman Society: From Republic to Empire." In *Patronage in Ancient Society,* edited by A. Wallace-Hadrill, 63–87. London, 1989.

Webster, T.B.L. *Monuments Illustrating New Comedy.* 3d ed. revised and enlarged by J.R. Green and A. Seeberg. 2 vols. London, 1995.

———. *Studies in Menander.* Manchester, 1950.

Wehrli, F. *Die Schule des Aristoteles: Texte und Kommentare.* 10 vols. Basel, 1944–59.

West, M.L. *Iambi et elegi graeci ante Alexandrum cantati.* 2 vols. Oxford, 1971–72.

White, P. "The Friends of Martial, Statius, and Pliny, and the Dispersal of Patronage." *HSCP* 79 (1975): 265–300.

———. "The Presentation and Dedication of the *Silvae* and *Epigrams.*" *JRS* 64 (1974): 40–61.

———. *Promised Verse: Poets in the Society of Augustan Rome.* Cambridge, Mass., 1993.

Wilamowitz-Moellendorff, U. von. *Antigonos von Karystos.* Philologische Untersuchungen, vol. 4. Berlin, 1881.

Williams, G. *Tradition and Originality in Roman Poetry.* Oxford, 1968.

Wiseman, T.P. *Catullus and His World: A Reappraisal.* Cambridge, 1985.

———. "*Pete nobiles amicos:* Poets and Patrons in Late Republican Rome." In *Lit-*

erary and Artistic Patronage in Ancient Rome, edited by B. Gold, 28–49. Austin, 1982. Reprinted in *Roman Studies: Literary and Historical,* 263–84. Liverpool, 1987.

Woytek, E. T. *Maccius Plautus,* Persa: *Einleitung, Text, und Kommentar.* Österreichische Akademie der Wissenschaften, Philosophisch-historische Klasse, Sitzungsberichte 385. Vienna, 1982.

———. "*Viri capitones.*" WS 7 (1973): 65–74.

Wüst, E., and A. Hug "Parasitos." *RE* 18 (1949): 1381–1405.

Zagagi, N. *Tradition and Originality in Plautus: Studies of the Amatory Motifs in Plautine Comedy.* Hypomnemata 62. Göttingen, 1980.

Ziehen, L. Παράσιτοι. *RE* 18 (1949): 1377–81.

Zwierlein, O. *Zur Kritik und Exegese des Plautus.* Vol.1, Poenulus *und* Curculio. Akademie der Wissenschaften und der Literatur, Abh. der Geistes- und Sozialwissenschaftlichen Klasse, no. 4. Stuttgart, 1990.

———. *Zur Kritik und Exegese des Plautus.* Vol. 2, Miles gloriosus. Akademie der Wissenschaften und der Literatur, Abh. der Geistes- und Sozialwissenschaftlichen Klasse, no. 3. Stuttgart, 1991.

Index of Works and Passages Cited

General Index

DATE DUE

Demco, Inc. 38-293